THE SEPHARDIC LEGACY

UNIQUE FEATURES
AND
ACHIEVEMENTS

T0351383

THE SEPHARDIC LEGACY

UNIQUE FEATURES AND ACHIEVEMENTS

HAIM HENRY TOLEDANO

University of Scranton Press
Scranton and London

Library of Congress Cataloging-in-Publication Data

Toledano, Henry, 1929-
The Sephardic legacy : unique features and achievements / Haim (Henry) Toledano.
   p. cm.
Includes bibliographical references and index.
ISBN 978-1-58966-205-6 (pbk.)
1. Sephardim. 2. Sephardim--Religious life. 3. Sephardim--Social life and customs. 4. Jews--Spain--History. I. Title.
BM182.T65 2010
909'.04924--dc22

                                                              2010013242

Distribution:
University of Scranton Press
Chicago Distribution Center
11030 S. Langley
Chicago, IL 60628

PRINTED IN THE UNITED STATES OF AMERICA

DEDICATION

This book is dedicated to the memory of the Jewish community of Meknes, Morocco, its rabbis, teachers, halakhic decisors, historians, poets, and communal leaders. Their works and leadership represent a continuation and preservation of the quintessential Sephardic erudition and piety, multidimensional creativity, leniency and tolerance, graciousness, and humility.

CONTENTS

PREFACE

The material in this volume brings together many fundamental elements and features of the Sephardic tradition as well as various aspects of the Judeo-Muslim cultural symbiosis. Each of the essays in this volume is a self-contained study of its particular topic and may be read independent of the others, but the choice of topics and their arrangement is deliberate. This book presents, in a logical and coherent way, what I consider to be the most important aspects of the Sephardic tradition—proceeding from a general introductory overview to a fuller discussion of the fundamental cultural achievements of the Sephardic legacy, and concluding with the impact of this legacy on the Sephardic Diaspora after 1492.

Specifically, the first three chapters are introductory in nature. They deal with a definition of Sephardim and Sephardic culture, unique and distinguishing features of Sephardic Judaism, and the historical and cultural factors that account for the flourishing of Jewish culture and science first in the East and later in Spain. Chapters four through seven deal in greater detail with the impact of Islamic civilization on the development of critical biblical exegesis; Hebrew philology and comparative Semitics; Hebrew poetry, both religious and secular, as well as other belletristic literature; the systematic and topical codification of Jewish Law; and Jewish philosophy. All of these developments were inspired and influenced by parallel Muslim models. Finally, the last two chapters demonstrate the extent to which the Sephardic legacy of the Golden Age continued to inspire and inform Sephardic culture and tradition, as well as the way of life in general after 1492, throughout the Sephardic Diaspora.

In summary, it might be safely stated that the overarching theme of most of these essays is the fact, attested to by all scholars in the field, that the Golden Age of Jewish culture and tradition, first in Baghdad and North Africa and then in Spain, would have been inconceivable without the stimulus and inspiration of contemporary Islamic civilization. This may sound incredible to us today in light of the present fierce hostility of Arabs and Muslims toward Israel and the Jews in general. But what must be remembered is the medieval historical context. The early centuries of Islamic civilization, the classical period, were marked by great tolerance on the part of Muslim rulers toward their non-Muslim subjects. It was a period when Jews, Arabs, and Christians lived side by side in a measure of harmony, participating in the same civilization, learning from it and contributing to it. As Bernard Lewis, put it, Islamic civilization, though usually known as Arabic, "was not brought ready-made from the desert, but was created after the [Islamic] conquest by the collaboration of many people. . . . . Nor was it even purely Muslim, for many Christians, Jews, and Zoroastrians were among its creators."

It is my pleasant duty to thank those who helped me in the preparation of this work. First and foremost, I wish to express my infinite gratitude to my wife Sylvia and my daughter Danielle, whose assistance was invaluable. Sylvia's meticulous editing is responsible for innumerable stylistic improvements. Danielle's coaching on the technical uses of the computer was absolutely indispensable. She patiently tutored me on the efficient use of the computer from the start, and remains on call whenever technical problems require her attention. My thanks also go to my colleague, Dr. Andrew Gluck, for his valuable editorial advice as well as his technical assistance in the esoteric techniques in the use of the computer. I also extend my thanks to Dr. Tsvi Yaakov Aranoff for his generous help in putting my essays into book form. Last but not least, I am particularly grateful to Mr. Jeffrey L. Gainey, Director of University of Scranton Press. His enthusiasm for publishing my book and his continued guidance throughout this process are greatly appreciated.

INTRODUCTION

Although my research and publications in recent years focused on various historical and cultural aspects of Moroccan Judaism, my interest in and passion for Sephardic culture in general has not abated. In an introduction to the material in this collection of essays on Sephardic culture, it seems appropriate to recount the evolution of my intense interest in Sephardic culture and tradition—beginning with my upbringing in the Jewish community of Meknes, Morocco where the legacy of the Spanish Golden Age of Jewish culture was part of every day's living experience, my rabbinic training in Yeshivat Keter Torah in Meknes, and through my academic career as both a student and a teacher at various universities.

I grew up in the Jewish community of Meknes, Morocco, a community where the Sephardic tradition was manifested in every aspect of religious life; liturgy; social, educational, and cultural institutions; and multidimensional rabbinic creativity. Thus, for example, the poetry of such great Spanish masters as Solomon Ibn Gabirol, Yehudah Halevi, and Moshe and Abraham Ibn Ezra was not only part of the synagogue liturgy, but constituted a prominent part of the popular repertoire of *piyyutim* sung to Andalusian and contemporary Arabic music at any and every social and festive occasion along with the poetic compositions of Moroccan *paytanim*—scholar-poets who preserved and amplified the Spanish poetic legacy. The community of Meknes also produced numerous rabbinic sages renowned for their vast erudition and genuine piety (*Yir'at shamayim amittit*). They were most representative of the Sephardic tradition in their tolerance toward all Jews without regard to their level of observance, in their lenient halakhic disposition, and in their most dignified personal comportment and deference to and respect for each other even when they differed in their halakhic views or other matters of consequence.

The yeshivot in Morocco, likewise, followed a curriculum of studies which emphasized, in addition to the Talmud and Halakhah, the study of the Bible and its commentaries, especially those of the Spanish school of biblical exegesis, with great preference for the commentaries of Abraham Ibn Ezra, Nachmanides (Ramban), and David Kimhi (Radaq). The curricu-

1

lum emphasized also the study of such theological classics as Yehudah Halevi's *Kuzari*, Bahya Ibn Paquda's *Hovat ha-Levavot* (The Duties of the Heart), and Maimonides' *Shemonah Perakim* (Eight Chapters).

Because my father was one of the eminent rabbis of the community, our home and his synagogue were frequently visited by many of his colleagues, including eminent rabbis and *dayyanim* (judges). Growing up in this environment, I had the chance to meet and know rabbinic leaders whose wisdom, erudition, piety, humanity, and humility left an indelible impression on me.

My rabbinic studies in Yeshivat Keter Torah instilled in me a great love and appreciation for the Sephardic approach to Torah study, which emphasized the halakhic orientation to all Talmudic studies. The program of study was always divided equally between the Talmud and Halakhah (of course, in addition to the Bible and its commentaries).

The particular Talmudic tractate to be studied at any given period was frequently chosen for the purpose of providing the background for whatever laws were being studied at the time. One of my teachers and mentors at Keter Torah was Rabbi Shalom Messas Z.Tz.L, the late Chief Sephardi Rabbi of Jerusalem, whose halakhic opinions were sought by rabbis and decisors from Jewish communities throughout the world. Likewise, most rabbinic tribunals in Israel, including that of Rabbi Obadyah Yosef, referred to him all difficult cases of *mamzerut*, deferring to his great expertise and lenient and compassionate rulings on the subject.

This is the community in which I grew up, the authentic Sephardic life that I experienced, and the rabbinic models I idealized. This rich background continued to inform, inspire, and guide the course of my life in my religious practice, my rabbinic studies, my halakhic disposition, and my academic career.

When I began my university studies in the United States, it was inevitable that my interest in Sephardic culture would influence the direction of those studies—beginning with a minor in medieval philosophy during my undergraduate years at Wayne State University in Detroit, Michigan, and culminating in a PhD from Columbia University with a major in Islamic civilization and a minor in medieval Sephardic culture. My first academic encounter with Sephardic culture was in a course on medieval Jewish philosophy at Wayne State University for which I wrote a research paper on "The Problem of Evil in Maimonides' *Guide of the Perplexed* and the Zohar."

Following graduation from Wayne with a BA in American History and Semitics, I was advised by several of my professors who were aware of my interest in pursuing graduate studies in Sephardic culture, "Go east young man." I began my graduate studies at Dropsie College in Philadelphia under a National Defense grant for the study of comparative religion. When I expressed interest in medieval Sephardic culture, I was informed that one cannot approach the subject without a fair knowledge of Arabic and Islam. Accordingly, I took courses in Arabic, Islam, Judeo-Arabic, and medieval Jewish philosophy in addition to courses in comparative religion required by the terms of the grant. Following my years at Dropsie College, I earned a PhD from Columbia University in Arabic language and literature, Islamic jurisprudence and theology, and medieval Hebrew culture and history.

During my various teaching positions in several American universities, I introduced and taught courses in Arabic, Aramaic, medieval and modern Hebrew literature, Jewish thought, and Islamic history. But it was at Hofstra University (1975–96)—as director of the Arabic, Hebrew, and Jewish Studies Program—that I was able to introduce and teach many courses bearing directly or indirectly on Sephardic culture. Courses included "The Bible and its Exegesis through the Ages," "Foundations of Jewish Culture and Tradition," "Judaism and Islam—Jews and Arabs," and "The Golden Age of Jewish Culture and Tradition." Clearly, these courses focused on topics similar to those covered in my public lectures and symposia (discussed below).

In the course of a long academic career spanning over thirty years—especially during my years at Hofstra University, my academic home for the last twenty years of my active teaching career—I lectured widely in various forums on many aspects of Sephardic culture and on Judeo-Muslim relations. The lectures were delivered most notably in a number of lecture series and symposia I had developed, directed, and participated in as a speaker at Hofstra University. They included "Project Sepharad," a series of sixteen two-hour lectures entitled "Sephardic Judaism: History, Culture, and Folklore" (1980); two colloquia on Maimonides, "Maimonides: Philosopher, Educator" (Dec. 10, 1985), and "The Political Philosophy of Maimonides" (March, 26, 1987); "The Sephardic Odyssey: 1492–1992," a ten-lecture series on the communities in the Sephardic Diaspora after 1492—"In Commemoration of the Quincentenary of the Expulsion of the Jews from Spain" (March–June, 1992); and a one-day symposium, "Rationalism and Mysticism in the Sephardi Tradition" (Nov. 22, 1992). In addition, I delivered a number of public lectures for the Hofstra University faculty, several student organizations, and various Jewish organizations and congregations. The lectures had such titles as "Jews and Arabs: Cousins or Enemies," "The Muslim Conquest and its Cultural, Linguistic, and Religious Impact," "The Cultural Interdependence of Judaism and Islam," "Sephardim before the Golden Age," "Return to the Source: Spanish Exiles in North Africa," "Zionism before Herzl," and "The Poetic and Pragmatic Legacy of Yehudah Halevi's Zionism."

Finally, from 1983 through 1986, I served as Scholar in Residence at several weekend conferences on the Sephardi experience—held annually at various congregations throughout the Northeast and sponsored by the Tarbuth Foundation for the Advancement of Jewish Culture. During the course of these weekend conferences, entitled "A Weekend with Yehudah Halevi," I covered various topics of Sephardic interest, in my lectures: "The Golden Age of Jewish Culture in Spain: An Overview," "Sephardic Culture in Spain: Unique Features and Contemporary Relevance," "The Great Loves of Yehudah Halevi: God, Zion, and the People of Israel," and "Special Customs and Rituals of the Sephardim."

I have often considered publishing some of these lectures, but circumstances always stood in the way. It is my aim in the present volume to make the content of most of these lectures available to the wider public. The chapters of this volume represent essentially a condensation of most of the above-mentioned lectures.

1.

SEPHARDIC CULTURE — DEFINITIONS

Sephardic tradition is a system of values, institutions, ethnic traits, and attitudes that has long constituted a common bond between the Jewish communities throughout the Mediterranean basin, and which continues today to bind all Sephardim wherever they may be. This tradition is fundamentally different from other Jewish traditions and experiences.

Sephardic tradition evolved among Jews living within the orbit of the Islamic world beginning in the early Middle Ages—during the eighth and ninth centuries. This system of values and institutions originated in the East where Jews first came in contact with Islamic and Arabic civilization and culture and were greatly influenced by them. From the East, this tradition crossed to the Iberian Peninsula where it reached its fullest and richest development, culminating in what has come to be known as the Golden Age of Jewish culture and creativity.

Indeed, it was the Jews of Baghdad, Qayrawan, and Andalusia who made some of the most lasting contributions in all fields of Jewish culture and creativity. Their masterworks in philology, poetry, liturgy, biblical studies, philosophy, theology, and Jewish law—including the three major codes of Jewish law of Rabbi Isaac Alfasi, Maimonides, and Rabbi Joseph Caro—have since become classics of Judaism cherished by Sephardim and Ashkenazim alike. They made these contributions in response to the intellectual and cultural challenges of Islamic civilization during its own Golden Age.

Following their expulsion from Spain, the Sephardim carried with them this rich and diversified legacy wherever they went, preserving it and amplifying it. During all these centuries, the Sephardim acquired certain ethnic traits and social tastes that set them apart from their Ashkenazi brethren. At the same time, they created their own communal, legal, and social institutions; they developed their own food, their own music, and their own forms of art.

It must be emphasized that this tradition did not begin in Spain nor did it end in 1492–97. In other words, it was limited neither to Spain nor to the Golden Age. It transcended regional and temporal boundaries. Geographically speaking, its intellectual center shifted from one place to another depending on the political, economic, and cultural significance of any given region at any given time. Thus, during the Abbasid Caliphate, when the newly founded capital of Baghdad (750 CE) became the center of Islamic power, commerce, and culture, it also became the center of Sephardic culture and tradition. It became the seat of the two famous Babylonian Yeshivot, as well as that of the formal head of the Jewish community under Islam, the Exilarch or *Resh Galuta* (literally, head of the exile).

Moreover, the great literary and cultural achievements of the Abbasids presented the Jews with a great intellectual challenge and led to their own corresponding achievements. Perhaps there is no better illustration of this than the literary and scholarly achievements of Saadiah Gaon (892–942), who may be justly regarded as the founding father of Sephardic culture. It was he who single-handedly forged the tools for the analytical studies of the Bible and its language through his many pioneering works on Hebrew and Arabic lexicography and grammar, his translation of the Bible into Arabic (*Tafsir*), and his critical and innovative commentary on the Bible. He also pioneered works in Hebrew poetry, liturgy, codification of Jewish law according to subject matter (following the model of Muslim codifiers), and Jewish philosophy. In short, all the Jewish sciences and literary genres which were to flower in Spain were begun by Saadiah.[1]

As the influence of the centers of learning in Baghdad began to decline, new Jewish centers of learning were emerging in Spain. During the first two centuries of Islamic rule in Spain, however, Spanish Jewry continued to depend for its spiritual guidance on the Babylonian Yeshivot in Baghdad. It was not until the days of Hasdai Ibn Shaprut (915–75) that Spanish Jewry began to develop its own culture. In this process, the role played by North African Jews was quite significant.[2] During the early medieval period, the Jewish communities of Fez and Qayrawan served as a cultural bridge between the great Babylonian Yeshivot and the newly emerging communities in Spain. These North African communities were in a good position to do this. Not only were their rabbis scholars in their own right, they were also in constant contact with both the Babylonian and Spanish communities, and commanded the respect of both. Indeed, responsa from the Babylonian Yeshivot to the Jewish communities of Fez, Qayrawan, and Sijilmasa address them with utmost reverence as great centers of learning.[3]

Moreover, Moroccan Jewry provided the young community in Spain with its first teachers in Hebrew poetry, philology, and rabbinic learning. From Morocco in the tenth century came the first Hebrew grammarians, linguists, and poets (Judah Ibn Hayyuj and Dunash Ibn Labrat, among others), and one of the first great Talmudists and Halakhists, Rabbi Isaac Alfasi, known as the Rab Alfes or the Rif. All were attracted to Cordova by the largess and patronage of Hasdai Ibn Shaprut. Ibn Hayyuj's philological discoveries revolutionized the scientific study of Hebrew grammar and lexicography; Ibn Labrat was the first to adapt features and conventions of Arabic prosody to Hebrew, thereby providing future Hebrew poets in Spain with an important tool and models for their poetry;[4] Alfasi headed the famous yeshivah in Lucena.[5] These three individuals may rightly be regarded as the founders of the Spanish school of Jewish learning and science that culminated in the Golden Age in Spain. Indeed, the Golden Age in Spain was preceded by a number of mini-Golden Ages in various parts of the Islamic world, in Baghdad, Qayrawan, Fez, and elsewhere—all of which contributed to and culminated in the Golden Age of Sephardic culture in Spain.

Finally, following the expulsion from Spain and Portugal, the center of Sephardic culture shifted to Turkey, Palestine, North Africa, and such cities in Christendom as Amsterdam, Venice, and Leghorn. Thus, the Sephardic tradition did not cease to exist after the expulsion from Spain and Portugal in 1492–97. As stated above, the Sephardim carried their legacy wherever they went, preserved it zealously, and amplified it by continuing to create in its spirit.

Solomon Freehof, an eminent American Jewish scholar, comments on the events of 1492 and the subsequent emergence of new centers of Sephardic culture:

> One of the outstanding examples in the long series of the Jewish recoveries is the cultural achievement of ex-Spanish Jewry. The last century of Jewish life in Spain had been a hideous succession of persecution, massacre and forced conversions, culminating in complete and absolute expulsion. If history did not tell us that it was true, it would be hard to believe that this Jewry, dragged down from its high eminence, pursued to the death, and then strewn like dust to the winds of the earth, should ever again become a living and creative force. But the fact is that the ex-Spanish Jews revived old Jewries, built new ones, and wrote

great literature almost wherever they came. Though their influence was felt wherever they settled in any considerable numbers—as far north as Hamburg and London, as far west as the New World—their greatest achievement was in the Near East, the Levant. Under Isaac bar Sheshet and Simon ben Zemach Duran, they had given new life to the Jewries of northwest Africa. Then, under a whole galaxy of scholars, they brought a new religious and cultural flowering to Egypt, Palestine, Asia Minor, and Turkey.[6]

Among the factors that made this continued cultural activity of the Sephardim after 1492 possible, two factors stand out. First is the tremendous pride the Spanish Jews took in their Judeo-Spanish cultural legacy. As a result, they carried this rich and diverse legacy with them wherever they went, preserving it, cherishing and cultivating it, and continuing to create in its spirit. Equally important was the fact that, in their new host countries, these Spanish exiles enjoyed warm hospitality, religious tolerance (indeed, in some cases, even religious autonomy), relative security, and new outlets for their talents—all of which afforded them the luxury and peace of mind to enable them to direct their energies and creativity to religious, intellectual, and cultural pursuits.

In conclusion, this tradition in all its richness and diversity is called Sephardi not because it was the exclusive patrimony of Spain. In fact, the Sephardic tradition is not derived exclusively from language, geography, or ethnicity. Rather, it has to do with the spirit and cultural elements of this tradition and is based exclusively on its values and ideals. It is called Sephardi because it matured and reached its fullest and richest expression in Spain, and because, following the expulsions of 1391, 1492, and 1497, it was cherished, preserved, and cultivated further by the Spanish exiles and their descendents wherever they found themselves, whether they spoke Ladino, Greek, or Arabic. Therefore, by definition, Sephardim are Jews who continue to adhere to and cherish this tradition. They include Jewish communities in North Africa, Turkey and other Balkan countries, the Middle East, Amsterdam, London, and now France, Canada, the United States, and South America.

WHO IS A SEPHARDI?

It might be recalled that during the late 1960s and the 1970s, one of the burning questions on the Israeli scene was "Who is a Jew?"—a question never resolved to the complete satisfaction of all concerned. The question of who is a Sephardi seems to be almost as controversial. Perhaps, to Ashkenazim, a Sephardi is simply one who is not Ashkenazi. But among Sephardim themselves, each group claims exclusive authenticity, and there are many such groups.

An eminent Sephardi leader of Yugoslav origin once asserted publicly that only Ladino-speaking Jews are authentic Sephardim. Such an assertion must be surprising if not insulting to the descendants of Spanish exiles who found refuge and hospitality in Algeria, Tunisia, Morocco, and other Arabic-speaking countries. Similarly, a well-known American Jewish writer once asked in the course of a public lecture, "By what right can Moroccan Jews call themselves Sephardim?" His statement betrays total ignorance of Moroccan Jewry's contribution to the preservation and development of Sephardic culture after 1492.

As stated above, Sephardic culture and tradition began not in Spain but in Baghdad and North Africa and, following the expulsions of 1391, 1492, and 1497, continued to thrive to a greater or lesser extent in all parts of the Sephardic Diaspora. Therefore, *Sephardism* can't be defined geographically, ethnically, or linguistically. The only valid definition is a cultural one. Accordingly, a more accurate definition of *Sephardim* includes all Jews who trace their origin and ancestry to Spain and Portugal, or to any of the other centers of Sephardic culture, and who share and cherish the Sephardic tradition and heritage as it was transmitted from one generation to another.

This definition is, of course, inclusive of diverse groups of Sephardim: the Ladino-speaking Sephardim of Turkey and other Balkan countries; the Spanish and Portuguese Sephardim of Amsterdam, London, and New York and other U.S. cities; the Middle East Sephardim of Egypt, Iraq, and Syria; and the Sephardim of North Africa. Regardless of the part of the Sephardic Diaspora they come from, all are equally Sephardim. They all follow Sephardic halakhic authorities and Sephardic liturgy, and most have made great contributions to the development and flowering of Sephardic culture during one historical period or another.

Obviously, Sephardim from various parts of the world differ from each other in the precise ways in which they express this tradition. This is especially true with regard to food, music, and folklore, which inevitably reflect local and regional influences. Yet, all cherish and take pride in a common spiritual and cultural legacy going back to the Golden Age of

Sephardic culture and creativity in Spain, and even to prior periods of development in Baghdad and North Africa.

To be sure, among the communities of Yemen and Iran, each has its own distinct culture and liturgy, as do Italian and Ethiopian Jews, and according to our definition, they are really neither Sephardim nor Ashkenazim. Nonetheless, these communities prefer to identify more with the Sephardic than the Ashkenazi tradition. Perhaps, they do so in consideration of the fact that Sephardic culture developed under the influence of Islamic civilization. Yemen and Persia were always part of that civilization, while Ethiopia and Italy were subject to Islamic influence at certain periods of their history.[7]

2.

DISTINGUISHING FEATURES OF SEPHARDIC CULTURE

This chapter will focus on what I believe to be certain distinguishing features or fundamental aspects of Sephardic tradition and culture, especially during the Golden Age of Judaism in Spain. But first, several historical observations on that period are in order.

One of the interesting and controversial aspects of Jewish life under Islam is the so-called *dhimmi* (protected minorities) status. This took several generations to evolve, but essentially, it was based on the precedent established by Muhammad in his agreement with the Jews of Khaybar, as well as on statements made by him or attributed to him by Muslim tradition. Of course, it was determined by other factors as well.[1] On the one hand, this *dhimmi* status entailed obligations on the part of the Jews as well as discrimination (financial, social, and political) against them. On the other hand, it entailed guarantees and protection by Muslim rulers. These guarantees were significant. They included protection of life and limb, religious and judicial autonomy, freedom of movement within the Islamic empire, and with but a few limitations, freedom of professions.

All in all, it was a mixed bag. Scholars are still debating whether all was well with the Jews in Islamic lands. A final verdict is not in yet. But, leaving scholarly debate aside, the way *dhimmi* status worked in real life was as follows: In times of political instability and under the rule of religious fanatics, Jews suffered many indignities, financial and social discriminations, and outright persecution. But in times of political stability and under enlightened rulers—particularly when the services of the Jews and their skills were badly needed by the rulers—they fared very well.

Such were the conditions of the Golden Age in Spain, Iraq, and North Africa. During this period, we witness the rise of Jews to political and economic prominence in Baghdad, Cordova, Cairo, Qayrawan, and elsewhere. We find Jews in Muslim courts in various official capacities as viziers, financial advisors and bankers, ministers of state, and—in the singular case of Samuel Ibn Nagrela (Hanagid, 993–1056)—even as a general at the head of Muslim armies.[2] Most important, during this period we witness a tremendous broadening of the cultural horizons of Judaism, resulting in the flourishing of Jewish science, philosophy, and poetry, all under the influence of contemporary Islamic culture and as a result of its inspiration. Some of the greatest masterpieces of Jewish culture and tradition were produced by the Sephardim during this period. These include works in liturgy, Hebrew poetry (both religious and secular), Jewish philosophy, Hebrew philology and grammar, analytical biblical commentaries, and legal codes. These works were and are cherished by Sephardim and Ashkenazim alike. They belong to the Jewish people as a whole.

I maintain, however, that underlying the achievements of the Sephardim, and underlying their separate way of life, have always been certain attitudes toward life and knowledge that are basic to Judaism. I refer to these attitudes as the distinguishing features or fundamental aspects of Sephardic Judaism. In my opinion, these features were directly responsible for making the Sephardic tradition unlike any other tradition and the Sephardic experience unlike any other experience. It is these features or attitudes that were responsible for making the Golden Age of Jewish culture in Spain unlike any other period in Jewish history. I may also add at the outset that these attitudes have been typical of Sephardic Judaism not only during the Golden Age in Spain but throughout its history (although most of my examples are from the Golden Age).

UNIVERSAL DIMENSION OF SEPHARDIC CULTURE

First and foremost, we find in this tradition an intellectual open-mindedness and broad-mindedness, a diversity of interests, and a positive attitude toward nonreligious sciences. The Sephardim showed a willingness and capacity to master contemporary sciences and synthesize them with Jewish concepts and ideals. They showed a readiness to meet the scientific and philosophical world of Muslim civilization head-on. They were confident that religion and knowledge—revelation and reason—were equally valid sources of Divine Truth. As such, they must of necessity confirm and reinforce rather than contradict each other. As a result of this positive attitude, no investigation was too daring; no philosophical speculation was too dangerous or threatening to their religious convictions. The interest of the Sephardim in medieval times covered every field of knowledge then known to man. Mathematics and medicine, astrology and astronomy, philosophy and philology, poetry and polemics—all wetted their intellectual appetite. Medieval Jewish scholars were humanists, men of universal knowledge.

Saadiah Gaon (892–942), Maimonides (1135–1204), and Rabbi Abraham Ibn Ezra (1092–1167) provide excellent illustrations of this versatile and universal dimension of Sephardic culture.

SAADIAH GAON

Because of his reputation for rabbinic scholarship, Saadiah Gaon was invited to head the prestigious Sura Academy in Baghdad, which was a rare honor for an outsider who had not risen through the ranks of the Yeshiva. He was a first-rate polemicist who single-handedly defended the legitimacy and binding authority of rabbinic tradition against the attacks of heretics and Karaites alike. Through his many pioneering works in Hebrew and Arabic lexicography and grammar, his translation (*Tafsir*) of the Bible into Arabic, and his critical and innovative commentary on the Bible, he forged the tools for the analytical studies of the Bible and its language.[3] He was the first rabbinic commentator to bring scientific and linguistic analysis to bear on the content of the Bible. His total mastery of the Bible is evident even in his philosophical work, *Beliefs and Opinions* (*Emunot ve-De'ot*), where he displays amazing skill in finding scriptural support for almost every detail of his philosophical and doctrinal arguments.[4] He also pioneered works in Hebrew poetry, liturgy, codification of Jewish law according to subject matter (following the model of Muslim codifiers), and Jewish philosophy.

MAIMONIDES

Rabbi Moshe ben Maymon (1135–1204), known popularly by his Hebrew acronym, Rambam, was a Talmudic scholar of the highest rank, an Aristotelian philosopher, and a physician in the Court of the famous Saladin. Commonly known today as Maimonides, he wrote treatises on sciences from logic to pharmacology. As a rabbinic scholar, he is famous for his responsa and for his commentary on the Mishnah, *Sefer ha-Ma'or*, his *Mishneh Torah*, the first systematic and comprehensive code of Jewish law written in concise and clear Hebrew. In the words of Isador Twersky, the *Mishneh Torah* is not only "the flower of Jewish jurisprudence," but also "covers physics, metaphysics, ethics, psychology, dietetics, astronomy, everything from creation to the end of days."[5]

As a philosopher, he is famous for his magnum opus, *The Guide of the Perplexed* (*Moreh Nebukhim*), the most important and influential work in Jewish philosophy. Also, in his commentary on the Mishnah, he articulated his Thirteen Principles of Faith, which were later composed as the popular liturgical hymn, *Yigdal*, which is now a standard prayer that appears in most prayer books.[6] As a physician, he wrote treatises on preventive medicine and pharmacology. Finally, as a communal leader whose authority and fame spread far and wide, he is famous for his epistles, notably The Epistle to Yemen (*Iggeret Teman*), and The Epistle of Martyrdom (*Iggeret ha-Shemad*). [7]

RABBI ABRAHAM IBN EZRA

Rabbi Abraham Ibn Ezra (1092–1161) was a poet, grammarian, biblical commentator, philosopher, astronomer, astrologer, and physician. He was a most prolific scholar and is alleged to have written no fewer than one hundred and eight works only some of which have survived. He is most famous, however, for his biblical commentaries, his poetry both secular and sacred, and his scientific works in astronomy and (especially) astrology. His biblical commentaries reflect his vast knowledge of philosophy, Hebrew grammar, mathematics, and astrology. Like Maimonides, he was a rationalist, asserting, "The Bible speaks only to intellectuals" (*lo nitenah torah ella le-anshei ha-da'at*). In the introduction to his commentary on the Pentateuch, he reviews four methods of biblical interpretation, and rejects all of them in favor of the plain literal and logical meaning of the text.

His commentary is characterized by an emphasis on etymological and grammatical explanations, a sophisticated historical and textual analysis, and a brief and concise style, at times even terse and enigmatic. This is especially typical of comments pertaining to his critical analysis of certain biblical passages, in which he often anticipates views associated with modern biblical scholarship. Because his views in these instances were radical departures from tradition, he did not state them explicitly, but only hinted at them, usually adding such statements as "*ve-ha-maskil yavin*" (and the intellectual will understand) or "*ve-ha-maskil yiddom*" (let the intellectual keep his understanding to himself).

So, at times one gets the impression that Ibn Ezra is addressing an exclusive audience. At other times he is sharp and sarcastic, as when he dismisses any *midrashic* interpretation with the statement, *"ve-derekh ha-midrash yadu'a"* (and the *midrashic* approach is well known), as if to say to the reader, "You and I know better." All these features make his commentary more difficult to understand. Indeed, studying Ibn Ezra's biblical commentaries requires special expertise. It is no wonder that "more than seventy super-commentaries" have been written on his biblical commentaries.

Tradition maintains that Moses wrote the entire Torah. On the basis of his textual and historical analysis, however, Ibn Ezra concludes that certain passages in the Pentateuch, such as, "And the Cananite was then in the land" (Gen. 12:6), and "In the mount where the Lord is seen" (Gen. 22:14), and "And Moses wrote" (Exod. 24:4; Num. 33:2; and Deut. 31:9–22), and "Behold his bedstead was a bedstead of iron" (Deut. 3:11), and " These are the words which Moses spoke unto all Israel beyond the Jordan" (Deut. 1:2), could not have been written by Moses and must necessarily be post-Mosaic additions or insertions. Marc Shapiro, in an exhaustive and thorough discussion of Maimonides' Eighth Principle regarding the "Revelation of the Torah," cites a number of rabbinic authorities from different periods who essentially agree with Ibn Ezra's analysis. Furthermore, these scholars argue that the notion that certain details pertaining to the narratives in the Torah were written by Joshua, Ezra, or other prophets is not incompatible with the traditional belief that the Torah is from heaven, divinely inspired, and that it was written by Moses. In the words of Rabbi Benjamin Ze'ev, quoted by Shapiro, "a few post-Mosaic prophetic insertions do not alter the fact that Moses is regarded as the author of the Torah."[8]

His versatility is also evident in his poetry. His secular poetry includes occasional poems, encomia, satiric verse, and witty epigrams, as well as poems of friendship, love, nature, and wine. His sacred poetry, both religious and philosophical, expresses his yearning for the knowledge and nearness of God. Much of his religious poetry is liturgical, and his poems of penitence (*selihot*) and supplications (*bakkashot*), as well as many of his hymns, have been included in the liturgy—especially the Sephardic liturgy for the High Holidays.[9]

Rabbi Abraham Ibn Ezra was interested in astronomy and astrology (a respected science at the time). He wrote twenty-four books on astrology in both Hebrew and Latin. He also translated one work from Arabic into Hebrew. In several of these books, he cites Plato, Aristotle, Claudius Ptolemy, as well as Egyptian, Persian, and Indian astrologers. Many of these works have been translated into Greek, Latin, and Arabic. Professor

Leopold Fleischer, in discussing his own publication of some of these books on astrology, writes, "The publication of these astrological works of Abraham Ibn Ezra is important because: a. we can more easily understand his [biblical] commentaries with their assistance, and b. they help us to recognize the personality of a great intellectual."[10]

Finally, Ibn Ezra was also important as a translator of many of the works of Spanish scholars and grammarians from Arabic into Hebrew for the benefit of Jews who were unable to read Arabic. During his travels in Italy, France, and England, after leaving Spain in 1140, he acted as a cultural bridge between Spain and the non-Arabic speaking Jewish communities, affording those communities the benefits and fruits of Spanish scholarship and culture.[11]

PRACTICE OF MEDICINE

Another illustration of the Jews' participation in medieval Islamic culture is their noticeable predilection for the practice of medicine. (Indeed, the Golden Age was the dream of every "Jewish mother." The concept of "my son, the doctor" obviously has a long history.) In the twelfth century alone, about fifty Jewish scholars are noted for their medical practice and medical writings. As S. D. Goitein puts it, "If medicine was a prominent constituent of Islamic civilization during its creative period, it was absolutely paramount in the life of so-called protected minorities, the Christians and the Jews."[12] This is all the more amazing when one realizes that, strictly speaking, their status as *dhimmis* did not permit them the practice of medicine. Yet, no other discriminatory law was less observed then this prohibition.

Christian and Jewish doctors are known to have been court physicians to Caliphs and other Muslim rulers in practically every Muslim country. Many others occupied leading positions in hospitals founded and maintained by Muslim rulers.[13] For example, Isaac Israeli (855–955) of Qayrawan, the first Jewish physician we hear of, received instruction in medicine from a distinguished Muslim doctor, and in turn, taught medicine to many Muslim as well as Jewish pupils. He also wrote many medical books that circulated in the East and earned him a considerable reputation. His books were translated into Latin in the eleventh century, and made their way to Europe where they served as textbooks for several centuries. Like many other Jewish physicians, he also wrote books on philosophy and science.[14]

There were other equally famous Jewish physicians including Rabbi Yehudah Ibn Quraysh (second half of the ninth century—a Hebrew grammarian and physician, who, along with Saadiah Gaon, is considered one of the founders of comparative Semitic linguistics), Yehudah Halevy, Abraham Ibn Ezra, and of course Maimonides, who devoted the last years of his life to the practice of medicine as the court physician of the famous Saladin, and who wrote numerous treatises on various aspects of medicine and pharmacology.

CENTRALITY OF REASON AND RATIONALISM IN SEPHARDIC THOUGHT

Another related distinguishing feature is the centrality of reason and rationalism and the place of eminence they occupied in the thought and philosophy of medieval Sephardic masters. It may be said that underlying all their achievements in science and philosophy, was their positive attitude toward human reason. For the Sephardim, the age of reason was not the seventeenth ant eighteenth centuries as in Europe, but the eleventh and twelfth centuries in Spain. They believed that reason was God's greatest gift to man, and it is at once man's privilege and obligation to use his reason to the fullest. Reason, for these medieval masters, was a source of Divine truth no less so than revelation itself. They saw in reason the yardstick against which they measured all things—including revelation.

Thus Saadiah Gaon considers reason—by which he means, "that which is derived purely from the mind"—as one of the "four roots of knowledge," the other roots being sense perception, inferential knowledge, and in the case of the Jews, the truth of tradition.[15] Abraham Ibn Ezra, in the introduction to his commentary on the Torah writes, "Reason is the foundation of everything. The Torah was not given to men who cannot reason and man's reason is the angel, which mediates between him and his God. It follows that wherever we find something in the Torah that is not contrary to reason we must understand it in accordance with its plain meaning and accept it as saying what it seems to say, believing that this is the true meaning."[16] Finally, Maimonides, in his explanations of the rationale for the commandments, asserts that it is impossible that God would have given any commandment which did not have a purpose or a rationale, and devotes no fewer than twenty-five chapters of the third part of *The Guide of the Perplexed* (chaps. 25–49) to offering a rationale for every commandment, including ceremonial commandments.[17]

This attitude toward reason had many ramifications: intellectual, scientific, philosophical, and theological. It led to the rise of Jewish philosophy and science as well as the development of sophisticated analytical and grammatical commentaries on the Bible, in many ways anticipating modern biblical scholarship. Also, as a result of this commitment to and faith in reason, there came into being a whole school of philosophical or rational interpretation of Scripture—or the rationalization of the irrational in the Bible. This school, which included philosophers as well as biblical commentators, culminated in the *The Guide of the Perplexed*, Maimonides' magnum opus, which is a systematic and comprehensive philosophical interpretation of the Bible and of Judaism in general. In fact, some see the *Guide* as simply a philosophical or Aristotelian midrash.

But Maimonides, though the greatest of them all, was by no means alone in dealing with rational explanation of the commandments; all the great medieval Sephardic scholars dealt with *Ta'ame ha-Mitzvot* in one context or another, some in their philosophical works, still others in their commentaries on the Torah.[18]

JOIE DE VIVRE IN SEPHARDIC LIFE AND CULTURE

The third of these distinguishing features of Sephardic tradition has to do with neither religion, nor philosophy, nor scholarship. Rather, it has to do with another plane of existence, namely the Sephardic attitude toward life. There is a religious point of view that glorifies self-denial and holds that the more one denies oneself, the better Jew one is. This was never the way of the Sephardim who believed that one can be a good Jew without going to extremes. They seem to have had always a very healthy and positive attitude toward the pleasures of life. Spanish Jews, and not only the masses, but even the very religious leaders and scholars, had a certain *joie de vivre*, which I believe is unique. Theirs was a very healthy attitude to all aspects of life—even the very earthly ones. Their piety and intellectual sophistication did not cause them to ignore life and its pleasures. The Sephardim—and I mean the pillars of orthodoxy, the giants among them— gave religion its due, but otherwise they enjoyed life for what it was. They partook of its pleasures and its joys without feeling the slightest guilt. They drank the cup of life to its last drop.

For us today, it is very difficult to imagine let alone accept such a phenomenon. One can hardly imagine, for example, the leaders of traditional or Orthodox Judaism writing love poetry for relaxation. Yet, in medieval Spain, this was a common experience. Moses and Abraham Ibn Ezra, Samuel Hanagid, Yehuda Halevi, and Ibn Gabirol all did just that. All of them went from one drinking banquet to another, wrote drinking poetry and wine songs, and nearly all indulged in writing love and even sensual poetry.

The same Yehudah Halevi, who in his religious poetry rises to sublime spiritual heights, the same Halevi who can feel so close to God as to say,

> Lord, where shall I find You?
> Your place is lofty and secret.
> And where shall I not find You?
> The whole earth is full of Your glory!

*****

> I have sought to come near You,
> I have called to You with all my heart;
> and when I went out towards You,
> I found You coming towards me.

– or –

> When I am far from You, my life is death;
> but if I cling to You, my death is life.

– or –

> Is there any savior but You?
> Any prisoner of hope but me?[19]

This same man who is God-intoxicated, so to speak, did not refrain from singing of wine, women, and love. In light and relaxed moments, he indulged in describing the beauty and enticing charm of a woman's face as well as the seductiveness of her physique, and the emotions these stirred within him. Yes, they sang of wine, women, nature, friendship, and God.

Some scholars argue that the language and style of such poems and the reality they describe are no more than the adaptation of the literary fashion of Arab poetry, and do not reflect the true attitudes or the real experience of the poets. This seems to this writer totally untrue, for there are many themes of Arabic poetry such as camels, desert scenery, and war poems that went untouched by Sephardic poets—for the simple reason that they were not part of their experience. If they were only imitating Arabic poetry, why would they have excluded such common themes of the Arabic models? It is true that Samuel Hanagid (Ibn Nagrela) wrote war poems, but his case is the exception that confirms the rule, for he was the only one who fought battles and won victories and therefore had the experience to write war poems. Actually, the secular poetry of the Jewish poets in Spain reflects the cultural reality in medieval Spain where Arab and Jewish poets would entertain themselves in nocturnal wine parties by reciting and discussing the poems of others, displaying their own compositions, and testing each other's poetic mettle in improvisational poetic games.[20]

This positive attitude to all aspects of life is supported by a careful examination of the sources. Thus, for example, in Ecclesiastes, we read, "A time for weeping and a time for laughing; A time for wailing and a time for dancing" (3:4), and, "So in a time of good fortune, enjoy the good fortune" (7:14).

The Talmud (BT *Nedarim*, 10a), referring to the biblical requirement that a nazirite (one who decides to consecrate himself unto the Lord) bring a sacrifice so that the priest "shall make atonement for him for that he sinned against a soul" (Num. 6:11), asks, "Just against which soul has he sinned? But it is only because he afflicted himself through abstinence from wine. Now, does not this afford an argument from the minor to the major [*kal va-homer*]? If one who afflicted himself only in respect to wine is called a sinner, how much more is one who ascetically refrains from everything? Hence, one who fasts [unnecessarily] is called a sinner."

In a similar spirit, the *Yerushalmi* in tractate *Kiddushin* (4:12) states, "In the future, a person will have to give an accounting for every good thing his eyes saw, but of which he did not eat." It then relates that Rabbi Elazar, "paying particular attention to this statement, set aside money so that he could eat every kind of food at least once a year." This healthy and balanced attitude toward the full enjoyment of life is reflected again in the liturgy of the Sephardim. In the *vidduy ha-Gadol* (long confession, attributed in many Sephardic mahzorim to Rabbenu Nissim) recited by the Sephardim during the repetition of the morning *amidah* of Yom Kippur, among the many sins enumerated for which we ask forgiveness are the following: "What Thou hast declared clean I have defiled, / And what Thou has declared unclean, I have treated as clean. / What Thou has forbidden, I have permitted, / And what Thou has permitted, I have forbidden." Clearly, it is as sinful to forbid oneself that which is permitted as it is to permit that which is forbidden.[21]

Yehudah Halevi states the case most eloquently in his *Kuzari* when he says, "Divine law imposes no asceticism on us. It rather desires that we should keep the balance and give every mental and physical faculty its due, without overburdening one faculty at the expense of another. . . . Our law as a whole is divided between fear, love and joy; through each of them you may approach your creator. Your contrition on the fast day does not bring you nearer to God than the joy of the Sabbath day and holy days, if the latter is the outcome of devotion."[22]

If Halevi states the case philosophically, Samuel Hanagid sums it up in a delightful wine poem. Here is a free translation of that poem:

Reward
(*'alekhem le-fo'alkhem*)

You owe your Maker righteous behavior;
And He owes you rewarding your endeavor.
Spend not your days in His service;
Some time devote to Him, some to yourself.
Give to Him half your day, the rest to your affairs.
    But give the wine no rest throughout your nights.

* * * * *

And since there is neither song, wine, nor friend in the grave,
Let these, O fools, be your life's reward.

I have made no attempt to reproduce the rhyme in this translation, but Professor Raymond Schendlin points out that "the formal rhyme in the Hebrew original, which occurs at the end of each verse as well as at the end of every hemistich but one, is *l* (vowel) *khem*, *khem* being a pronominal suffix meaning "you"—so that drumming in our ears we hear, "you . . . you . . . you." Scheindlin points out also that this rhyme scheme is a strong indication as to where Hanagid wants man to concentrate his efforts.[23] I recall with amusement the excited reaction of our professor at Columbia University, Isaac Barzilay during a seminar on medieval Hebrew literature. After reading this poem of Hanagid, Professor Barzilay commented, "This was a Jewry full of the joy of life. I assure you that the Vilna Gaon would have never written anything like this."

To sum up then, these distinguishing features of Sephardic tradition and culture are, namely, the readiness of the Sephardim to face the philosophical and scientific challenge presented them by Islamic civilization head-on, participate in it, and contribute to it; their positive attitude toward human reason and the eminent place it occupies in their thought; and finally, their healthy and balanced attitude toward life, its blessings and pleasures. All these unique features combined to make the medieval Sephardic experience in Spain truly the Golden Age of Jewish history.

AESTHETICS IN SEPHARDIC LIFE AND TRADITION

Another aspect of Sephardic culture worth mentioning in this connection is the aesthetic aspect of religion, a certain romantic quality typical of Sephardic folklore and observances of religious rituals. To appreciate this, we must understand the role of aesthetics in Arab civilization. It permeates every aspect of Islamic culture, which is essentially a folk culture. This aesthetic tradition is manifest in various oral arts, such as popular music, song, and poetry, as well as in decorative arts, such as jewelry, calligraphy, embroidery, and leather crafts. Moreover, this aesthetic element is accessible to all, not confined to museums. One encounters it in such everyday objects as silver and copper trays, carpets, and bookbinding, as well as in the architecture and decoration of private homes.

Because Sephardic Jews were part of this civilization, it is only natural and even inevitable that their culture was influenced by its aesthetics. What is extremely interesting is that this aestheticism left its impact on the religious observances of the Sephardim, their rituals, and their ceremonies. It even made its way to the synagogue proper. Examples of the influence of Arab architecture and decorations are evident in the Transito and Santa Maria la Blanca Synagogues in Toledo, Spain, the Sephardic synagogue in Florence, Italy, the Nahon and Suiri synagogues in Tangier, and the Sadoun synagogue in Fez, Morocco.[24]

In the Near East and North Africa, the Torah mantle or cover (*mappah* or *parokhet*) are made of velvet embroidered with metallic (usually golden) threads. In Morocco, talit and tefilin bags are likewise made of velvet embroidered with metallic threads, as are mezuzah covers. Likewise, Near Eastern Sephardim house the Torah in a cylindrical case (tik) decorated with elaborate silver filigree and Hebrew inscriptions. Moroccan and Near Eastern *Tapuhim* or *Rimonim* (Torah finials) and other sacred and ceremonial objects are engraved with multicolored enamel decorations in geometric patterns, typical of Islamic architectural and decorative art.

During the holyday of *sukkot*, Moroccan Jews decorate the *lulavim* (palm branches) with shiny threads of lively colors. Likewise, for *Simhat Torah*, Moroccan synagogues were decorated with oriental tapestries, multicolored lights, palm branches, and flowers and greenery of all types, creating the aura of an oriental palace. Also, on the morning of *Simhat Torah*, each child carried a tall candle to the synagogue. The lit candles of various colors and designs, which were set next to the *tebah* or *bimah*, added to the ambiance and festive atmosphere, while the traditional sweet and lively melodies of Moroccan liturgy blended harmoniously with the artistic and colorful décor.[25]

Needless to say, one of the best illustrations of this aesthetic aspect of medieval Judeo-Arabic culture is the Hebrew poetry produced by Spanish Jews in medieval Spain. S. D. Goitein calls it "the acme of Jewish–Arab symbiosis." Likewise, Bernard Lewis observes that "Hebrew poetry, in the medieval golden age, follows very closely on the prosody and technique of Arabic poetry and indeed on its whole system of symbol and allusions." And though written in a non-Islamic language and script, "medieval Hebrew poetry and much of the prose literature belong to the same cultural world as Arabic and other literatures of Islam."

It is worth noting in this connection that the poetic legacy of Andalusian Jewry was preserved and enriched by Sephardim (who continued to create in its spirit) in various parts of the Sephardic Diaspora. Thus, for example, Syrian and Moroccan rabbis composed *piyyutim* or *pizmonim* (religious poems and songs) for all occasions in both Hebrew and Arabic. Most Moroccan rabbis considered the composition of *piyyutim* and *melitsah* (rhymed prose) a desirable achievement of a *talmid hakham* (rabbinic scholar). One popular aspect of these *piyyutim* or *pizmonim* is that they were sung both in the synagogue and in the homes on holidays and family celebrations to classical and contemporary Andalusian and Arabic music. In general, Sephardic music reflects local or regional musical traditions. Thus, the melodies associated with Sephardic liturgy, for example, derive from Andalusian, Greek, and Near Eastern music.

3.

HISTORICAL AND CULTURAL ROOTS
OF SEPHARDIC JUDAISM

The Roots of Sephardic culture and tradition go back to the historical encounter between Judaism and Islam. In a sense, they were the product of the challenge and opportunities presented by Islamic civilization to the Jews living within its orbit and the Jewish response to that challenge. Maimonides often refers to Muhammad as the madman (*meshuga'*), yet ironically, were it not for Muhammad, there might very well have been no Maimonides. For the Golden Age of Jewish culture and creativity in Spain, which produced Maimonides and other luminaries, would have been inconceivable without Islam.[1]

Why so? Because it seems that ever since the emergence of Islam in 622 CE in the Arabian Peninsula, the fortunes of the Jews in Muslim lands were to be forever intertwined with those of the Arabs and the Arabic or Islamic civilization—for better or for worse. The encounter between Judaism and Islam during the Golden Age of Islamic civilization illustrates the better aspect of this symbiotic relationship. It was most productive and mutually beneficial to Jews and Arabs alike. It was marked by a humanistic spirit, sophistication of thought, and intellectual daring on the parts of both peoples. Above all, it was marked by the readiness of the Jews to participate in and contribute to their contemporary culture.[2]

The question that arises then is why and in what ways was this encounter between Judaism and Islam in the Middle Ages so unique? Or, to put it differently, what events or political and cultural factors were responsible for or determined the great development of Sephardic culture during this period? I believe that fundamentally there were several such factors. They are (a) Muhammad's encounter with the Jews of Arabia and the consequences of that encounter, (b) the Islamic conquest and expansion in its multidimensional aspect, and its impact on the Jews living under Islam, and (c) the cultural, linguistic, and scientific achievements of both the Abbasids in Baghdad and the Umayyads in Spain, and the impact of their inspiration on the parallel development of Jewish culture.

MUHAMMAD'S ENCOUNTER WITH THE JEWS OF ARABIA

Muhammad's encounter with the Jews of Arabia and his relations with them is rather a complex subject and was determined by many factors—political, economic, and religious. It was stormy and ambivalent, cordial at the beginning and hostile at the end. Marked by hostility on one hand and tolerance on the other, this relationship had mixed implications for future Judeo-Muslim relations. In order to appreciate the consequences of this relationship, a brief historical background is in order.

The Arabian peninsula of pre-Islamic times had a substantial Jewish settlement which exercised a decided influence on the general population in many respects—economically, politically, and culturally. By the time of Muhammad (around 610 CE), there were large concentrations of Jews in Mecca, Medina (known in pre-Islamic times as Yathrib), and Khaybar, with three Jewish tribes (or confederations of clans) in Medina alone. These Jews were possessed of great Jewish learning. They were well versed in the Bible, Talmud, and Midrash.[3] Indeed, Arab historians saw in the presence of Jews in Arabia at this juncture an "act of Divine Providence" for it facilitated the acceptance of Muhammad's message.

Muhammad came in contact with the Jews of Arabia, learned much from them, and was immensely impressed by the teachings of Judaism.[4] More than once, the Prophet himself had suggested that much of what he taught he learned from others, presumably the Jews of the Arabian Peninsula.[5] In fact he conceived himself as another link in the chain of the prophets of Israel, with a special message for the Arabs in Arabic. Initially, he even tried to model his religion on Judaism and even included many of its concepts and practices in Islam. And when faced with the stiff opposition of his fellow Meccans, he appealed to the Jews to affirm the validity of his prophecy.

For their own reasons, the Jews denied him such recognition, and that led to the ultimate deterioration in their relations—with tragic consequences for the history of both peoples. Most tragic was the fate of the three Jewish tribes of Medina. Muhammad forced two of them, the Banu Qaynuqa and Banu Nadir into exile, and had all the males of the third one, the Banu Qurayza put to death.[6] This stage in the relation between Muhammad and the Jews of Arabia is reflected in all the negative and hostile references to the Jews in the Koran.

Thus, Muhammad's encounter with the Jews of Arabia had mixed results. On the negative side, Muhammad's statements in the Koran against the Jews, even when taken out of the context of battle and passionate debate, were believed by Muslims to be divinely inspired. As such, they served as a model and precedent for Muslim hostility against the Jews. They could and were often invoked by zealous Muslims against the Jews. In a sense, Muslims never forgave the Jews for rejecting Muhammad.

On the positive side, however, this tradition of intolerance and hostility was tempered by recognition on the part of Muslims that Jews were granted a revelation; they were "People of the Book (*ahlu al-kitab*)," and as such were to be granted a measure of tolerance. This measure of tolerance was based on the agreement made by Muhammad with Jews and Christians, and on many sayings, authentic and spurious, transmitted in his name in oral tradition (*hadith*). This led eventually to the establishment of the general principle that adherents of monotheistic religions (including Zoroastrians) should be allowed to live under Muslim domination. S. W. Baron rightly points out that, as a result, the Jews were never treated as "aliens" under Islam.[7]

A more important positive result of Muhammad's encounter with the Jews of Arabia, and one that bears more directly on the development of Sephardic culture was the impact of this encounter on the teachings of Muhammad and Islam. As noted above, Muhammad was so impressed by the teaching of Judaism as practiced by the Jews of Arabia that he tried to model Islam after Judaism. Thus, Islam's belief in absolute monotheism, divine revelation and prophecy, and its central concepts of God as the Creator and Provider all betray Jewish origins. Even the religious rituals of the confession of faith, public prayer, charity, and fasting, four of the "Five Pillars of Islam," were all inspired and informed by parallel Jewish practices.

Likewise, the Koran teems with references to biblical concepts, narratives, and characters of the Hebrew Bible. For example, the Koran mentions frequently such typical Jewish institutions as the rabbis or Jewish scholars (*ahbar*), the Sabbath, the Torah, and divine presence (*sakina*). Abraham is the subject of chapter 14, and is mentioned seventy times in over twenty other chapters; chapter 12 deals with Joseph, who stands out as a substantial figure reflecting possible traces of midrashic stories; "Jonah" is the title of chapter 10.

The figure towering above all others, however, the one with whom Muhammad identified himself, is that of Moses, the messenger of God. His name is mentioned more than one hundred times throughout the Koran. Likewise, the Koran contains legends, maxims, and theological ideas traceable to the Talmud and Midrash.[8] Similarly, many of the legislative reforms instituted by Muhammad in the Koran, such as the forbidden marriages, the prohibition against usury, and the emphasis on kindness and charity— all have their prototypes in the Hebrew Bible. Finally, the position of the Koran in Islam parallels that of the Torah in Judaism. Just as the Torah is the Holy Book of Judaism, so is the Koran the Holy Book of Islam—a book which contains God's revelation and is therefore the fundamental source of its beliefs, ethics, law, and religious life.

Subsequent developments in Islam, such as the *Shari'ah* and *Hadith* (oral tradition), also have their Jewish parallels. Both faiths seem to have followed parallel developments. Just as Judaism continued to develop after the canonization of the Bible, producing a vast corpus of rabbinic literature (Mishnah, Talmud, Midrash, legal codes, and so on), so Islam developed and changed enormously following the death of Muhammad until it became an elaborate system of ideas, institutions, customs, rites, and religious practices. Indeed, the resemblances of many features of both traditions are most striking. For example, *Halakhah* (Jewish law) and *Shari'ah* (Islamic law) are legal systems that have much in common in their conception of the law as God-given, in their all-embracing scope which minutely regulates all aspects of life, and the place accorded to the law in everyday personal, public, and private life. The very names *Halakhah* and *Shari'ah* mean the same thing, "the path to be followed", that is, the way of life.

Likewise, both systems developed an oral tradition, called *Hadith* in Arabic and *Torah she-be' al peh* in Hebrew, and both systems regard this oral tradition as being of divine origin—as authoritative as the Torah and the Koran respectively. Also, in both systems, this oral tradition consists of legal and nonlegal parts (*Halakhah* and *Haggadah* in Judaism; legal and nonlegal *Hadith* in Islam), and in both traditions, the nonlegal material assumes the form of maxims, short anecdotes, and ethical teachings.

Similarly, although the Muslims created their legal system when they had a political state, *Shari'ah*, like *Halakhah*, was developed by what

S. D. Goitein aptly calls "a completely free and organized republic of scholars." Also, the study of even purely legal matters is regarded by both religions as worship and a religious duty.[9] Finally, *Kiyas* (analogy) which is one of the four main official sources of Islamic law (the other three being the Koran, the oral tradition, and *Ijma'*—the consensus of scholars) derives both etymologically and conceptually from the Talmudic hermeneutical principle of *hekesh*.[10]

In fact, Islam is so permeated with the spirit of Judaism that Professor Goitein describes it as being "of the very flesh and bone of Judaism." Bernard Lewis, speaking of this affinity between Judaism and Islam in a different context, writes,

> But underlying them all there was something more powerful—an affinity of religious culture which made it possible for Jews, even emancipated, liberal West European Jews, to achieve an immediate and intuitive understanding of Islam. . . . The Judaeo-Islamic affinities include such things as inflexible Monotheism, austerity of worship, the rejection of images and incarnations, and, most important of all, submission to an all-embracing divine law, enshrined in scripture, tradition and commentary, which regulates and sanctifies the most intimate details of daily life. Not only are the sacred texts similar in spirit, but they were written in cognate languages. The same word, *din*, means religion in Arabic, law in Hebrew. The connection between the two meanings is obvious to any Jew or Muslim.[11]

Why is all this significant? What does all this have to do with the development of Sephardic culture? It is significant because it explains the unique phenomenon of the readiness of the Jews, during the height of Arab-Muslim civilization, to participate fully in Muslim culture without the slightest religious scruples. Their motto, as it were, was "Anything religious Muslims can do, we can do." As a result, for the first time since biblical times, Jews wrote secular poetry on wine, women, and love. Why? Because if pious Muslims can do it, so can the Jews.

At the same time, science and philosophy thrived among the Jews. It was engaged in not by free thinkers or libertines, but by such luminaries as Saadiah, Maimonides, and Abraham Ibn Ezra, the very pillars of Jewish orthodoxy at the time. This is indeed a unique case in Jewish history. As Goitein puts it, "The basic fact about Jewish-Arabic thought is that Greek science and Greek methods of thinking made their entrance into Jewish life mainly through the gates of Arab-Muslim literature. With the Arabic-writing Jewish doctors, mathematicians, astronomers and philosophers of the ninth and tenth centuries, science, in the Greek sense of the word, for the first time became known and practiced among the bulk of the Jewish community."[12]

Similarly, Bernard Lewis, discussing examples of Islamic influence on Judaism, writes, "The notion of a theology, of a formulation of religious belief in the form of philosophical principles, was alien to the Jews of Biblical and Talmudic times. The emergence of a Jewish theology took place almost entirely in Islamic lands. It was the work of theologians who used both the concepts and the vocabulary (either in Arabic or calqued into Hebrew) of Muslim *kalam*."[13]

Perhaps, in order to appreciate the magnitude of this phenomenon, we need to compare the encounter between Judaism and Islam with other historical encounters, namely the encounter with Hellenic culture in Hellenic times, and the encounter with the modern European secular culture of the Enlightenment. In Hellenic times, the study of Greek wisdom was discouraged as reflected in the Talmudic dictum, "Find an hour which is neither day nor night and study Greek wisdom" (BT *Menahot*, 99b). The second encounter with modern European secularism of the Enlightenment was also opposed by Jewish orthodoxy. Yet, as noted above, in medieval times, Jews had no problem engaging in the same Greek sciences and philosophy, as Goitein puts it, "through the gates of Arab-Muslim literature."

So, why did Judaism accept so readily the fruits of Islamic civilization? It is simply this. Unlike Hellenism, Islam was not pagan, and unlike modern European secularism, Islam was not secular. That is why the nature of Islam was instrumental to the development of Jewish culture during the Golden Age. Islam being what it is—almost a replica of Judaism—presented no threat to Judaism. After all, was not Islam "of the very flesh and bone of Judaism," (as Goitein puts it)? So, anything a pious Muslim can do, a pious Jew or a rabbi can do. Therefore, if a great Muslim jurist and thinker like Ibn Rushd can study Aristotle, so can Maimonides. And if a pious Muslim can indulge in secular poetry of wine, women, and friendship, so can Halevi and others. And so they did. It is a bit ironic that the rabbis seem to have gotten their *hekhsher* for studying science and philosophy or writing secular poetry from the Muslims.[14]

THE ISLAMIC CONQUEST AND EXPANSION AND ITS IMPACT ON SEPHARDIC CULTURE

The second major factor that had a considerable impact on the development of Sephardic culture is the Arab-Muslim conquest in all but one of its aspects. People usually tend to think of the Islamic conquest in pure territorial and military terms. Actually, the Arabs conquered souls and cultures as well as territories. Thus, in addition to the military and territorial or geographic aspect, the Arab conquest had linguistic, cultural, and religious aspects as well, and all these were equally amazing and most remarkable in terms of their scope and extent—and in terms of the relatively short time in which they were achieved.

In a sense, the multidimensional nature of the expansion and conquest corresponds to and reflects what S. D. Goitein calls the "Four Faces of Islam." These are (a) Islam as the self-realization of the Arab nation, (b) Islam as a great monotheistic religion, (c) Islam as a body politic, and (d) Islam as a civilization.[15] All aspects of the Islamic conquest but the religious one had a salutary and beneficial impact on Jewish life and culture. All but the religious aspect presented the Jews living under Islam with multiple challenges and unique opportunities, and the Jews rose to the challenges and seized the opportunities.

TERRITORIAL EXPANSION

At the beginning of Muhammad's career, he was so scorned by his fellow Meccans that he was forced to emigrate to Medina in 622 CE (the year of the *Hijra*); yet, barely eight years later, Mecca prostrated itself before him, and by the time of his death in 632, all of Arabia submitted voluntarily to Islam. By 750, a little over one hundred years after his death, a series of spectacular victories under able caliphs and generals carried the Arabs across all of the Near East and North Africa, all the way to Morocco, Spain, and France in the West, to the gates of Constantinople and as far across Central Asia up to the Indus River in the East. From the shores of the Atlantic to as far east as China, the reach of Islam was greater than even the Roman Empire at its zenith. The reasons for such spectacular expansion are many, but our concern here is the impact of this geographical expansion on Jews and on Jewish history and culture.

First of all, during the conquest, Jews regarded the Arabs as liberators from oppressive Byzantine rule, and helped the Arab-Muslim conquerors in various ways in such places as Jerusalem, Alexandria, and Toledo. By and large, Jews not only welcomed the Arab conquerors, but assisted them actively. In many cases, they relieved them of the administration of the newly acquired territories, leaving them free to pursue further conquests. For example, the gates of Toledo in Spain were opened to the Arabs by the Jews (on Palm Sunday) while Christians were at church. Also, the conquerors entrusted the administration of the military garrisons of Elvira, Seville, and Cordoba to the Jews.[16]

The helpful role of the Jews elicited feelings of gratitude on the part of the conquerors, and helped influence their attitude toward their Jewish subjects. For example, when the second caliph Omar first occupied Jerusalem, he maintained the status quo of not allowing Jews in Jerusalem. But after the Jews helped him locate and clean the site of the Jewish Temple, on which site the Mosque of Omar was later built, he broke his agreement with the Christians and allowed Jews to settle in Jerusalem.[17] The helpful role of the Jews in the conquest no doubt also influenced the relatively good treatment accorded them by the so-called Pact of Omar. Its terms, as they evolved over time, granted them certain basic freedoms and protections. These included the protection of life, limb, and property; religious, cultural, educational, communal, and judicial autonomy; freedom of movement within most of the Muslim empire; and freedom of occupation, with the exceptions of high government office and the practice of medicine (limitations which were observed mainly in the breach).

It is true that as "protected minorities" (*dhimmis*), their official status under the Pact of Omar, Jews and Christians were subjected to a number of financial (in the form of special taxes) and social disabilities. These were irksome and even humiliating. Nevertheless, as S. W. Baron points out, "the majority of Jews undoubtedly viewed all the financial and social disabilities and even the irksome humiliations [mandated by the Pact of Omar] as but a minor price they had to pay for their freedom of conscience and their ability to live an untrammeled Jewish life within the confines of their own community."[18]

Secondly, the Jews were encouraged by the conquerors to settle in the new garrison cities (*amsar*) such as Fustat in Egypt and Qayrawan in Tunisia, giving rise to totally new Jewish communities. Thus, the Arab territorial expansion led to a parallel Jewish geographical expansion. Ancient communities were revived and new vibrant ones came into being. Old dormant communities such as Jerusalem, Tripoli, Aleppo, Damascus, and Alexandria were quickened back to life. Thus, for example, under the Byzantines, Jews were forbidden to settle in Jerusalem, but Omar, the second caliph, allowed them to return to Jerusalem—albeit in limited numbers.[19] In no time, however, the Jewish community in Jerusalem grew by leaps and bounds. Similarly, Al-Baladhuri, the first Arab historian of the conquest, informs us that in Tripoli, which was completely deserted by its Christian inhabitants, the first Umayyad caliph Mu'away settled a large number of Jews, "and it is they who live in that harbor to the present day." (Al-Baladhuri died in 892.)[20]

What is even more important is that new Jewish communities came into being in the new Arab cities of Baghdad, Fustat, Qayrawan, and Fez. All became great centers of Jewish life and learning. For example, Baghdad, the capital of Iraq, from its foundation as the "City of Salvation" in 762 by the Caliph Al-Mansur, attracted many Jewish settlers. It had two separate Jewish quarters with a large affluent Jewish community. It also became the site of the two famous Babylonian academies of Sura and Pumbedita, as well as the seat of the official head of the Jewish community under Islam, the Exilarch or *Resh Galuta*. The renowned medieval traveler, Benjamin of Tudela who visited Baghdad in 1148, found there some 40,000 Jews maintaining twenty-eight synagogues.[21]

In North Africa, likewise, the newly built cities of Qayrawan and Fez became great centers of Jewish life and scholarship. The Jews in Qayrawan, reinforced by numerous arrivals from Egypt and Palestine, had a fully developed community life at the time of the Fatimid rise to power in 909.[22] The community of Qayrawan experienced its Golden Age before that of Spain. It produced such great rabbinic scholars as Rabbi Jacob ben Nissim Ibn Shahin (d. c.1006), his son, Rabbi Nissim ben Jacob (d. 1062), Rabbi Hushi'el ben Elhanan (d. early part of the eleventh century), and his son, Rabenu Hananel (d. 1057), all of whom were celebrated rabbinic scholars whose works constituted a major contribution to medieval rabbinic scholarship and culture.

Rabbi Jacob ben Nissim's many queries from Sherira Gaon (d. 1000) elicited the latter's response in his famous Epistle (*Iggeret Sherira Gaon*), which is one of the major sources for the history of the Talmudic and Geonic periods. His son, Rabbi Nissim ben Jacob, probably the greatest of the "sages" of Qayrawan, was a prolific writer. One of his books, *Sefer Mafte'ah Man'ulei ha-Talmud* (The Key to the Locks of the Talmud) was the first attempt to systematize the study of the Talmud by providing sources for *baraitot* and *mishnayot*, as well as references for quotations encountered in Talmudic study. Rabbi Hushiel ben Elhanan was an Italian rabbi who settled in Qayrawan, and became the head of its great yeshiva, while his son and successor Rabenu Hananel, a major medieval rabbinic scholar, is best known for his commentary on the entire Babylonian Talmud.[23]

Similarly, in Morocco, the newly founded capital of Fez—from its inception in 808 by the Shi'ite Idrisid dynasty—became a major center of Jewish culture. Among its residents were some of the most illustrious Jewish scholars and writers of the tenth and eleventh centuries, such as Dunash Ibn Labrat, Yehudah ben David Ibn Hayyuj, Rabbi Isaac Alfasi, and Maimonides. In fact, the Jewish communities of Fez and Qayrawan played a crucial role in transmitting Jewish scholarship from Baghdad to Spain, and Fez provided the emerging community in Spain with its first Hebrew grammarian (Ibn Hayyuj), its first Hebrew poet (Ibn Labrat), and one of its first great rabbinic scholars and its first codifier of Jewish law (Rabbi Isaac Alfasi).[24] Finally, in Spain, the once oppressed Jewish communities under Visigothic rule were revitalized and soon became the greatest center of Jewish learning, replacing those of Babylonia and culminating in the Golden Age of Jewish science and creativity.

ECONOMIC TRANSFORMATION

Somewhat connected to the territorial expansion of the Arab conquest is an economic expansion. During the eighth and ninth centuries, Islamic society witnessed what S. D. Goitein describes as a great "bourgeois revolution," characterized by commerce, industry, and bureaucratic organization.[25] Again, the Jews under Islam rose to the challenge presented them by this form of Muslim capitalism, participating in it fully and profitably. They underwent a complete economic transformation. As Goitein puts it, "The Jews too, so to say, died as an agricultural people during the seventh and eighth centuries, but, unlike other ancient populations, returned to life as a nation of merchants and artisans." Goitein adds, "The Jews took their share in the great Middle Eastern mercantile civilization."[26] They were active in international trade and commerce, and were prominent as courtiers and court bankers.

Most telling examples of this are the remarkable careers of Joseph ben Phinehas and Aaron ben Amram as court bankers under the Abbasid Caliph Al-Muqtadir in Baghdad from c.911 through 924, surviving the rise and fall of many Muslim viziers. Walter Fischel, in his important book, *The Jews in the Economic and Political Life of Medieval Islam*, gives a detailed account of the amazing careers of these two Jewish merchants of Baghdad and the many indispensable financial services they were able to provide to Al-Muqtadir by virtue of their personal wealth, their commercial skills, and their many Jewish connections with other merchants and banking houses throughout the Muslim Empire.[27]

Why and how is this relevant to the development of medieval Sephardic culture? The answer is simply this. Wealthy and prominent Jews, following Muslim examples, became patrons of Jewish learning and culture. Hasdai Ibn Shaprut (915–75) and Samuel Ibn Nagrela, known better as Samuel Hanagid (993–1056), the two most important courtiers in Muslim Spain, by virtue of their wealth and prominence, were great patrons of Jewish learning and scholarship.[28]

Even Maimonides was able to devote himself completely to his studies and the preparation of his works only because, for many years, he was supported by his brother David who dealt in precious stones, affording Maimonides the luxury of living a life free from care. Only after David died in a shipwreck in the Indian Ocean while on a business trip (around 1169), did Maimonides feel the need to seek a livelihood in order to support himself—and his brother's widow and daughter. Since he was strongly opposed to communal support of Torah scholars, he decided to take up the practice of medicine—which he had studied during his family's stay in Fez, Morocco—as a means of gaining a livelihood.[29] He practiced medicine for the rest of his life, later becoming the court physician of the famous Saladin. In a letter written at a late date, Maimonides talks of the devastating effect his brother's death had on him and describes his brother: "My brother, my pupil. He went to trade so that I might remain at home and continue my studies. My one joy was to see him."

LINGUISTIC EXPANSION

Arabic spread from Arabia to many of the conquered territories. It accompanied the conquerors and became the official language of the conquered populations. A number of explanations have been offered for the "wonder" of Arabic expansion. While S. D. Goitein found it difficult to account for the comparatively rapid and almost complete diffusion of the Arabic language in the countries of Southwest Asia and North Africa, he nonetheless suggests that one of the most important factors is "the fervent attachment of the Arabs to their beloved language, an enthusiasm which simply infected the populations which came under their sway." In addition, Goitein mentioned "the merits inherent in that highly developed language itself."[30]

Bernard Lewis, on the other hand, suggests that the remarkable spread of Arabic in the conquered countries was facilitated by the garrison towns (*amsar*) that the Arab conquerors wisely established at the edge of the desert as their main bases. Such were the new towns of Kufa and Basra in Iraq, Fustat in Egypt, and Qayrawan in Tunisia. As Bernard Lewis explains, these garrison towns "played a vital role in the establishment and consolidation of Arab influence in the conquered lands." That is, explains Lewis, while the Arabs were a minority in the provinces as a whole, they formed the dominant element in the *amsar*, where Arabic became the chief language. Moreover, these garrison towns served as markets for the agricultural produce of the neighboring districts; through them, Arabic spread to the surrounding countryside. Soon, Lewis adds, "each of the Arab garrison cities developed an outer town of artisans, shopkeepers, clerks, and workmen drawn from the subject populations, supplying the needs of the Arab ruling class."[31] Incidentally, the *amsar* strategy was one among many other factors that account for the spectacular ease and success of the Arab conquest.[32]

Speaking of the impact of the spread of Arabic on the Jews, S. D. Goitein states, "The first and most basic aspect of Jewish-Arab symbiosis is the simple fact that the great majority of the Jews, like the rest of the populations of the Caliph's Empire, adopted the Arabic language. . . . In the main, the process was completed around 1000." Goitein adds that Arabic "was adopted by the Jews at a time when the Arabs had already developed a national literature and a religious terminology. . . . Therefore, the acquisition of the Arab language by the Jews meant also their adoption of Arab ways of thinking and forms of literature, as well as Muslim religious notions."[33] As a result, Goitein continues, "Arabic was used by the Jews for all kinds of literary activities, not only for scientific and other secular purposes, but for expounding and translating the Bible or the Mishnah, for theological and philosophical treatises, for discussing Jewish law and ritual, and even for the study of Hebrew grammar and lexicography." Examples in all these fields abound.

Saadiah Gaon, Yehudah Halevi, Solomon Ibn Gabirol, Maimonides, and Abraham Ibn Ezra—all wrote their philosophical works in Arabic. Saadiah's translation of the Bible into Arabic was named by him *Tafsir*, commentary, for it was indeed more than a translation. Maimonides' *siraj*, his commentary on the Mishnah, was also written in Arabic. Saadiah Gaon, Samuel ben Hofni Gaon, and Hai Gaon, three of the great *Geonim*, all wrote their legal monographs in Arabic,[34] and finally, Saadiah, Yehudah Ibn Qurysh, Yehudah ben David Ibn Hayyuj, and Jonah Ibn Janah, all wrote their works on Hebrew grammar and lexicography in Arabic. Most of these works were written in Judeo-Arabic, which, according to Goitein, was not a specific Jewish idiom, but rather Arabic as developed in the post-classical period.[35]

CULTURAL EXPANSION

As a result of the Arab conquest, the Arabs came into contact with and assimilated many different cultures. They fell heir to the ancient civilizations of Mesopotamia and Egypt, assimilated the Persian and Greco-Roman cultures, and acted as transmitters of Greek science and philosophy. Thus, Islamic civilization incorporated within itself many elements of diverse origins, including Christian, Jewish, and Zoroastrian ideas of revelation and prophecy, legal religion, eschatology and mysticism, and most especially Greek science and philosophy. But despite the diversity of its origins, Islamic civilization was no mere juxtaposition of previous cultures, but rather a new creation, in which the Arabs fused and molded all these elements in a new and original Arabic civilization. As Bernard Lewis observes, "It was the Arabisation of the conquered provinces rather than their military conquest that is the true wonder of the Arab expansion." By the eleventh century, Lewis continues, "Arabic had become not only the chief idiom of everyday use from Persia to the Pyrenees, but also the chief instrument of culture, superseding old culture languages like Coptic, Aramaic, Greek, and Latin"[36]

In the process of Arabization and Islamization of these foreign cultures, Islam developed its own legal system, philosophy and science, mysticism and Sufism, new religious sciences (such as the *hadith* or oral tradition and Koranic commentaries), and Arabic philology and poetry. Islamic civilization reached its apogee under the Abbasid Caliph Harun Al-Rashid (813–33) in Baghdad, and the Caliphs Abd Al-Rahman III (912–61) and Hakam II (961–76), his son—successive Umayyad Caliphs in Cordova.

Influenced by the remarkable cultural and literary achievements of the Arabs, the Jews of Arab lands developed a multidimensional culture of their own. It may be safely stated that all the great achievements of medieval Sephardic culture were the result of the influence and inspiration of Islamic civilization, and in many cases were modeled on corresponding Islamic prototypes.

Responding to the cultural challenge presented by Islamic civilization, the Jews produced compendia of highly organized legal codes, beginning with the systematically organized legal monographs of Saadiah Gaon and other *Geonim* and culminating in Maimonides' monumental code, the *Mishneh Torah*; highly sophisticated Jewish philosophy and theology represented in the works of Saadiah, Abraham Ibn Daud, Solomon Ibn Gabirol, Yehudah Halevi, and Maimonides; and biblical exegesis, striking new pathways in more directions, and characterized, in the words of Nahum Sarna, by "a uniqueness and originality, a vitality and a pioneering quality that set it apart from anything that came before or after." They also developed Hebrew philology and comparative Semitic linguistics, and composed sublime Hebrew poetry, both secular and religious, adopting and effectively using all features and conventions of Arab prosody in their Hebrew poetry.[37]

Perhaps all this was possible because the process of absorption and Arabization of the legacy of Greece and other cultures by Islam was completed, in the main, by the end of the tenth century, precisely at the time when Jews began taking their part in the new civilization. It just happened that, as noted above, at this juncture in history, around 1000, Arabic became the language of the majority of the Jewish people, replacing Aramaic. The acquisition of Arabic therefore meant also the acquisition of all the elements of contemporary Arab culture, including science, philosophy, Arab ways of thinking and literary forms, and Muslim religious notions.[38] As Bernard Lewis puts it, when speaking of the adoption of Arabic by the Jews, "What was more important was the sharing of the language and the cultural values expressed in it—the whole frame of reference that made possible a degree of communication, indeed of cooperation, that is comparatively rare in the history of the Jewish Diaspora."[39] Also, at the same time, new science and learning had taken root in the well-to-do, educated classes of Muslim society, and it became then a question of survival for Judaism, whether or not it could stand the test of being interpreted in progressive and contemporary terms. Needless to say, Judaism stood the test of the Islamic challenge and emerged immensely enriched by the experience.

As noted at the outset, the only aspect of the Islamic expansion that did not have an impact on the Jews was the religious one. An interesting contrast is provided by the impact of the Islamic conquest on other religions. Thus, for example, the Persian religion, Zoroastrianism entirely disintegrated—practically the entire nation embraced Islam. Likewise, many Christians, having spent their energies in sectarian struggles, now largely gave up Christianity for Islam. Many found the simplicity of the absolute and inflexible monotheism preached by Islam more appealing and convincing than the complicated doctrine of the Trinity. Some simply emigrated.[40] But Jews and Judaism, unlike the Persians and Christians, gained in strength and numbers under Islam.[41]

Perhaps the simplest reason for this is that Jews had very few incentives to give up Judaism for Islam. Neither coercion nor conviction could drive them to embrace Islam. Contrary to the implication of the popular notion of the Muslims offering the Koran in one hand and the sword in the other, with rare exceptions, no forced conversions took place during the conquest. The religious aspect was not prominent in the minds of the Muslims during the conquest. Thus, compared to the zeal of Muhammad's preaching, no preaching was carried on by the Arab conquerors. In fact, conversions were even discouraged so as not to diminish the number of taxpayers, since Muslims were free from general land taxes.[42] Nor was there anything in the Islamic religion or theology that was more appealing to the Jews than Judaism for, as we have seen, many of the Islamic notions about God and revelation, as well as many religious institutions and practices owe their origin to Jewish sources.[43]

Finally, although many Jews embraced Islam for convenience—that is, in order to advance themselves in Islamic society—actually being Jewish did not prevent many Jews from rising to positions of eminence in the Islamic Empire. As we have seen, many Jews rose to positions of power and influence both under the Abbasids in Baghdad and under the Spanish Umayyads. Nor were the Jews driven to embrace Islam in order to escape the status of subject under Islam—as was the case with many Christians. For, as Bernard Lewis points out, for the Jews, "the Islamic conquest merely meant a change of masters, in most places indeed for the better."[44] On the other hand, all but the religious aspects of the Arab conquest presented the Jews under Islam with multiple challenges and unique opportunities on all levels—geographically, economically, linguistically, and above all culturally. And the Jews rose to every challenge and seized every opportunity, and in the process enhanced Jewish life and culture, imparting to it a uniqueness and originality that set it apart from anything that came before or after.

4.

BIBLICAL EXEGESIS AND HEBREW PHILOLOGY IN MEDIEVAL SPAIN

Beginning with the early part of the tenth century, we witness the development and ultimate flourishing of Hebrew philology and comparative Semitic linguistics, Hebrew poetry both religious and secular, and biblical studies characterized by critical independence and intellectual daring. Basically, the development of Hebrew philology, biblical exegesis, and Hebrew poetry are all connected. As Nahum Sarna, the eminent biblical scholar put it, "The course of Hebrew rebirth and efflorescence in Spain proceeded in three distinct directions—poetic composition, linguistic studies, and biblical exegesis. In actual fact, however, it is not always easy to separate the disciplines since all three are inextricably intertwined, and they reacted one upon the other."[1] He continues, "The ability to write Hebrew poetry, when Hebrew was not the vernacular, required a thorough mastery of the biblical text, a keen sensitivity to the distinctive peculiarities of biblical prose and poetry, and a fine perception of the meaning of words and the subtleties of their use." Likewise, he adds, "No biblical interpretation could be convincing if it ignored sound philology, [so] the Spanish Jewish grammarians carefully studied the Bible to extract from it the laws of the language."[2] For convenience, this chapter will focus on biblical exegesis and Hebrew philology; Hebrew poetry will be the subject of a separate chapter.

BIBLICAL EXEGESIS

Speaking of the flourishing of biblical studies in medieval Spain, Sarna writes, "It was in biblical studies, in all their manifestations, that the intellectual history of Spanish Jewry found its most fundamental and concrete articulation." In describing the uniqueness of biblical exegesis in Spain, he adds, "Unlike the experience of Jews of Christian Europe, the

41

study of Scriptures in Spain did not become [solely] the consolidation of past learning. . . . [Rather,] an element of contention and controversy was allowed to penetrate, and a considerable admixture of critical independence and intellectual daring imparted a quality of excitement to biblical studies."[3] He observes, "The diversity and multiplicity of approach, the acute sensitivity to difficulties [exhibited for example in Abraham Ibn Ezra's commentary on the Torah], the forging of the essential tools of scholarship, and the extraordinary degree of sophistication—all these characterized the Sephardi contribution to biblical scholarship and led to a remarkable and unparalleled efflorescence in the field." [4]

This glorious and sophisticated tradition of which Sarna speaks is evident in the biblical commentaries of such Sephardic luminaries as Saadiah Gaon, Abraham Ibn Ezra, Moses Ibn Gikatella (Ibn Chiquitilla), Nachmanides (Ramban), Bahia Ibn Asher (known popularly as Rabbenu Bahia), Isaac Arama, David Kimhi, and Isaac Abrabanel.[5]

Some of the major factors that led to the flourishing of biblical studies in Spain and elsewhere are these:

- The anti-Rabbanite polemics of the sectarian Karaites stimulated the study of the Bible. In their rigorous attack on rabbinic teachings and rabbinic law, the Karaites used the Bible, studying its language and its contents. In order to repudiate the Karaites' attacks, the Rabbanites also had to master the Bible and its language—to beat them at their own game, so to speak. Thus, for example, Saadiah Gaon, who defended the legitimate and binding authority of rabbinic tradition against the attacks of the Karaites, had an unparalleled mastery of the Bible and its language—evident in all his writings, especially in his philological and exegetical works.

- Muslim anti-Jewish polemics frequently involved attacks on the Bible and inevitably generated apologetics and counter-polemics from the Jews, all of which led to further study and reexamination of the Bible.

- The spread of rationalism of the period fostered a spirit of criticism, which soon found expression in a skeptical approach to Scriptures. Also, the encounter between Islam, Judaism, and Christianity produced not only polemics and religious propaganda, but also generated criticism and skepticism among Muslims themselves. In fact, the very Islamic notion that other monotheistic faiths (Judaism and Christianity) also possessed divine truth could not help but encourage skepticism among certain Muslims. As a result, the rational and critical approach to everything typical of the times deeply affected the exegetical approach to the Bible and the Koran as well. Thus, for example, the Muslim heretics Ibn Al-Rawandi (who died at the end of the ninth century or the beginning of the tenth century) questioned certain fundamental tenets of Islam such as the prophecy of Muhammad, and the "inimitability of the Koran" (*I'jaz al-Kor'an*).[6] Similarly, Hivi ha-Balkhi (of Balkh in today's Afghanistan), described by S. W. Baron as a rabbanite extremist, raised as many as two hundred arguments against the Bible. (Incidentally, Saadiah fought him, answering all his objections.)[7]

• In addition, the repeated boastings by the Muslims that the Arabic of the Koran represented linguistic purity and literary elegance in its most excellent form, must have stimulated a corresponding desire among the Jews to promote the Hebrew Bible as the model of literary excellence.

All these internal and external factors led inevitably to the analytical, critical, and rational examination of the Bible represented in the works of the above-mentioned Sephardi commentators of the Bible.[8]

HEBREW PHILOLOGY

Together with the study of the Bible, there came into being the study of its language—and the study of language in general. An additional factor leading to the development of Hebrew philology was the example and the challenge presented by the development of Arabic philology. As noted above, the adoption of Arabic by the Jews led to the study of Hebrew grammar and lexicography.[9] As Bernard Lewis point out, "Jews studying Hebrew in order to achieve a better understanding of the Hebrew Bible followed many of the procedures devised by Muslims examining Arabic for the parallel purpose of studying the sacred text of the Qur'an."[10] Also, the meticulous regard of the Arabs for their language and the great attention they paid to proper grammatical and stylistic usage must have developed among the Arabic-speaking Jews a high degree of linguistic consciousness and aesthetic appreciation which they in turn applied to Hebrew. Thus, Jewish scholars, taking Arabic grammar and lexicography as their model, explored, examined, and described the Hebrew of the Bible (and eventually that of the Mishnah as well). S. D. Goitein put it this way: "For the first time, the pronunciation, the grammar and syntax, and the vocabulary of Hebrew were treated scientifically and analytically, and, so to speak, were brought under control; thus, Hebrew became a disciplined and well-organized means of expression under the influence of Arabic."[11] But the Hebrew philologists did not confine themselves to the study of Hebrew. Fluent in Arabic, Hebrew, and Aramaic, they were best qualified to undertake the comparative aspects of all three languages, thus laying the foundation for the field of comparative linguistics.

The impact of all these factors on the development of Hebrew philology in Spain was reinforced by the policies of Abd Al-Rahman III (912–61) and his son Abd Al-Hakam II (961–76), Caliphs of Cordova. In their desire to make Cordova an independent center of Islamic learning and culture, they cultivated various fields of scholarship, including linguistic studies, through the import and patronage of scholars. Inspired by the example of both caliphs, the Jewish aristocracy followed suit. Thus, Hasdai Ibn Shaprut (915–75), court physician and advisor to both caliphs, wanted likewise to liberate Spanish Jewry from its spiritual and cultural dependence on Babylonia. To that end, he invited scholars and rabbis from Baghdad, North Africa, and southern Italy to Spain, supported them, and established academies for them. Cultured, scholarly, wealthy, and powerful, he became the leading patron of Hebrew studies in Cordova, which was soon to become the Mecca for Jewish scholars who could be assured of hospitable welcome from Jewish courtiers and men of means.[12] Among those attracted to Cordova by his largess and his patronage were Dunash Ibn Labrat (c.920–c.990), Judah Ibn Hayyuj (c.950–1000), and Rabbi Isaac Alfasi, known as the Rif (1013–1103).

All these factors contributed to the flourishing of Hebrew philology in medieval Spain. The story of the development of Hebrew philology is most remarkable in that it laid the foundations for other achievements of the Golden Age. For example, it facilitated the production of poetry in pure classical biblical Hebrew. It also contributed to the biblical commentaries that emphasize textual and grammatical analysis such as those of Abraham

Ibn Ezra and David Kimhi (Radak). Moreover, it provides a good illustration of the history of ideas and how they move from one geographical center of Jewish life to another.

While Hebrew philology thrived and flourished in Spain, it really began in Baghdad and Tahert (in what is Algeria today). The first pioneer in the field of Hebrew philology (as in many other fields) was Saadiah Gaon. His pioneering work in this field was his translation of the Bible into Arabic, which as its name *Tafsir* (commentary) indicates, was more than a mere translation. It was the first translation of the Bible into Arabic, and has remained the standard Bible for Arabic-speaking Jews. According to S. D. Goitein, Saadiah's translation "became a sacred text, which was copied, and later printed, beside the Hebrew original and the old Aramaic version."[13]

Saadiah also wrote a critical and, in many ways, innovative commentary on several books of the Bible. Also, in addition to many linguistic annotations in his biblical commentary, he also wrote three separate works on the subject. Of these works, his *Egron* provides a dictionary of a substantial part of the Hebrew language, and, in particular, a rhyming dictionary of word-endings designed especially for the benefit of Hebrew poets. The subject of his third work, *Sefer Tzahut ha-Lashon ha-Ivrit*, was Hebrew grammar. Like all his other writings, Saadiah's works on Hebrew grammar and lexicography attest to his extensive knowledge and the great vigor with which he applied himself to whatever task he undertook. Thus, the first Spanish linguist, Menahem Ibn Seruq (910–70), a protégé of Hasdai Ibn Shaprut in Cordova, speaks of Saadiah's "accuracy in his interpretation and the comprehensiveness of his linguistics." Similarly, the renowned Spanish Hebrew grammarian, Jonah Ibn Janah (see below), praises Saadiah's great work in the field.[14]

The next Hebrew philologist of note was a contemporary of Saadiah, Judah Ibn Quraysh from Tahert (in today's Algeria). He lived at the end of the ninth century and the beginning of the tenth. Not much is known about him. He is believed to have been a physician by profession. As far as is known, he was the very first comparative linguist. He studied the relationship between Hebrew and its cognate languages, Aramaic and Arabic. He is most famous for his Epistle (*Risalah*) to the Jewish community of Fez regarding the merit of resuming the age-old tradition of reading each verse of the weekly portion of the Torah (*parashah*) twice in Hebrew and once in Aramaic. The Jewish community of Fez had decided to discontinue the practice, arguing that they no longer needed the Aramaic translation.[15]

The subject of the *Risalah* and its purpose are spelled out by the author in his description of the work: "Epistle of Yehudah Ibn Quraysh to the Jewish community of Fez concerning the revival of the study of the Targum [Aramaic translation], and the love of it, and the enjoyment of its benefits, and the blameworthiness of its rejection."[16] In his attempt to demonstrate the importance and benefits to be derived from resuming the discontinued practice, Ibn Quraysh discusses the relationship between the language of the Bible and those of the Mishnah and the Talmud. More importantly, in the last part of the Epistle, he discusses the relationship between Hebrew, Aramaic, and Arabic, in terms of vocabulary, morphology, and grammar, and formulates rules determining various consonantal changes among them.[17]

This Epistle is very important for a number of reasons. First and foremost, it tells us something about its author. We learn of his great proficiency in languages, his originality, and his sure instinct which led him in the right direction, although the study of the Hebrew language was in its infancy at the time.[18] Second, the Epistle was the first treatise on comparative linguistics ever written, and as such its interest is universal.[19] But, most importantly, the Epistle is significant for the considerable impact it had on the future of Hebrew philology. As a result of the *Risalah* and subsequent works influenced by it, Spanish Jews inherited a well-established tradition in the use of cognate languages for the study of Hebrew and biblical exegesis. Merely one generation after his Epistle reached the community of Fez, we find there two linguistic scholars famous for their research in Hebrew philology.[20] They are Dunash Ibn Labrat and Judah Ibn Hayyuj. Both flourished outside North Africa, namely in Spain, but both had acquired their learning in Fez and were directly influenced by Ibn Quraysh's Epistle. They adopted and perfected his approach.

As noted above, both Ibn Hayyuj and Ibn Labrat were attracted to Cordova by the patronage of Hasdai Ibn Shaprut. While the philological discoveries of Ibn Hayyuj revolutionized the scientific study of Hebrew grammar, Ibn Labrat, a grammarian and a linguist, was the first to adapt features and conventions of Arabic prosody to Hebrew, thereby providing future Hebrew poets in Spain with an important tool and models for their poetry,. The former, together with his Spanish disciple, Jonah Ibn Janah, discovered and developed the principle that—just as in Arabic—all Hebrew words were derived from (or went back to) three root letters. Speaking of the respective contributions of both grammarians, Sarna writes, "There is certainly unanimous agreement on the role of Judah ben David Ibn Hayyuj (950–1000) as the real founder of Hebrew grammar as we know it today." Of Ibn Janah he says, "Basing himself on the master's discoveries, a younger contemporary, a scholar of true genius, soon outstripped all others in the field."[21] Other Hebrew philologists of note were Samuel Ibn Nagrela, Moses Ha-Cohen Ibn Gikatella (or Ibn Chiquitilla), and Abraham Ibn Ezra.

Samuel Ibn Nagrela, known as Samuel Hanagid, in addition to being a great Talmudist, poet, and statesman, was also a grammarian and lexicographer of note. According to Abraham Ibn Ezra, Hanagid wrote no fewer than twenty-two philological treatises.[22] Ibn Gikatella was the first Spanish Jew to translate the scientific works of Ibn Hayyuj and Ibn Janah from Arabic to Hebrew. He was also a grammarian and biblical commentator in his own right.[23]

Abraham Ibn Ezra's forte, on the other hand, lay in his thorough familiarity with the entire field of grammatical, lexicographical, and exegetical scholarship, including that of the Karaites, from Saadiah to his own day. According to Sarna, because Ibn Ezra was an anthologist and a synthesizer rather than an innovator, he "had the great merit of salvaging for future generations much of what otherwise would have certainly disappeared beyond reclaim."[24] Ibn Ezra was also important as a translator of many of the works of Spanish scholars and grammarians from Arabic to Hebrew for the benefit of Jews who were unable to read Arabic. As noted above (chap. 2, n. 11), during his travels in Italy, Provence, France, and England, after having left Spain in 1140, he acted as a living cultural bridge between Spain and the non-Arabic-speaking Jewish communities, affording them the benefits and fruits of Spanish scholarship and culture.

This, in brief outline, is the remarkable story of the development of Hebrew philology. It began simultaneously in Baghdad and in Tahert, Algeria. It was brought to Spain by two Moroccan scholars, Ibn Labrat and Ibn Hayyuj, and was perfected by Jonah Ibn Janah, a Spanish disciple of Ibn Hayyuj. Translated to Hebrew, it was thus made accessible to non-Arabic-speaking Jews by another Spanish scholar, Ibn Gikatella. Finally, it was carried and transmitted to Europe by another great Sephardi, Abraham Ibn Ezra, who in his own person (and in his own life) constituted a living bridge between Sephardim and Ashkenazim, thus making the philological achievements of the Sephardim part of the legacy of all Jews.

It might be appropriate to conclude this discussion of the development and flowering of Hebrew philology with a very insightful comment by S. D. Goitein, who wonders why the Jews did not develop Hebrew philology before, say in Talmudic times? After all, he observes, the Jews had all the requirements for developing their philology while on their own soil: the rabbis of Talmudic times were versed in two or even three languages; the canon of biblical literature was finally fixed in mishnaic times; the powerful faculty of abstract and syllogistic thinking displayed in the Talmud, if applied to the study of language, would have made the rabbis excellent linguists; and finally, the work of the *masoretes* shows that its creators had a very fine "ear" and an excellent faculty of observation of linguistic facts.

Yet, despite all these favorable conditions, no genuine Hebrew philology was created by the Jews while on their own soil. The reason suggested by Goitein for this lack of interest in philology among Jews before their encounter with the Arabs is the concentration on ideas coupled with an innate disregard for the importance of a national language, which were characteristics of old Israel—in contrast to the Arabs. Thus, he concludes, "It was the contact with the Arabs—'the worshippers of language,' as they have been called—that directed the Jewish mind to a field of activity for which, as it was proved subsequently, it was particularly gifted, and which bore its mature first fruits to the benefit of the national language of the Jewish People itself."[25]

5.

HEBREW POETRY IN MEDIEVAL SPAIN

Under the Umayyad and the Abbasid dynasties, we witness a renaissance of poets and poetry among Arabs. According to Bernard Lewis, "Under the Umayyads [661–750], the orally transmitted poetry of pre-Islamic Arabia was codified and served as the model for further development. Under the Abbasids [750 onwards], Arabic poetry was enriched by Persian influence."[1] As was the case with various other aspects of Arabic culture, the flourishing of its poetry led to a corresponding development—the flourishing of Hebrew poetry.

Speaking of the impact of the Arab influence on the development of Hebrew poetry, Bernard Lewis observes, "In literature and the arts, the Muslim influence on the Jews is enormous, and it is almost entirely one way. Hebrew poetry, in the medieval golden age, follows very closely on the prosody and technique of Arabic poetry and indeed on its whole system of symbol and allusions. Though written in a non-Islamic language and script, medieval Hebrew poetry and much of the prose literature belong to the same cultural world as Arabic and other literatures of Islam."[2] S. D. Goitein calls the Hebrew poetry in medieval Spain "the acme of Jewish–Arab symbiosis." According to Goitein, "the most perfect expression of the Jewish–Arab symbiosis is not in the Arabic literature of the Jews, but in the Hebrew poetry created in Muslim countries, particularly in Spain." He adds that "it was the influence of Arabic on Hebrew which made the rise of medieval Hebrew poetry possible," and that apart from the general impact of Arabic on Hebrew, "the very forms and motifs of Hebrew poetry . . . were indebted to the Arabic model."[3]

In addition, as noted above (in chap. 4), the intensive and analytical study of the Bible and the development of Hebrew philology facilitated the production of Hebrew poetry in pure classical biblical Hebrew. In fact, many of the medieval Hebrew poets such as Saadiah Gaon, Dunash Ibn Labrat, Samuel Hanagid, and Abraham Ibn Ezra were themselves linguistic scholars (even as Solomon Ibn Gabirol, Yehudah Halevi, and Abraham Ibn Ezra were philosophers as well).[4]

Saadiah Gaon initiated the process in his *Egron*, compiled specifically for the benefit of Hebrew poets. The *Egron* provided them with a rhyming dictionary of word-endings. In addition, Saadiah composed *azharot* (a poetic versification of the commandments) and *bakkashot* (supplications). His *bakkashot* received high praise from Abraham Ibn Ezra in his commentary on Ecclesiastes (5:1); he said of them, "No other author had composed their like." Moreover, these *bakkashot* seem to have acquired the status of quasi-formal prayers; thus, Maimonides was asked whether it was necessary to stand—as one stands in the *amidah* prayer—when reciting the *bakkashot* of the Gaon.[5]

As noted above (chap. 4, p. 46), Dunash Ibn Labrat (Saadiah's disciple) was the first to adapt features and conventions of Arabic prosody to Hebrew, thereby providing future Hebrew poets in Spain with important tools and models for Hebrew poetry.[6] Ibn Labrat's poetry and his achievements as a grammarian were ultimately surpassed by the works of greater poets and greater grammarians. His claim to fame, however, rests in his having ushered in the new Hebrew poetry in Spain. Interestingly, his religious poem for the Sabbath, "*Deror yikra le-ben 'im bat . . .* (He will proclaim freedom for all his children, and will guard them as the apple of His eye)" achieved universal popularity, and it is sung to this day at the Sabbath tables of Sephardim and Ashkenazim alike. By the time of Samuel Hanagid, only a few generations after Ibn Labrat, Hebrew poetry was flourishing in Spain. In the words of Abraham Ibn Daud in his *Sefer Ha-Kabbalah*, "In the days of Hasdai the Nasi they began to chirp, and in the days of Samuel the Nagid they sang loudly."[7]

Uniqueness of Hebrew Poetry in Spain

Religious poetry had been an important branch of Hebrew literature before Islam as part of synagogue service. But the Hebrew poetry in medieval Spain was unique in many ways, all of which were due to Arab influence. First of all, it was the first instance of secular Hebrew poetry written about nature, friendship, wine, women, and love. It became fashionable and was practiced by most prominent poets. Secondly, the writing of poetry became a respectable profession, commanding patronage and sophisticated audiences. To be sure, the first steps were hesitant due to religious scruples about using the "holy tongue" (*lashon ha-kodesh*) for secular poetry, but contemporary Arab culture provided the necessary reassurance. Seeing that religious and even pious Muslims wrote secular poetry in the language of their Holy Book, the Jews felt it was appropriate for them to do the same in Hebrew.

In addition to these things, Spanish poets saw in the writing of Hebrew poetry a national challenge of sorts. The Arabs boasted that Arabic was the most eloquent language as evidenced by the elegance and beauty of Arabic poetry. The Jewish answer was, as it were, "Anything the Arabs can do in Arabic, we can do in Hebrew, and do it even better." That is why, while medieval Jewish scholars wrote most of their works in Arabic (or Judeo-Arabic), when it came to writing poetry, they chose to do so in Hebrew. Logically, it would have been much easier for them to write in Arabic, as they were adopting the very forms and motifs, as well as all stylistic features of Arabic poetry. Yet, they chose to write their secular poetry in Hebrew because they felt that in doing so they were in fact strengthening the Jewish sense of self-respect.[8]

Thus, most of the themes that ran through the Arabic models were adopted by Hebrew poets, as if to prove that Hebrew—no less than Arabic—was capable of expressing any idea or motif which was regarded by Arab contemporaries as proper for poetic formulation. As a result, poets like Yehudah Halevi, rises to sublime spiritual heights in his religious poetry:

> Lord, all my longing is before You,
> even though it does not pass my lips.
> Grant me Your favour for even a moment, and I will die.
> If only You would grant my wish!

– and –

> [O God], I have sought to come near you,
> I have called to You with all my heart;
> And when I went out towards You,
> I found You coming towards me.[9]

And this same Halevi does not hesitate to come down to earth, so to speak, when he sings of his beloved Spanish maiden of golden hair whose love consumes his captivated heart. Thus, religious poets indulged freely in writing secular and even erotic poetry.

But even the religious poetry of medieval Spanish poets was innovative. Religious poetry of pre-Islamic times, although rich and imaginative, was essentially static, undisciplined, and sometimes even bizarre.[10] It was from the Arabs that Jews learned the notion of pure classical language. Accordingly, they took the language of the Bible as their model. Its pronunciation, grammar, spelling, vocabulary, syntax, and methodology were studied assiduously in all Islamic countries. In addition, Hebrew poets made full and effective use of all stylistic features and conventions of Arabic poetry including meter, rhyme, imagery, similes, and metaphors—all of which were new to Hebrew poetry.

As a result of all these innovations, Hebrew poets in Spain produced a body of poetry unsurpassed in elegance of form, depth of feeling and emotion, and simplicity of expression. Speaking of the literary qualities of this poetry, S. D. Goitein writes, "A poem by, perhaps, Yehudah Halevi—graceful in form, unfailing in wording, forceful in feeling and thought, overwhelms the reader with that complete harmony which is the surest indication of true culture. This applies especially to religious poetry which is our most precious heritage from Hebrew–Arab Spain."[11]

But the Spanish Jews wrote not only Hebrew poetry but other genres of belletristic literature as well. Judah Al-Harizi (c.1165–1225) wrote Hebrew *maqamat*, a literary genre created by the Arabs around the tenth century. The *maqama* is a narrative in rhymed prose interlaced with short metrical poems and witty discourse. Al-Harizi said that he composed his book, *Tahkemoni* (which contains fifty such *maqamat*) *to* prove that it was possible to use Arabic literary forms in Hebrew. He also translated into Hebrew the Arabic *maqamat* of Al-Hariri (1054–1121), considered to be the greatest Arab writer of *maqamat*.[12]

Likewise, Moses Ibn Ezra—having undertaken an extensive study of the nature of poetry and its forms, the creative process involved in writing poetry, and the intellectual qualities of poets—went on to write a comprehensive treatise on poetry in general, and Hebrew poetry in particular. He included in it a historical and critical overview of the Hebrew poets who lived before him, notably Samuel Hanagid and Solomon Ibn Gabirol. Following the convention of the times, he wrote this work in Arabic and called it *Kitab Al-Muhadara wal-Mudhakara* (The Book of Conversation and Discussions/Debates), but the Hebrew translator of the work called it simply *Shirat Yisrael* (The Poetry of Israel). It is a unique treatise in that it is the only treatise of its kind to have been written on the subject by anyone during the Golden Age.[13]

In my opinion, the most famous of Spanish Hebrew poets were Samuel Hanagid, Solomon Ibn Gabirol, Moses Ibn Ezra, Yehudah Halevi, and Abraham Ibn Ezra. They all wrote secular poetry about friendship, nature, wine, women, and love, especially in their youth. Halevi speaks for them all when he writes:

> My youth has done its pleasures until today,
> But when shall I do good for my own soul?
>
> (*Ne'uray 'ad halom 'asu le-nafsham,*
> *U-matay gam ani e'eseh le-veti.*)[14]

All wrote stirring religious poetry marked by love for the people of Israel, the Torah, the Land of Israel, and the God of Israel. Yet, each of these poets is noted for something special and a unique contribution. Following are brief descriptions of the works and the unique aspects thereof from each of these poets, with excerpts from their verses.

SAMUEL HANAGID (993–C.1055)[15]

Samuel Hanagid, in addition to being a diplomat, statesman, Talmudic scholar, and a philologist, was also a prolific poet. His poetry came in three poetic collections: *Ben Tehilim, Ben Mishlei,* and *Ben Kohelet.* Among the first Hebrew poets to write secular Hebrew poetry, he wrote songs of nature, love, and friendship—all motifs popular in Arabic poetry. Israel Zinberg calls him the founder of secular Hebrew poetry.[16] He also composed poems of praise and glory, mourning, morality, and meditation, as well as poems brimming with deep Jewish nationalism. But most of all he is famous for his delightful wine poems—and the long war poems that he wrote on the battlefield.

According to Raymond P. Scheindlin, Hanagid "seems to have devoted more attention to this subject [wine poetry] than any other poet of the Golden Age," and the number of wine poems found in his *diwan* (collection of poems written by one author) is substantial.[17] Hanagid is the only Spanish Hebrew poet to have written poems of war, for he was the only one to have had battlefield experience; he was commander of King Habus's armies. His long martial poems are indeed unique in the Golden Age in Spain. Here is a sampling of his poetry:

Israel, Arise
(*Malkah Resha'ah*)

Terminate your reign, wicked queen.
Sarah, the despised, rule over your enemies.
Gazelle of Senir, your slumber has been long
On your bed of pain. Awake, arise,
Raise yourself; there is reward for your righteousness.
Cure yourself; there is balm for your injuries.[18]

The Power of the Pen
(*Tevunat 'ish be-Mikhtavo*)

Man's wisdom is at the tip of his pen,
His intelligence is in his writing,
His pen can raise a man to the rank
That the scepter accords to a King.[19]

A Wine Poem
(*Me'oddam be-Mar'ehu*)

Red to the eye, sweet to the drinker,
It is poured out in Spain but its bouquet reaches India.
When it is in the bowls, it is feeble; but once it goes to the head,
It holds sway over swaying heads.

The wretch whose heart's blood is mixed with his tears
Banishes his sorrows with the grape's blood.
As the goblets make the rounds, passing from hand to hand,
It seems as if the friends are casting lots for a diamond.[20]

War
(*Kerav*)

War is at first like a beautiful girl
with whom all men long to play,
but in the end like a repulsive hag
whose suitors all weep and ache.[21]

Samuel's position as vizier to King Habus entailed leading the army of
Granada, which was constantly occupied in warfare with Arab Seville. Here
are excerpts from some of his war poems:

The Battle of Alfuente
(*'Ve-Yatsa Av'* from *Elo'ah 'oz ve-El Kanno ve-Nora*)

[When God came to his rescue, after defeating Ibn Abbas, he composed
this song and called it *Shirah* (Song). The great victory took place on Friday, the first of Elul in the year 4798 (August 4, 1038).]

Then Av—the month of ancient woe departed,
and Elul arrived, speeding good fortune.[22]
Ibn Abbas pitched his tents on the mountain side,
and we pitched ours in the pass,
taking no heed of his army,
as though it were a passing caravan.
Then he drew near and, with many words,
tried to incite my men against me.
But when my adversary saw that my company
spoke with my voice, as one man,
he uncovered spears, swords, and lances,
and prepared his weapons for battle.
My enemy rose—and the Rock rose against him.
How can any creature rise against his creator?
Now my troops and the enemy's
drew up their ranks opposite each other.
On such a day of anger, jealousy, and rage,
men deem the Prince of Death a princely prize;

And each man seeks to win renown,
    though he must lose his life for it.
The Earth's foundations,
    overthrown like Gomorrah, reeled to and fro.

* * * * *

As the sun came out, the earth rocked on its pillars
    as if it were drunk.
The horses lunged back and forth
    like vipers darting out of their nests.
The hurled spears were like bolts of lightning,
    filling the air with light.

* * * * *

The blood of men flowed upon the ground
    like the blood of rams on the corners of the altar.
Still, my gallant men scorned their lives, preferring death.
These young lions welcomed each raw wound
    upon their heads as though it were a garland.
To die—they believed—was to keep the faith;
    to live—they thought—was forbidden.
And what was I to do with no escape,
    no prop or stay, and all hope gone?
While my foes, on this bitter day, poured out blood like water,
    I poured out my prayer to God,
who degrades all evildoers and makes them fall
    into the pit which they have dug;
to God, who on the day of battle will make the enemy's
        drawn swords
    and darting arrows pierce his own heart![23]

Short Prayer in Time of Battle
(*Re'eh Ha-Yom be-Tsarati*)

[A year after the death of Ibn Abbas, Samuel faced an even more formidable enemy, Isma'il Ibn Abbad at the head of the army of Seville. The battle between the forces of Hanagid and those of Ibn Abbad flared up near the Sengil River on Thursday, the thirteenth of Tishrei in the year 4800 (October 4, 1039). It was then that he composed the following verses, which he recited instead of the afternoon service of the day.]

> See my distress today; listen to my prayer, and answer it.
> Remember Your promise to Your servant; do not disappoint
> my hope.
> Can any hand do me violence, when You are my hand and
> my shelter?
> You once made me a pledge and sent me good tidings with Your
> angels.[24]
> Now I am passing through deep waters—lift me out of my terrors.
> I am walking through searing fire—snatch me from the flames.
> If I have sinned—what am I, what are my sins?
> I am in danger and cannot pray at length.
> Give me my heart's desire; oh, hasten to my aid.
> If I am not deserving in Your eyes—
> do it for the sake of my son and my sacred learning.[25]

Samuel emerged victorious in this war as well; the enemy chief, Ibn Abbad, was killed and his army defeated. Samuel then sang a great and splendid hymn of praise to God; he called it *Tehilah* (Praise).

The Victory over Ben Abbad
(*Hali Ta'as be-khol Shanah Pe'ulim*)

Will you perform for me every year deeds
Like those you executed for the princes and patriarchs?

* * * * *

You, my rock, you it is right to praise.
    You are God, and from your hand comes power.
You seduce the cowards at their last hour,
    And, in the day of vengeance, you remove the dross.
I shall tell your glory in the gates
    And give thanks to your name in the congregations.

I shall recount your marvels in the assembly of the pious,
    And your wonders among those who wear fringes.

About a year ago, on a day of terror like this,
    You redeemed me, and made the wicked my ransom.
Now that Ben Abbas has met his death,
    So Ben Abbad approaches and fear takes hold of me.
Both have pursued me, but the first was a common man,
    While on this one's head sits the crown of majesty.

* * * * *

There is strife and hatred between him and my king
    Each rules his land far from the other.
Both are like cedars among the kings,
    And all the earth's monarchs are mere saplings.

* * * * *

Then he set out to wage a trial of strength
    And arrayed his armies upon the frontiers.
He took a city and a kingdom in his path,
    And there was none to prevent him, none to protest.

* * * * *

We crossed over into his land in strength
    To revenge ourselves on our despoiled princes.
Warriors went with us like savage lions,
    And a multitude like a swarm of locusts.

* * * * *

When I saw this army so superior
    To the slaughtered and reviled force of Amalek,
When I saw great warriors afraid
    And the mighty men of battle trembling,
Captains going to war with reluctance
    And princes refusing to take up the fight;

* * * * *

Then I raised my hand in the name of God,
    The honoured, the awesome, acclaimed by his seventy armies.
At this time of distress I mentioned his name in my heart,
    To implore thereby him who dwells in the skies,
To overcome the power of the foe with the force of the Rock,
    For he can take an army in the palm of his hand.

* * * * *

On the night of the sixth day we pursued them
    Like a ravening bird, like a swarm of bees.
We struck down their mighty men and their king;
    Their captains and their servants were dead men.

* * * * *

We captured our captors, and those that thought
    To destroy us were themselves destroyed.
They imagined that we should be their possession,
    But they themselves were possessed by our hands.

* * * * *

To the God of strength, who appears in the storm cloud,
    And in the whirlwind against the keepers of idols,
Who has not given his glory to others,
    Nor transferred his praise to images,
To him I have already composed a song;
    And now this song of praise that is bright like the stars,
Like the style of its sister, well-set in lines,
    According to the number of the psalmist's praises.

* * * * *

Sons of my people, sing with me this poem of praise
    Placed at the head of all panegyrics.
See that its words are ordered correctly
    In the mouths of old men and children.

And when in the future your sons ask
    What it is, then you will reply;
"A song of praise to God who redeemed his friend,
    Who composed it for the redeemed to recite.
It is a song of praise, great and glorious,
    For the God of glory, and his great deeds."[26]

SOLOMON IBN GABIROL (C.1021–57)[27]

Solomon Ibn Gabirol wrote many works in philosophy, ethics, and biblical exegesis, but he is most famous for his poetry, especially religious poetry. Like all Hebrew Spanish poets, he wrote secular and religious poems. His secular poems are very personal; they bemoan his suffering, his poverty, and are in general very egocentric, arrogant, and individualistic. But his real greatness lies in his religious poems, which are marked by concision, delicacy, humility, and an outpouring of the soul. It was he who introduced into Hebrew poetry the poem addressed to the soul, by which he generally meant man's intellectual aspiration to discover God. And whereas in his secular poetry Ibn Gabirol stands as individual qua individual, in his sacred poetry he represents the national spirit of the people of Israel, and addresses God as the spokesman of his people, addressing Him as the God of Abraham, Isaac, and Jacob. The crown jewel of his poetry, however, is his *Keter Malkhut* (The Kingly Crown), which is, no doubt, the greatest Hebrew religious poem of the Middle Ages. Noteworthy also as part of his poetic legacy is his *Azharot*, the poetic versification of the 613 commandments, which he composed at the age of sixteen. Here is a sampling of his poetry:

Separation from the Torah
(*'Al 'Eres Devay*: 3)

You enquire gracefully of a man sick at heart,
"Why do you wear sackcloth and put ashes on your head?"
I do not mourn or grieve for someone who had died,
For every man dies. He gives no ransom instead.
But I am grief-stricken, because, being ill,
I cannot go to hear the Sefer Torah read.[28]

On the Death of Rab Hai
(*'Al Mot Rab Hai*: 2)

Weep, my people, put on sackcloth and sorrow,
Break all the instruments of music and song,
For Rab Hai, our master, the last remnant
Left to us in the world, has gone.
What shall we bemoan and lament first of all,
And for what shall we first grieve and mourn?
For the ark which now lies hidden in Zion,
Or for Rab Hai, buried in Babylon?[29]

I am the Master
(*Ani ha-Sar*)

I am the master, and song is a slave to me;
The harp of all poets and minstrels am I.
My song is a crown to all kings of the earth,
And a miter on the heads of the noble and high.
Though my body treads on the earth here below,
My spirit soars to the clouds in the sky.
Sixteen though am I, yet my wisdom excels
The wisdom of one who is eighty well-nigh.[30]

Humble of Spirit
(*Shefal Ru'ah*)

Humble in spirit, lowly in knee and stature,
But in fear and awe abounding, I come before Thee.
And in Thy presence to myself appear
As a little earthworm.
O Thou, who fillest the earth and whose greatness is endless,
Shall one like me laud Thee? And how shall he honor Thee?
The angels in heaven do not suffice,
How then one like me?
Thou hast wrought good and hast magnified mercies,
Wherefore the soul shall magnify praise to Thee.[31]

The Soul and its Maker
(Shehi la-El)

Bow down before God, my precious thinking soul,
   and make haste to worship Him with reverence.
Night and day think only of your everlasting world.
   Why should you chase after vanity and emptiness?
As long as you live, you are akin to the living God:
   just as He is invisible, so are you.
Since your Creator is pure and flawless,
   know that you too are pure and perfect.
The Mighty One upholds the heavens on His arm,
   as you uphold the mute body.
My soul, let your songs come before your Rock,
   who does not lay your form in the dust.
My innermost heart, bless your Rock always,
   whose name is praised by everything that has breath.[32]

At Dawn I Look to You
(Shahar Avakeshkha)

At dawn I come to You, my Rock, my strength;
   I offer You my dawn and evening prayers.

Before Your majesty I stand in fear,
   Because Your eye discerns my secret thoughts.

What is there that man's mind and mouth
   Can make? What power is there in my body's breath?

And yet the songs of man delight you; therefore I
   Will praise You while I still have breath from God.[33]

THE KINGLY CROWN (KETER MALKHUT)

Before quoting passages from *Keter Malkhut*, several comments
on this most majestic poem of Ibn Gabirol seem in order.

Keter Malkhut is at once a philosophical, scientific, and above all religious poem. Its basic theme is the contrast between the greatness of God and his creation and the insignificance of man. It is written in a rhythmic rhymed prose of biblical simplicity (with no Arabic meter). It is divided into a series of systematically constructed stanzas, each concluding in a thematically appropriate biblical quotation. The poem is arranged in three parts or three cycles. The first celebrates the attributes of God in lyrical language and sublime splendor. The second describes the wonders of God's creation as conceived in the scientific and philosophical ideas of the time. In the final cycle, Ibn Gabirol turns, in the words of Bernard Lewis, "from the universal [and Divine heights] to human depths—from worship and adoration to confession, penitence, and supplication. The poem ends with a hymn of glory at once personal and universal to the greatness of God."[34]

A common feature of medieval Hebrew poetry is the technique or literary device of *shibbutz* (literally, inlay), that is, the intertextual insertions of biblical phrases or fragments of phrases, giving them a totally new meaning in the new poetic context, a meaning that is strikingly different from the original one in the Bible. Ibn Gabirol is fond of (and masterful in the use of) this literary device. He makes effective and clever use of it throughout the poem *Keter Malkhut*, where many verses are infused with such associative biblical insertions or allusions, and each stanza concludes with a thematically appropriate biblical quotation.

The following examples are good illustrations of Ibn Gabirol's use of *shibbutz*. The last verse in the first stanza of the poem describes the reward in the world to come reserved by God for the righteous. "Thine is the reward which Thou has set aside for the righteous and hidden it." This verse is then followed by the biblical quotation, "And Thou sawest that it was good and has kept it hidden (*va-tere 'oto ki tov hu va-titzpenehu*)." Now, in its original biblical context (Exod. 2: 2), the phrase refers to Moses' mother who, upon giving birth to Moses, "saw how beautiful he was and she hid him." Note that the Hebrew verbal forms *va-tere* and *va-titzpenehu* are the forms for the third-person feminine singular and refer to Moses' mother; but the same verbal forms can be used for the second-person masculine singular, which is how Ibn Gabirol uses them addressing himself to God.[35]

Similarly, in stanza 15, Ibn Gabirol describes the sun, its numerous functions and benefits, and its daily journey rising in the morning in the east and setting in the evening in the west. The last verse of this stanza reads, "And at dawn she lifts up her head and bows it at evening to the west." This is followed by the biblical quote, "In the evening she goes, and on the morning she returns (*ba'erev hi ba'ah u-ba-boker hi shavah*)." Again, in its original context (Esther 2:14), the phrase refers to Queen Esther who would go to King Ahasuerus in the evening, and return (to the harem) the next morning. It is to be noted that the Hebrew verb *'ba'ah*, when applied to the sun, also means "to set." Further, the Hebrew word used by Ibn Gabirol for sun is *hammah*, which is a feminine noun. Accordingly, the verbs *tarim* (lift up) and *tikkod* (bow) are also in the feminine forms; my translation therefore reflects the Hebrew gender of *hammah*.[36]

Here are passages from the first and the last parts of the poem:

The Kingly Crown
(***Keter Malkhut***)

Preamble

> By my prayer a man shall profit
>> For in it he will learn righteousness and purity.
> In it I tell the wonders of the living God,
>> Briefly and not at length.
> I put it at the head of my praises
>> And I called it The Kingly Crown.

Part I: The Praises of God

> Marvellous are Thy works; and that my soul knoweth right well.
> Thine are the greatness and the strength and the splendor and the glory and the majesty.
> Thine O God is the kingdom and the rising above all things and the richness and the honour.
> Thine are the higher and the lower creatures, and they bear witness that they perish and Thou dost endure.
> Thine is the might whose secrets our thoughts are wearied of seeking, for Thou art so much stronger than we.
> Thine is the mystery of power, the secret and the foundation.
> Thine is the name that is hidden from the wise,
> the strength that sustains the world over the void,
> the power to bring to light all that is hidden.

Thine is the mercy that rules over Thy creatures and the
goodness preserved for those who fear Thee.
Thine are the secrets that no mind or thought can encompass,
and the life over which decay has no rule,
and the throne that is higher than all height,
and the habitation that is hidden at the pinnacle of mystery.
Thine is the existence from the shadow of whose light every being
was made to be, and we said, "Under His shadow we shall live."
Thine are the two worlds between which Thou didst set a limit,
the first for works and the second for requital.
Thine is the reward which Thou has set aside for the righteous
and hidden, and Thou sawest that it was good and has
kept it hidden.

Part III: Prayer and Penitence
(from stanza 33)

My God, I am abashed and ashamed to stand before Thee, for I
know
that according to the magnitude of Thy greatness,
so is the measure of my baseness and vileness.
According to the potency of Thy power, so is the
feebleness of my power;
according to Thy perfection, so is the deficiency
of my knowing.
For Thou art One, Thou art living, Thou art mighty,
Thou art enduring, Thou art great, Thou art wise,
Thou art God.
And I am clods and worms, dust of the earth,
a vessel full of shame, a dumb stone,
A fleeting shadow, "a wind that passeth away and
cometh not again," an adder's venom.

* * * * *

(from stanza 34)

O my God, I know that my sins are too numerous to count,
and that my guilt is too great to be told,
But I shall tell of them that which is like a drop in the ocean,
and I shall confess them—Perhaps I may still

the clamor of the waves and their tumult.
"Then hear Thou in heaven and forgive!"

* * * * *

(from stanza 36)

I am unworthy of all the mercies and all the truth that
Thou hast dispensed to Thy servant, but indeed,
O Lord my God, I praise Thee.
For Thou hast put a holy soul in me—and with my evil deeds
I soiled it, and with my evil imagining I profaned and defiled it.
But I know that if I have sinned, I have injured not Thee
but myself;
Yet my cruel tempter stands firm by my right hand, to tempt me,
not letting me refresh my spirit or prepare my rest.

* * * * *

(from stanza 38)

O my God, if my sin is too great to bear,
what wilt Thou do for Thy great name?
If I cannot hope for Thy mercies,
who but Thou will have pity on me?
Therefore, though Thou kill me, I shall hope in Thee,
And if Thou search out my sin, I shall flee from
Thee to Thee,
and hide myself from Thy wrath in Thy shadow,
I shall hold on to the skirts of Thy mercy, until
Thou hast pity on me.
"I will not let Thee go except Thou bless me."
Remember that of clay Thou didst make me,
and with these afflictions didst Thou try me.
Therefore do not visit my acts upon me,
nor make me eat the fruit of my deeds.
Soften Thy wrath upon me, and do not cause my last
days to draw near,
until I make ready provision to return to my place;
Do not speed me from the earth, with the kneading-trough
of my sins bound up upon my shoulders.

And when Thou dost put my sins into one of the scales,
put my afflictions in the other.
And when Thou rememberest my wickedness and rebellion,
remember my misery and my misfortunes.

* * * * *

(from stanza 39)

May it please Thee, O Lord my God, to come back
to me with Thy mercy,
and to bring me back with perfect penitence before Thee.
Prepare my heart and open Thine ear to my supplication.
Open my heart with Thy law, and plant Thy fear in my thoughts.
Pronounce good decrees over me,
and abrogate evil decrees from upon me.
Do not bring me into temptation, nor let me fall into dishonour.
Save me from all evil encounters,
and hide me in Thy shadow "until these calamities be overpast."
Be with my mouth and with my mind,
and guard my ways lest I sin with my tongue,
Remember me in the remembrance of Thy people,
and in the building of Thy temple,
to see good befall Thy chosen,
and make me worthy to enter Thy sanctuary,
Which now is desolate and destroyed, to cherish its
stones and its dust,
and the clods of its ruins, and rebuild its desolation.[37]

MOSES IBN EZRA (1055–1135) [38]

In his youth, Moses Ibn Ezra wrote a voluminous amount of secular poetry, but later in life, he devoted himself solely to liturgical poetry and penitential hymns (*selihot*). The difficult circumstances of his life had a deep impact on the quality and mood of his poetry. His youthful feeling of the joy of life later gave way to sorrow over misfortune. The joyous singer, who in young manhood had been filled with a love of life, became the sorrowful, humble composer of religious hymns, summoning men to repentance and piety. He wrote some three hundred *piyyutim* (religious hymns) and *selihot* (penitential poems).

One of the special qualities of his *selihot* is that they are written in a very simple, pure, and easily understood Hebrew, so that they evoke in the reader the same feeling of contrition expressed by the poet both on his own behalf and on behalf of the Jewish people. Interestingly, one of Abraham Ibn Ezra's criticisms of Hakalir's *piyyutim* is that his language is convoluted, full of riddles and metaphors, and grammatically sloppy so that it is very difficult even for the scholar, let alone the average congregant, to understand. Abraham Ibn Ezra insists that liturgical poetry must be written in simple and grammatically correct biblical Hebrew without any admixture of Aramaic or Talmudic Hebrew, in exactly the same pure and simple Hebrew used by the Sages in composing the core prayers.[39] Moses Ibn Ezra achieves this goal superbly in his penitential poems. It is no wonder that later generations called him *Ha-Sallah* or *Ha-Salhan*, the preeminent composer of *selihot*. His popular hymn introducing the *Ne'ilah* service on Yom Kippur provides an excellent illustration of this quality. It is a hymn that is chanted by all Sephardim before the *Ne'ilah* service with great fervor and devotion.

> *El nora 'alilah, El nora 'alilah*
> *Hamtzi lanu mehilah, Be-sha'at ha-ne'ilah.*
> God of awe, God of might
> God of awe, God of might
> Grant us pardon in this hour
> As Thy gates are closed this night.
>
> We who few have been from yore
> Raise our eyes to heaven's height,
> Trembling, fearful in our prayer
> As Thy Gates are closed this night.
> *El nora 'alilah, El nora 'alilah . . .*

* * * * *

> Pouring out our soul we pray
> That the sentence Thou wilt write
> Shall be one of pardoned sin

As Thy gates are closed this night.
El nora 'alilah, El nora 'alilah . . .

* * * * *

Remember generations of our sires
Strong in faith they walked in Thy light,
As of old renew our days,
As Thy gates are closed this night.
El nora 'alilah, El nora 'alilah . . .

Gather Judah's scattered flock
Unto Zion's rebuilt site,
Bless this year with grace divine,
As Thy gates are closed this night.
El nora 'alilah, El nora 'alilah . . .

Michael, Prince of Israel
Gabriel, the angels bright,
With Elijah, come, redeem,
As Thy gates are closed this night.

El nora 'alilah, El nora 'alilah
Hamtzi lanu mehilah, Be-sha'at ha-ne'ilah.[40]

Here is a sampling from the rest of his poetry:

The Rose
(*Kotnot Passim lavash ha-Gan*)

The garden put on a coat of many colours,
    and its grass garments were like robes of brocade.
All the trees dressed in chequered tunics
    and showed their wonders to every eye.
The new blossoms all came forth in honour of Time renewed,
    came gaily to welcome him.
But at their head advanced the rose, king of them all,
    for his throne was set on high.

He came out from among the guard of leaves
    and cast aside his prison clothes.
Whoever does not drink his wine upon the rose-bed—
    that man will surely bear his guilt![41]

Wine Song for Spring
(*Zeman ha-Kor*)

The cold season has slipped away like a shadow.
    Its rains are already gone, its chariots and its horsemen.
Now the sun, in its ordained circuit, is at the sign of the Ram,
    like a king reclining on his couch.
The hills have put on turbans of flowers,
    and the plain has robed itself in tunics of grass and herbs;
It greets our nostrils with the incense
    hidden in its bosom all winter long.

Give me the cup that will enthrone my joy
    and banish sorrow from my heart.
The wine is hot with anger;
    temper its fierce fire with my tears.
Beware of Fortune: her favors
    are like the venom of serpents, spiced with honey.
But let your soul deceive itself and accept her goodness in the
        morning,
    even though you know that she will be treacherous at night.

Drink all day long, until the day wanes
    and the sun coats its silver with gold;
and all night long, until the night flees like a Moor,
    while the hand of dawn grips the heel.[42]

Let Man Remember
(*Yizkor Gever*)

Let man remember all the days of his life
He moves at the grave's request.

He goes a little journey every day
And thinks he is at rest;
Like someone lying on board a ship
Which flies at the wind's behest.[43]

Slaves and Masters
(*Kebarim Min Zeman*)

There are graves of a primeval age
In which people sleep eternally.
No jealousy, no hatred exists there.
There is no love among neighbours, no enmity.
And when I see them, I cannot determine
Which were slaves, which had the mastery.[44]

The Soul
(*Nafshi 'Ivvitikh ba-Laylah*)

With all my soul I long for You in the night.

My soul longs for the home of her soul,[45]
she yearns for her fountainhead,
she pines for her holy dwelling—
she will travel there day and night.

* * * * *

I have had my fill of sleepless nights, tossing on my
sick-bed.
My feet have hurried me to the holy houses of worship
even *when deep sleep falls upon men
and they have visions in the night.*
I was a fool, I blundered all the days of my childhood;
I am ashamed that I wasted my youth;
that is why *tears are
now my food, day and night.*[46]

* * * * *

You who invoke the Lord's name—
call a solemn assembly, wash yourselves,
hallow yourselves, purge your hearts of dross,
stand fast, do not be silent *day and night*.

[God:] "My daughter, know that I shall yet endow you
  with My grace;
I shall gently lead you to My dwelling and install you there.
You have no kinsman closer than I:
Now go and sleep through the night."[47]

With A Bitter Heart Greatly Shaken
(*Be-Levav Mar Me'od Nishbar*)

With heart purified, greatly shaken,
    I approach God at the time of my arising;
It counsels me and guides me
    To confess my transgressions.
Behold, to expiate my iniquities,
    I offer my fat and my blood;
And I make confession and supplication,
    For my sinfulness, and for the sinfulness of my people.

* * * * *

O God, cause wrath to depart,
    And lift up Thy steps to the ruins.
With the waters of love, Oh, blot our guilt;
    Tear in pieces the records of sin.
Oh, show grace to Thy servant, that day when before Thee,
    He stands among Thy creatures to be judged—
The day that the pure are made known
    Before the Lord of Hosts,
That their souls may dwell among the holy ones
    As a sign and a wonder—
The day that a voice passes among my people,
    Crying; "Who are they that go?"[48]

Selihah, Supplication
(Ana ke-'ab Zedoni Timhehu)[49]

O Lord, disperse my wrongdoing as a cloud,
and *"Forgive Thou my guilt, although it is great."*

Yet what is recorded before God my Father can not be deleted.
The thought in His heart is not as my thought,
To wipe out what stands for the day I am judged,
when "the writing is written of God,"
　　　"Forgive, then, my guilt, although it is great."

O Rock, shouldst Thou probe and examine the ways man conceals,
a furrow of guilt he is ploughing by day and by night
Or shouldst Thou examine his sins and transgressions,
From the sole of his foot to his head dwells his guilt.
　　　"Forgive, then, my guilt, although it is great."

My thinking builds up then breaks down in my heart
on this day when my failures cry out to my face.
Yet within me I know that the Lord
may forgive in His tender, compassionate mercy.
　　　"Forgive, then, my guilt, although it is great."

* * * * *

Turn back from their exile Thy people in darkness.
Thy messenger send with good tidings of promise,
foretelling the day that shall be when Thy wrath is at end
and Israel comfort shall find, for they shall at length understand.
　　　"Forgive, then, my guilt, although it is great."

May Israel's horn grow in strength,
for he is oppressed and downtrodden,
and strengthen Elijah to come as Messiah's precursor.
In all things to which he may turn may he so succeed
and so prosper,
that everywhere it shall be known there comes the Messiah of God.
　　　"Forgive, then, my guilt, although it is great."

Selihah, Supplication
(*Le-Mitvaddeeh Hattotav*)

He whose days are consumed in sorrow,
and his years in vanities frittered,
confesses his sins and avows his transgressions profuse.
In the midst of assailants he cries from attack of his foes
    "Let us fall into the hand of the Lord
    For great are His mercies."

From my earliest days I have trailed along sin as with ropes of decoy.
But now I turn back and repent me,
for how can I know when my fatal day may draw nigh?
Fasting, I offer my flesh as a sacrifice, my tears as a libation;
perchance my Lord will show mercy, "for his mercies are not at an end."
    "Let us fall into the hand of the Lord
    For great are His mercies."

YEHUDAH HALEVI (1075–1141)[50]

According to many scholars, the poetry of Yehudah Halevi represents the zenith of Spanish Hebrew poetry.[51] He is generally considered to be the greatest of all post-biblical Hebrew poets, truly *ne'im zemirot yisrael*, "the sweet singer of Israel." His poetry has a certain mystical quality to it. It is filled with yearning for the nearness of God.

His poetry also shows his mastery of the Hebrew Bible on the one hand, and the Arabic poetic conventions and motifs on the other. At home with halakhah and aggadah, he draws freely on both. His mastery of the Bible is evident in the ease and cleverness with which he twists biblical expressions and phrases to serve his poetic needs. But what makes his poetry unique above all is his intense nationalism. It is permeated with boundless love for his people, for the Torah and its commandments, for the God of Israel, and for the Land of Israel—the land of his dreams.

Yehudah Halevi enjoys playing on words in his poems, recalling wordplays found in the Bible, and he is a master at it. In the liturgical poem

"Redemption" (*Ein Zulatekha Lig'ol*), he complains, "*Ve-lammah ba-mer-hak, 'amad dar shahak?*" (Why then stands He afar off, [He] that dwells in the Skies?) He then adds, "*Ve-rodi dahak-we-dodi rahak*" (While my ruler oppresses, my beloved is afar). Using the same two words in both hemistiches of the verse, but reversing the order of the first consonants of the words in the first hemistich, *rodi dahak* (my ruler oppresses), he obtains *dodi rahak* (my beloved is afar) in the second hemistich, thus lending a poetic punch to Israel's complaint that God seems to stand afar in times of need.[52]

Perhaps one of the best illustrations of Halevi's propensity for word play is a line in his liturgical poem, "*Hashem Negdekha Kol Ta'avati*" (Before Thee, O Lord is My Whole Desire), chanted by Sephardim during the morning service of Yom Kippur. The verse toward the end of the poem reads, "*Ve-Eikhah e'ebod Yotzri, be'odi asir Yitzri ve-'eved ta'avati?*" (And how then shall I serve my Maker, while a captive to my lust, a slave of my desire?)[53] The words *yotzri* (my Maker) and *yitzri* (my lust) rhyme and alliterate, yet the contrast in meaning is all too striking. Likewise, in the same line, the words *e'ebod* (shall I serve) and *'eved* (slave) derive from the same Hebrew verb, *la'avod*, while in this context they provide a dramatic contrast between serving God and being a slave to desire.[54] This verse is surely one of the most beautiful lines in this heartfelt and moving poem. Another beautiful expression in this same poem is the penultimate verse:

> *Ani mi-ma'asim sholal ve-'arom,*
> *Ve-Tzidkatekha levadah hi khesuti.*

> I am despoiled and naked of good works,
> Thy righteousness alone my covering.

Perhaps Heinrich Heine, the renowned German poet, was right when he wrote in his well-known poem, "Jehudah Halevi,"

> Pure and just, without the least fault,
> Is his song, as is his soul.
> When God created
> This soul, satisfied with his work,
> He kissed the first-born;
> And the echo of that kiss

Lives in every song of the poet
Anointed with God's grace.[55]

Indeed, the echo of that divine kiss rings throughout Halevi's religious poetry. Here is a sampling:

Zion Complains to God
(*Yedidi Hashakhahta?*)

My love, have you forgotten how you lay between my breasts?
Then why have you sold me forever to my enslavers?
Did I not follow you through a barren land?
Let Mount Seir and Mount Paran, Sinai and Sin be my witnesses![56]
There my love was yours, and I was your delight.
Then how can you now bestow my glory upon others?
I am thrust into Seir, driven towards Kedar,[57]
tested in the furnace of Greece, crushed under the yoke of Media.
Is there any savior but you? Any prisoner of hope but I?
Give me your strength, and I shall give you my love.[58]

The Servant of God
(*Mi Yiteneni 'Eved Elo'ah 'Oseni*)

If only I could be the servant of God who made me,
My friends could all desert me, if he would but befriend me.

My maker, and shepherd, I, body and soul, am your creation.
You perceive all my thought; you discern my intention.
You measure my journeying, my steps, my relaxation.
If you help me, who can throw me down?
If you confine me, who but you can break my bonds?

My inner heart yearns to be near you,
But my worldly cares drive me away from you.
My paths have strayed far from the way you pursue.
O God, help me to follow your truth. Give me instruction.
Lead me gently in judgment. Stay your conviction.

* * * * *

Incline my heart to serve in your kingdom's service.
Cleanse my thoughts that I may know your divineness.
Do not delay your healing power in the days of my sickness.
Answer, my God. Do not chastise. Do not withhold reply.
Employ me again as your servant. Say, "Here am I."[59]

My Heart is in The East
(*Libbi Ba-Mizrah*)

My heart is in the East and I am at the edge of the West.
Then how can I taste what I eat, how can I enjoy it?
How can I fulfil my vows and pledges, while
Zion is in the domain of Edom, and I am in the bonds of Arabia?
It would be easy for me to leave behind all the good things of Spain;
It would be glorious to see the dust of the ruined Shrine.[60]

Jerusalem
(*Yefeh Nof Mesos Tevel*)

Beautiful heights, joy of the world, city of a great king;
For you my soul yearns from the lands of the West.
My pity collects and is roused when I remember the past,
Your glory in exile, and your temple destroyed.
Would that I were on the wings of an eagle,
So that I could water your dust with my mingling tears.
I have sought you, although your king is away,
And snakes and scorpions oust Gilead's balm.
I shall cherish your stones and kiss them,
And your earth would be sweeter than honey to my taste.[61]

Mount Avarim
(*Shalom Lekha Har Ha'Avarim*)

I greet you Mount Avarim. I greet you from all sides.
On you was gathered the best of men;
you received the most precious of graves.
If you do not know him, ask the Red Sea that was divided in two;

Or ask the bush, ask Mount Sinai, and they will reply:
"He was not a man of words,
and yet he was faithful to the mission of God."
I have vowed to visit you soon, if God will be my help.[62]

Ode to Zion
(*Tzion Halo Tish'ali*)

O Zion, will you not ask how your captives are—
the exiles who seek your welfare, who are the remnant of your flocks?
From west and east, from north and south, from every side,
accept the greetings of those near and far,
and the blessings of this captive of desire, who sheds his tears
like the dew of Hermon and longs to have them fall upon your hills.

I am like a jackal when I weep for you affliction; but when I dream
of your exiles' return, I am a lute for your songs.

* * * * *

Oh I would pour out my life in the very place where
once the spirit of God was poured out upon your chosen ones.
You are the seat of royalty, you are the throne of the Lord—
Though slaves now sit upon your princes' thrones.

If only I could roam through those places where
God was revealed to your prophets and heralds!
Who will give me wings, so that I may wander far away?
I would carry the pieces of my broken heart over your rugged mountains.
I would bow down, my face on your ground; I would love
your stones; your dust would move me to pity.
I would weep, as I stood by my ancestors' graves.
I would grieve, in Hebron, over the choicest of burial places!
I would walk in your forests and meadows,
stop in Gilead, marvel at Mount Abarim;

Mount Abarim and Mount Hor, where the two great luminaries
(Moses and Aaron) rest, those who guided you and gave you light.

* * * * *

It would delight my heart to walk naked and barefoot among
the desolate ruins where your shrines once stood;
where your Ark was hidden away, where your
cherubim once dwelled in the innermost chamber.

* * * * *

Happy is he who waits and lives to see your light rising,
your dawn breaking forth over him!
He shall see your chosen people prospering, he shall rejoice
in your joy when you regain the days of your youth.[63]

ABRAHAM IBN EZRA (1089–1161)[64]

Abraham Ibn Ezra was typical of his period. He mastered many
skills, excelling in them all, and wrote treatises on many scientific and religious subjects. But he is most famous for his biblical commentary, which
though "laconic and opaque" in style, reflects Ibn Ezra's wide interest in
and mastery of grammar, science, and philosophy. As a poet, he was versatile as both a secular and religious poet. He enriched medieval Hebrew
poetry by introducing the new elements of humor and wit, light satire, and
lampoon. His secular poetry includes occasional poems, satiric verse, and
witty epigrams, in addition to poems of friendship, nature, love, and wine.
His sacred poetry, both religious and philosophical, is marked by his religious humility before the Creator, and his yearning for the knowledge and
nearness of God. Much of his religious poetry is liturgical, and his penitential poems (*selihot*) and supplications (*bakkashot*)—as well as many of
his hymns—have become an integral part of the liturgy, especially the
Sephardic liturgy for the High Holidays. Here is a sampling of his poetry:

Songs of Nations
(*Shirat Ha-'ummot*)

The Arabs always sing about love and passion.
Rome's songs celebrate the battlefield and vengeance.
Full of profound thought and rich in knowledge are the songs of
Greece.
The people of India compose riddles and fables.
And the Jews sing songs of praise and glory to God Almighty.[65]

The Patron
(*Ashkim Le-vet Ha-Sar*)

When I come to the Patron's house early in the morning,
    they say, "He has already ridden away."
When I come in the evening,
    they say, "He has already gone to sleep."
He either climbs into his carriage or climbs into bed—
    woe to the poor man, born to misfortune!

Out of Luck
(*Beli mazzal*)

The heavenly spheres and the constellations
    strayed from their path when I was born.
If my business were in candles,
    the sun would not set until I died!
However I struggle, I cannot succeed,
    for my stars have ruined me:
If I were a dealer in shrouds,
    No one would die as long as I lived.

The Old Cloak
(*Me'il Yesh Li*)

I have a cloak that is like a sieve
    to sift wheat and barley.

I spread it out like a tent in the dark of night,
    and the stars shine through it;
through it I see the moon and the Pleiades,
    and Orion, flashing his light.
I am tired of counting all its holes
    which are shaped like the teeth of a saw.
No thread can hope to mend its gaps
    with warp and woof.
If a fly landed on it with its full weight,
    it would quickly regret its foolishness.
O God, give me a robe of glory in exchange—
    this would be properly tailored![66]

I Glorify You Lord of all Souls
(*Agadelkha Elohei Kol Neshamah*)

I will Glorify You Lord of all Souls;
and praise You in fear and awe abounding.
As I stand in the midst of your congregation,
to exalt Your name, my Rock,
I bow and bend my head and stature in reverence.

* * * * *

Who is it in The East or the West
who can fathom the secrets of his Creator?
Exalted beyond all praise is He
who created all with great wisdom.
May He be glorified among His holy and mighty people!
And may His great name be hallowed throughout His World![67]

Penitential Prayer
(*Eshtahaveh Appayim Artzah*)

I bow down with my face to the ground,
    for there is nothing lower than it.

I throw myself down before the Supreme One,
    highest of the high.
What but my spirit shall I bring when I approach Him,
    it comes from Him,
He gives it life in the choicest part of my body,
    and a man has nothing dearer than his soul.
There is no end and no beginning to His glory—
    how then can my tongue glorify Him?
He is farther from me than the farthest heaven,
    and closer than my flesh and bone!
I come to you now, my God,
    Because none but You can be of help.

* * * * *

What more can I hope to know,
    knowing that You created me for my good?
Your acts of love are beyond number,
    but my sins outnumber the sand of the seashore.
How shall I lift up my eyes to You?
    They, too, are sinful.
What more can my lips say?
    They, too, have done wrong.
My wanton heart has done to me
    what no enemy could have done.
Guts of anger seize me as I think of it—
    woe to me, I have disobeyed.
My evil passions led me astray;
    I had no wish to anger You.
My wrongs have wronged no one but me,
    and none but You will keep faith with me.
Show me the right path
    for it is You who have taught me all I know.
I have heard myself speak the words of my heart:
    may You hear them in heaven![68]

CONCLUDING COMMENTS

In concluding this chapter, it must be pointed out that the religious poetry of medieval Hebrew poets, which, according to Goitein, is "our most precious heritage from Hebrew-Arab Spain," remains a living legacy to this day, especially among the Sephardim. Its best poems constitute an integral part of Sephardic liturgy for the High Holidays and numerous special occasions. Thus, for example, the special liturgical poems (called *piz-monim*, *piyyutim*, *bakkashot*, or *selihot*)—chanted by the Sephardim on Rosh Hashanah, Yom Kippur, and the *selihot* services during the month of *Elul*—are all gems of medieval religious Hebrew poetry composed by Solomon Ibn Gabirol, Yehudah Halevi, and Moses and Abraham Ibn Ezra, among others.

In addition, on *Shabbat Zakhor*, the Sabbath before Purim, all Sephardim sing Halevi's long historical poem, "*Mi Kamokha*," which is essentially a masterful poetic rendition of the story of Purim. Likewise, on the seventh day of Passover, many Sephardim sing Halevi's poem of redemption, "*Yom Le-Yabbashah . . . Shirah Hadashah ShiBbehu Ge'ulim*" (The day the depths were turned into dry land, A new song sang the redeemed), celebrating the miraculous crossing of the Red Sea by the Israelites.[69]

On Shavu'ot, the *Azharot* of Ibn Gabirol are chanted by all Sephardim, either at the conclusion of the morning service or before the afternoon service. A number of special *kinot* (lamentations), notably "*Tzion Halo Tish'al*," "*Halanofelim Tekumah*," and "*Eikhah Tzon Ha-Haregah*" by Yehudah Halevi, and "*Nir'eh Le-Helil 'al Shibrenu*" by Moses Ibn Ezra are all part of the *Tish'ah be-av* (the ninth of *Av*) service of the Sephardim.

Besides for the liturgy for the High Holidays, Shavu'ot, and other special occasions, some medieval religious poems have become part of the popular repertoire of *piyyutim* or *pizmonim* sung by many Sephardim at all types of social gatherings. These *piyyutim* include "*Yedidi Hashakhahta?*" (Israel Complains) by Yehudah Halevi; "*Shehi La-El Yehidah Ha Hakhamah*" (Bow down before God, my precious thinking soul), "*Shefal Ru'ah Shefal Berekh ve-Komah*" (Humble in Spirit, lowly in knee and stature), and "*Shahar Avakeshkha Tzuri u-Misgabi*" (At dawn I come to you my Rock, my strength) by Solomon Ibn Gabirol; and "*Agadelkha Elohei Kol Nashamah*" (I glorify You, Lord of all souls) by Abraham Ibn Ezra. All these are popular *piyyutim* that appear in numerous anthologies of *piyyutim* and *bakkashot* from Morocco and elsewhere.[70]

Finally, poems for the Sabbath such as "*Deror Yikra l-Ben im Bat*" (He will proclaim freedom to all his sons) by Dunash Ibn Labrat; "'*Al Ahabatekh Eshteh Gevi'i, Shalom lakh Shalom Yom ha-Shevi'I*" (To love of thee I drink my cup; Peace to thee, Peace O seventh day), and "*Yom Shabbaton ein Lishko'ah*" (O let us never forget the beloved Sabbath day) by Yehudah Halevi; and "*Ki Eshmerah Shabbat El Yishmereni*" (As I observe the Sabbath, so will God guard me) and "*Tzame'ah Nafshi Lelohim le-el Hai*" (My whole soul thirsts for the Living God) by Abraham Ibn Ezra all figure prominently in most prayer books of Sephardim and Ashkenazim alike as *zemirot* (songs) for the Sabbath.

6.

SEPHARDIC CODIFICATION OF JEWISH LAW

Beginning with the early Geonic period, we witness a progressive tendency toward the codification of halakhah. This tendency began with the *Halakhot Pesukot* of Rabbi Yehudai Gaon and the *Halakhot Gedolot* of Rabbi Simeon Kayyara, and culminated in the four major codes of Jewish law: the *Sefer ha-Halakhot* of Rabbi IsaacAlfasi, the *Mishneh Torah* of Maimonides, the *Arba'ah Turim* of Rabbi Jacob ben Asher, and the twofold work of Rabbi Joseph Caro, the *Bet Yosef* and the *Shulhan Arukh*.

According to Menahem Elon, the codificatory attempts that began with the Geonic period "produced three main types of codificatory literature: (a) books of *halakhot,* (b) books of *pesakim,* and (c) a combination of both."*[1] Elon points out that the two basic types of codificatory literature, *halakhot* and *pesakim,* differ fundamentally in their approach to the problem of codification of Jewish law, as well as in their literary form. Books of *halakhot* state the final conclusion or ruling after a brief and concise discussion that cites and explains the sources on which the halakhic conclusion is based, while books of *pesakim* state the final halakhic ruling categorically without any discussion and without indicating the sources on which the ruling is based.

The two types differ in their literary forms as well. Books of *halakhot* follow the order of the tractates of the Talmud, whereas books of *pesakim* are organized topically, setting forth in one place all the relevant laws, which in their original sources may be scattered throughout various parts of the Talmud and post-Talmudic literature. According to Elon, the outstanding example of *halakhot* is Alfasi's *Sefer ha-Halakhot*, while the *Mishneh Torah* of Maimonides represents the outstanding example of

---

* This and all other excerpts from Elon's work, *Jewish Law: History, Sources and Principles,* © 1994, by Menachem Elom, and published by the Jewish Publication Society, are reprinted with the permission of the publisher.

pesakim. Elon explains that books of *halakhot* are "naturally organized to correspond with the organization of whatever literary source contains the material on which the statement of the law is based." And therefore, "Alfasi's *Sefer ha-Halakhot* is organized according to the order of the tractates of the Talmud," whereas a code that sets forth the halakhic conclusions, with no discussion of source, "is organized topically because that is the most convenient and useful arrangement." This was the method used by Maimonides in the *Mishneh Torah*.[2] Elon adds that "in the course of time, a third type developed, which blended the qualities of each of the other two."[3]

MOTIVATING FACTORS FOR THE
CODIFICATION OF JEWISH LAW DURING THE GEONIC PERIOD

In the introduction to his *Mishneh Torah*, and also in the introduction to his *Sefer ha-Mitzvot* (The Book of the Commandments), as well as in several of his responsa and his epistles, Maimonides lists what Elon describes as "the familiar reasons" that led in all periods to the writing of compendious but concise codes, namely, "the vastness of the halakhic material, the difficulty of understanding the sources and of finding one's way in them, and the social and historical milieu."[4] Clearly, the same considerations seem to have motivated codifiers of all periods. In the case of the Geonic codificatory literature, there was an additional consideration, according to Elon. That is, in their ongoing ideological battle against the Karaites, the *Geonim* (beginning with Yehudai Gaon) composed works aimed at clarifying, and summarizing the entire corpus of the Oral Law in a clear and concise formulation.[5]

CODIFICATION DURING THE GEONIC PERIOD

According to Elon, while the codificatory literature of the Geonic period took several forms, a feature common to them all is that they were all books of *halakhot*—that is, their declared aim was to present halakhic conclusions and final rulings after a concise discussion of the underlying Talmudic and post-Talmudic sources.[6] Saadiah Gaon, however, was the first to introduce systematic and topical classification of the law in his innovative form of halakhic monographs. His model was followed by Samuel ben Hofni Gaon, and Hai Gaon, and together their works provided a model of systematic classification and topical arrangement of subjects for Maimonides and those who followed his footsteps in terms of topical arrangement.

EARLY BOOKS OF HALAKHOT

The first two works to aim at codification of Jewish law were the *Halakhot Pesukot* (Settled Laws) of Rabbi Yehudai Gaon, head of the Sura academy (c.757–61), and the *Halakhot Gedolot* (Great Laws) written two generations later by Rabbi Simon Kayyara from Basra, Babylonia (c.825). Elon notes that *Halakhot Pesukot* is the first classic book of *halakhot*. It influenced subsequent codificatory literature and opened an era in the codification of Jewish law. Its statements of the law are prefaced by a concise discussion of the sources on which the laws are based, and are arranged by subject—Sabbath, festivals, Passover, interest and usury, betrothal and divorce, and so on—but its organization follows the order of the tractates of the Talmud. It encompasses all parts of *halakhah*, but only those applicable at the time it was written. Elon points out that by omitting inapplicable laws, Yehudai Gaon "set an example for all subsequent codificatory literature, which, with limited exceptions, was also confined to codifying only the laws having practical relevance at the time they were written." Elon observes further that *Halakhot Pesukot* "substantially facilitated subsequent halakhic research, and that this advantage, together with the recognition of the great authority of the author, led to its widespread circulation throughout the Diaspora."

Halakhot Gedolot resembles *Halakhot Pesukot* in many respects. Like *Halakhot Pesukot*, it is arranged by subjects, and its organization follows the order of the tractates of the Talmud. It also prefaces the statement of the laws with a discussion of the sources on which the laws are based. *Halakhot Gedolot*, however, is more comprehensive in that it includes even laws that had no applicable relevance at the time such as the laws of sacrifices. Moreover, its sources include, in addition to the Talmud, *Halakhot Pesukot*, *Sefer ha-She'iltot* of Rab Aha of Shabha, and Geonic responsa.[7]

Nevertheless, although the laws in these two works were arranged by subjects, because they were organized in the order of the tractates of the Talmud, not all the material pertaining to a particular subject was brought together in one place. In addition, these two works were composed in the very style of the Mishnah and the Talmud, not distinguishing between gen-

eral principles and details. Nor did their authors bother to provide introductions to all major halakhic topics before going into details. It was not
until Saadiah Gaon, about a century later, that systematic codification began
in earnest. In fact, according to Simha Assaf, Saadiah considered these earlier works most primitive because of these deficiencies. On the other hand,
Saadiah—who was a man of science and a great systemizer, and who, according to Assaf, was influenced greatly by Arabic literature—aimed at introducing a logical and scientific organization even in his halakhic works
(no doubt following the model of the handbooks of Islamic law).[8]

Saadiah's halakhic works include commentaries and introductions
to the Talmud and to specific halakhic subjects. However, his major halakhic works are his innovative monographs on various subjects—*Sefer
ha-Yerushot* (Book of Inheritance), *Sefer Shetarot* (Book of Contracts),
Sefer ha-Matanot (Book of Gifts), *Sefer ha-Pikkadon* (Book of Deposits
and Pledges), as well as monographs on ritual slaughter and *terefot* (animals
unfit for consumption because of physical defects), interest and usury, and
ritual purity and impurity.[9]

Clearly, Saadiah chose for these works a new form, the monograph,
an exhaustive summary of the laws on a single subject. The monographs
ushered in a new literary form, different from all previous code books. In
addition, all of Saadiah's monographs were written in Arabic. These innovations were followed by two leading Babylonian *Geonim*, Samuel ben
Hofni Gaon in Sura (977–1013), and Hai Gaon (939–1039), who also wrote
halakhic monographs in Arabic. The works of Saadiah, like those of Samuel
ben Hofni Gaon and Hai Gaon who followed his approach, were clear, thorough, and topically organized with each topic preceded by an introduction
and a summary of general principles. Saadiah follows these introductions
and summaries by setting out the subjects in minutest detail.[10]

POSSIBLE INFLUENCE OF SAADIAH'S MONOGRAPHS
ON MAIMONIDES' *MISHNEH TORAH*

Both Elon and Assaf believe that the systematic and exhaustive
treatment and topical classification of the law in Saadiah's monographs, as
well as in those of Samuel ben Hofni Gaon and Hai Gaon who followed
his approach, were later of great help to Maimonides in composing his
monumental code, the *Mishneh Torah*. According to Elon, the goal Maimonides set for himself in writing his *Mishneh Torah* was to create "a code

that (1) includes all the laws of the halakhic system, (2) classifies and log-ically arranges the law, (3) couches [formulates] the law in original, clear, and easy Hebrew, and most importantly, (4) states the law categorically, without reference to source or to contrary views."[11]

Commenting on Maimonides' second aim of topical classification of the law, Elon observes that while it is true that in the earlier works of *Halakhot Pesukot, Halakhot Gedolot*, and Alfasi's *Sefer ha-Halakhot*, which were arranged in the order of the tractates of the Talmud, "the ma-terial began to be arranged topically . . . and Maimonides was influenced by this development, the earlier works were only a modest first step; not all the material relating to the topic were covered, and only a small number of topics were so treated." But he adds, "Some *Geonim*, as we have seen, wrote monographs on various topics, like *Sefer ha-Yerushot* [Book of In-heritance] by Saadiah Gaon, *Sefer Arvut ve-ha-Kabbelanut* [Book of Or-dinary and Special Contractual Suretyship] by Samuel ben Hofni Gaon, and *Sefer ha-Mikah ve-ha-Mimkar* [Book of Purchase and Sale] by Hai Gaon and others; and it is a fair assumption that the concentration of ma-terial on a particular subject in each of the monographs greatly assisted Maimonides in his efforts to classify the law and organize it topically." And while these monographs "encompassed only a few subjects and there was as yet no comprehensive work encompassing all the areas of Jewish law, fully classified and topically arranged," as Elon correctly points out, these monographs, nonetheless, provided Maimonides (and indirectly Joseph Caro) with a model for systematic and topical arrangement of the laws, one of the goals that Maimonides set for himself in composing the *Mishneh Torah*.

Indeed, Simha Assaf suggests that from the list of Saadiah's mono-graphs it may be assumed that he did not think the time was ripe for com-posing a comprehensive code of Jewish law covering all aspects of halakhah. Assaf, goes on to say that Saadiah must have believed that the composition of such a comprehensive code required much preparatory re-search which could be achieved by the preparation of separate monographs, each devoted to one of the various topics of Jewish law, so that each mono-graph would explore thoroughly all aspects of a particular topic. If Assaf's assumption is correct, Saadiah's monographs, as well as those of Samuel ben Hofni Gaon and Hai Gaon, truly prepared the ground for the *Mishneh Torah*. Indeed, as noted above, both Elon and Assaf agree that the exhaus-tive treatment and the systematic arrangement and topical classification used in the monographs of these three illustrious *Geonim* were later of great help to Maimonides in his monumental code *Mishneh Torah*.[12]

Assaf, however, goes further, asserting that Saadiah's *Sefer ha-Yerushot* as well as his *Siddur* (prayer book) manifest an additional characteristic that became one of the principles in Maimonides' approach to his codification in *Mishneh Torah*, namely, that of stating the law categorically without citing any sources or contrary opinions. That is, unlike his approach in the other monographs where he provides documentation from Scripture and the Talmud, Saadiah states his legal decisions as settled laws in his *Sefer ha-Yerushot* and in the halakhic part of his *Siddur*, "referring neither to any passage from the Talmud, nor mentioning the name of a single sage from the Mishnah or the Talmud." Thus, according to Assaf, in this respect too, "Saadiah paved the way and provided a fine model for Maimonides."[13]

Assaf suggests that Saadiah might have changed the format in his later works by providing references to the sources of the law because his earlier method of omitting citations of his sources may have aroused opposition—very much like that directed at Maimonides on account of his similar lack of reference to the sources of the rulings in his *Mishneh Torah*. Elon, however, disagrees with Assaf's assumption, and, quoting an article by S. Abramson, argues that the original *Sefer ha-Yerushot* "as Saadiah wrote it [like all his other works] included documentation from Scripture and the Talmud," while the printed *Sefer ha-Yerushot* "is merely an abridgment" of the original. The abridgment, according to Abramson, as quoted by Elon, "omitted the documentation from Scripture and the Talmud, and left only the rules derived from them."[14]

THE *SEFER HA-HALAKHOT* OF RABBI ISAAC ALFASI

As the Geonic period came to an end, a number of factors once again gave rise to the need for a code that covered the entire halakhic system in a succinct and definitive way. Among these factors were (a) the increased volume of responsa and legislative enactments (*taqqanot*) produced by the *Geonim* in various fields of the law, which involved the continuing expansion of the law not only in Babylonia, but also in North Africa and Europe, and (b) the emergence of numerous additional Jewish centers of learning, which inevitably led to marked differences in laws and customs. These factors among others led to the composition of what Elon calls "one of the greatest and most important works in the halakhic system—a work that left its mark on the study and determination of Halakhah in every subsequent generation."[15] This work is the *Sefer ha-Halakhot* (Book of the Laws) by Rabbi Isaac Alfasi, known in Hebrew by his acronym, Rif (Rabbi Isaac of Fez).[16]

According to Elon, "Alfasi's work was the crowning masterpiece of this genre of codificatory literature; and, thanks to its scope and contents as well as to the personality of its author, it became the authoritative code of the halakhic system." Thus for example, Maimonides in his introduction to his commentary on the Mishnah, after discussing the codificatory literature of the *Geonim*, went on to say, "The *Halakhot* by the great master, Rabbenu Isaac, of blessed memory, succeeded in replacing all of them [that is, the other codes of the *Geonim*] since it included all the decisions and laws that are needed in this era, i.e., the era of exile. In this work, he cleared up all the errors that had crept into the rulings of his predecessors. I have found difficulty in only a few rulings, certainly not amounting even to ten."[17]

Alfasi's achievements were also appreciated by the halakhic authorities of France and Provence. Thus, Rabad of Posquiere, the keen critic of Maimonides, wrote of Alfasi, "I would rely on Alfasi, of blessed memory, even if he were to say that right is left." Elon observes that the status of Alfasi as a major halakhic authority was "authoritatively established" by the rule of decision-making that Rabbi Joseph Caro set as the basis of determining the law in his works, the *Bet Yosef* and the *Shulhan Arukh*. Caro resolved that "the three pillars of halakhah upon which the House of Israel rests are Alfasi, Maimonides, and Asheri." In his preface to the *Bet Yosef*, he says that when two of them agreed on any point of the law, Caro determined the law "in accordance with their view, except for those few instances where all or most of [the other] halakhic authorities disagreed with that view and a contrary practice had therefore become widespread." In this way, Elon adds, "many of Alfasi's rulings found their way into the authoritative *corpus juris* of the Halakhah where they remain to this day."[18]

Alfasi was regarded in his generation as the leading rabbinic authority in Spain, and he left a legacy of hundreds of responsa to queries addressed to him from all the communities of Spain and North Africa. His major work, however, is *Sefer ha-Halakhot*, which generally follows the pattern of *Halakhot Gedolot* of Rabbi Simeon Kayyara, although it differs from it in some significant aspects.

Like *Halakhot Gedolot*, Alfasi's work is arranged in the order of the tractates of the Talmud. But unlike Kayyara's work, which includes some laws that had no practical application in exile (such as the laws of sacrifices), Alfasi's work is confined strictly to that portion of the law that retained practical relevance after the destruction of the Temple. Therefore, the work does not encompass the entire Talmud, but only three of the six "orders,"—specifically, *Moed*, *Nashim*, and *Nezikin*, together with tractate *Berakhot* (which covers the laws of blessings and prayers) in the order of *Zera'im*, and tractate *Holin* (which deals with dietary laws and ritual slaughter) in the order of *Kodashim*. The laws that are scattered through the orders of *Kodashim* and *Taharot* and still have practical relevance, such as the laws of ritual defilements of priests, and the laws relating to Torah scrolls, *mezuzah*, phylacteries (*tefilin*), and fringes (*tzitzit*) were codified by Alfasi in a separate work entitled *Halakhot Ketanot*.

Alfasi adhered to the principle of treating only laws having practical application so meticulously that he omitted even materials contained in the three orders he covers if they were not practically applicable. For example, he omitted chapters 5–8 in tractate *Pesahim* because they deal with the Pascal sacrifice, no longer applicable in exile. Similarly, he treated only the last chapter in tractate *Yoma* (chapter 8) which deals with the five privations prescribed for the Day of Atonement and the rules of repentance; he did not treat the seven other chapters that deal with the Temple ritual of the day.[19]

Also, like Kayyara, Alfasi concisely discussed the relevant Talmudic sources before stating his final conclusions. But Alfasi went much further. His discussions of the sources are much more extensive than in the books of *halakhot* by Kayyara and other *Geonim*. Alfasi's work includes the general structure of the Talmudic discussion, thus providing the student of his *halakhot* with a recapitulation of the main points of the pertinent Talmudic sources.

Occasionally, Alfasi undertook one additional important function, namely, that of resolving many halakhic problems that had previously been disputed. He did this by discussing the meaning of the Talmudic passage and the various views regarding a particular ruling derived from it, and then stating his own supporting or opposing opinion. Likewise, in the face of the vast halakhic material contained in the Talmud and in the rest of Talmudic literature, as well as the extensive halakhic literature of the Geonic period, Alfasi had to decide between conflicting opinions. Generally, Alfasi applied the rules for decision-making found throughout the Talmud and augmented by the *savoraim* and the *Geonim*. Not infrequently, however, he disagreed with the law established by the *Geonim* and with Simeon Kayyara's conclusions in *Halakhot Gedolot*. Alfasi frequently quoted the Jerusalem Talmud, but when it conflicted with the law in the Babylonian Talmud, he followed the latter. Finally, *Sefer ha-Halakhot* also includes a certain amount of Talmudic aggadah if he felt it served as a basis for halakhic rules governing conduct—but not if it were merely speculative or held only anecdotal significance.[20]

CONCLUSION

In evaluating the significance of Alfasi's *Sefer ha-Halakhot*, Elon writes that "Alfasi's advantage over other *halakhot* books is that his work includes the main points of Talmudic discussion—both the halakhic and the aggadic portions." This unique quality, according to Elon, "earned his *Sefer ha-Halakhot* the additional title 'The Abridged (or Small) Talmud' (*Talmud Katan*); and the author himself apparently intended his work to be just that, in order to make it easier for people to engage in Talmudic study."[21]

It must be pointed out, however, that despite the nearly universally acclaimed greatness of Alfasi's work, and notwithstanding its many innovative features, in terms of the lack of a systematic arrangement and topical classification of the laws, it represents a step backward from the halakhic monographs of Saadiah and the other *Geonim* who followed his approach. In fact, it might be convenient to divide the *halakhot* works of the Geonic period and Alfasi's work into two sub-categories or types. On the one hand, we have the *Halakhot Pesukot*, *Halakhot Gedolot*, and Alfasi's *Sefer ha-Halakhot*, all of which follow the order of the tractates of the Talmud. On the other hand, we have the halakhic monographs of Saadiah, Samuel ben Hofni, and Hai, all of which adopt a more systematic and topical classification of the laws on any single topic, and provide exhaustive treatment of all the laws pertaining to each topic.[22]

THE *MISHNEH TORAH* OF MAIMONIDES

Elon begins his chapter on Maimonides' *Mishneh Torah* by noting that "the turn toward codification of halakhah, manifested in Alfasi's *Sefer ha-Halakhot*, continued to gather momentum until it brought about a significant change in the methodology of codification." Elom wrote that steps in this new direction "appear to have commenced as early as the beginning of the twelfth century, immediately following the death of Alfasi." He goes on to say that the supreme expression of this change "was achieved in the monumental and most original halakhic code ever written, namely, the *Mishneh Torah* of Maimonides."[23] As evidence of this change in the methodology of codification, Elon cites a responsum by Ri Migash, who was the foremost student of Alfasi and his successor as the head of the yeshiva in Lucena, as well as the leading halakhic scholar of his time in Spain.

Ri Migash was asked whether a judge who does not have an adequate knowledge of the Talmud and does not understand even the basis of the applicable law or its source in the Talmud is permitted to make legal rulings on the strength of responsa and books of *halakhot*, and whether it is proper to rely on the decisions of such a judge. Ri Migash's response to this query was that books of *halakhot* were not merely reference works to be consulted only in case of doubt regarding a given legal issue, as Paltoy Gaon had asserted (in a responsum) in mid-ninth century. Rather, Ri Migash maintained, "a book of *halakhot* carries weight in its own right, and it is not necessary to study the Talmudic sources." Recourse to books of *halakhot*, asserted Ri Migash, "is superior to the research and analysis of the Talmud itself as a means of ascertaining the Law." This is so, he explains, because in the search for a legal rule in the vast Talmudic literature, there is always the risk that a judge might misunderstand something and draw improper distinctions, whereas when he bases his decision on "the clear and easily grasped formulation of the codifier, the judge can at least be certain that he has based his decision on the law as declared by a learned halakhic authority." Elon explains that Ri Migash went so far because he believed that "no one in our time has attained such distinction in the Talmud as to be qualified on that account to make authoritative pronouncements on the law."

After discussing Ri Migash's responsum at some length, Elon makes several observations. First, he observes that the explicit statement of Ri Migash "indicates the palpable change in attitude on the part of some halakhic authorities as to the course and proper place of codification of Jewish law." Next, Elon adds that considering the high esteem in which Maimonides held Ri Migash, the forthright and far-reaching statement by the latter that a code is a better basis for making legal decisions than the Talmud itself must have "encouraged Maimonides to undertake the important and difficult task of composing a code of Jewish law in such a form and on such a scale that it suffices, even standing alone, as a basis for making legal rulings and deciding cases."[24]

Clearly, responding to the encouragement provided by Ri Migash's responsum, as well as other motivating factors (see below), Maimonides, in the words of Elon, "performed the task with prodigious genius and much artfulness by pioneering a new form of codificatory literature: a book of *pesakim*—authoritative, concise statements of legal rules."[25]

As an overarching justification or motivation for writing his code, Maimonides cites the nation's need for a code. In a letter to his outstanding disciple, Joseph ben Judah Ibn Aknin, he writes,

> [I am letting you] know that I have not composed this work in order to aggrandize myself among the Jews, or to attain any glory. The One-Whose-Name-Is-To-Be-Blessed knows that at first I labored on it only for my private use, to gain some respite from probing, debating, and searching out whatever I may need. Now that I have become old, thanks to God and may He be praised that I am alive, a zeal for the Lord of Hosts has taken hold of me, seeing that the people are without a legal code that would contain only the correct determinations, free from differences of opinion and from errors. So I have acted solely for the honor of Him-Whose-Name-Is-To-Be-Blessed.

After quoting this letter, Elon observes, "Truly, Maimonides did prepare for the people a 'legal code'—the best crafted and most comprehensive book of *pesakim* in the history of Jewish law."[26]

Referring to Maimonides' statement on the national need for a code, Isadore Twersky writes that the main thrust of this statement is that "Maimonides insists that there is an intrinsic, deeply felt, jurisprudential need for a code. The very nature of the law . . . calls for a *diwan*, a systematic book of rulings which encompasses all areas of halakhah. The nation requires 'a compendious book.'" In discussing other possible contributing motives for Maimonides' writing of his code, Twersky adds, "Codes of law were common in the Islamic world, and inasmuch as Maimonides was generally aware of the surrounding tendencies, this could have provided a stimulus."[27]

Twersky comments, "The anti-Karaite tendency, striving to achieve and underscore unity and uniformity in halakhah, should also be taken into account. Yet the motive which Maimonides pinpoints here [in the letter to Ibn Aknin], the independent legal–literary requirements, is quite persuasive and self-sufficient. There was a vacuum, and Maimonides sought to fill it. The sense of originality and primacy is clearly manifest in this work and was perceived by others as well."[28]

MAIMONIDES' OWN ACCOUNTS OF THE
PURPOSES AND FEATURES OF THE *MISHNEH TORAH*

As noted above, according to Elon, Maimonides set himself four basic objectives in the preparation of the *Mishneh Torah*:

1.   To compile the entire corpus of Jewish law from the Torah up to his own day, and to rework this material scientifically and systematically.

2.   To select and arrange the material topically.

3.   To set forth the law categorically and prescriptively, without associating it with particular sages, without mentioning conflicting opinions, and without source references.

4.   To achieve a polished literary style that clearly and succinctly expresses the contents of the concepts expounded. [29]

Commenting on Maimonides' own statements explaining the goals he set himself in composing his code, Twersky observes, "Given the general reticence and autobiographical shyness that constricts so much of medieval Jewish writing, it may be unequivocally asserted that Maimonides was unusually articulate in commenting upon the purposes, methods, and characteristics of the *Mishneh Torah*."[30]

Maimonides stated his goals boldly and clearly in detail in his introduction to *Sefer ha-Mitzvot* (Book of the Commandments), in his introduction to the *Mishneh Torah*, and in several of his responsa and epistles written to those who sought his guidance or took issue with him. The following is a sampling of his statements with regard to his four objectives.[31]

After listing, in his introduction to the *Mishneh Torah*, the motivations for writing his code, including the vastness of the halakhic material, the difficulty of understanding the sources and of finding one's way in them, and the social and historical milieu, Maimonides adds, "Therefore, I, Moses ben Maimon, the Sephardi, bestirred myself and, relying upon the Creator blessed be He, have made a thorough study of all these books [mentioned previously], and have determined to compose a work containing the results derived from all these books concerning what is prohibited and what is permitted, unclean and clean, as well as the other laws of the Torah" (Elon, *Jewish Law*, p. 1185, n. 90).*

On the all-encompassing scope of the *Mishneh Torah*, Maimonides, in his introduction to his *Sefer ha-Mitzvot* (ibid., p. 1187), writes,

> I deemed it advisable to compile a compendium that will include all the laws and precepts of the Torah, with nothing missing from it . . . so that this compendium would include all the laws of the Torah of Moses, our teacher, whether or not they have practical relevance in this time of exile. . . . Such is my goal in this work: to be brief yet comprehensive, so that the reader might encompass all that is found in the Mishnah, the Talmud, the *Sifra*, the *Sifrei*, the *Tosefta*, and all the enactments of the *Geonim*, of blessed memory, who came afterwards, as well as all that they have explained and commented upon concerning what is prohibited or permitted, ritually impure and pure [and so on]. . . . In short, there should be no need for any book written since the Torah other than this one from which to ascertain anything required in the entire Torah, including both biblical and rabbinic laws.

The topical arrangement and classification of the laws, no doubt, presented Maimonides with a formidable challenge. In his introduction to *Sefer ha-Mitzvot*, he describes the task (ibid., p. 1195) as follows:

> As I directed my attention toward this goal, I began thinking about how the organization of this work and the arrangement of its parts should be accomplished. . . . Then it became clear to

---

* This and the following excerpts are quoted from Elon's *Jewish Law* (used throughout this chapter). Therefore, the quotations will be folowed by *ibid*. and the page number(s)—and the note number, where applicable.

me that it would be best to organize this work into groups of *halakhot* rather than according to the tractates of the Mishnah, e.g., "The Laws of Tabernacle" (*sukkah*), "The Laws of the Palm Branch" (*Lulav*), "The Laws of *Mezuzah*," [and] "The Laws of Fringes" (*tzitzit*); and that I should divide every such general section of *halakhot* into chapters and paragraphs, in the format of the Mishnah, so that for example, "The Laws of Phylacteries" (*Tefillin*) would consist of chapters one, two, three, and four, with each chapter being divided into paragraphs, so as to facilitate memorization by those who wish to learn any part of it by heart.

In his letter to Phinehas ben Meshullam of Alexandria, Maimonides points out how tedious this task was (ibid., p. 1216–17):

Only a great scholar like yourself can understand the toil involved in this work. Most students will imagine that it [simply] follows the order of the Talmud, merely omitting the questions and answers. I can certify that many chapters in it contain *halakhot* distilled from ten or more places in the Babylonian and Jerusalem Talmud and in *baraitot* [*Tosefta* and halakhic midrashim]. I have not followed the order of the Talmud or the Mishnah, but under each topic I have gathered all the relevant laws regardless of their source, so that the laws relating to that subject should not remain scattered throughout the sources. This was my ultimate aim in this work; for no one in the whole world can remember everything in the three main sources of the laws—the Babylonian and Jerusalem Talmuds and the *baraitot*.

Clearly, Maimonides composed the *Mishneh Torah* in comformity with these principles. He called his work *Mishneh Torah* (Recapitulation of the Torah), and also *Ha-Yad ha-Hazakah* (The Mighty Hand). According to Elon, the name *Mishneh Torah* has the same meaning as "Deuteronomy," which in Greek means "Recapitulation of the Law." And, as he puts it, "Just as the biblical Moses recapitulated the Torah in the Book of Deuteronomy, so Moses Maimonides recapitulated the halakhah in his day." The work contains fourteen books, a number expressed in Hebrew by the letters *Yod-Dalet*, forming the first word of the other title, *Yad ha-Hazakah* (The Mighty Hand), an allusion to the concluding verse of the Torah: "For all the great might [literally, the mighty hand] and awesome power that Moses displayed before all Israel" (Deut. 34:12). Each book of the *Mishneh Torah* is divided into sections, each section is in turn divided into chapters, and each chapter is divided into paragraphs, totaling eighty-three sections, one thousand chapters, and nearly fifteen thousand paragraphs in all.

Each book is called *Sefer* (Book of) followed by the general subject treated in the book. Each section is entitled *Hilkhot* (Laws of) followed by the name of the specific topic covered, and each paragraph is called ha-lakhah (law; pl. halakhot). For example, book 4 which deals with family law is called *Sefer Nashim* (Book of Women), and is divided into five sections as follows:

1. *Hilkhot Ishut*, "Laws of Matrimony" (twenty-five chapters).
2. *Hilkhot Gerushin*, "Laws of Divorce" (thirteen chapters).
3. *Hilkhot Yibbum va-Halitzah*, "Laws of Levirate Marriage and Re-lease Therefrom" (eight chapters).
4. *Hilkhot Na'arah Betulah*, "Laws of Virgin Maiden" (three chapters).
5. *Hilkhot Sotah*, "Laws of Suspected Wife" (four chapters).

In concluding this section, Elon comments (ibid., p. 1203), "It was probably thanks to this great work of Maimonides in putting together a so-phisticated and systematic code that his successors—Jacob ben Aher who wrote the *Sefer ha-Turim*, one hundred fifty years later, and Joseph Caro, the author of the *Shulhan Arukh*, about four hundred years later—were able to classify into clear and well-defined categories the halakhic material that accumulated since Maimonides, making only minor changes in the system of classification." Elon adds, "If not for the achievement of Maimonides, it would be impossible today to find a path through the vast accumulation of halakhic material."

The great innovation of Maimonides involved an additional revo-lutionary objective of the *Mishneh Torah*, namely, the creation of what Elon describes as "a new genre of codificatory literature—a systematic halakhic work presenting legal rules categorically in prescriptive form, with no ref-erence to sources or contrary opinions." Maimonides explains the method and motives of the new genre in his introduction to the *Mishneh Torah* (ibid., p. 1204, n. 64) thus:

> I decided to put together the results obtained from all those [pre-vious] works, as to what is forbidden or permitted, [ritually] pure or impure, together with the other laws of the Torah, all in plain

and concise language. Thus, the entire Oral Law, systematically arranged, will become familiar to all, without citing arguments and counterarguments—one person saying one thing and another something else. Rather, [the law will be stated] clearly, pointedly, and accurately, in accordance with the conclusions drawn from all these compilations and commentaries that have appeared since the time of Moses to the present, so that all the laws, whether [Biblical] precepts or enactments adopted by the Sages and Prophets, will be accessible to old and young alike.

Elsewhere in his introduction to the *Mishneh Torah* (ibid., p. 1185, n.12), Maimonides categorically states this revolutionary objective more explicitly:

In brief, a person will not need to have recourse to any other work to ascertain any of the laws of Israel. This work is intended as a compendium of the entire Oral Law, including the enactments, customs, and decrees instituted from the days of Moses, our teacher, until the redaction of the Talmud, as expounded for us by the *Geonim* in all the works composed by them since the completion of the Talmud. Hence I have entitled this work *Mishneh Torah* [Recapitulation of the Torah], for the reason that a person who first reads the Torah and then this work will know from it all of the Oral Law, and there will be no need to read any other book [written] between them.

In his introduction to *Sefer ha-Mitzvot* (ibid., p. 1204, n. 66), Maimonides adds,

In this compendium, I will try, as is my custom, to avoid mentioning differences of opinion and rejected teachings: and I will include in it only the established law, so that this compendium will include all the laws of the Torah of Moses, our teacher, whether they have practical relevance in the time of the exile or not. It also appears to me to be advisable to omit citation of the bearers of the tradition as support and proof [for the various laws]: thus, I will not say with each and every law, "These are the words of this Rabbi," or "This Rabbi says this—and so." . . . All this [I will do] for the sake of brevity. . . . Instead, I will mention in a general way at the beginning of this compendium all the Sages of the Mishnah and the Talmud, of blessed memory, and I will say that all the laws of the Torah— namely, the Oral Law—have been received and handed down from person to person [going back] to Ezra, [and thence] to Moses, our teacher. Together with the leader of every generation that received the tradition, I will also mention the outstanding persons in his generation who were associated with him in the imparting of the Oral Teaching.

After quoting the above passages from *Sefer ha-Mitzvot*, Elon notes (ibid.), "Maimonides, in fact, did this in his Introduction to the *Mishneh Torah* and thereby gave assurance that the source of the authority of the Jewish law is the Torah given at Sinai and the chain of tradition, and that his work, notwithstanding its categorical and monolithic style, does not pretend to be the source of legal authority but rather is a compendium containing all the halakhic laws as crystallized up to his times."

In discussing this innovative aspect of Maimonides' code, Elon observes, "His third objective was attained in consequence of two characteristics to be expected in someone of his stature—a capacity for boldness, and a readiness to pioneer beyond the conventional." Elon then adds (ibid., p. 1203), "The codification of Jewish law involves a fundamental problem: Can the Jewish legal system, which is, by its very nature, a continuous chain of tradition harking back to the Torah, tolerate a code containing only a definitive and categorical statement of each law, with no citation of differing opinions and without source references?" Yet this is precisely what Maimonides meant to accomplish, as is evident from the above-quoted statements, no doubt due to his "capacity for boldness and his readiness to pioneer beyond the conventional," as suggested by Elon. It is no wonder that this revolutionary aspect of his code aroused the strongest opposition on the part of his critics. (See "Criticism of Maimonides and His Response" below).

Maimonides' fourth basic objective for the *Mishneh Torah* involved the question of language and style; his goal was the clear and succinct formulation of its content in an easily understood Hebrew. Thus, in his *Sefer ha-Mitzvot* (ibid., p. 1206), he writes, "I also found it advisable not to compose it [the *Mishneh Torah*] in the style of Scripture, since that sacred tongue is limited for us now to express the laws in all their complexity. I also will not compose it in the language of the Talmud [Aramaic], because only a few of our people now understand it [Aramaic], and even those who are expert in the Talmud find many of its words strange and difficult. Instead, I will compose it in the style of the Mishnah, so that it will be easily understood by most people."

After quoting the above passage, Elon comments (ibid.), "The style of the *Mishneh Torah* reveals that the statement just quoted reflects the modesty of a great man. Although the Mishnah did serve as a basis for the style of the *Mishneh Torah*, the stylistic structure of the *Mishneh Torah* was an innovation in Jewish legal literature. It is characterized by two features: (1) lucid and pleasant Hebrew legal style; and (2) clear and precise legal draftsmanship, easy to read and to understand. The creation of this Hebrew legal style is one of the prime achievements of the codificatory work of Maimonides. Indeed, it has not been equaled to this day."

Elon adds, "It was the good fortune of the Hebrew language that in writing the *Mishneh Torah*, Maimonides departed from his previous practice in regard to the language in which the work was written. All his other works had been written in Arabic. . . . The Hebrew of the *Mishneh Torah* . . . is Maimonides' own [not that of a translator]; it is a precious treasure, a Hebrew legal style of wonderful beauty and precision." Thus, when "the dear and honored elder," the student Mar Yoseph, requested Maimonides to translate the code into Arabic, Maimonides replied (ibid., p. 1208, n. 76),

> It would also be well for you to learn this lesson from this work in the sacred tongue in which we composed it; for it is easy to understand and well suited for self-instruction; once you master one section, you will be able to understand the whole work. I do not want, under any circumstances, to publish it in Arabic, because it would then lose all its beauty. I now would like to render the *Commentary on the Mishnah* and the *Sefer ha-Mitzvot* into the holy tongue; how much less would I be likely to turn this code into Arabic! Do not in any way ask this of me.

ADDITIONAL COMMENTS ON THE SCOPE OF THE *MISHNEH TORAH* AND SOME OF ITS UNIQUE FEATURES

Commenting further on the all-inclusive scope of Maimonides' code, Elon observes that Maimonides was aided in this enormous labor by commentaries and books he had previously written, especially his classic commentary on the Mishnah, which, as Maimonides himself asserts, was based on the halakhic midrashim, the *Tosefta*, the Talmud and the Geonic literature, and the *Sefer ha-Mitzvot*, which he wrote as a preparatory exercise for the *Mishneh Torah* (ibid., pp. 1187–88). Elon then enumerates a number of major features of the *Mishneh Torah*:

(1)   In reworking the material that he had assembled, Maimonides examined on the basis of "old texts" the nature and the accuracy of various legal rules that had been established by his predecessors—and also pointed to errors in the texts that had been responsible for erroneous halakhic conclusions.

(2)   As noted in several of Maimonides' statements in his introduction to his *Sefer ha-Mitzvot* (quoted above), Maimonides intended to cover in his work the entire *corpus juris* of the Jewish legal system, whether or not some laws have practical relevance in this time of exile.[32]

(3)   Maimonides' code includes principles relating to Jewish thought, theology, and ethics, and to the mental and physical aspects of human conduct. He believed that these subjects also deserved to be covered in a book of *pesakim*, and he set them forth in numbered paragraphs, in the classic code style in *Sefer ha-Madda'* (The Book of Knowledge), the first book of the *Mishneh Torah*. Maimonides' integrating philosophy, faith, and ethics with the law characterizes even the purely halakhic sections of his code. Sometimes he prefaces a legal topic with a relevant historical–ethical introduction, and in other instances, he concludes a legal topic with pertinent comments and philosophical reflections.[33]

Similarly, Twersky quotes several statements of Maimonides in his letter to Joseph Ibn Shim'on and in *Ma'amar Tehiyyat ha-Metim* (Essay on The Resurrection of the Dead) illustrating this aspect of the *Mishneh Torah*, and then adds, "It is clear that Maimonides intended from the outset not only to compile rules in respect to that which is forbidden and permitted, clean and unclean, but also to elucidate 'Torah principles' and 'theological fundamentals,' to set forth 'true and exact opinions,' and to indicate how each person can understand 'the ultimate goal of precepts,' according to his capacity." Twersky also notes that this purpose of Maimonides was realized "not only in the distinctly speculative parts of *Sefer ha-Madda'*, but also in the incidental *dicta*, the exegetical notes that sometimes appear to be digressions, in the intellectual–ethical explanations of laws as means of perfecting body and soul."

In describing the contents of Book One, the Book of Knowledge, Twersky writes:

> Book One (*Madda'*, Knowledge) contains Maimonides' sum-mary of the essential beliefs and guiding concepts which provide the ideological and the experiential substructure of Judaism. He explains that he could not compose a comprehensive work on the details of practical precepts while ignoring the fundamentals of essential beliefs, those commandments which are the "roots" (*ikkar*) of Mosaic religion and which should be known before anything else. . . . He was, therefore, compelled to prefix an ex-tended philosophical–theological prolegomenon to his massive Code of Law, thereby underscoring the unity of the philosophi-cal and the legal components of Judaism. . . . The systematic treatment of metaphysics and ethics, the structuring of separate sections of laws of study and laws of repentance, the devoting of a section to idolatry, which includes a history of religion and a rigorous review of superstitions or magical practices which must still be uncompromisingly rejected—all this combines to produce a new and exciting book which is an introduction to, as well as an integral part of, the entire Code. It is literally a foun-dation, a cornerstone of an imposing edifice.[34]

Elon concludes his discussion on the scope of the Mishneh Torah thus (ibid., p. 1194): "The arduous labor involved in finding and 'unveiling' every law in the vast Talmudic literature—where a law is mentioned only incidentally in the course of a debate dealing essentially with an entirely different subject—was described by Maimonides himself in a letter to *Dayyan* Phinehas ben Meshullam of Alexandria, recounting an incident in Maimonides' own life."

After quoting the said letter, Elon adds, "The difficulty and the bur-den of responsibility involved in finding, assembling, and reworking the entire *corpus juris* of the Halakhah was acknowledged and appreciated even by those halakhic authorities who strongly took issue with the other basic guidelines followed by Maimonides in writing the *Mishneh Torah*."

Thus, Rabad, a severe critic of Maimonides, after criticizing (in one of his glosses) one of Maimonides' rulings as having no basis . . . adds, "And for the life of me, if he had not achieved such prodigious accomplishment in gathering together the statements of the *gemara*, the Jerusalem Talmud, and the *Tosefta*, I would have convened a public council against him." Elon, then, concludes, "The merit of Maimonides' great accomplishment in finding, assembling, and reworking the corpus of Jewish law seems to have stood him in good stead."[35]

CRITICISM OF MAIMONIDES AND HIS RESPONSE

In his letter to his disciple, Joseph ben Yehudah, Maimonides indicates that he anticipated all sorts of criticism emanating from various sources,[36] but that he was optimistic that it would not continue beyond his lifetime, and that in the future, "when envy and egocentric ambitions will subside, all Jewry will use it [the Code] exclusively and, without doubt, will not turn to any other book of *Halakhot*." After quoting Maimonides' statement, Elon observes that "Maimonides' ambition and optimistic wish was in substantial measure fulfilled." However, Elon adds that "the main controversy around Maimonides' work did not turn on the points raised in his letter to Joseph ben Yehudah. Many halakhic authorities, although they understood, appreciated, and were impressed by the greatness of Maimonides' work, were strongly opposed to a code intended to be the sole source for determining the law and reaching decisions, in which the law is stated categorically and monolithically without referring to the sources or the contrary opinions." This opposition, Elon continues, gathered strength and made increasing headway.

CRITICISM OF THE *DAYYAN* (JUDGE)
PHINEHAS BEN MESHULLAM OF ALEXANDRIA

Maimonides' correspondence with Phinehas ben Meshullam of Alexandria is of great significance to the controversy regarding Maimonides' approach in the *Mishneh Torah*, for in defending his approach against the latter's criticism, he also provides several rationales for his approach, and even concedes the validity of one of the criticisms. Phinehas ben Meshullam objects to Maimonides' approach of stating the laws categorically without indicating the sources underlying them, "for that would cause the names of the *tanaim and amoraim* to be forgotten," and could lead some students to abandon the study of the Talmud altogether.

Replying to this criticism which, according to Elon, "tended to deny the *Mishneh Torah* its essential purpose as a code," Maimonides was rather outspoken. He writes (ibid., pp. 1216–17),

> Let me tell you first, that I have never said (Heaven forbid): "Do not occupy yourselves with the Talmud or the *Halakhot* [Book of Laws] of Rabbi Isaac [Alfasi]—or anyone else . . . ." As to what you say about the names of the sages, I did mention the names of most of the Sages—*tanaim* and *amoraim*—at the beginning of the work [in the introduction]. . . . *Geonim* and great masters before me have written books and made legal pronouncements in Hebrew and Arabic [he clearly refers to previous books of *halakhot*, including the halakhic monographs of Saadiah Gaon, Samuel ben Hofni Gaon, and Hai Gaon]. But in codifying the entire Talmud and all the laws of the Torah, I have had no predecessor since our sainted master [Rabbi Judah Ha-Nasi] and his colleagues. Because this [work] is comprehensive, is the Heavenly Name on that account profaned? How astonishing!

Maimonides goes on to explain the difference between the literary form of a book of *pesakim* (*hibbur*, composition) and a commentary (*perush*). Then he offers several rationales for his approach. First, he points out that his omission of the names of the Sages followed the precedent of Rabbi Judah Ha-Nasi's way of writing the Mishnah.[37]

Maimonides cites yet another rationale for his approach, one rooted in the Jewish historical reality of the time, namely, the ongoing bitter conflict with the Karaites who attacked the validity and authority of the Oral Law. One of their arguments, according to Maimonides, was that they saw the Oral Law "as the product of various individuals and imagine[d] that the Oral Law was not transmitted but rather made up by particular individuals." Therefore, as Elon put it, Maimonides found it "desirable and even necessary that a book of *pesakim* should reflect Jewish law's monolithic nature . . . and that the *halakhot* be seen not as something handed down by individuals but as grounded in the 'thousands and tens of thousands' who received it from 'thousands and tens of thousands.'"[38]

Finally, in his letter to Phinehas ben Meshullam, Maimonides concedes the validity of one criticism, namely, that the topical arrangement of the *halakhot* in the *Mishneh Torah* resulted in the fact that "halakhic rules from ten or more places in the Babylonian and Jerusalem Talmuds and the *baraitot*" were sometimes assembled in one chapter, in consequence of which "it was often difficult to ascertain the source of a given law, whether for the purpose of academic–theoretical study or for adjudicating an actual case." Maimonides expresses his regret for not having written a companion piece to the *Mishneh Torah*, and declares his intention, "God willing," to write such a companion work "that gives the source reference of every relevant law located elsewhere in the Talmud other than in the main body of law on the topic." For example, most of the laws of the Sabbath are easily found in Tractates *Shabbat* and *Eruvin*, but some Sabbath laws are scattered in Tractates *Avodah Zarah*, *Pesahim*, or *Zevahim* and *Keritot*.

Following a detailed discussion of Maimonides' reply to Phinehas ben Meshullam, Elon summarizes Maimonides' explanation thus: "This detailed explanation once again clearly summarizes Maimonides' objective in writing the *Mishneh Torah*—that the work was to have a unique status in determining the law as crystallized in his day, and that it was to be the sole source for ascertaining the law for purposes of conduct and adjudication. A categorical statement of the law, without attribution of source or reference to contrary opinions was designed to enable his work to attain that status."[39]

For one reason or another, Maimonides never got around to writing this companion work. It was left to the Rashba and to Joseph Caro, several centuries later, to implement Maimonides' plan to write a book of *pesakim* and provide it with a companion or complementary work citing the sources and discussing the various opinions pertaining to each legal issue. (See a full discussion of this development below).

CRITICISM OF RABAD AND ASHERI

As noted above, the opposition to Maimonides' approach "gained strength and increasing headway." Most representative of this opposition is that of Rabad and Asheri. According to Elon, Rabad appreciated some of the extraordinary merits of the *Mishneh Torah*, expressed agreement with many of the laws in it, and was in no way jealous of its fame. What he really objected to was Maimonides' method of declaring the law categorically without citing the sources and without setting out the range of opinions on each legal issue, information which Rabad deemed to be "vital to the very essence of Jewish law and the methodology of halakhic decision-making."[40]

Elon adds that Rabad attacked this feature of Maimonides' code in the first of his critical glosses (*hasaggot*) to Maimonides' introduction to the *Mishneh Torah*. His attack was directed at Maimonides' "revolutionary" (and pretentious sounding) statement that he entitled the work *Mishneh Torah* "for the reason that a person who first reads the Torah and then this work will know from it all of the Oral Law, and there will be no need to read any other book [written] between them." After quoting Rabad's gloss, Elon explains Rabad's position thus:

> In Rabad's opinion the *Mishneh Torah* statement of only a single unattributed view deprives the judge of the means to make up his own mind and impairs his power of decision. . . . The judge may be aware of an opinion opposed to the one stated in the *Mishneh Torah*, but he cannot know which opinion should prevail, because he does not know the weight of the nameless authority whose view is set forth in the *Mishneh Torah*. . . . The effect is to deny to the judge the power of independent judgment essential to his basic function, which is to decide the case before him.[41]

Introducing Asheri's criticism of Maimonides, Elon observes that the criticism of Maimonides' codificatory methodology continued after the time of Rabad and his colleagues, and that some of that criticism even came from halakhic authorities who esteemed Maimonides' work highly and made considerable use of it in their own writings. According to Elon, the severest reaction—and one having the greatest consequence—came about a century later from one of the great halakhic codifiers and commentators, Asheri.[42]

Asheri categorically rejected Maimonides' objective. According to him, the aim of a codificatory work is not to be a self-sufficient source; it is rather to be used in connection with Talmudic sources of the law it seeks to summarize. Only by keeping close to the sources of a legal rule can one arrive at the true meaning of the rule stated in the code.[43] Elon notes further that in several places, Asheri adds that "an opinion stated without attribution of sources or supporting Talmudic citations is entitled to less weight than an opinion based on proofs adduced from the Talmud."[44]

Elon concludes his discussion of Maimonides' *Mishneh Torah* by pointing out that even though Maimonides' objective was not accepted, the *Mishneh Torah* profoundly influenced the codification of Jewish law. Maimonides was the "second pillar" upon whom Joseph Caro based his legal pronouncements in the *Bet Yosef* and the *Shulhan Arukh*.

POST-MAIMONIDEAN CODIFICATION

Summing up the evolution of codificatory literature from the days of Paltoy Gaon, Elon delineates three phases of development:

1) In the ninth century, Paltoy Gaon was firmly opposed to according an independent status to books of *halakhot*, and insisted that they were to be used only in cases where it was difficult to find in Talmudic literature the solution to particular problems.

2) Some three centuries later, Ri Migash reached precisely the opposite conclusion. He maintained that the books of *halakhot* should be the main source of determining the law, and that they were preferable to the complicated discussions of the Talmud. This attitude of Ri Migash attained its high point in the *Mishneh Torah* of Maimonides.

3) The third phase is represented by Rabad in Maimonides' own lifetime, and by Rabad's successors thereafter, particularly Asheri, a century later, who reverted to the position of Paltoy Gaon.

Elon continues (ibid., p. 1230), "[As a result,] the halakhic authorities began to search out new and different codificatory methods that would be consistent with the purpose of halakhic codification, namely, to help find and determine the law. In these efforts, they sought to preserve the essential characteristics of Jewish law—awareness by the judge of the multiplicity of opinions vital to the correct decision in the particular case before him."

This quest for the right form of codification led eventually to the development of a third form of codificatory literature, one that combines desirable features of books of *halakhot* and *pesakim*. This development took two different directions, the first was the path pioneered by Rashba and perfected, several centuries later, by Joseph Caro, and the second was the form adopted by Rabbenu Jacob Ba'al ha-Turim.

THE CODIFICATORY METHODOLOGY OF RASHBA[45]

Rashba's code, *Torat ha-Bayit* (The Law of The House) is in fact two complementary books, *Torat ha-Bayit ha-Arokh* (The Long *Torat ha-Bayit*) and *Torat ha-Bayit ha-Katzer* (The Short *Torat ha-Bayit*). In the Long *Torat ha-Bayit*, Rashba discusses in detail the relevant Talmudic and post-Talmudic sources, while in the Short *Torat ha-Bayit*, he states the laws categorically—that is, the bare legal conclusions arrived at in the Long *Torat ha-Bayit*, without citation of sources or attribution of authority. Its form was thus different from that of all other books of *halakhot*, and, according to Elon, "was the precursor of what was destined to become, some two centuries later, the accepted methodology of codification."

By this original and innovative "dual method," Rashba solved the fundamental problem of codification of halakhah faced by his predecessors since the days of Maimonides. On the one hand, codifiers felt the practical need for a book of categorical rulings, without citation of sources or reference to contrary opinion. On the other hand, they wanted to avoid the danger that such formulation may sever the law from its sources, lead to errors in the interpretation of the categorically stated law, and, as a result, impede a judge's consideration of divergent opinions when ruling on an actual case.[46]

Rashba's code is divided into seven "houses" (*batim*), each of which is in turn divided into "gates" (*she'arim*). Rashba prefaced his work with a table of contents that contains a concise précis of the subject treated in each "house" and in each "gate." He called the table of contents *Mevo ha-She'arim* (The Introduction to the Gates), and explained the objective of his elaborate organization thus: "I have divided this work into seven houses and I will divide each house into gates, in order to make the reader's task easier so that he should feel at home in the Law of the House. . . . Therefore, I called this work *Torat ha-Bayit*.[47]

Rashba's code is limited in scope, however. Both the long and short versions of *Torat ha-Bayit* treat what is generally classified as "religious law," which includes ritual slaughter, animals unfit for food (*terefot*), salting the meat, and forbidden mixtures. Because of its limited scope, according to Elon, Rashba's experiment of two complementary works remained an isolated effort and had no immediate effect on subsequent codificatory literature. Only two centuries later was his "dual method" emulated and perfected by Joseph Caro in his complementary works, the *Bet Yosef* and the *Shulhan Arukh*.

THE *SEFER HA-TURIM* OF RABBI JACOB BEN ASHER

In introducing his discussion of *Sefer ha-Turim*, Elon notes that "from the days of Maimonides, codifiers of the Halakhah wrestled strenuously with the problem of methodology," and that instead of emulating Maimonides' experiment, codifiers made various attempts "to draft codes in the style of books of *halakhot*, whether following the order of the Talmudic tractates, the biblical commandments, or organized topically." They did so, according to Elon, because Maimonides' model of a self-sufficient and consolidated code "reawakened and even intensified the fear that a definitive statement of the law could lead to a severance of the law from its sources and could restrict the range of judicial opinion by omitting reference to divergent opinions." Elon notes further that while all the various forms of codification succeeded in preserving the link with the sources and providing the judge with the full range of halakhic opinions, the great majority of them "did not fulfill the essential codificatory objectives: easy style, simple language, logical organization that made it easy to find the law, a clear and unequivocal statement of the law, and comprehensive coverage of the entire *corpus juris* currently applicable."[48]

Finally, Elon concludes that this state of affairs gave rise to "an urgent and vital need to develop a suitable method for the codification of Jewish law," and that, in the first half of the fourteenth century, "a work exemplifying such a method was both successful and well received." This work, according to Elon, was the *Sefer ha-Turim* (The Book of Rows), also called the *Turim*, or the *Arba'ah Turim* (The Four Rows), written by Jacob ben Asher, who is also called after the name of his work, Jacob Ba'al ha-Turim (Jacob the author of the *Turim*) or simply Ba'al ha-Turim (the Author of the *Turim*).[49]

APPROACH AND METHODOLOGY OF THE *TURIM*

According to Elon (ibid., p. 1283), Jacob ben Asher set himself two goals, the first of which was "to restore definitiveness to Jewish law, and to express the law clearly and unequivocally." His second goal was to find a suitable method of codification, which, "would enable the law to be clearly, definitively and categorically stated without attribution of authority or citation of sources, yet, at the same time, would maintain the continuity of the law, preserve the link with the sources, and keep alive the knowledge of the wide spectrum of opinions within it."

He chose a middle course between a book of *halakhot* and one of *pesakim*. But unlike Rashba who did so by way of two complementary works, Jacob ben Asher combined the two literary forms in a single work. His method was first to state the law briefly, in a form only slightly changed from the original Talmudic formulation, and generally without indicating the source in the Talmud or the names of the Talmudic Sages involved. In this respect, Elon observes, *Sefer ha-Turim* is a book of *pesakim*. But then, immediately after stating the law in this manner, he sets out briefly "the essence of the various relevant opinions of prior authorities, identifies the author of each opinion— whether one of the *Geonim* or one of the *rishonim* of the Jewish centers of Germany, France, or Spain—and then indicates with which opinion he agrees."[50]

According to Elon, Jacob ben Asher "took the rulings of Alfasi as his basis for determining the law: and when Maimonides or others . . . disagreed with Alfasi, the *Turim* discusses the various opinions and generally follows the decision of the author's father . . . [based on] the principle of *hilkheta ke-vatra'ei*, i.e., that the law is in accordance with the views of the latter authorities." Elon adds that "as far as Jacob ben Asher was concerned, his father was the latest authority whose decision was therefore definitive and binding."[51]

Evaluating the methodology of Jacob ben Asher, Elon writes (ibid., p. 1286), "Thus, in this middle way, Jacob ben Asher found the desirable solution to the problem of codifying Jewish law: on the one hand, a categorical and prescriptive statement of the basic legal principle, without attribution of authority or citation of source, and, on the other hand, a presentation of the various opinions of the post-Talmudic authorities on the ramifications of the principle, and his conclusion as to how the law should be declared definitively." Finally Elon observes that "a careful study of the *Turim* reveals that essentially it is modeled on the codificatory method of Rabbi Judah Ha-Nasi in the Mishnah."[52]

STRUCTURE AND ORGANIZATION OF THE *TURIM*

In deciding on the form and structure of his work, the principal aim of Jacob ben Asher, according to Elon, was to make it easy to use, "so that the reader may run through it" and "so that every point may be easily found." For this reason, he did not follow the sequence of the tractates of the Talmud, as his father had done; nor did he adapt an arbitrary pattern of organization. Instead, he organized his work according to subject matter. (See ibid., pp. 1257–88.) His work is divided into four rows (*Turim*) each of which is divided into sections called *halakhot*, which in turn are subdivided into chapters, called *simanim*. The names of the four *Turim* and the content of each *Tur* are as follows:

1) *Tur Orah Hayyim* (The Path of Life) contains all the laws governing a person's daily life, such as the laws of benedictions, fringes (*tzitzit*), phylacteries (*tefillin*), prayers, Sabbath, and festivals.

2) *Tur Yoreh De'ah* (It Will Teach Knowledge) discusses matters of "religious law" (*issur va-heter*), such as the laws of ritual slaughter, animals unfit for food (*terefot*), other forbidden foods, idolatry, usury and interest, menstruant women (*niddah*) and ritual bath, vows and oaths, circumcision, visiting the sick, and burial and mourning.

3) *Tur Even ha-Ezer* (The Stone of the Helper) treats family law. It is divided into many sections covering such subjects as "procreation" which, *inter alia*, deals with forbidden marriages and includes the laws of *agunah* (chained women); marriage (*ketubbah*) and divorce; levirate marriage (*yibbum*) and release therefrom (*halitzah*); and wives suspected of infidelity (*sotah*).

4) *Tur Hoshen Mishpat* (The Breastplate of Decisions) contains the great bulk of civil law and certain parts of criminal law.[53]

Elon observes that the pattern of *Hoshen Mishpat* differs from the organization of the same material in the *Mishneh Torah*. Thus, for example, the civil code in the *Tur* begins with the laws of judges, followed by the laws of evidence, followed by various areas of civil law such as loans, partnerships, acquisition, sales, inheritance, and so on, and concludes with the laws of theft and robbery, torts and informers, and assault and battery (a total of 426 chapters). Maimonides' arrangement of laws dealing with civil and criminal law (what Elon calls *Mishpat Ivri*), on the other hand, follows almost a diametrically opposite pattern, beginning with Book of Damages (*Sefer Nezikin*), and concluding with the Book of Judges (*Sefer Shofetim*) dealing with the laws of Sanhedrin and the laws of evidence.[54]

COMPARATIVE EVALUATION OF THE *SEFER HA-TURIM* AND THE *MISHNEH TORAH*

In comparing the codes of Maimonides and Jacob ben Asher, Elon goes on to point out additional significant differences—relating to the scope, structure, and style—between their respective codes. In terms of scope, Elon points out that in covering only those laws that were currently applicable, Jacob ben Asher reverted to the example set first by Yehudai Gaon and followed by the great majority of codifiers, while Maimonides' *Mishneh Torah* was unique in treating the entire corpus of halakhah (ibid., p. 1300, n. 269). As another example of the difference in scope between the two codes, Elon cites the fact that less than one-third of the *Mishneh Torah* is devoted to civil and family law, while approximately one-half of the *Turim* (*Even ha-Ezer* and *Hoshen Mishpat*) is devoted to the same area of the law (ibid., p. 1300).

In terms of structure and organization, Elon thinks that the classification in the *Turim* is much more refined than that of the *Mishneh Torah*. Thus, for example, Maimonides divides the halakhic material on civil law into four books (*Nezikin*, *Kinyan*, *Mishpatim*, and *Shofetim*), which were subdivided into nineteen sections. The *Tur Hoshen Mishpat*, on the other hand, divides the same material into fifty-eight sections, and while the analytical division in the *Turim* into sections is sometimes too fine, Elon thinks "this division, generally speaking, was a forward step in the classification of Jewish law" (ibid., pp. 1293–94).

Finally, in terms of methodology and style, Elon observes (ibid., p. 1301) that "it is true that the *Mishneh Torah* is, in some respects, a superior work, [and that] it excels the *Turim* in consolidation of the laws into complete and homogeneous units and particularly in clarity and beauty of style and diction." However, he adds, "The *Turim* succeeded in concentrating in a convenient and well-organized form the entire *corpus juris* of Jewish law (so far as it still had practical applicability) as it had developed, and in classifying and organizing the law into clear and well-defined subject areas, so that both students and judges could easily find whatever was necessary for their study or rulings." Most significantly, Elon continues, the *Turim* "successfully achieved a middle course between a book of *pesakim* and a book of *halakhot*."

In summing up the importance of the *Turim*, Elon observes that Jacob ben Asher realized his aspiration to create a work "that the reader may quickly find and act in accordance with what is to be found there, not deviating from it to the right or to the left." As a result, the *Turim* was accepted in a large part of the Jewish world, and although a part of the eastern Jewish communities continued to accept Maimonides' *Mishneh Torah* as the authoritative code, according to Elon, the great Jewish centers of Germany, Italy, and Poland followed the rulings of the *Turim*. Finally, Elon concludes, "the contents and even the topical arrangement of the *Turim* served, two centuries later, as the basis for the most widely accepted halakhic code, the *Shulhan Arukh* of Joseph Caro."[55]

JOSEPH CARO'S WORKS: THE *BET YOSEF* AND THE *SHULHAN ARUKH*

The era between Jacob ben Asher and Joseph Caro witnessed the decline and even destruction of some Jewish centers in the Diaspora and the rise of new ones that took their place and carried on their traditions. Thus, for example, the center in Germany was shaken to its foundations by the outbreak of the Black Death in the middle of the fourteenth century (1348–50), and by ensuing pogroms against the Jews, while the Jewish center in Poland was built from the ruins of the Jewish communities of Germany.

Likewise, the persecution and oppressive laws against the Jews in Spain intensified in the second half of the fourteenth century, reached a high point of mass forced conversions to Christianity in 1391, continued through the fifteenth century, culminating in the expulsion of 1492, which in turn resulted in the destruction of the Jewish community in Spain.

The Jews of Spain found refuge in a number of Jewish centers, primarily in North Africa, the Middle East, Turkey, the Land of Israel, Egypt, and Italy. As a result, Salonika, Constantinople, and Cairo—among many others—were transformed into great centers of Jewish learning, and the High Court of Safed became renowned as a leading halakhic tribunal throughout the Jewish world. Many of the leading halakhic authorities became exiled wanderers, among them Joseph Caro, son of Ephraim.[56]

According to Elon (ibid., p. 1312), these migrations and wanderings of entire Jewish communities produced a number of social and halakhic effects. "Jews began to long for the Final Redemption and for a restored and renewed supreme halakhic authority that would once again consolidate the Jewish people scattered throughout the Diaspora." He quotes Caro's description of the condition of Jewish law in his day (in his introduction to *Bet Yosef—Tur Orah Hayyim*) bemoaning the fact that due to the "terrible trials and tribulations" endured by the Jewish people, the Torah has become not two torahs, but "has been fragmented into innumerable Torahs." Elon then comments, "The wounds of exile and dispersion had left their scars on Jewish law; the one Torah had become not two but innumerable Torahs, and the Jews of that generation needed a book such as this [the *Bet Yosef*] that collects all the laws and reveals their sources so that a correct conclusion can be reached as to what the Halakhah prescribes." Elon notes that there were many halakhic authorities in that generation, "but of them all, Joseph Caro alone undertook this momentous task so vitally needed by both his and later generations."

CARO'S METHODOLOGY

According to Elon, Caro "succeeded in transforming Rashba's 'dual methodology' into the accepted approach to halakhic codification by the adoption of that methodology for the creation of his great code: a single work made up of two parts—*Bet Yosef* and the *Shulhan Arukh*." And although the two parts are separate and distinct in form and content, taken together they were meant to achieve a single overall objective, namely, that of combining the desirable features of books of *halakhot* and books of *pesakim*. Caro believed that a halakhic code must have two components: one that cites all the sources and differing opinions, and another that presents a single statement of the law—final, categorical, and monolithic. Caro describes clearly his theory of the "double" code in his introduction to the *Shulhan Arukh*.[57]

THE *BET YOSEF*

Bet Yosef (The House of Joseph) was Caro's first, and in terms of scope and content, his major work. He composed it as an extension of or a commentary on the *Turim*. In his introduction to the *Bet Yosef*, he clearly and explicitly describes the two objectives of his work. The first was to collect all the halakhic material up to his time concerning "the laws currently applicable . . . and to present all the different opinions bearing on the law." His second objective was to determine the law by selecting which of the many conflicting opinions to follow, thus laying the foundations of his *Shulhan Arukh*. He describes his first objective thus: "To complete a work that includes all the laws currently applicable, together with an explanation of their roots and origins in the Talmud, as well as an exposition of the different opinions of all the authorities, omitting none."[58]

As noted above, both Rashba and Jacob ben Asher tried to solve the problem of codification of Jewish law by combining features of the books of *halakhot* and of *pesakim*, but took two different approaches in doing so. Rashba chose a "dual methodology" of writing two complementary works, one stating the law categorically, and a companion work citing and discussing the sources and all the different opinions bearing on the law. Jacob ben Asher chose, instead, to combine features of books of *pesakim* and *halakhot* in a single work. By attaching the *Bet Yosef* to the *Turim*, Caro in fact followed the organization and classification of the *Turim* while adopting the "dual methodology" of Rashba. Caro explains why he wrote the *Bet Yosef* as a commentary on the *Turim* thus: "I decided not to write the book as an independent work, so that I would not have to repeat what my predecessors wrote; I therefore decided to attach it to one of the famous codes . . . the book of the . . . *Turim* of Rabbenu Jacob ben Asher because it [the *Turim*] includes most of the opinions of the authorities" (ibid., p. 1314, n.14). In a footnote, Elon adds that Caro stated that he had originally intended to attach his work to Maimonides' *Mishneh Torah* "since he is the most famous halakhic authority in the world," but he gave up the idea because Maimonides gives only one opinion and Caro would have had to set out at length the opinions and the rationales of all other authorities.[59]

Thus, Caro chose to attach his *Bet Yosef* to the *Turim* only for reasons of convenience, and it is safe to assume that were it not for this practical consideration, his ideal choice would have been to attach it to the *Mishneh Torah* of Maimonides, whom he considered the "most famous halakhic authority in the world." Elon points out that by attaching his work to the *Turim*, Caro has spared himself "the burden of repeating the opinions of the halakhic authorities already collated in that work [the *Turim*]; he needed merely to indicate the Talmudic source of the laws stated in the *Turim*, explain and sometimes criticize the various opinions presented there, and occasionally correct errors that had found their way into the text."

After explaining in detail his methodology in dealing with the opinions stated in the *Turim* (quoted at length by Elon), Caro proceeds to set out "a detailed listing of more than thirty halakhic works by leading halakhic authorities—commentaries, novellae, responsa, and codes—whose statements and opinions are presented and discussed in *Bet Yosef*."[60]

CARO'S METHODOLOGY IN DETERMINING THE LAW

Elon observes that after a thorough description of his first objective in writing the *Bet Yosef*, Caro went on to describe his second objective: to determine the law (which he describes as his "ultimate purpose") by selecting which of the many conflicting opinions to follow. Elon then (ibid., p. 1317) sums up Caro's description of his second objective as follows: "Logically, when there are differences of opinion among the halakhic authorities, it would seem that the law should be determined by adducing arguments and proofs from the Talmudic sources and appraising the merits of each opinion. . . . [But] Caro contended that as a practical matter it [this methodology] was almost impossible to employ. He gave two reasons: (1) all the *rishonim* based their opinions on arguments and proofs, and 'who can be so audacious as . . . to decide between them by appraising arguments and proofs?'; and (2) such a course would involve an exceedingly long journey 'too onerous to ever complete.'"

In view of these considerations, Elon continues, "Caro chose a different and original method to determine the binding legal rules." Elon then quotes Caro's own description of his method:

> Since I concluded that the three pillars of instruction upon which the House of Israel rests [*ammudei hora'ah*] are Alfasi, Maimonides, and Asheri, of blessed memory, I resolved that when two of them agree on any point I will determine the law in accordance with their view, except for those few instances when all or most [of the other] halakhic authorities disagree with that view and a contrary practice has therefore become widespread.
>
> When one of the above-mentioned three pillars expresses no opinion on a particular matter and the other two do not agree, we will turn to Nachmanides (Ramban), Rashba, Ran, the Mordekhai, and Semag . . . and declare the law in accordance with the view of the majority of these authorities.
>
> When none of the above-mentioned pillars expresses an opinion, we will declare the law according to the well-known halakhic authorities who have expressed an opinion on the particular matter. . . . This method is the most feasible (literally, the royal road—*derekh ha-melekh*); it is correct, easy to apply, and the most efficient solution to the problem.[61]

After quoting Caro's description of his approach in determining the law in full, Elon makes the following evaluative comments: (1) Caro's criterion for determining the law on a question disputed by halakhic authorities "was not an evaluation of the arguments on the merits of the question, but rather a technical and mathematical formula based on the number of proponents of a particular opinion among a pre-selected group of halakhic authorities." (2) Caro understood and emphasized that his method was not ideal but was chosen only because of its utility as "the most feasible . . . and . . . efficient solution." (3) Elon states that "this methodology for decision-making was better than relying on an appraisal of the merits of each question, both because of the substantive difficulty involved in making a choice from among the different opinions, and because the laborious efforts required to reach a conclusion as to every single issue would have been a never-ending process. . . . Instead, Caro, in effect, established pre-selected 'judicial benches.' The first 'bench' was composed of Alfasi, Maimonides, and Asheri; the second consisted of one or two of them together with Nahmanides, Rashba, Ran, the Mordekhai, and Semag." (4) Elon thinks this was "a good method in view of the personal attributes and stature of those who constituted the 'benches.' It was efficient because the 'benches' were permanent and always in session, and the opinions of the 'judges' could be found in the books they have written." In sum, concludes Elon, "it was the vast increase in halakhic material and the multitude of differences of opinion among the halakhic authorities that led Caro to adopt his methodology."[62]

THE SHULHAN ARUKH

Caro, like Maimonides, believed that for a code of Jewish law to be convenient and efficient, it was essential that it present the law clearly, categorically, and definitively. Accordingly, he saw his *Bet Yosef* as only one part of his solution to the problem of codifying Jewish law. Therefore, after composing his *Bet Yosef*, he provided Jewish law with a classic book of *pesakim*, as complementary on it.[63]

Elon points out that Caro made his position with regard to the need of a book of *pesakim* very clear in his defense of Maimonides against the criticism of Rabad, which was that in omitting the sources for his rulings in the *Mishneh Torah*, Maimonides had "forsaken the methods of all authors who preceded him." Caro responded to Rabad's stricture thus:

But I say that the Master's [Maimonides'] reason was that if he had wanted to follow the method of the authors who preceded him, what purpose would there have been in writing anything beyond what had already been written by Alfasi, whose rulings he generally followed? Therefore, he intended to introduce a new method: to state the law clearly and briefly in the style of the Mishnah, so that every intelligent person thereafter can rely on Maimonides' statement of the law. And should some great scholar not be prepared to accept that choice without first weighing the matter himself—who prevents him from studying the Talmudic literature and the other halakhic works? It follows that the method Maimonides adopted is of benefit to everyone except the scholar who stands head and shoulder above the rest of his generation, and even for such a person it is of value, because if he must make a quick decision, he can rely on Maimonides' opinion, and even if he is not pressed for time, it is no small matter for him to know Maimonides' opinion.[64]

STRUCTURE OF THE *SHULHAN ARUKH*

The *Shulhan Arukh*, like the *Turim*, is divided into four parts: *Orah Hayyim, Yoreh De'ah, Even ha-Ezer,* and *Hoshen Mishpat*. This design clearly follows from the fact that the laws stated in the *Shulhan Arukh* are "distillations of Caro's conclusions reached in the *Bet Yosef* which follows the arrangement of the *Turim*."

Elon notes, though, that although the *Shulhan Arukh*, like the *Turim*, is arranged topically, "the analytical breakdown of the various subjects, i.e., the sections within each part is somewhat different from that of the *Turim*." The general tendency in the *Shulhan Arukh* is to "subsume numerous subsidiary topics under a single general heading," whereas the same material in the *Tur* is subdivided into numerous sections, each with its own heading. Thus, for example, in the *Tur Hoshen Mishpat*, the material contained in chapters 39–74 consists of seven sections, each with its own heading. In the *Shulhan Arukh*, on the other hand, they all appear under the heading, "Laws of Lending," which, according to Elon, is a more appropriate arrangement since all of the seven sections in the *Tur* "are really subdivisions of the central subject in the laws of loans."[65]

Language and Style

In terms of language and style, Caro intended the *Shulhan Arukh* to be a book of "clear and definitive statement of the applicable law, without discursive debate or argument," and, according to Elon, "a comparison of the *Shulhan Arukh* with previous books of *pesakim* will reveal that the *Shulhan Arukh* is more categorical and concise than all of them." In most respects, Caro followed the example of Maimonides in the *Mishneh Torah*. Like Maimonides, he omitted references to the sources of the law, the many different opinions, the considerations that led him to his conclusions, and the names of the authors of the laws stated in the *Shulhan Arukh*. But, unlike Maimonides, Caro also omitted any additional comments not strictly necessary to the bare statement of the law. As noted above, Maimonides frequently incorporated rationales or explanations into his statement of the laws, and he sometimes even added a relevant philosophical or ethical preamble or epilogue to his exposition of the law (such comments can also be found in the *Turim*). By contrast, Caro, in his desire for the utmost conciseness, omitted all such comments; his statement of the laws themselves was also as terse as possible.

Following a comparative discussion of four parallel examples of the law from the *Mishneh Torah*, the *Turim*, and the *Shulhan Arukh* with regard to their respective formulation and style in stating the law, Elon concludes,

> The method of the *Shulhan Arukh* is distinct from that of the other codes. The *Shulhan Arukh* states the substance of the law briefly, sometimes adopting the formulation of the *Turim* for this purpose. However, when clarity is particularly needed, the *Shulhan Arukh* frequently prefers Maimonides' text; and in these instances is more expansive than the *Turim*. The *Shulhan Arukh* presents only the normative rule; in contrast to Maimonides and the *Turim*, it includes neither rationales for the law nor any philosophical considerations. Laws are generally stated without attribution of source, and with no reference to contrary opinions.

Elon adds that the differences between the codes stems from the different approaches of their authors to codification.[66]

Notwithstanding his high praise of both the *Turim* and the *Shulhan Arukh*, Elon's highest praise is reserved for the *Mishneh Torah*. Continuing his comparative evaluation of the major codes, he writes (ibid., p. 1340),

> Nevertheless, it should be reiterated that Maimonides' *Mishneh Torah* remains the preeminent code in terms of structure and style. No author of a book of *halakhot* or *pesakim*—not even the *Shulhan Arukh*—has succeeded in producing a work so uniformly excellent in clarity and design, beauty of style, and unity of structure as the *Mishneh Torah*. The *Mishneh Torah* is a unified tightly constructed work, written in consistently beautiful and clear Hebrew. The *Shulhan Arukh*, on the other hand, contains a variety of styles with a confusing mixture of Hebrew and Aramaic; the work as a whole lacks the uniformity and harmony that distinguishes every part of the *Mishneh Torah*.

THE CRYSTALLIZATION OF THE METHODOLOGY OF CODIFYING JEWISH LAW

In concluding his discussion of Caro's *Bet Yosef* and the *Shulhan Arukh*, Elon comments (ibid., p. 1341),

> Joseph Caro's methodology for codifying the *Halakhah* was the culmination of the efforts of a number of predecessors. Had it not been for Maimonides' bold and revolutionary innovation in the twelfth century—a monolithic book of *pesakim* containing a categorical statement of legal rules with no reference to sources or contrary opinions—or for the originality of Rashba's thirteenth-century undertaking . . . a book of *pesakim* as a companion to a book of *halakhot* or to Jacob ben Asher's venture in the fourteenth century combining both these genres into one *magnum opus* in the *Turim*, it is unlikely that Joseph Caro's twofold work *Bet Yosef* and *Shulhan Arukh* would have been accepted or even written.

He goes on to say, "The need for a code of Jewish law was recognized equally by Maimonides, Rashba, Jacob ben Asher, and Joseph Caro, and the background giving rise to the need was the same for each of them: the difficulty of finding one's way through the halakhic sources, the diffusiveness of the laws, and the proliferation of conflicting views as to specific provisions."[67]

CONCLUDING COMMENTS

Finally, it must be pointed out that with the exception of the *Turim* by Jacob ben Asher, all the major codes discussed in this chapter, including Saadiah Gaon's innovative and original halakhic monographs (which became the model for topical organization of *halakhah*), Alfasi's *Sefer ha-Halakhot*, Maimonides' *Mishneh Torah*, Rashba's twofold work of *Torat ha-Bayit ha-Arokh* and *Torat ha-Bayit ha-Katzer*, and Joseph Caro's monumental complementary works of *Bet Yoseph* and the *Shulhan Arukh* were all the works of Sephardic codifiers. According to Elon, even Jacob ben Asher took the rulings of Alfasi as the basis for determining the law and followed the opinion of his father, the Asheri (considered the leader of Ashkenazic Jewry), only when Maimonides and/or others disagreed with Alfasi's rulings—hence the title of this chapter: "Sephardic Codification of Jewish Law."[68]

7.

MEDIEVAL JEWISH PHILOSOPHY

As with various developments of Sephardic culture discussed in the previous chapters, medieval Jewish philosophy was inspired and informed by Arabic culture. As S. D. Goitein astutely points out, "The basic fact about Jewish–Arabic thought is that Greek science and Greek methods of thinking made their entrance into Jewish life mainly through the gates of Arabic–Muslim literature. With the Arabic-writing Jewish doctors, mathematicians, astronomers, and philosophers of the ninth and tenth centuries, science, in the Greek sense of the word, for the first time became known and practiced among the bulk of the Jewish community."[1]

Alexander Altman sums it up by stating categorically that "medieval Jewish philosophy is the offspring of Arabian culture."[2] According to him, it was the intellectual climate of Islamic thought that largely inspired and informed the rational bent of medieval Jewish philosophy. It is true that the encounter between Judaism and Greek civilization goes back to the days of Philo of Alexandria who wrote works on philosophy. But his work and conclusions had very little direct influence on subsequent Jewish thought, mainly because they were not sufficiently rooted in Jewish lore, for his knowledge of that lore was deficient. It is also true that many of the theological problems confronted by Islamic religious philosophy for the first time, as a result of the influx of Greek thought, were not entirely new to Jewish thinkers. Judaism had already faced them in some measure at a previous stage in the history of Jewish thought—when it had its first encounter with Hellenistic civilization in Talmudic times.

As a result, there are numerous questions touched on in rabbinic literature that properly belong to the realm of theology. But, as Abraham Halkin observes, "The rabbinic manner of dealing with its problems, by finding support in a biblical verse, or by reconciling seemingly contradictory verses, however definitely it may represent an earnest desire to understand a certain problem or to solve a certain difficulty, cannot be called formal theology."[3] In a similar spirit, Bernard Lewis notes, "The notion of a theology, of a formulation of religious belief in the form of philosophical principles, was alien to the Jews of Biblical and Talmudic times. The emergence of a Jewish theology took place almost entirely in Islamic lands. It was the work of theologians who used both the concepts and the vocabulary (either in Arabic or calqued into Hebrew) of Muslim *kalam*."[4]

Nine centuries after Philo, however, we witness a reawakening of Jewish philosophy under the impact of Arab philosophy, which in turn was the result of Islam's encounter with Greek thought.[5] Altmann observes, "It was inevitable that the acquisition of this vast treasure of Greek thought should initiate a period of profound scientific and philosophic activity." He said that, because the Islamic world was virtually in complete possession of the Greek legacy, it assumed the leadership in the cultural sphere. Altmann adds, "The Jews living under Islamic rule took a prominent part in all branches of science, and soon evolved a philosophical movement of their own, which persisted throughout the Middle Ages and reached down into the Renaissance period."[6]

One of the central premises of the Islamic and Jewish philosophers was their conviction that religion and speculative knowledge, revelation and reason, were equally valid sources of Divine Truth, and as such must of necessity confirm and reinforce rather than contradict each other. As Raphael Patai puts it, "Saadiah sounds the theme that was to become the leitmotif of medieval Jewish philosophy: there is no conflict between Reason and Revelation, that is, between philosophical speculation and the teachings of Judaism as revealed in the Bible."[7] Accordingly, one of the pressing problems that preoccupied Jewish philosophers (as it did Muslim philosophers, especially the Mu'tazilites) was how to reconcile reason and revelation, or philosophy and religion. They were all firm believers in the truth of Scriptures as they were in the teachings of certain Greek philosophers, which reached them in a Muslim-Arab garb. They believed that two truths cannot contradict each other, and therefore the teachings of the Bible and of the philosophers, though cast in different idioms, must contain the same truth. Their task then, as they saw it, was to show—by using the reasoning faculty—that these two seemingly different truths were fundamentally identical. They achieved this aim either by means of allegorical interpretation of biblical passages which seemed to contradict reason, or by showing that logical reasoning proves the biblical teachings right and the views of the philosophers wrong.

Thus, for example, Maimonides uses both methods in *The Guide of the Perplexed*. He devotes most of the first part of the three parts of the *Guide* to allegorical interpretation of the Bible in order to reconcile its teachings with philosophy. On the other hand, when dealing with the question of Aristotle's view of the eternity of the world as opposed to the biblical notion of "creation out of nothing," he rejects Aristotle's view in favor of the biblical theory of "creation in time," arguing that since neither doctrine is demonstrable with certainty, he opts for the biblical one, for it has on its side the authority of prophecy.[8]

Muslim philosophical writings may be classified into three categories or phases of development. They are *kalam*, Neoplatonism, and Aristotelianism. Then, there is also the anti-philosophical thought of the intellectual mystic Al-Ghazali. Medieval Jewish philosophy is representative of all the major phases of Islamic thought. Thus, Saadiah was the outstanding representative of Jewish *kalam*, Isaac Israeli and Solomon Ibn Gabirol were the outstanding representatives of Jewish Neoplatonism, and Abraham Ibn Daud and Maimonides represent the Aristotelian phase of Jewish philosophy, that is to say, the Aristotelianism of al-Kindi (late ninth century), al-Farabi (c.870–950), and Avicenna (Ibn Sina, 980–1037)—who attempted to combine Neoplatonism with Aristotelianism. Finally, al-Ghazali's thought influenced the anti-philosophical thinking of Yehudah Halevi and Hasdai Crescas. This chapter, however, will focus on the works of Saadiah Gaon, Maimonides, and Yehudah Halevi, representatives of the Jewish philosophical parallels of *kalam*, Aristotelianism, and al-Ghazali. A systematic presentation of these works is beyond the scope of this work. What is attempted here is simply presenting a general idea of the motivations for the composition of these works, for whom they were meant, and some of the main ideas or teachings of these major Jewish thinkers. For a more systematic review of these works, there are numerous analytical and exhaustive studies available.

SAADIAH GAON

In its initial phase, medieval Jewish philosophy followed the model of the Arabic *kalam* (literally, speech, but meaning dogmatic theology). Saadiah Gaon, the earliest Jewish philosopher in the Arab orbit, was the outstanding representative of Jewish *kalam*. As the head of the Sura Academy, Saadiah Gaon was the intellectual representative of Jewry and Judaism in his generation. As such, he felt a personal responsibility to educate his people and to interpret for them Judaism in light of contemporary scientific and cultural currents. Indeed, as Alexander Altmann points out, Saadiah was "the pioneer of the scientific learning of the Middle Ages."[9] Hebrew grammar and lexicography did not exist before him; and while the Bible had been translated into Aramaic and Greek before, he was the first to translate it into Arabic and the first to write a commentary on it.

As stated at the beginning of this work, Saadiah single-handedly forged the tools for the analytical study of the Bible and its language through his many pioneering works on Hebrew and Arabic lexicography and grammar, his translation of the Bible into Arabic (*Tafsir*), and his critical and in many ways innovative commentary on the Bible (*Sharh*). He also pioneered works in Hebrew poetry, liturgy, and codification of Jewish law in his original topically arranged halakhic monographs.[10] But, according to Isaac Husik, his greatest work, "that which did the most important service to the theory of Judaism, and by which he will be best remembered, is his endeavor to work out a system of doctrine which should be in harmony with the tradition of Judaism on the one hand, and, with the most authoritative scientific and philosophic opinion of the time on the other."[11]

Saadiah's philosophical work, *Emunot ve-De'ot* (Beliefs and Opinions) gives full and comprehensive answers to all the problems that agitated the minds of his contemporaries. Alexander Altmann points out that Saadiah's work is not a work of academic research and speculation, but a collection of living answers to living problems. Thus, Altmann adds, the phrase which so often occurs in it—"someone may ask"—is not a rhetorical phrase designed to introduce the author's own trend of argument, but the echo of some real question or objection which Saadiah had met either in a book or in a personal discussion.[12] Altmann concludes, "The answer which Saadiah's book evolves is not that of any particular philosophical system, but the interpretation of Judaism in the light of reason (*'akl*). It is Saadiah's conviction, eloquently expressed, that Judaism teaches nothing contrary to 'Reason,' and that, furthermore, its fundamental principles, such as Creation, Unity of God, the rational character of the Law, Freedom of the Will, the Future Life, can be demonstrated by the 'speculation' (*nazr*) of Reason."[13]

SOURCE OF SAADIAH'S INSPIRATION AND MODEL

Saadiah's conception of reason as well as his basic premise that there is no conflict between reason and revelation was inspired and informed by the Mu'tazilite schools, described by Altmann as the "free thinkers of Islam" who introduced the method of ta'wil (allegorical interpretation) as a means of harmonizing faith and reason.[14]

Saadiah's book is arranged following the Mu'tazilite model, whose works typically consist of two main divisions on the unity and justice of God. Indeed, the Mu'tazilites like to speak of themselves as "the people of unity and justice" (ahl al-'adl wal-tawhid).[15] Following some preliminary considerations on the nature and sources of knowledge, the first sections in Mu'tazilite works proceed to prove the existence of God by showing that the world cannot have existed from eternity and must have been created in time. Creation implies a Creator. This is usually followed by arguments proving the unity and incorporeality of God, and a discussion of the divine attributes with the purpose of showing that God's unity and simplicity is not affected by them. This section concludes with a refutation of opposing views, such as those of the dualists and trinitarians. The section on the justice of God centers around the doctrines of man's free will, reward and punishment, and problems of a more dogmatic nature—eschatological or otherwise. Saadiah's *Book of Beliefs and Opinions* (or to use Altmann's preferred translation—*Book of Doctrines and Beliefs*) follows the same plan and structure. His indebtedness to the Mu'tazilites is not limited, however, to the plan and arrangement of his book. Many of his arguments for the existence of God and Creation in time, as well as his discussion of divine attributes, are all taken directly from them.[16]

Another doctrine associated with *kalam* is that of the "atomic theory of existence." It is held by some of the Mutakallimun, especially the Asharites (but, according to Maimonides, it was held by most of the Mutakallimun). The supporters of this theory were opposed to the Aristotelian theory of matter and form, and substituted for it the "atomic theory." According to them, all existence is composed of atoms, which form the substance (matter), and the atoms are characterized by certain properties such as form, color, size, and so on, which they call accidents. These properties are constantly changing as their duration is only temporary (in an atom of time, as it were). This doctrine denies the necessity of cause and effect and the validity of natural law; it makes God directly responsible for everything that happens every moment of existence. According to these Mutakallimun, God creates continually and is not hampered by any such thing as natural law, which is merely our name for that which we are accustomed to seeing. In this conception of the natural process, miracles cease to be miraculous.

Among the Jewish philosophers who followed the system of *kalam*, not all adopted the atomic theory of existence. It is not clear, however, whether Saadiah adopted it. Abraham Halkin says that the most notable Jewish representative of *kalam*, Saadiah Gaon, does not incline to the theory, preferring a variety of the Aristotelian concept of matter and form. Isaac Husik notes, however, that "Saadiah does not speak of matter and form as constituting the essence of existing things; he does speak of substance and accident, which might lead us to believe that he held the atomic theory."[17]

PURPOSE OF THE BOOK

Saadiah wrote his philosophical work with the aim of offering guidance to his People.[18] In the opening chapter, his prolegomenon, he states the purpose of his work, what drove him to write it, for whom it is intended, and what he hoped to achieve with it. He informs the reader that he was induced to write his book because he found that the beliefs and opinions of men were in an unsatisfactory state. He explains that while some of the people are fortunate enough to possess the truth, know that they have it and rejoice at having it, there are others who, when they have the truth, know it not and doubt it; others adopt erroneous opinions believing them to be true, while still others vacillate continually going from one opinion or belief to another. This, Saadiah writes, gave him pain, and he thought it his duty to use his limited knowledge to help them. Thus, he writes,

> My heart grieved for my race, the race of mankind, and my soul was moved on account of my own people Israel, as I saw in my time many of the believers clinging to unsound doctrines and mistaken beliefs while many of those who deny the faith boast of their unbelief and despise the men of truth, although they are themselves in error. I saw men sunk, as it were, in a sea of doubt and covered by the waters of confusion, and there was no diver to bring them up from the depths and no swimmer to come to their rescue. But as my lord had granted unto me some knowledge which I can use for their support, and endowed me with some ability which I might employ for their benefit, I felt that to help them was my duty and guiding them aright an obligation upon me.[19]

In order for his book to achieve his educational goal most effectively, Saadiah intended "to place the subject matter throughout the book within the grasp of the reader and not beyond it; to speak a language which is easy and not difficult; to adduce only the principle proofs and arguments, not their ramifications, so that the reader may find his way about without too great difficulty." In other words, he intended the book to benefit all readers and not only the intellectual elite.[20]

Saadiah further spells out precisely what he hoped his book will accomplish: "If both the scholar and the learner follow this path, the certainty of him that feels certain will increase; the doubt of him that is in doubt will vanish; the believer who blindly relies on tradition will turn into one basing his belief on speculation and understanding; those who put forward erroneous arguments will be silenced; those who are obstinate and defy evidence will be shamed; and the righteous and upright will rejoice."[21]

After stating the purpose of his writing the book and what he hopes to achieve with it, Saadiah proceeds to discuss a number of ideas or principles which he believes to have a bearing on the subjects of his book, such as the nature of doubt and belief, the roots or sources of all human knowledge, the need to confirm the teachings of Judaism by means of inquiry and philosophical speculation, and the all-important principle that there is no conflict between reason and revelation, that is, between philosophical speculation and the teachings of Judaism as revealed in the Bible.

In the third section of the prolegomenon, Saadiah discusses the sources of truth and certainty, which he describes as "the origin of all knowledge and the fountain of all cognition." He affirms that there exist three sources of knowledge. First, is the knowledge derived from our sense perception (that is, that which man perceives by his five senses). Second, is knowledge derived from reason (that which is derived purely from the mind, applied especially to judgment of values, as the approval of truth and the disapproval of falsehood). In addition to these two sources of immediate knowledge, there is a third source based on these two. It is inferential knowledge or logical inference by which we are led to believe something we have not directly perceived by our senses or a matter concerning which we have no immediate knowledge via reason—because we infer it from something else which we have perceived or of which we do have immediate certainty via reason. Thus, we believe that man has a soul though we have never seen it, because we infer its presence from its activities or functions, which we do see. These three sources are universal and are not peculiar to a given race or religion, though there are some persons who deny the validity of some or all of them. He affirms that Jews believe in them and in still another source of truth—namely, authentic tradition.[22]

Saadiah then dismisses the objections of some people—who believe that inquiry and speculation lead to unbelief—as the opinion of ignorants: "Only the ignorant think thus." He asserts further that a Jew is not forbidden to speculate and philosophize about the truths of religion. What is forbidden, he explains, is to "brush aside the prophetic Scriptures and rely [exclusively] on our personal judgment in our speculation on the origin of Space and Time." For, he argues, one may find the truth or one may miss it, and "even if he finds the truth of religion and clings to it, he is never sure that he will not depart from it should doubt arise in his mind and weaken his belief."

In any case, he adds, the discovery of truth through speculation takes time, and until a person finds it, he is without a religious guide. But if we hold fast to the commandments of the Bible, our own rationalization on the truth of religion will be of great benefit to us. First, such speculative investigation of the facts of religion will give us a reasoned and scientific knowledge of the teachings of the Bible; second, it will enable us "to refute those who attack us on matters connected with our religion." Hence, Saadiah concludes, it is not only our privilege but our duty to confirm the truth of religion by reason.

Finally, Saadiah tackles the obvious question that some may ask: If the truth of religion can be discovered through reason, what need was there for revelation? He offers two answers: (1) God knew that arriving at the truths of religion through speculation and inquiry takes time; it is a gradual process and is achieved in stages, and meanwhile man needed religious guidance which is provided by revelation. (2) Not everyone has the capacity or the patience to complete the task of speculation, and for such people revelation is a necessity.[23]

After dealing with preliminary themes in his prolegomenon, Saadiah proceeds to discuss in the body of his book such fundamental principles of Judaism as the existence of God, His unity, Creation in time, the rational character of the Law, freedom of the will, reward and punishment, the nature and function of man's soul, the afterlife, and other related matters. For the purpose of this chapter, we will focus on several of those principles.

THE EXISTENCE OF GOD

The most fundamental fact of religion is the existence of God. We know it from Scripture, but Jewish and Muslim philosophers alike felt the need to prove it by reason. Since no one has seen God or has an intimate certainty of His existence, the method used to prove it is that of "logical inference." Hence Saadiah proceeds to prove the existence of God starting from things we know with certainty and proceeding step by step through logical inference until he achieves the object of his inquiry. Like most of the Mutakallimun, he proves the existence of God by proving philosophically that the world was created in time out of nothing, and creation implies the existence of a Creator.

In typical Mu'tazilite style, he opens the body of his work with an extensive discussion of creation. He maintains that the world was created in time, that its creator was other than itself (that is, it did not create itself), and that it was created ex nihilo. He explains that the world and all things in it are directly accessible to our senses and judgment, but we cannot know how long it has been in existence nor how it came to be, and therefore we must prove that by a chain of reasoning. Saadiah suggests that there are several possible explanations as to the origin of the world:

- The world just as it is must have existed from eternity, in which case no one made it and we have no proof of the existence of God.

- The world in its present form must have proceeded from some primitive or prime matter, but such hypothesis only removes the problem back in time. Where did the primitive matter come from? Has it existed from eternity or was it created in time?

- The third alternative is that whether the world was developed from a prime matter or not, it or the primitive matter from which it proceeded was created in time. If so, there must have been someone who created it, since nothing can create itself.

Essentially, Saadiah proceeds to prove by logical inference that only the third explanation is valid, and creation in time necessitates a Creator. He offers four proofs of creation (the first based on Aristotelian principles and the other three on *kalam*) too complex to go into here. He then proceeds to refute twelve other cosmogonic theories which differ from his own. These range from theories that uphold the eternity of the world through theories which are skeptical about the capacity of human knowledge to demonstrate either creation in time or eternity of the world, to theories which, while accepting the principle that a Creator created the world in time, deny that it was created out of nothing.

An example of the last theory is that of emanation held by Neoplatonists. According to this theory, God created the world, not out of nothing but out of Himself, that is, the world emanated from Him, as light from the sun, in a number of emanations. Saadiah objects to this theory thus: Why would an eternal substance which is limited neither by form, condition, measure, place, or time change into a body subject to these limitations? "How could the just who does no injustice decree that part of His being be subjected to these calamities?" Such hypothesis, he continues, is conceivable only in one of two ways: either He deserved it for having done some wrong, or He did not deserve it, and it was an act of violence and injustice which He would have inflicted upon Himself. Saadiah dismisses both possibilities as being equally absurd. He explains that the only reason those who hold this opinion do so is that they find it difficult to believe that something can come out of nothing. He acknowledges the difficulty, but answers that that is precisely why we ascribe creation ex nihilo to God alone. To demand that we show how this can be done is to demand that we ourselves become creators.

Husik sums up Saadiah's arguments and conclusion thus: "The only alternative left now is that the author of the universe is an intelligent being, and that nothing outside of him is eternal. He alone is responsible for the existence of the world, which was at one time nothing. Whether he first created a matter and then from it the universe, or whether he made the world outright is of secondary importance."[24]

The Nature of God

All medieval philosophers—Jews, Muslims, and others—were preoccupied with the problem of the nature of God. All agree that man cannot know exactly what His nature is, but all try to establish what He is not. Jewish and Muslim philosophers were especially concerned to establish His unity, incorporeality, and simplicity (that is, His noncomposite nature—hence the importance attached to the problem of divine attributes). Accordingly, having proven the existence of God, Saadiah proceeds to prove His incorporeality, unity, and simplicity. His proof for God's incorporeality is that God, as the cause of all corporeal existence cannot Himself be corporeal, for if He were corporeal, there should have to be something beyond Him which is the cause of His existence. As for His unity it is implied in His being incorporeal. An incorporeal being cannot be subject to the corporeal attributes of quantity and number, and hence cannot be more than one. Another argument for the unity of God offered by Saadiah is that a unitary effect cannot be the result of two separate causes. The universe is one and its parts cannot be separated.[25]

Having proven God's existence, incorporeality, and His unity, Saadiah turns his attention to discuss His most essential attributes: life, omnipotence, and omniscience. Saadiah's position is that the attribution of these qualities to God does not imply a plurality in God, for these attributes are inherent in the concept of God as the Creator of all things. We cannot conceive of a Creation ex nihilo unless He is all-powerful. Power implies life, and the thing made cannot be perfect unless its maker knows what it is going to be before he makes it. Our reason discovers these three concepts with one act of thinking effort, for they are all inherent in the concept of Maker. There is no gradual inference from one to another. In reality all these qualities are united in Him, but we are forced to speak of them as separate only because of the limitations of human language.

Saadiah's discussion of these attributes includes a criticism of Christian theologians' attempt to equate them with the Trinity. He argues that by saying that there are several attributes in Him distinct one from the other, they are saying in effect that He is corporeal. Also, he adds, if His attributes are distinct parts within His being, why limit them to only these three? Why do they not add power, or hearing and seeing? He explains that Christians quote Scripture in their support; for example, the verse in II Samuel (23:2), "The Spirit of the Lord spoke through me and His word was upon my tongue." They claim that "Word" denotes His attribute of wisdom, and "Spirit" His life as distinct persons. "But they are mistaken," Saadiah asserts. "There are other similar instances which they cite, and in their ignorance of Hebrew take metaphorical expressions literally." If they are consistent, he continues sarcastically, "they should add many more persons in the Godhead, in accordance with the many phrases of the Bible concerning the hand of God, the eye of God, the glory of God, the anger of God, the mercy of God and so on."[26]

BIBLICAL ANTHROPOMORPHISM

Having proven that God is one in the two important senses of the word—He is one in the sense that there is no second God beside Him, and He is one in His essence, that is, He is simple and not composed of parts—Saadiah proceeds to discuss biblical anthropomorphism. He insists that all anthropomorphic nouns and verbs in the Bible are figurative and not to be taken literally, "for it is the custom of language to apply such terms metaphorically to certain ideas like elevation, providence, acceptance, declaration, command, favor, anger, power, wisdom, mercy, and dominion." With regard to the interpretation of the Bible, Saadiah makes the general remark that whenever a verse of Scripture appears to contradict reason, there is no doubt that it is figurative.[27]

Finally, Saadiah explains at the end of the chapter on creation that the creation of the world was not the result of a need or a compulsion on the part of God, but an act of His free will. God created the world for two reasons: to manifest His wisdom through the order and harmony of creation, and to bestow happiness upon His creatures by giving them the opportunity of serving Him through the observance of the Law.[28]

CLASSIFICATION OF THE COMMANDMENTS

Saadiah opens the chapter on the commandments by stating that the purpose of the commandments and prohibitions is simply God's kindness toward His creatures. "He offered them a gift by means of which they are able to obtain complete happiness and perfect bliss." He then raises the question: Why does not God simply bestow on men perfect bliss and happiness without imposing on them the burden of the observance of commandments and prohibitions? He explains that it is precisely the quality of God's goodness, which demands that man be given the opportunity to win his own reward, for reason judges that the joy and happiness is much greater for one who earns it through his own efforts.[29]

Saadiah classifies the commandments of the Torah into two categories. The first category is "rational laws" (*mitzvoth sikhliyyot*) which have their basis in reason—our reason recognizes such acts as right or wrong, good or bad, through a feeling of approval and disapproval. Man would have been able to discover such commandments by means of reason even if they had not been revealed. The second category is "traditional laws" (*mitzvoth shim'iyyot*), ritual and ceremonial laws such as dietary laws and the observance of the Sabbath and holidays, which do not have their basis in reason, and are inherently neither right or wrong, but are made so only by the fact that they are commanded by God. Saadiah asserts further that while the basis of traditional laws is the fact that they were commanded by God, it is still possible upon close examination to discover in these laws a certain intrinsic value and rationality. For example, the commandment to refrain from work on the Sabbath provides man with the opportunity to devote himself to spiritual matters. On the other hand, revelation is necessary not only for traditional laws, but also for the rational ones. For reason grasps only abstract principles and general norms. The details necessary for the application of these principles are provided by means of revelation.[30]

Saadiah adds the interesting and original notion that Jewish law contains three elements, all of which are necessary for effective teaching. They are the commandments and prohibitions themselves, the reward and punishment consequent upon obedience or disobedience, and examples of historical characters in which the laws and their consequences are illustrated. Finally, Saadiah maintains that the written law alone would not accomplish its purpose without belief in tradition, and concludes by arguing against the possibility of the abrogation of the Law.[31]

GOD'S JUSTICE AND MAN'S FREE WILL

In chapter 4, Saadiah deals with the question of man's freedom of choice. He argues that since God gave man commandments, rewarding or punishing him in accordance with his conduct, justice dictates that man be allowed to exercise his free will. Unless God is unjust, in order for man to be accountable for his action, his behavior must result from his free choice. In addition to the dictates of reason, Saadiah adduces other proofs for his position: (a) everyone is conscious of the freedom of his actions and is not aware of any force constraining him in his voluntary acts; (b) the Bible testifies to this when it says, "I have set before you life and death . . . therefore choose life (Deut. 30:19); and (c) the rabbinic tradition also confirms it in the dictum: "Everything is in the hand of God except the fear of God" (T. B. Berakhot, 33b).[32]

Next, Saadiah deals with the problem of God's foreknowledge versus man's exercise of his free will. The problem is this: If God knows beforehand how an individual will act in a given situation, does not that knowledge in fact determine man's choice, thus depriving him of the exercise of his free will? Saadiah's answer is that God's knowledge is not the cause of man's actions, and hence does not restrict his freedom of choice; God merely knows what the outcome of man's deliberations would be.[33] Having established that God does not interfere with man's freedom of action, Saadiah asserts that any passage in the Bible which seems to indicate the contrary is not properly understood and must be interpreted in accordance with the evidence he has adduced from various sources, including the Bible itself, in support of man's freedom of choice.

One such problematic passage is God's promise to Moses, "I will harden the heart of Pharaoh . . . . But Pharaoh will not hearken unto you (Exod. 7:3–4)." Saadiah interprets the passage to mean, not that God forced Pharaoh to refuse to let the children of Israel out of Egypt, but rather that God gave him strength to withstand the plagues without succumbing to them, as did many of the Egyptians. Saadiah applies the same approach to other passages in the Bible which appear to imply determinism.[34] To put the problem in contemporary terms, in order for social order to exist, it is essential that man be held accountable for his actions, but if man is to be held responsible for his actions, such actions must be the result of his choosing his behavior freely.

Saadiah deals also with the problem of the "prospering of the wicked and the suffering of the righteous." The problem is raised by Job as well as the Talmudic sages. Saadiah's answer to the problem follows that of the rabbis, namely, that the reward or punishment in the next world is given for the preponderant element of one's conduct. Thus, a righteous man is punished for his few bad deeds in this world in order not to diminish his reward in the world to come for his good deeds. On the other hand, the wicked man is paid for his few good deeds in this world, while the full punishment for his bad deeds is reserved for the world to come.

Saadiah offers several new answers for the prospering of the wicked. A sinner is sometimes well treated and his life is prolonged for one of the following reasons: to give him a chance to repent; to use him to punish others more wicked than he is (such as the role of Assyria described in Isaiah 10:5–11); that he may beget a righteous son as did Ahaz, the father of Hezekiah; or for the sake of a righteous relative, as in the case of God's saving Lot for the sake of Abraham.[35]

NATURE AND FUNCTIONS OF MAN'S SOUL

Saadiah infers the existence of man's soul logically from its activities which are directly visible. He views man as a composite of body and soul. The soul cannot act on its own and is therefore placed in the body, which serves as its instrument. As to the nature of the soul, Saadiah's view is that it is a fine substance created by God at the same time when the human body is completed. It has no eternal existence before the body as Plato thought, for nothing outside God is eternal. Nor does the soul enter the body from the outside, but is created with and in the body. When connected to the body, it has three functions: appetite, which controls growth and reproduction; Spirit, which controls emotions; and reason, which controls knowledge. The soul does not depend for its knowledge on the body, which without the soul has neither life nor knowledge, but it uses the body as an instrument for its functions.[36]

THE AFTERLIFE

As for the existence of an afterlife (*olam ha-ba*), Saadiah claims that it can be proven from reason, from Scripture, and from tradition. First, it is unlikely that the full measure of happiness intended for man's soul is what it gets in this world only. Many a soul suffers and sees no happiness in this world; justice dictates that there must be reward or compensation in another world. Second, if there were no afterlife, why would Isaac have been ready to sacrifice himself, or why should God have expected him to do so? The same applies to Hananiah, Mishael, and Azariah who preferred to be thrown into the fiery furnace rather than worship the golden image of Nebuchadnezzar. Finally, tradition and rabbinic literature are filled with references to a future world. Saadiah proceeds to quote several of these references (Mishnah *Avot*, chap. 4, and T. B. Berakhot, 17a).[37]

CONCLUSION

These examples of Saadiah's discussion of the fundamental principles of Judaism provide ample illustration of his speculative and rational approach to the tenets of Judaism. It should be noted also that throughout the book, once he establishes a given doctrine on the basis of reason, he then proceeds to quote Scripture and Tradition in support of that doctrine, no doubt in his attempt to repudiate Karaism.

MAIMONIDES

With Moses Maimonides, medieval Judaism reached its high-water mark. His was the most curious and systematic mind of medieval Jewry. His interests and works are many and diverse, covering most fields of rabbinic learning as well as secular sciences and philosophy. He was as renowned for his *Mishneh Torah*, the first major comprehensive and topically arranged code of Jewish law,[38] as he was for his philosophical magnum opus, *The Guide of the Perplexed*. If Saadiah Gaon was the first Jewish philosopher in Arab lands, Maimonides was, by general consensus, the most significant Jewish philosopher of the Middle Ages, and according to Arthur Hyman, *The Guide of the Perplexed* is the most important philosophic work produced by a Jew.[39]

Like his predecessors, Maimonides assumed that philosophy and religion teach the same truth, but according to Abraham Halkin, Maimonides was "far more conscious than Ibn Daud of disagreements of the two sources of truth, more conscientious in threshing the difficulties out, and more desirous of arriving at a valid synthesis."[40] He is considered not only the greatest Jewish philosopher, but also one of the two greatest creative minds of the medieval world in general, the other being Averroes (Ibn Rushd, 1126–98), a younger contemporary of Maimonides, considered the greatest Muslim philosopher, who dominated the Aristotelian phase of medieval Muslim and Jewish philosophy alike.[41]

In discussing the influence of Muslim philosophers on Maimonides, Hyman notes that "Maimonides considered himself in the tradition of the [Arab] Aristotelians, adapting and developing their teachings in accord with his own views, but he differed from them in the works he produced." The Muslims had composed commentaries on Aristotle's works, summaries of his views, and independent philosophic treatises, while Maimonides produced no pure philosophic work of his own, and devoted himself to specific issues, particularly those bearing on the interrelation of philosophy and religion.[42] Similarly, Isaac Husik observes that the *Guide* is not a treatise of science or philosophy. The latter are presumed. Maimonides "introduces philosophic principles, Aristotelian or kalamistic, only with a view to their relation to Jewish theology. And he either accepts them, provisionally or absolutely, if he regards as proven, as true and useful," in which case he shows by proper interpretation that similar principles are taught in the Bible and the Talmud. If he refutes them as untenable, "he contents himself by proving that Aristotle or the Mutakallimun, as the case may be, did not prove their point." His refutation of Aristotle's doctrine of the eternity of the world in favor of the biblical one of creation ex nihilo is a case in point. Leo Strauss put it succinctly thus: "One begins to understand the *Guide* once one sees that it is not a philosophic book—a book written by a philosopher for philosophers—but a Jewish book written by a Jew for Jews."[43]

While the *Guide* constitutes the major statement of Maimonides' philosophy, some of his philosophic and theological views appeared also in a variety of his other writings, notably, in his introductory essays in his commentary on the Mishnah (the introductions to *Avot*, and to the eleventh chapter of *Sanhedrin*), as well as the first book and the last section of his *Mishneh Torah*.[44] However, according to Husik, the treatment of philosophical and theological subjects in his other writings is "popular and elementary, and is intended for popular consumption." There, Maimonides lays down the results of his speculation in their simplest form without discussing their origin or the arguments pro and con, whereas his approach in the *Guide* is more sophisticated and intended for an exclusive audience.[45]

PURPOSE OF THE BOOK

Maimonides' purpose in composing the *Guide*, like that of Saadiah and other predecessors, was to harmonize Judaism with philosophy, to reconcile the Bible and the Talmud with Aristotle. He did this for the good of Judaism, and in the interest of a rational and enlightened faith. Unlike Saadiah's *Book of Doctrines and Beliefs*, which was intended for an inclusive readership, the *Guide* was addressed to an intellectual elite. Indeed, initially, it was addressed to one individual, his favored disciple, Joseph ben Yehudah Ibn Shim'on, especially known for the Dedicatory Epistle attached to the *Guide*, which Maimonides addressed to him.

Ibn Shim'on's relationship with Maimonides began when both were in Morocco, Ibn Shim'on in Ceuta, and Maimonides in Fez where his family had sought refuge from the Almohads. After Maimonides settled in Egypt, Ibn Shim'on followed him to Cairo where he studied under him. At some point, Ibn Shim'on left Cairo for Aleppo, and since oral instruction was no longer possible, Maimonides decided to send him some lessons in philosophy which he had been preparing. These lessons were designed as a manual or guide for his friend in the problems of the Bible and religion in general. He continued to send these discourses chapter by chapter to his favored disciple.[46] In a sense, then, *The Guide of the Perplexed* was the result of this "correspondence course" between Maimonides and his disciple, and was intended also, no doubt, for those equal to Ibn Shim'on in intelligence as well as intellectual preparation and achievement, as outlined in Maimonides' Dedicatory Epistle.[47]

Clearly, the *Guide* is intended for the likes of Ibn Shim'on, Jews who are firm in their religious beliefs and practice and who, having come in contact with science and philosophy, are troubled by doubts, confusion and perplexity, stemming from apparent disagreements of philosophical teachings with the ideas expressed in biblical and rabbinic writings. Maimonides' specific purpose is to show such Jews that the difficult biblical terms and similes susceptible of being misunderstood have a spiritual meaning besides the literal one, and that it is the spiritual meaning that applies to God. Maimonides is emphatic in asserting that his *Guide* is not intended for the masses, beginners in philosophy, or even rabbinic scholars who confine themselves to the legalistic aspect of the Law, and not to the "science of the Law," its true sense, as Maimonides put it. Thus, in his Dedicatory Epistle addressed to Ibn Shim'on, Maimonides writes, "Your absence drove me to compose this treatise, which I composed for you and for those like you, however few they are." Similarly, in his introduction to the first part, he states, "It is not the purpose of this treatise to make its totality understandable to the vulgar or to beginners in philosophy, nor to those who have not engaged in any study other than the science of the Law—I mean the legalistic study of the Law. For the purpose of this treatise and all like it is the 'science of the Law' in its true sense."[48]

The *Guide* opens with a discussion of biblical expressions apt to present theological problems because of their anthropomorphism. Then Maimonides discusses the nature of God, especially the problem of divine attributes. He concludes the first part of the *Guide* with a summary and refutation of the views of *kalam* philosophers (Mutakallimun). The second part of the work is devoted to proofs of the existence of God, His unity and incorporeality, proofs of creation of the world ex nihilo, the nature and function of prophecy, and the differences between the prophecy of Moses and that of the other prophets. Finally, in the third part of the *Guide*, Maimonides turns his attention to the problem of evil, divine providence and man's free will, and the rationale of the commandments. Two of the last chapters outline the higher religion of the "perfect man" which consists of true knowledge of God. Given the limited scope of this chapter, we will touch briefly only on some of the major issues, especially those with regard to which Maimonides disagrees with Saadiah.

ALLEGORICAL INTERPRETATION

Maimonides' overarching theme and basic premise in the *Guide* is that the Bible does not contradict science and philosophy. If some biblical terms or parables seem to indicate otherwise, it is only because they are not understood properly. He maintains that anything in the Bible that seems to clash with or contradict reason must not be understood in its literal meaning, but must be interpreted allegorically. Therefore he begins by explaining biblical terms susceptible of being misunderstood. Indeed, he devotes no fewer than forty-nine chapters in the first part of the *Guide* to allegorical or symbolic interpretations of many biblical terms and similes, thus elevating allegorical or symbolic interpretation to an important exegetical principle. An example of his exegesis is his commentary on the term *image of God* (*tzelem Elohim*), in the first chapter of Genesis. Some have argued, Maimonides states, that since man was created in the image of God, it follows that God, like man, has a body. He refutes that argument by explaining that the term *tzelem* refers always to a spiritual quality. Hence the "image of God" in man refers to his essence, that is, his reason—not his physical likeness.[49]

Essentially, then, the *Guide* is a work of philosophical or even Aristotelian exegesis. Leo Strauss explains, in his introductory essay to the *Guide*, that such exegesis was required because, according to Maimonides, many biblical terms and all biblical similes or parables have an apparent or outer meaning and a hidden or inner one, and that "the gravest errors as well as the most tormenting perplexities arise from man's understanding the Bible always according to its apparent or literal meaning." The *Guide*, Strauss continues, is then devoted to the "difficulties of the Law" or to the "secrets of the Law," the most important of which are the Account of the Beginning (the beginning of the Bible) and the Account of the Chariot (Ezek. 1 and 10). Strauss adds that "the *Guide* is then devoted primarily and chiefly to the explanation of the Account of the Beginning and the Account of the Chariot."[50]

The reason the Bible was written in the form of allegories and parables is because it was intended for all Jews, intellectuals and simpletons alike. Therefore it is written in a language that can be understood on two levels. The simple or outer meaning is sufficient for the average persons, the masses. Hence the simple meaning does not contain speculative or metaphysical matters, for presenting those who are not intellectually mature with physics and metaphysics would not only confuse them but even destroy their belief entirely. "It is like feeding an infant on wheat and meat and wine." On the other hand, with the proper exegetical method (provided by Maimonides) those who are well prepared intellectually may derive the deeper or allegorical meaning of the Bible.[51]

Maimonides identifies the Account of the Beginning (*ma'aseh bereshit*) and the Account of the Chariot (*ma'aseh merkavah*) with physics and metaphysics. This presents him with a serious problem. According to the Mishnah (Hag. 2:1), one may not teach the Account of the Beginning to two persons, and the Account of the Chariot even to one, unless he is wise and able to understand the matter by himself. Moreover, Maimonides himself codifies the mishnaic rule in his *Mishneh Torah* (*Hilkhot Yesode ha-Torah*, 2:12; and 4:10–16). How, then, could he write a book devoted to an explanation of the "secrets of the Law" when putting something in writing is the equivalent of teaching in public, in violation of the very Law whose secrets he sets out to explain?

Leo Strauss lists other apparent violations of the Law by Maimonides in his *Guide*, namely, his studying the works of idolaters, which he admits to have studied thoroughly, and his seeking reasons for the Commandments, to which task he devotes twenty-six chapters in the third part of the *Guide*—both forbidden by the Law. Strauss adds that all these irregularities have one and the same justification: Maimonides transgresses the Law "for the sake of heaven"—that is, in order to uphold or to fulfill the Law.[52] Strauss adds, "Still, in the most important case he does not, strictly speaking, transgress the Law, for his written explanations of the secrets of the Law is not a public but a secret explanation."

According to Strauss, Maimonides achieves such secrecy in three ways. First, every word in the *Guide* is chosen with exceeding care, and since very few men are able or willing to read with exceeding care, most men will fail to perceive the secret teaching. Second, Maimonides deliberately contradicts himself with regard to a number of issues.[53] And lastly, the "chapter headings" of the secret teachings are not presented in an orderly fashion but are scattered throughout the book. That is why the plan of the *Guide* is so obscure. The book is not divided explicitly into sections and subsections, but is divided into three parts and each part into chapters without appropriate headings indicating the subject matters of either the parts or the chapters.[54]

One might add that Maimonides addressed the *Guide* to his disciple, Ibn Shim'on; this means that in its formal aspect, the work is a personal communication with one student. In addition, in the Dedicatory Epistle, Maimonides relates Ibn Shim'on's intellectual history, showing thereby that he was able to reason for himself, thus fulfilling the mishnaic conditions for studying the "secrets of the Law."[55]

DIVINE ATTRIBUTES

Having disposed of difficult biblical terms and similes, Maimonides takes up the problem of divine attributes, to which he devotes the next eleven chapters of the first part of the *Guide* (50–60). As it was pointed out above in connection with Saadiah's treatment of the subject, all medieval philosophers—Jews, Muslim, and others—were preoccupied with the question of the nature of God. Medieval Jewish and Muslim philosophers attached great importance to the problem of divine attributes in their concern to establish God's unity, incorporeality, and simplicity (the non-composite nature of His essence). The problem is that the Bible describes God by many attributes, while at the same time stating that He is one. But every statement, which asserts a predicate of a subject, introduces thereby the element of multiplicity. But if He is one in the sense of being simple, how can a multiplicity of attributes be ascribed to Him without implying the element of multiplicity in His essence?

Maimonides asserts that it is not permissible to ascribe to God in any positive sense even the formal attributes of existence and unity. According to Arthur Hyman, "Medieval philosophers held that attributes applied to substances are of two kinds: essential and accidental. Essential attributes are those that are closely connected with the essence, such as existence and life; accidental attributes are those independent of the essence, such as anger and mercifulness." Hyman adds that medieval logicians "agreed that accidental attributes introduce multiplicity into that which they describe, while they disagreed concerning essential attributes." Some held that essential attributes are implicitly contained in the essence and, hence, do not introduce multiplicity; others, including Avicenna, held that they provide new information, hence produce multiplicity.[56]

As we have seen above, Saadiah held that the important attributes of existence, life, power, and wisdom are implied in the concept of God as the Creator. Maimonides, on the other hand, accepted Avicenna's view regarding the essential attributes. Accordingly, he concluded that essential attributes must be interpreted as negations, that is, if God is said to be existent, it means that He is not nonexistent; while accidental attributes must be interpreted as attributes of action, that is, if it is said that God is merciful, it means that God acts mercifully. In other words, essential attributes are those that exclude from God some imperfection, and accidental attributes describe the effect of His actions on His creatures.

Isaac Husik observes the curious fact that Maimonides, a most systematic and logical thinker, appears to have abandoned any logical organization in the *Guide*. Most medieval philosophers (Saadiah, Bahya, and Ibn Daud) first prove the existence of God and only then proceed to discuss His nature and attributes, while Maimonides begins with a discussion of anthropomorphic terms and attributes before proving the existence of God. Husik suggests that this inversion of logical order was deliberate, for the Jews for whom he wrote his *Guide* did not doubt the existence of God. But a great many of them had an inadequate idea of His spiritual nature. Therefore, Husik continues, "Maimonides cast logical considerations aside and dealt with that which was nearest to his heart." For his purpose was "to teach a spiritual conception of God, anything short of this is worse than idolatry."[57]

MAIMONIDES ON *KALAM*

Before taking up his Aristotelian proofs of the existence of God, Maimonides had to dispose of the proofs presented by the Mutakallimun of which he disapproved. He devotes the last chapters of the first part of the *Guide* (I, chaps. 71–76) to a systematic presentation and refutation of their views and their methodology. He claims that, upon examining their works, he found that, with but slight differences between the various schools of *kalam*, all Mutakallimun are alike. Their method is to first establish that the world was created in time, and then argue that creation implies the existence of a Creator. They then proceed to infer that He is one and incorporeal. All the Mutakallimun, Maimonides asserts, follow this method, and they are imitated by those Jews who follow in their footsteps.[58] First, he attacks their methodology, asserting that "every argument deemed to be a demonstration of the temporal creation of the world is accompanied by doubt and is not a cogent demonstration except among those who do not know the difference between demonstration, dialectics, and sophistic argument."[59]

Although Maimonides himself believed in creation in time, he nevertheless objected to the Mutakallimun's approach to proving the existence of God by proving creation. His argument is that creation in time cannot be demonstrated with scientific rigor; it is disputed by the philosophers and is clouded with doubts. It is therefore not safe or prudent to build so important a structure as the existence of God upon an insecure foundation. He prefers to make the proof of the existence of God independent of the problem of the world's creation, so that if the latter proved to be nondemonstrable, the belief in the existence of God would not thereby be affected. Accordingly, he bases his proofs of the existence of God on the Aristotelian theory of the eternity of the world, showing thereby that the existence of God is demonstrable regardless of whether creation or eternity of the world turns out to be the correct opinion concerning the origin of the world.[60] But once he proves the existence of God, he immediately takes up the question of creation in time, arguing that since eternity had not been demonstrated with certainty, he opts for creation because of its being such a central belief in Judaism.[61]

PROOF OF THE EXISTENCE OF GOD

Having refuted the Mutakallimun's approach—that is, proving the existence of God from creation in time—Maimonides begins the second part of the *Guide* by laying down twenty-five prepositions culled from the physics and metaphysics of Aristotle and his Arab commentators, which he deemed necessary to prove the existence, unity, and incorporeality of God. To those he adds a twenty-sixth preposition, the eternity of the world (only provisionally) to prove that the existence of God is demonstrable regardless of whether or not the world came into being in time after having been nonexistent.

Maimonides offers several proofs of the existence of God current in his day, the most important of which is the one from motion. He notes that in the sublunar world things constantly move and change. This motion must have a mover, for according to Aristotle (preposition 25), matter cannot move itself. This mover must have another mover, and this will lead us to infinity which is impossible, for according to another Aristotelian prepo-sition (preposition 3) cited by Maimonides, there cannot be an infinite chain of cause and effect. Maimonides argues further that the motion in the sub-lunar world is ultimately caused by the celestial motion of the spheres, which comes to an end with the motion of the uppermost celestial sphere. The motion of that sphere is caused by a mover that is not moved by an-other mover—again because there cannot be an infinite chain of cause and effect. This mover is called Prime Mover (or Unmoved Mover), and it is the last mover in a chain of causes producing motion.[62]

By way of illustration, Maimonides suggests the following exam-ple. A draft of air is blowing through a hole in the wall, and a stick is used to push a stone in the hole to close it. In such a situation, the stone is moved by the stick, the stick is moved by the hand, and the hand is moved by the sinews and muscles of the human body. Now the reason for the motion of the stone in the first place is the draft of air, which is caused by the motion of the lowest celestial sphere, whose motion is in turn caused by the suc-cessive motions of the other spheres. The chain of things moved and mov-ing comes to an end with the last of the celestial spheres. This sphere is set in motion by a principle which, while it produces motion is itself not moved. This is the Prime Mover, which Maimonides identifies with God.[63]

Maimonides then turns to a discussion of the nature of the Prime Mover. He suggests four possibilities. The Prime mover of the uppermost sphere may be (a) a body external to the sphere, (b) a separate incorporeal substance, (c) an internal corporeal power divisible with the division of the sphere, or (d) an internal indivisible power. By process of elimination, he shows that the Prime Mover cannot exist within the sphere, which elimi-nates the last two possibilities. He also shows that the first possibility is, in fact, impossible, for if the mover of the sphere is another body, it is likewise in motion and must have another to move it, which, if a body, must yet have another mover and so on ad infinitum, which is impossible. Hence the only possibility left is that the Prime Mover exists apart from the sphere and must be incorporeal. Maimonides shows further that there cannot be two incorporeal movers. Thus, Husik observes, Maimonides has "proved with one stroke God's existence as well as His unity and incorporeality."[64]

CREATION EX NIHILO

As stated above, once Maimonides proves the existence, unity, and incorporeality of God even according to the hypothesis of the eternity of the world, he immediately takes up the question of creation in time. After a lengthy and intricate discussion of the pros and cons of both doctrines—creation in time and the eternity of the world—he concludes that neither is demonstrably certain, and therefore decides in favor of the biblical doctrine of creation in time. He explains that, had Aristotle provided compelling proof for his view, he (Maimonides) would not have found it difficult to interpret figuratively those biblical passages which speak of creation, just as he did interpret the passages regarding God's corporeality. But he asserts, "The eternity of the world has not been demonstrated," therefore he saw no reason to reject the biblical theory, nor any need to interpret figuratively the biblical texts that speak of creation.[65] In addition, Maimonides argues, "the belief in eternity as Aristotle sees it—that is the belief according to which the world exists by necessity . . . and that the customary course of events cannot be modified with regard to anything—destroys the Law in its principle, necessarily gives the lie to every miracle, and reduces to inanity all the hopes and threats that the Law has held out." In other words, Maimonides rejects the eternity theory not only because Aristotle failed to prove his view compellingly, but also because Maimonides finds the biblical theory superior, the more so since it has on its side the authority of prophecy. This issue is so important for Maimonides that he devotes to it many chapters in the second part of the *Guide*, since, as he says, the theory that God created the universe out of nothing is "undoubtedly a basis of the law of Moses our Master, peace be upon him. And it is second to the basis that is the belief in the unity of God."[66]

PROPHECY

Having laid the philosophical foundations of religion in proving the existence, unity, and incorporeality of God, as well as purposeful creation in time, Maimonides proceeds to the more properly religious doctrines of Judaism, beginning with prophecy, to which he devotes the last chapters of Part II of the *Guide* (32–48). He begins his discussion of prophecy by listing three theories as to how prophecy is acquired:

• The view of the common people, among pagans and Jews alike, who hold that God arbitrarily chooses any person, be he young or old, wise or ignorant, and inspires him with the prophetic spirit. They concede, however, that the potential prophet must be of good and moral character.

- The view of the philosophers who believe that prophecy is a human gift and requires natural aptitude, hard preparation and study. Maimonides adds that according to this view, a superior individual who is perfect with respect to his rational and moral qualities, and whose imaginative faculty is in its most perfect state, and when he has been prepared—he will necessarily become a prophet.

- The view of Scripture, which specifies the same level of development of the natural faculties, as do the philosophers, but adds dependence on God. Thus, a man may have all the qualifications—that is, he may be fit for prophecy and prepared for it—and yet be prevented from prophesying if God, by way of punishment, does not desire that he should.[67]

Maimonides shares with Aristotelian philosophy the view that prophecy results from the close natural relation between the potential prophet and the Active Intellect. However, he maintains that a naturally endowed potential prophet requires God's will (or grace) before he can prophesy, and that the figurative form in which prophecies are delivered is the result of the imaginative faculty of the soul in addition to the intellectual capacity. Accordingly, Maimonides defines prophecy as an emanation from God, which—through the intermediary of the Active Intellect—flows first upon man's intellectual faculty and overflows from it upon the imaginative faculty.[68]

Arthur Hyman observes that "while a well-developed imaginative faculty is of a little significance for the illuminative experience of the prophet, it is central to his political function . . . . For Maimonides, the primary function of prophets other than Moses is to admonish people to adhere to the Law of Moses; this requires that the prophet use the kind of imaginative language and parables that appeal to the imagination of the masses."[69]

According to Maimonides, Moses was the greatest of all the prophets. His prophecy is so different from that of other prophets that he and they had virtually only the name *prophet* in common. Moses' prophecy was in fact unique and without equal. He alone, because of his superiority to all the prophets before and after him, is called the prophet of the Law.

No one before him said to the people, "The Lord sent me to you that you may do so and so." "Abraham taught the people and explained to them by means of speculative proofs that the world has but one deity, [and] that He created all the things that are other than Himself. . . . But he never said, 'God has sent me to you and has given me commandments and prohibitions.' All the prophets after Moses, on the other hand, simply preached to the people urging them to obey the Law of Moses. This shows, according to Maimonides, that the Law will never change for 'The Law of the Lord is Perfect'" (Ps. 19:8).[70]

In addition to this, Maimonides enumerates four distinguishing features of Moses' prophetic experience itself as compared with that of all other prophets:

- Other prophets receive their prophecy in dream or vision; Moses received his while awake.

- Other prophets received their prophecy in allegorical form; Moses received his directly.

- Other prophets were filled with fear when they received prophecy; Moses was not.

- Other prophets received prophecy intermittently; Moses received it whenever he wished.[71]

MAIMONIDES ON MIRACLES

Toward the end of Part I of the *Guide*, Maimonides writes, "There is no doubt that there are things that are common to all three of us, I mean the Jews, the Christians, and the Muslims: namely the affirmation of the temporal creation of the world, the validity of which entails the validity of miracles and other things of the kind."[72] Similarly, one of his objections to Aristotle's doctrine of eternity is that it does away with the possibility of miracles.[73] Thus, Maimonides disagrees with Aristotle regarding the validity of biblical miracles, just as he does with his theories concerning the origin of the world and how prophecy is acquired.[74]

Maimonides accepts miracles as means by which God realizes His purpose in the universe. But his conception of miracles is far from being identical with the naïve faith according to which God becomes a constant miracle worker, as it were. He does not accept all miracles at face value. He explains them as having been preordained from eternity as part of God's plan for the universe. That is, when God created the laws of nature, he pre-programmed them so that they would produce all the miracles that were to occur (and be recorded in the Bible) when they were needed.[75]

Thus, Maimonides notes that "the Sages . . . have made a very strange statement about miracles in *Bereshit Rabbah* and *Midrash Kohelet*. This notion consists in their holding the view that miracles too are something that is, in a certain respect, in nature." They say, he continues, that "when God created that which exists and stamped upon it the existing natures, He put it into these natures that all the miracles that occurred [in the Bible] should be produced in them at the time when they occurred." Maimonides adds that this statement "indicates the superiority of the man who made it and the fact that he found it extremely difficult to admit that a nature may change after the Work of the Beginning, or that another volition may supervene after that nature has been established in a definite way."[76]

In other words, when God created the world, He created at the same time the laws of nature (presumably for the benefit of man and science, so that man may arrange his affairs intelligently and predictably). He intended these laws to be permanent, not subject to substantial change. Yet, in His omniscience, He knew that at certain junctures in the history of Israel there would arise the need for a temporary suspension of or intervention in the laws of nature. Therefore, to avoid undermining the reliability and predictability of these laws by frequent interference, he established from the beginning as part of these laws the occurrence of certain miracles at certain times in history. The *midrashim* quoted by Maimonides in support of this novel and original interpretation of biblical miracles are amazingly explicit on the matter, and therefore worth quoting in full.

> Rabbi Jonathan said: The Holy One, blessed be He, has posed conditions on the sea: that it should divide before Israel. That is [the meaning of the words]: And the sea returned to its strength when the morning appeared. Rabbi Jeremiah, son of Elazar, said: The Holy One, blessed be He, has posed conditions not only to the sea but to all that has been created in the six days of the Beginning. That is [the meaning of the words]: I, even my hands have stretched out the heavens, and all their hosts have I commanded. I have commanded the sea to divide; the fire not to

harm Hananiah, Mishael, and Azariah; the lions not to harm Daniel; and the fish to spit out Jonah.

Maimonides adds, "All other miracles can be explained in an analogous manner."[77]

THE PROBLEM OF EVIL

The problem of evil, physical as well as moral, preoccupied all medieval philosophers—Jews, Muslims, and Christians alike. If God is good, and He created the world and everything in it including matter, what is the source of evil? A number of answers were suggested including the one identifying evil with matter. Since Maimonides believed in creation in time, he could not identify evil with matter, for matter is also created by God, and all that God created is good. Therefore, Maimonides declares categorically that "all evils are privations." That is to say, evil is nothing but the negation or absence of good, as for example, darkness is the absence of light. Maimonides maintains that only positive things can be created, and all positive things are good. Thus, he explains that, with regard to man, for instance, his illness, his poverty, or his ignorance are evils with regard to him, and all of them are privations of the normal state of things. Similarly, all evils that men do to each other are due to negations—that is, they are the absence of wisdom, knowledge, and ethical nobility.[78]

Maimonides observes that many people think there is more evil than good in the world. But, their mistake, he explains, is that they view the world from the perspective of the individual man and his suffering rather than from that of the world at large. "Every ignoramus imagines that all that exists exists with a view to his individual sake . . . as if there were nothing that exists except him." Man forgets that he is only a small fraction of the world, and all that exists is in existence because of the will of God.[79] Man should be grateful to God, for his very existence is "a great gift and benefit on the part of God, because of the properties with which He has singled him out and perfected him."[80]

In any case, Maimonides asserts that all evils befalling man fall under three categories, which are either infrequent or self-inflicted:

- Natural evils—that is, evils that are inherent in man's nature (as a being subject to generation and decay) and natural forces in general, such as illness, diseases, death, earthquakes, and floods—all of which are vulnerabilities that man is subject to on account of natural causes. They are inevitable and inseparable from existence. Maimonides' view is that to demand that man of flesh and blood shall not be subject to these vulnerabilities is a contradiction in terms. But, he adds, the evils of this first category are comparatively few.

- Social evils—that is, evils inflicted by men on each other, such as wars and the tyrannical domination of some of them over others. The source of these evils, as stated before, is the absence of wisdom, knowledge, nobility of character, and ethical behavior. These evils are more frequent than those of the first category, yet these too are not too frequent.

- Personal evils—that is, various human vices. According to Maimonides, the most common evils are the ones that man brings upon himself by self-indulgences and formation of bad habits. Therefore, most of the evils in the world are caused by man, and can be remedied by proper training.[81]

THE JUSTICE OF GOD

One of the problems that engaged religious thinkers of all times is the apparent injustice in "the suffering of the righteous and prospering of the wicked (*Tzadik ve-ra' lo, rasha' ve-tov lo*)." The problem is raised by Job and the Talmudic sages, as well as Saadiah and others. Maimonides deals with the problem in connection with his discussion of divine providence. Saadiah, echoing the rabbinic notion of *yissurim shel ahavah* (afflictions of love), explains that God may cause suffering to a righteous person in order to reward him fully in the hereafter.[82] Maimonides rejects this principle, stating that only an unjust God would act in this manner, asserting that every pain and affliction is a punishment for a prior sin. Maimonides also uses his theory of providence in his interpretation of the book of Job. He construes the characters of the book as representing the varying attitudes toward providence as he outlined them in his discussion of it.[83]

GOD'S OMNISCIENCE VERSUS MAN'S FREE WILL

Another vexing problem that exercised the minds of most medieval Jewish philosophers is the seeming contradiction between the doctrine of God's foreknowledge and that of man's free will. If God knows beforehand how an individual will act in a given situation, does not that knowledge in fact determine man's behavior, thus depriving him of his free choice? Various solutions have been suggested for this problem. Saadiah's unconvincing answer, for example, is that God's foreknowledge is not the cause of man's choice; He merely knows what the outcome of man's deliberations will be.

Gersonides argues that God's omniscience embraces all events of this world, but not the outcome of contingent acts of man that cannot be predicted by any type of knowledge, not even divine knowledge. Maimonides, on the other hand, maintains that God's omniscience embraces all events of the world, past and future, including the outcome of particular contingent events in the future, including acts that result from man's exercise of his free will. Maimonides' solution to the problem, however, is that God's knowledge is so different from our knowledge that we have no way of knowing how He knows, just as we are unable to know His essence, for His essence and His knowledge are one.[84]

As stated above, Saadiah asserts that any biblical passage which seems to indicate any restriction on man's free choice is not properly understood, and must be interpreted in accordance with the evidence he adduced from various sources, including the Bible itself, in support of man's free will. One such problematic passage is God's promise to Moses, "I will harden the heart of Pharaoh . . . . But Pharaoh will not hearken unto you (Exod. 7:3–4). Maimonides' explanation of this passage is that God did indeed cause Pharaoh to refuse to let Israel go, but this was part of his punishment for drowning all Jewish male children in the river (an act of his own choice). God forced him to refuse to let the children of Israel go in order to visit upon him the full measure of his due punishment—the ten plagues.[85]

EXPLANATION OF THE COMMANDMENTS

The last major topic Maimonides considers in the *Guide* is the reason and purpose of the commandments of the Bible, particularly the ceremonial ones which apparently have no rational meaning. He disagrees with Saadiah and other Mu'tazilite philosophers who divide the commandments into two categories: rational commandments (*mitzvoth sikhliyyot*), such as the prohibition against murder and theft, which the human mind can discern without revelation; and traditional commandments (*mitzvoth shim'iyyot*), ritual and ceremonial laws, such as dietary laws and the observance of the Sabbath and holidays, which are neutral from the point of view of reason, and can be known only through revelation. Maimonides asserts, however, that it is impossible that God would have given any commandment that did not have a purpose or a rationale. He devotes no fewer than twenty-five chapters of the third part of the *Guide* (chaps. 25–49) to offering rationales for every commandment, including the ceremonial ones. He argues that all divine commandments are the product of God's wisdom, although some are easily intelligible (*mishpatim*) and others are intelligible only with difficulty (*hukkim*), and he concedes that there are some particular commandments for which he has been unable to grasp the rational meaning.[86]

He attributes to the Talmudic sages the view that "any particular commandment or prohibition has a useful end." Therefore he maintains, "One should seek in all the Laws an end that is useful in regard to being." However, he concedes that while the generalities of the commandments necessarily have a cause and have been given because of certain utility, their details are that in regard to which it was said of the commandments [by the rabbis] that they were given merely for purifying the people. By way of illustration, he offers the laws of slaughtering (*shehitah*). "The killing of animals because of the necessity of having good food is manifestly useful," he states. But "the prescription that they should be killed through having the upper and not the lower part of their throat cut, and having their esophagus and windpipe severed at one particular place is, like other prescriptions of the same kind, imposed with a view to purifying the people."[87]

As to the general purpose of the Law, Maimonides states that the Law as a whole has two purposes: the well-being of the soul (intellect), and the well-being of the body. He explains that the well-being of the soul consists in the acquisition by the multitude of correct opinions— true beliefs according to their respective capacity. As to the welfare of the body, it is achieved through the "abolition of [people] wronging each other" and the acquisition "by every human individual of moral qualities that are useful for life in society."[88]

Maimonides sums up his classification of the commandments thus: "Every commandment from among the 613 commandments exists either with a view to communicating a correct opinion, or to putting an end to an unhealthy opinion, or to communicating a rule of justice, or to warding off an injustice, or to endowing men with a noble moral quality, or to warning them against an evil moral quality. Thus all [the commandments] are bound up with three things: opinions, moral qualities, and political civic actions."[89]

Although rationales for general moral and ethical laws, as well as true beliefs, are easy to find, it is more difficult to explain numerous ritual and ceremonial laws found in the Bible. In his effort to explain these laws, Maimonides proves to be most original. Thus, he explains many of them as reactions to pagan beliefs and practices. Further, he postulates that the punishments prescribed in the Torah for following pagan ways correspond to the contrary benefits believed by the pagans to be gained from their practices.[90]

Maimonides also articulates the thesis that sacrifices are an inferior form of worship (prayer being superior), but were ordered as a concession to the state of mind of the Jews at the time of Moses. God recognized that the people of Israel in Egypt were used to sacrifices as the only form of worship, and that it would have been difficult and unrealistic to prohibit them outright. Therefore the Bible commanded sacrifices but restricted the time and place for them and permitted only the priests to offer them, thus sublimating sacrifice worship by diverting it toward Him. The negative attitude of the biblical prophets toward sacrifices seems to support Maimonides' thesis.[91]

CONCLUSION

According to Arthur Hyman, *The Guide of the Perplexed* in its Hebrew translation determined the course of Jewish philosophy from the thirteenth century on, and "almost every philosophic work for the remainder of the Middle Ages cited, commented on, or criticized Maimonides' views."[92] Hyman adds that, in addition to its significance for medieval Jewish philosophy, the *Guide* had "a formative influence on modern Jewish thought." Maimonides, Hyman continues, "provided a first acquaintance with philosophic speculation for a number of philosophers of the Enlightenment period [*haskalah*] and served as a bridge for the study of more modern philosophy. Among modern thinkers who were influenced in some way by Maimonides, Hyman lists Moses Mendelssohn, Solomon Maimon, Nachman Krochmal, Samuel David Luzzatto (who opposed Maimonides' rationalism), Herman Cohen, and Ahad Ha'am. Hyman adds that "Maimonides became a symbol for their own philosophic endeavors: he had attempted to introduce the spirit of rationalism into Jewish teachings during medieval times, just as they tried to do in their times."[93]

Yehudah Halevi

Unlike most medieval Jewish philosophers, Yehudah Halevi's aim in his book, the *Kuzari*, was not to reconcile Judaism with philosophy; he felt no need for that. Rather, his aim was to defend Judaism and the honor of his people against the dominant and powerful religions of his time, Christianity and Islam, as well as against Aristotelian philosophy and the threat it presented to Judaism, a threat he was the first to recognize. In his opening comment on Halevi's philosophy, Israel Zinberg writes,

> An entirely new path for Jewish philosophy was attempted by the celebrated poet of Zion, Jehudah Halevi. Halevi considered it pointless to seek, as Saadiah Gaon had done in his day, a reconciliation or compromise between speculative thought and faith, to show that the philosophic and the secular sciences do not contradict the foundations of Judaism. It was clear to him that the essence and chief value of the Jewish religion consist not in the fact that it may be philosophically substantiated with the aid of logical theories and arguments, but rather in its moral content and in its educative power. The meaning and importance of the Torah consist, in Halevi's view, not in the fact that speculative thought and its conclusions are not inconsistent with it, but that it gives something that philosophy does not and cannot give.[94]

But Halevi was defending a persecuted race and a despised faith not only against the philosophers, but also against the more powerful professors of Christianity and Islam. As Isaac Husik puts it, Halevi "is the loyal son of his race and his religion, and he will show that they are above all criticism, that they are the best and the truest there are. In contrasting Maimonides with Halevi, Husik adds,

Maimonides, too, found it necessary to defend Judaism against the attacks of philosophy. But in his case, it was the Jew in him who had to be defended against the philosopher in him. It was no external enemy but an internal one who must be made harmless, and the method was one of reconciliation and harmonization. It is still truer to say that with Maimonides both Judaism and philosophy were his friends, neither was an enemy. He was attached to one quite as much as to the other. And it was his privilege to reconcile their differences, to the great gain, as he thought, of both. Judah Halevi [on the other hand] takes the stand of one who fights for his hearth and home against the attacks of foreign foes. He will not yield an inch to the adversary. He will maintain his own. The enemy cannot approach.[95]

According to D. Z. Baneth, Halevi had only two concerns in his criticism of philosophy: to diminish the enormous prestige which the Aristotelian doctrine still enjoyed, and to demonstrate that Aristotle's teachings are inadequate to satisfy the demands of religious and ethical consciousness. As for Halevi's stand against Christianity and Islam, it was, no doubt, influenced if not determined by his contemporary circumstances. He was born and grew up in difficult times, toward the end of the Golden Age, at the beginning of the Christian Reconquista of Spain from the Arabs. Those were times of intense conflict between Muslims and Christians, both in Spain and in the Holy Land, with the Jews feeling somewhat trapped in the middle. As certain Spanish cities (Toledo, Cordova) changed hands, the Jews, and Halevi among them, felt like a football in that game. Thus Halevi complains often in his poetry of being caught between "Edom and Arab," or "Edom and Ishma'el"—that is, Israel and Jerusalem being under the Crusaders (even as northern Spain was under Christian rule), while Andalusia was under Muslim rule.[96]

This same concern is clearly behind the writing of his philosophical work, the *Kuzari*. He is painfully aware that Muslims and Christians not only divide the world between them but are also assured of the respect and esteem of each other as the two super powers, whereas the Jews are despised and oppressed and have no land to call their own. This hurts him badly. His goals in his work are to show that earthly success of a religion does not prove its superiority, and that, as a matter of fact, the most despised religious community happened to be in possession of absolute religious truth.

This is most evident in the full Arabic title of his work: *Kitab al-hujja wa-**dalil**—fi nasri al-din al-**dhalil*** (The Book of Argument and Proof in Defense of the Despised /Scorned Religion). The words for proof (***dalil***) and despised (***dhalil***) rhyme and alliterate, thus one word refers to the other; the proof is the answer to the scorn and the spiritual oppression it produces. By playing on the words ***dalil*** and ***dhalil***, Halevi is suggesting the central theme of the entire book, namely, that the temporal power and esteem enjoyed by Christianity and Islam is no proof of their spiritual superiority, and that, in fact, the despised religion happened to be superior and in possession of absolute religious truth.

Halevi manages to prove his thesis by having the king of the Khazars choose Judaism (over Christianity, Islam, and Aristotelian philosophy), notwithstanding its temporal low status among nations. This theme is repeated with several variations throughout the work. For example, Halevi asserts that Israel is "the pick of mankind," by which he means "the religious choice of mankind," that is, those in possession of the divine gift of religious truth which is not transferable or acquired by adoption. In the same vain, he tells the king of the Khazars that "Israel amidst the nations is like the heart among the other organs; it is the most sick and the most healthy of them all."[97] (See full discussion of these and other related doctrines below.)

THE *KUZARI*—A DESCRIPTION

The *Kuzari*, scholars believe, is the most original Jewish work of the Middle Ages, and its influence is felt to this day. To be sure, Maimonides' *The Guide of the Perplexed* is a work of greater intellectual profundity, but it is not as original and certainly not as aesthetic as Halevi's work. Abraham Halkin writes that Judah Halevi, the most beloved medieval Jewish poet, "is the most independent and original thinker of the Jewish–Arabic period."[98]

Likewise, in describing the *Kuzari*, Eliezer Schweid writes, "While the *Kuzari* is an apologia rather than a systematic philosophic treatise, it is based upon an original crystallized and unified conception of Judaism, developed by Halevi in the course of a thoroughgoing confrontation with philosophy."[99]

In assessing the works of medieval Jewish thinkers, S. W. Baron writes, "Even more ardently and outspokenly Jewish was Yehudah Halevi.

His quasi-Platonic dialogue before the Khazar king (written about 1140) was devoted entirely to an apologia for Judaism and the presentation of a new comprehensive philosophy of Jewish and world history." Baron adds that whatever conviction Halevi's arguments carried with non-Jews, "they certainly helped strengthen the morale of the Jewish people, then being ground between the millstones of warring Islam and Christianity. The problem of exile loomed large in the eyes of all contemporaries."[100]

The *Kuzari* is written in the form of a dialogue between the king of the Khazars and a Jewish scholar (*haber*) who is Halevi's spokesman throughout the book. Halevi bases his dialogue on the historical fact of the king of the Khazars' conversion to Judaism, four centuries before Halevi's time. The story is told in the correspondence between Hasday Ibn Shaprut, the Jewish minister and patron of learning in Cordova, and the King of the Khazars.[101] Halevi uses this historical fact as a springboard and framework for his presentation of Judaism. As Husik puts it, "Instead of working out his ideas systematically, he wanted to give the subject dramatic interest by clothing it in dialogue form. And he was fortunate in finding a historical event which suited his purpose admirably."[102]

However, as Isaac Heinemann points out in his commentary on Book I of his abridged edition of the *Kuzari*, the historical description of this event was of no use to Halevi. According to the historical facts, "the king was against heathendom from the beginning, hesitating only as to which of the three monotheistic religions to adopt; it is a dream which makes him decide in favor of Judaism. The discussions are not initiated by the king; he only listens to the Christian and Moslem in order not to offend powerful neighbors. He has no difficulty in accepting Judaism seeing that the two younger faiths are at one in recognizing it."

Halevi, however, uses only the core elements of the historical event: the dream, discussions, and the king's conversion, and manipulates them to suit his purpose. In Halevi's version, Heinemann adds, "The king only learns from the dream that there exists a course of action which is pleasing to God, i.e., an absolute religion; it is only after listening to the representatives of all religions that he attains to the belief that the least popular religion is the true one; thereby he succeeds not only in arousing the human sympathy of the reader but also in shifting the general center of the interest of the whole story: everything now depends on the content and argument of the expositions given by the representatives of the three religions."[103]

As if to underscore the fact that the king opts for Judaism despite its low status (a despised religion) among nations, in Halevi's version the king is initially contemptuous of Judaism and has no intention of seeking the opinion of a Jewish scholar, given the low status of the Jews. It is only after learning from the Christian and Muslim representatives that both faiths rely on the prophetic tradition of Judaism in order to authenticate their own religions that he decides to consult a Jewish scholar—who ultimately succeeds in convincing him that the least popular religion happened to be in possession of absolute religious truth.

The *Kuzari* is divided into five books: Book I is intended to present a general description of Judaism as a whole; Books II–IV serve as a supplement and as a completion of the argument; and Book V is almost purely philosophical in character and serves as a defense of Judaism. Halevi's arguments proceed not in a straight line but in widening and broadening concentric circles, through questions and answers. The king converts at the beginning of the second book; the rest of the dialogue affords Halevi the chance to elaborate on his presentation of Judaism.

According to Heinemann, the *Kuzari* "falls into two unequal sections: the opening dialogue (in Book I) brings indirect proof of the truth of Judaism, both through the indication of flaws in the other three religions and through the establishment of the fact that the other biblical religions are able to bring evidence of unequivocal miracles only from the history of Israel. The second part is a direct justification of the doctrines of Judaism."[104]

HALEVI'S PRESENTATION

Heinemann notes that "although Halevi's presentation of the non-Jewish views is strictly objective, it is, nonetheless, part of the general plan. It is intended to supply an indirect proof of the truth of Jewish teaching. Each of the three opposing conceptions contains both points of agreement and of disagreement with Judaism. J. H. [Jehudah Halevi] attempts to prove that the points of agreement are evident and that the points of disagreement are controversial."[105]

Halevi's plan unfolds in several steps designed to serve as the underpinnings of his purpose, namely, proving the superiority of Judaism. First, as noted above, he manipulates the historical facts to have the king of the Khazars opt for Judaism not as a result of a dream but only after listening to the representatives of the three religions, and becoming convinced thereby that only Judaism is in possession of the absolute religious truth. Next, he has the king of the Khazars declare that "the human mind does not incline to believe that God has intercourse with man, except by a miracle which changes the nature of things, so that man may recognize that God alone is able to do so." Such a miracle, the king adds, "must also have taken place in the presence of great multitudes who saw it directly,"[106] a claim that neither Christianity nor Islam can make.

Finally, as Eliezer Schweid puts it, in presenting the doctrines of Christianity and Islam, Halevi underscores the fact "that they cannot base their doctrines on an unequivocal historical revelation such as the one granted to Israel at Sinai, when 600,000 people were granted the experience of prophecy, and found with a certitude that the intellect cannot attain, that God spoke to man and commanded him to observe the laws of the Torah. Christianity and Islam must, therefore, have recourse to the historical tradition of Judaism." Schweid adds that Halevi recognizes the presence of authentic Jewish elements in Christianity and Islam, and the vital role that these religions play in history. "However, insofar as they have diverged from the Torah and sought to supplant it, they are falsehoods which can neither be substantiated by the tradition of Israel, nor claim authentic historical validity of their own traditions."[107]

One might add that the dialogue form of the *Kuzari* affords Halevi the opportunity to weave into the unfolding dialogue some of his bold doctrines about Judaism and the Jews, which first shock and startle the king of the Khazars only to have him acknowledge their validity upon hearing Halevi's compelling explanations. Such doctrines include these: "Israel is the pick of mankind," "Israel amidst the nations is as the heart amidst the organs," and prophecy is the unique privilege of the Jewish people and is possible only in or about "the Land of prophecy,"—the Land of Israel. The king's acceptance of Halevi's doctrines is the more impressive given his initial contemptuous attitude toward Jews and Judaism.

According to Heinemann, "The question that the king sets before the four debaters is briefly this: which are the ways known to you of approach to God, by which we may attain nearness to God in this world and immortality in the world to come?" Finding neither the answer of the philosopher nor that of the Christian and Muslim scholars convincing, he saw himself "compelled to ask the Jews," the descendants of the Israelites, for he saw that "they constitute in themselves the evidence of a divine law on earth."[108] Accordingly, he invited a rabbi and asked about his belief.

Halevi's first answer to the king lays the groundwork for the course of his entire dialogue with the king. His answer does not refer to God as the Creator of the world, as the king expected him to do. Rather, he begins his discourse with the king by saying, "I believe in the God of Abraham, Isaac, and Israel, who led the Israelites out of Egypt with signs and miracles; who fed them in the desert and gave then the (Holy) Land . . . who sent Moses with the Law, and subsequently thousands of prophets, who confirmed His law by promises to those who observed, and threats to the disobedient. We believe in what is contained in the Torah—a very large domain."[109]

This claim, which is particular to the Israelites and excludes essentially all non-Jews, is clearly Halevi's first step leading to his central doctrine that "Israel is the pick of mankind." The king is disappointed, but the Jewish scholar begs his indulgence and the dialogue continues. Later in the dialogue, Halevi elaborates further on the centrality of the "exodus from Egypt" and the "revelation at Sinai" as constituting the basis of Jewish belief. He points out to the king that when Moses spoke to Pharaoh, he did not say "the God of heaven and earth" nor "my Creator and thine sent me" but "The God of the Hebrews sent me to thee"— the God of Abraham, Isaac, and Jacob. Likewise, when God spoke to the assembled people of Israel at Mount Sinai, He did not say "I am the Creator of the world and your Creator" but "I am the God you worship, who hath led you out of the land of Egypt." Halevi then adds that he spoke to the king in a similar manner, by mentioning that which is "convincing for him and for the whole of Israel, who knew these things [Exodus and Revelation], first through personal experience, and afterward through an uninterrupted tradition, which is equal to experience."[110]

ISRAEL, THE PICK OF MANKIND

When the king asks if Jewish belief is confined to Jews, Halevi proclaims his central doctrine that "Israel is the pick of mankind." He replies, "[Yes.] Any Gentile who joins us sincerely shares our good fortune, but he is not equal to us. If the Torah were binding on us because God created us, the white and the black man would be equal since He created them all. But the Torah (is binding) because He led us out of Egypt and remained attached to us. For we are the pick of mankind."[111]

It is to be noted that by "pick of mankind," Halevi means "the religious choice of mankind,"—those in possession of the divine gift of religious truth bestowed on them via the gift of prophecy, which, in Halevi's view, God conferred exclusively on the Jewish people. The king is startled by what he perceives as arrogance on the part of Halevi. Halevi asks for the king's forbearance, however, and proceeds to prove the preeminence of his people. He declares, "For me it is sufficient that God chose them as His community and people from all the nations of the world; that the Divine power descended on the whole people, so that they all became worthy to be addressed by Him." He then goes on to flesh out the "pick of mankind" doctrine by tracing the picking process, so to speak, to Adam from whom the gift of prophecy was transmitted, through Seth, to only one man in each generation until the Patriarch Jacob, when all his twelve sons became worthy of prophecy, and ultimately all the Israelites assembled at Sinai were worthy of being addressed directly by God.[112]

Just as Adam's prophetic gift was not transmitted to all his sons but only to Seth, likewise, not all the sons of Noah, Abraham, and Isaac inherited that gift. Thus, the pick of Noah's descendants was Shem, that of Abraham was Isaac (not Ishma'el), and only Jacob (not Esau) inherited his father's prophetic gift. This theory of the "pick of mankind" with its biological selectivity serves Halevi's purpose well. The claim that the gift of true religion is bestowed selectively on a particular group of mankind and cannot be transferred or acquired by adoption of the faith means that the Jews, as the chosen people, cannot have been replaced by Christians as the latter claim. And since the Arabs claim to descend from Ishma'el, Halevi discredits the Islamic claim as well by making Isaac the sole heir of Abraham's prophetic gift. Thus, with one bold stroke, Halevi defends Judaism, and achieves status for the Jews. At the same time, he denies Christianity and Islam their claims of superiority.

Both faiths concede the chosenness of the Jewish people, but claim to have replaced them as the bearers of God's revelation. By his "pick of mankind" doctrine, Halevi pulls the rug from under them, as it were. Salo Baron sums up the implication of the "pick of mankind" doctrine thus: "Arguing on the basis of historical facts rather than mere reasoning, as in his general philosophy, the great poet insisted that Israel is physically and spiritually the chosen people. . . . That is why a proselyte may well become pious and learned, but he cannot attain the gift of prophecy reserved for born Jews."[113]

Halevi's Explanation of the Sin of the Golden Calf

As Heinemann points out, Halevi seeks to extenuate even the sin of the golden calf "because this is the very sin which is often stressed by the Fathers of the Church and by Islam, and to which the loss of the preferential position of Judaism is attributed (Book I, #4)." Halevi stresses the fact that "there is a great difference between actual worship of idols and the justifiable need for a perceptible symbol of God's presence" (Book IV, #5). He explains the sin historically. Because we no longer admit any cult images, he reasons, we are easily inclined to overestimate the seriousness of the sin committed at a time when the worship of images was widespread. "The whole affair appears to us repulsive," he argues, "because nowadays the majority of nations have abandoned the worship of images; it was less objectionable at that time, because all nations were then idolators." The Israelites, he argues further, "had been promised that something visible would descend on them from God on which they could depend, as they followed the pillars of cloud and fire when they departed from Egypt." In similar manner, "they turned toward the cloud which hovered over Moses while God spoke to him; they rose and worshipped God in its presence."

And then Moses ascended the mount in order to receive the tablets which he was to bring down to them inscribed, and then to make an ark toward which they should direct their gaze during their devotions. The people waited for his return, expecting every moment to see him return. But when Moses tarried for forty days, "then distrust overpowered a section of the people and they began to divide into parties and factions." They simply wanted an "object of worship [as a symbol] toward which they could turn, like the other nations, without, however, prejudicing the supremacy of Him who had brought them out of Egypt." Their sin, Halevi concludes, "consisted in the manufacturing of an image, which was forbidden to them, and in attributing Divine power to a thing made and chosen by themselves without the order of God."[114]

After discussing Halevi's excuse of the sin of the golden calf, Heinemann observes, "In this way Yehudah Halevi is able to show that the sin of the golden calf rests on that fundamental error which he is constantly challenging (#77, end); the belief that man can find the way to God by the strength of his own reasoning, not needing revelation; in the case of the golden calf this belief is said to have been represented by 'astrologists and soothsayers.'" Heinemann concludes his commentary on the subject thus:

"Yehudah Halevi's treatment of the question has therefore not only the apologetic force that comes out in #97, end, but also a definite systematic significance; the latter is clearly emphasized in the king's summary (#98). That summary is as follows: 'Thou confirmed the opinion I formed through meditation and through what I saw in my vision: that man can only attain the Divine "order" through Divine "ordinance" viz. through actions ordained by God.'"[115]

It may be noted that Halevi's historical approach in explaining the sin of the golden calf was most original and, as Heinemann points out, "rare in medieval Judaism." He anticipates Maimonides who uses a similar historical approach in explaining the sacrifices and certain ceremonial commandments.

YEHUDAH HALEVI—A RACIST?

Does Halevi's "pick of mankind" doctrine, and particularly his assertion that a proselyte cannot attain the gift of prophecy make him a racist, as some have suggested? Not necessarily so. I believe that Halevi adopts this doctrine only to deny Christianity its claim that since the advent of Jesus, prophecy and religious truth had passed to his followers—that is, that Christians replaced the Jews as the chosen people (Book I, #34). Halevi asserts that the "gift of religious truth" is neither transferable nor acquired by adoption (Book IV, #23); at the same time, he denies the Muslims' claim that Muhammad is the "seal of the prophets" who abrogated every previous law. That Halevi is not a racist in the usual sense of the word is evident from the fact that he presents the heathen king as worthy of divine apparition.

David Z. Baneth, dealing with the same issue writes,

His theory of Israel's special religious faculty bears an unmistakable resemblance to modern racial theories. But unlike those theories, which are outgrowth of a sense of racial superiority, his doctrine does not attempt to construct evidence that would fit the doctrine. Rather, it rests on the (for him) given facts, immediately evident and established by the Bible, according to which true knowledge of God, prophecy, and supernatural providence can be found only in Israel. Nevertheless, he is far from wanting to press this theory rigorously. Unlike Ghazali, who, in keeping with Islamic dogma, excludes infidels from salvation, Judah Halevi, faithful to Jewish tradition, acknowledges that the righteous of other nations also have a share in eternal bliss. He even softens his basic notion by saying that a proselyte can be equal to a born Jew in every respect except for the ultimate supreme gift of prophecy, and he apparently feels that this last barrier also will fall in the days of the Messiah when, even as a seed acts to transform the soil from which it synthesizes its plant, Israel too will have transformed all the nations into its own likeness.[116]

Isaac Julius Guttmann echoes Baneth's view almost verbatim, and also points out that racism would defeat the main purpose of the *Kuzari*, which was to convert the king of the Khazars to Judaism.[117]

Finally, Isaac Heinemann, in his introduction to his abridged edition of the *Kuzari*, deals with the same issue. He writes,

By interpreting the free will of God displayed in the selection of Israel and Palestine as a causal necessity, Jehudah Halevi invests the notion of selection with a crudeness that he himself finds undesirable (Book I, # 28—Your words are poor after having been rich) and that, in fact, detracts from the weight of his psychological justification of religion, to which we have just referred; the fact that he does not insist in his story on this exclusiveness of the religious prerogative, formulated by him in Book I, #115, speaks well for him and for his rootedness in the real Bible heritage: he presents the heathen King of the Khazars as honoured by Divine apparition![118]

The above scholarly citations seem all to agree that while, on the face of it, the "pick of mankind" doctrine has racial overtones, when considered in the context of the rest of the *Kuzari*, and considering that the entire book is premised on the fact that the heathen king of the Khazars is "honored by divine apparition," a case cannot be made that Halevi is a racist.[119] To recapitulate, it is my personal view that Halevi may be considered a racist only in as much as he insists that Judaism and the Jews possess superior religious truth bestowed on them by God through the exclusive gift of prophecy.

As Salo Baron observes, all medieval Jewish philosophers sought to establish in various ways the exclusivity, or at least the unique character of Old Testament prophecy. Baron notes further, "In fact, the idea of selection [of Israel as the chosen people] permeates all medieval Jewish philosophy, whether it be amply discussed, as in Halevi, or merely referred to or implied, as in most writers." (See chap. 7, n. 141 below for a detailed discussion of Baron's observation.)

Indeed, in my opinion, Halevi's doctrine of prophecy was designed simply to deny the claims of Christianity and Islam to religious superiority. This is evident from the full Arabic title of his philosophical work, *The Book of Argument and Proof in Defense of the Despised/Scorned Religion.* His goal was to defend the honor and dignity of his faith and his people. His approach was based on the notion that the best defense is a good offense. Accordingly, he formulated a doctrine of prophecy which enabled him in one stroke to achieve status for the Jews, and at the same time to deny Christianity and Islam their claims to have replaced the Jews as the chosen People—nothing less and nothing more.

ISRAEL, THE HEART AMONG THE NATIONS

A corollary to the "pick of mankind" doctrine is the one that proclaims that "Israel amidst the nations is like the heart amidst the organs. . . . It is the most sick and the most healthy of them all." The king requires further clarification of what may have sounded to him a strange notion, and Halevi's spokesman, the rabbi, is ready to oblige. Husik's summary of Halevi's explanation is clear and succinct:

> The heart is more sensitive than the rest of the body in disease and in health. It feels both more intensely. It is more liable to disease than the other organs, and, on the other hand, it becomes aware sooner of agencies dangerous to its health and endeavors to reject them or ward them off. So is Israel among the nations. Their responsibility is greater than that of other nations and they are sooner punished. "Only you have I loved out of all the families of the earth," says Amos (3:2), "therefore will I visit upon you all your iniquities." On the other hand, God does not allow our sins to accumulate as he does with the other nations until they deserve destruction. "He pardons the iniquities of his people by causing them to pass away in due order." As the heart is affected by the other organs, so Israel suffers on account of their assimilation to the other nations. Israel suffers while other nations are at peace. As the elements are for the sake of minerals,

the minerals for the sake of the plants, the plants for the sake of the animals, the animals for the sake of man, so is man for the sake of Israel, and Israel for the sake of the prophets and the pious men. With the purification of Israel the world will be improved and brought nearer to God.[120]

HALEVI'S CRITICISM OF PHILOSOPHY AND PHILOSOPHERS

In the fifth book of the *Kuzari*, Halevi takes up polemics with the philosopher whom he did not properly challenge in the first book. His spokesman, the rabbi, presents his pupil, the king of the Khazars, with a brief sketch of the Aristotelian philosophy of his day, and at the same time criticizes its weaknesses. As stated above, according to Baneth, Halevi's attack on philosophy "had only two concerns: first, to diminish the enormous prestige which the Aristotelian doctrine still enjoyed; and second . . . to demonstrate that Aristotle's teachings are inadequate to satisfy the demands of religious and ethical consciousness."[121]

For Halevi, the only basis for faith is immediate religious experience, not speculative reasoning. Religious life is above all rooted in experience. Its terms may not be reconstructed in terms of pure theory; they must be sought in experience. The Jewish people have this experience through the gift of prophecy which is unique to them.[122] (See the section on prophecy below.)

Halevi maintains that Aristotle's conclusions are valid only with regard to mathematics and logic, but have no validity with regard to religion.[123] The God of Aristotle leads only to the God of metaphysics, not to the God of religion. As Baneth puts it,

> He [Halevi] makes a very sharp distinction between rationalistic and theistic concepts of God. For the philosopher, whose sole aim is to gain a speculative knowledge of all things, God is merely one object of knowledge among many others; he considers ignorance of God no more harmful than, say, a misconception about the position and form of the earth. . . . Thus, the God of Aristotle is different from the God of Abraham, whom the believer senses and perceives out of his deepest yearnings. His greatest joy is to be near Him; his greatest agony to be separated from Him. To such a God one can surrender with all one's soul, and one can go to one's death joyously for His sake. The philosopher, by contrast, has no incentive to tolerate so much as

one petty annoyance for the sake of his God, who does not even
have knowledge of His own existence. The ethics of the philosophers also lack a firm foundation because they do not believe in
divine retributive justice.[124]

In Halevi's view, philosophy does not bring one closer to God, nor does it
entail a way of life designed to bring man near God.[125]

In his attempt to diminish the prestige enjoyed by Aristotelian
teachings, Halevi dismisses the entire theory of the "four elements" and
the alleged composition of all things out of them as a pure assumption, having no empirical basis. He raises many objections to the doctrine: "Whoever
saw a fiery or aery body enter the matter of plant and animal so as to war-
rant us in saying that the latter are composed of the four elements?" He
asks, or "whoever saw plants resolve into the four elements?" Finally, he
asks, "How can philosophers maintain such a thing, since they believe in
the eternity of the world, that it always existed as it does now?"

Halevi also directs his criticism and even sarcasm against the Arab
Aristotelians, Al-Farabi and Avicenna, who worked up a doctrine, which
combines Aristotle's theory of motion with the emanation theory of Ploti-
nus. Halevi considers this doctrine purely mythological. It is all pure con-
jecture, he says, and there is not an iota of proof in it. People believe it and
think it is convincing simply because it bears the name of Greek philosophers.[126]

But Halevi does not have a totally negative attitude toward philosophy. In general, he concedes its validity in matters which can be demonstrated in the same absolute manner as propositions of mathematics and
logic. The problem, as he sees it, is that because philosophers had established their credibility in logic and mathematics, people tend to accept
everything they say concerning physics and metaphysics. Also, Halevi was
very well acquainted with philosophy. Indeed, according to Husik, Halevi
"shows a better knowledge of Aristotelian ideas than his [Jewish] predecessors, and is well versed in Neo-Platonism. While he attacks all those
views of philosophers which are inconsistent to his mind with the religion
of Judaism, he speaks in other respects the philosophic language, and even
makes concessions to the philosophers."[127]

Furthermore, notwithstanding his criticism of philosophers, Halevi
appreciates and even praises them for their behavior and their achievements. Thus, later in the dialogue, he acknowledges the personal virtues of
the philosophers in their renunciation of wealth, rank, and the pleasure of

children in order not to be distracted from study.[128] Toward the end of Book V, he praises their human wisdom, quoting Socrates as saying to Athenians, "O my people, I do not deny your knowledge of God, but I confess that I do not understand it. As for me, I am only wise in human matters." Then, after attacking the attempt by the Arab Aristotelians to link the Neoplatonist doctrine of emanation with Aristotle's theory of motion, he adds, "Yet, they cannot be blamed, nay, deserve thanks for all they have produced in abstract speculations. For their intentions were good; they observed the laws of reason, and led virtuous lives. At all events, they have earned this praise, because the same duties were not imposed on them as they were on us when we were given revelation, and a tradition which is tantamount to revelation."[129]

In describing Halevi's criticism of philosophy, Baron writes,

[Yehudah Halevi] felt the insufficiency of speculation in solving the riddle of existence. While criticizing extreme rationalism along the lines of Gahazali's "Incoherence of the Philosophers," he nevertheless deeply approved the ultimate need and value of knowledge. He merely contended that the human quest for knowledge, if unsupported by revelation, was doomed to failure, because revelation alone opened up avenues to absolute truth without error or defect. Time and again, his Jewish spokesman assured the king of Khazaria: "Heaven forbid that there should be anything in the Bible to contradict that which is manifest or proved [by reason]. Yet, the "philosophers" erred not only because their quest for knowledge was cold and impersonal—in one of his famous poems, Halevi decried Greek wisdom as bearing "no fruits; only flowers"—but also because their knowledge itself had no direct relationship to the essence of things.[130]

In the same spirit, after noting that Halevi, like al-Ghazali, was aware of the inadequacy of metaphysical reasoning, Halkin adds,

Halevi was far from being anti-rationalist. On the contrary, to the extent to which he believed its reasoning valid, he utilized the method and the conclusions of philosophy. Moreover, it was his purpose to make his own doctrine rationally demonstrable. But he objected to the position taken by philosophy on matters which, in his mind, were within the domain of religion and hence superrational. He did not feel that its evidence for the existence of God was adequate. He resented its conception of God as an inactive, disinterested force, and its indifference to religious works or to the relative validity of one religion as over against another. He disagreed entirely with the conceit of philosophers that by their efforts or methods they could attain the rank of prophecy, or the true knowledge of God, and the bliss which that elevated state bestows on man. The precious gifts that living with God brings to man are acquired not by man's intellect but by knowing and doing what God has taught. The basic capacity to lead such a life is bestowed by Him. It is "a Divine matter" as Ha-Levi calls it, a special talent or quality which God grants.[131]

HALEVI AND AL-GHAZALI ON PHILOSOPHY AND PHILOSOPHERS

Scholars have shown that some of Halevi's attacks against philosophy (expressed in the *Kuzari*) are similar to those of al-Ghazali.[132] But along with similarities, there are significant differences between the two thinkers as well. What is evident is that Yehudah Halevi is quite familiar with al-Ghazali's views and draws heavily upon them, but at times he adapts them to his own purposes which are different than those of al-Ghazali. Sometimes, he simply disagrees with al-Ghazali.[133]

The following are some examples of the similarities and differences between Halevi and al-Ghazali:

SIMILARITIES

Both Halevi and al-Ghazali were well acquainted with philosophy, but rejected it as a way of life for themselves. Both insist that the only basis of faith is immediate religious experience, which is superior to speculative reasoning. Both argue that the faculty of prophecy is the highest form of knowledge, and that it is not granted to everyone—certainly not to philosophers.[134] Both believe that because philosophers establish credibility with regard to logic and mathematics, people tend to accept anything they say concerning physics and metaphysics.

DIFFERENCES

Baneth, in his seminal article on Halevi and al-Ghazali quoted above,[135] calls attention to a number of significant differences between

Halevi and al-Ghazali. He notes that "both authors share the same general viewpoints, just as they are motivated by the same basic tendency." But if one compares their respective reasoning in detail, "the surprising result is that in his polemics, Judah Halevi turns out to be independent of his precursor [al-Ghazali] in nearly every respect."[136]

Here are examples of some of the major differences discussed by Baneth:

- In connection with Halevi's contrast between the God of Aristotle and the God of Abraham (see above), Baneth notes that Halevi makes a very sharp distinction between rationalistic and theistic aspects of God. He adds that "Ghazali never emphasized the contrast between philosophers and believers with the same clarity and acuity."[137]

- On the question of creation in time, Baneth observes that Halevi "goes beyond Ghazali. While Ghazali apparently thinks that he can provide not only dialectical but also adequate philosophical proof for the origin of the world in time, Judah Halevi boldly asserts that the proofs for and against the eternity of the world counterbalance each other."[138] It is worth noting that Halevi adds, "If, after all, a believer in the Torah finds himself compelled to admit an eternal substance and the existence of many worlds prior to this one, this would not affect his belief in that this world was created at a certain epoch, and that Adam and Noah were the first human beings."[139]

- Baneth points out that while the two thinkers do not differ in principle in their attitude toward metaphysics, there is a significant difference in their practical attitude. Metaphysical views do not play a crucial role in Ghazali's religious doctrines, whereas in the *Kuzari* certain metaphysical concepts and basic Aristotelian views are used abundantly for the purpose of providing a philosophical foundation. Baneth attributes this difference in part to the different tendencies of the two works. Most of al-Ghazali's writings, he explains, "merely want to awaken

the religious impulse and channel it into the right path—
in other words, to serve the purpose of practical theology."
Halevi, on the other hand, "wants to validate the truth of
Judaism and, especially, to integrate the concept of Israel's
chosenness with the scholarly world view of his time."[140]

- Al-Ghazal's view regarding man's free will is that man is
capable of willing, but he cannot will whatever he wants.
He can will only what God has determined for him. Baneth
observes that "such a rigorous determinism was compati-
ble with Islam, whose meaning by its very name, is sub-
mission (to the divine will). . . . Judaism, on the other hand,
the religion of the pious deed, is founded upon free will
and cannot be reconciled with determinism." As a result,
Baneth continues, "virtually all Jewish thinkers, including
Halevi, have come out on the side of free will."[141]

- Baneth also points out the difference between al-Ghazali's
universalism and Halevi's particularism or nationalism.
Baneth explains that while al-Ghazali regards Islam as the
true religion and bases his views as much as possible on
the koranic revelation, "his religious theories, unlike Judah
Halevi's, are not inextricably linked with his own religion
by virtue of their essence. Given the role he assigns to revelation, it is irrelevant whether that revelation is the one
communicated to Mohammed or some other revelation."
On the other hand, unlike most of the systems of the Jewish religious philosophers who show a tendency toward
universalism, "Judah Halevi's unique achievement is precisely that he clearly recognized the problem of the special
historic status of Judaism and attempted to solve it with
the philosophical methods of his day."[142]

- Halevi is categorically against the asceticism advocated
by al-Ghazali, which requires withdrawal from the world,
rigorous self-discipline, and the uprooting of all worldly
desires from one's spirit. Such withdrawal from the world,
Baneth explains, is "alien to Judah Halevi. The description

of Jewish piety in the *Kuzari* begins: In our view, a pious man is not one who detaches himself from the world lest he become a burden to the world and the world to him, or lest he come to hate life, which is a gift of God. . . . On the contrary, he loves life and wants to live to a ripe old age because it affords him an opportunity to deserve the world to come."[143]

In describing the religious duties of Judaism, Halevi declares, "The Divine law imposes no asceticism on us. It rather says that we should keep the balance and grant every mental and physical faculty its due, without overburdening one faculty at the expense of another. . . . Our law, as a whole, is divided between fear, love, and joy; through each of them thou mayest approach thy God. Thy contrition on a fast day does no more to bring thee nearer to God than thy joy on the Sabbath and holy days, if the latter is the outcome of devotion."[144]

HALEVI ON MIRACLES

All medieval Jewish philosophers proceed from the general to the particular, starting with proofs of the existence of God, creation, mankind, Israel, revelation, and so on. Halevi reverses the process and bases his religious views on miracles rather than on reasoned considerations. For him, miracles are manifestations of God's free will and the only proof of His sway over all happenings in the world. Above all miracles, Halevi places in the forefront two historical miracles: the Exodus from Egypt, and the Revelation at Sinai. His reason is that these two miracles had been experienced by many (600,000) and therefore constitute the best scientific and historical proof of God's concern for men, and His relation to them.

As Halkin puts it, "The revelation on Mount Sinai, an undoubted fact, as judged by medieval standards of historical knowledge, is at once the firmest proof of the existence of God, the most valid evidence of the election of Israel, and the clearest statement of the correct and only method of attaining the coveted degree of God's favor and love."[145] Halevi's spokesman, the rabbi, put it succinctly thus: "O prince of the Khazars, when thou didst ask me about my creed, I made mention to thee of what is convincing for me and for the whole of Israel, who knew these things [Exodus and Revelation], first through personal experience, and afterward through an uninterrupted tradition, which is equal to experience."[146] This brings us to the fact that Halevi's teachings are based on the concept of immediate religious experience—that is, prophecy—and its superiority over deductive reasoning.

HALEVI ON PROPHECY

Halevi defines prophecy as an "inner sense" which enables the prophet to apprehend spiritual reality in the same way as the ordinary man apprehends physical reality by means of his senses. Because the prophet experiences directly the presence of God, he is superior to the philosopher who has only an indirect theoretical knowledge of Him. Philosophy, in Halevi's view, has nothing to do with prophecy.[147] Indeed, for Halevi, the prophet is the highest type of man; he is above ordinary man as man is above animals, and animals are above plants (Book I, # 37–43). And since, in Halevi's view, God granted the gift of prophecy only to His chosen people, that makes the Jews superior to all nations.[148] And just as prophecy is possible only among Jews, so it is also possible only in or about the Land of Israel, "the land of prophecy."

In summing up Halevi's view of prophecy, Schweid concludes, "The prophetic faculty is a faculty beyond human reason, and constitutes a generic distinction between the prophet and the ordinary man, parallel to the distinction between man and animals. This faculty is hereditary and unique to the people of Israel. It is only through the intermediacy of Israel that the other nations can approach God, just as it is only through the intermediacy of the prophets that the people of Israel can come close to Him. This is the cornerstone of Halevi's doctrine of particularity of the people of Israel."[149]

THE PREEMINENCE OF THE LAND OF ISRAEL

Having convinced the king of the preeminence of the people of Israel, Halevi proceeds to prove to the king that just as the people of Israel are superior to all the nations, by virtue of the exclusive gift of prophecy, so is the Land of Israel superior to all other countries, as "the land of prophecy." He explains that just as some lands can produce better grapes— that is, they are better suited by their climate and the quality of their soil for producing wine—so is the Holy Land better suited for prophecy, not only because of its physical factors and its location at the center of the earth, but also because it was the exclusive land of prophecy, the land where God chose to manifest His "divine power" or "divine influence" (*Ha-Inyan ha-Elohi*).

Halevi further states that precedence belongs to those particular people who represent the "pick" and "heart" of mankind, and that the land also has its part in this and so have the religious acts connected with it, which he compares to the cultivation of a vineyard that is necessary for it to produce grapes. But he adds, "No other place could share with this pre-eminent people the influence of Divine power, whereas other hills are also able to produce good wine." To the king's objection that prophets like Abraham, Ezekiel, and Daniel prophesied outside Israel, Halevi responds: "Whosoever prophesied, did so either in Palestine or for its sake, viz. Abraham [in order] to reach it, Ezekiel and Daniel on account of it, to prepare for the return."[150]

Halevi admits that the gift of prophecy was retained as an asset of many of Abraham's descendants in Palestine only as long as they remained in the land and observed the necessary conditions, viz. purity, worship, and sacrifices, and, above all, the reverence of the Shekhinah. For the divine influence, one might say, singles out him who appears worthy of being connected with it, such as prophets and pious men.[151]

Halevi's response to the king's reproach—that the Jews, including Halevi, fall short of their religious duty by remaining in the Diaspora—is that this was a justified reproach. He also suggests that the same reproach could already have been leveled against the majority of the Jews in Babylonian exile, who, in order not to leave their homes and their affairs, chose to remain in Babylon and did not join those who returned to the Holy Land under Zerubbabel. Halevi believes that this sin is the reason why earlier prophecies that the Second Temple would fully equal the first were not fulfilled.[152]

THE SUFFERING OF ISRAEL

Halevi's doctrines of the "pick" and "heart" of mankind prove to his and the king's satisfaction that the "despised religion" is in possession of absolute religious truth. He also attempts to reconcile the chosenness of the Jewish people and their suffering in exile. God, he declares, has "a secret and wise design concerning us, which should be compared to the wisdom hidden in the seed which falls into the ground." Just as the seed appears to be rotting in the ground, but is in reality preparing for growth, so the unusual suffering of the Jews is not evidence of the inferiority of the Jewish faith, but of its superiority. The suffering of Israel is the sanctification of the name of God, and its purpose will be understood at the time of redemption. Halevi points out that there are "prominent men among us who could escape this degradation by a word spoken lightly, become free men, and turn against their oppressors, but do not do so out of devotion to their faith."[153]

Moreover, Halevi argues, Christians and Muslims also glorify the martyrs of their faith far above the conquerors; the nation of martyrs [Israel], likewise, towers above conquering empires. (Book I, # 113). In addition, Halevi refers to numerous religious compensations for the suffering of the Jews, such as being cleansed from their sins,[154] the reward and compensation awaiting the pious in the world to come,[155] and the attachment to the divine influence in this world.[156]

HALEVI ON THE COMMANDMENTS

The rationalist medieval Jewish philosophers, notably Saadiah and Maimonides, see the test of truth in rationality. Accordingly, for them the most important laws in the Bible are the rational commandments. Even the traditional or ceremonial laws, in their views, would turn out to be rational if only we knew the reasons for their having been commanded. In the absence of such knowledge, it is the task of the philosopher to guess or suggest appropriate rationales. Both Saadiah and Maimonides did just that, and Maimonides proved to be a master in this art.[157]

Halevi takes a dramatically opposite attitude. If the only important laws in religion were social and ethical ones, he asks, why should Christians and Muslims fight each other to death—shedding untold human blood? After all, there is hardly any difference between them regarding ethical theory and practice. It is only the ceremonial practice that separates them, he concludes. To be sure, ethical laws are important in any religion, but they are not peculiar to religion as such. They are a necessary condition of life. Society cannot exist without them. Halevi concedes that rational laws are "the basis and preamble of the Divine law, preceding it in character and time. They are indispensable in the administration of any human society; even a gang of robbers must have a kind of justice; otherwise, their confederacy cannot last."[158]

Religion, on the other hand, has peculiar practices. It is not sufficient to observe rational commandments alone. When the prophets of Israel
denounce the cult of sacrifices and proclaim that what God wants of man
is a pure heart and ethical conduct, what they mean is that ceremonial laws
alone are not sufficient. But surely a man is not fully an Israelite if he observes only the social and ethical laws and disregards the ceremonial
ones.[159] Therefore, Halevi considers the person who observes and performs
the commandments without seeking a rationale for their observance superior to one who does, but the latter is not blameworthy for doing so.[160]

HALEVI ON DIVINE ATTRIBUTES

Although Halevi presents God in personal terms as having close
personal relation with Israel, he does not conceive Him in anthropomorphic
terms. On this issue he does not yield one inch to other medieval Jewish
philosophers. He discusses the attributes of God, dividing them into three
categories: active, relative, and negative.

He describes as active attributes expressions such as low, high,
rich, jealous, revengeful, merciful, and so on. These attributes reflect the
visible acts or the effects of God's acts in the world, which we judge on
the basis of an analogy to our own acts. When man attempts to remove
misery, we call his action pity. Hence attributes as merciful and the like
are actional, meaning that it is the acts which suggest their being labeled
as such.

Relative attributes, according to Halevi, refer to expressions such
as blessed, praised, extolled, excellent, holy, and so on; they derive from
man's attitude toward God. "They are taken from the reverence paid to Him
by mankind. God is blessed because men bless Him." Negative attributes,
on the other hand, refer to such expressions as One, First, Last, living, and
so on. These adjectives, Halevi explains, are given to Him in order to negate
their contrast, but they do not denote God's essence. When we say God is
living, we do so to exclude its negative, dead. In reality, God cannot be
said to be living or dead "for we cannot understand life unaccompanied by
sensibility and movement; God is above these."[161]

But Halevi does not object to speaking of God in human images,
for images such as the prophets envisaged by virtue of their creative power
are indispensable for implanting in our souls the proper awe of God.[162]

THE POETIC ASPECT OF THE *KUZARI*

Halevi's *Kuzari* is distinguished from all other medieval Jewish philosophical works by its aesthetic aspect. In addition to the general poetic aspect of its dialogue form, there are some passages which are truly poetic. One such passage is Halevi's description of the religious behavior of the pious Jew. He describes such a person as "a prince [who is] obeyed by his senses and by his mental as well as physical faculties, which he governs like a city. . . . He concedes to the senses their fair share according as he requires them, using hands, feet, and tongue for necessary or useful action." Pursuing the "prince" metaphor further, Halevi adds,

> Thus, when he has satisfied each of them, giving to the organic limbs the necessary amount of rest and sleep, to the animal ones waking and movements in worldly occupation, he calls up his troops as a respected prince calls up his disciplined army, to assist him in reaching the higher or Divine degree, which is to be found above the degree of the intellect. . . . The will obeys his admonition and resolves to execute it. It [the will] directs first the organs of thought and frees them from all worldly ideas which filled them before; it charges the imagination to produce, with the assistance of memory, the most splendid pictures possible, in order to approach the Divine power which it seeks, e.g. the scene of Sinai, Abraham and Isaac at Moriah, the Tabernacle of Moses, the Temple service, the presence of [God's] glory in the holy house, and the like. The pious man then orders his memory to retain all these, and not to forget them. After this preparation, the will power stimulates all his organs to work with alertness, pleasure and joy. They stand without fatigue when occasion demands; they bow down when he bids them to bow; they sit at the proper moment. The eyes look as a servant looks at his master; the feet stand straight; all limbs are frightened and anxious to obey their master, paying no heed to pain or fatigue.

Halevi is as poetic in his discussion of the significance of the Sabbath and holy days, culminating in the Fast of Yom Kippur. He begins by comparing the three daily prayers to the three daily meals; just as the latter provide nourishment for the body, the former do the same for the soul, and "the blessing of one prayer lasts until it is time for the next, just as the strength derived from lunch lasts until supper." But "the further the soul of the pious man is removed from the time of prayer, the more it is darkened by coming in contact with worldly matters." He adds,

> Prayer, to be sure, purges his soul from all that has passed over and prepares it for the future; but in spite of this arrangement no week elapses in which both—his soul and body—are not satiated with weariness, oppressive elements having multiplied in the course of the week; and these cannot be cleansed away except by consecrating one day to service and corporeal rest. On the Sabbath, therefore, the body makes good what it lacked during the six days, and prepares itself for the week to come, and the soul remembers what it lacked as long as it looked after the body; it cures itself of past illness and provides against future sickness. . . . He then provides himself with a monthly remedy on the season of atonement for all that may happen during this period [prayer for Rosh Hodesh]. He further observes the three festivals and the very holy Fast Day [Yom Kippur] on which he casts off his former sins and makes up what he may have missed on the weekly and monthly days [of atonement]. . . . The fast of this day is such as to bring him near the angels, because it is spent in humility and contrition, standing, bowing, praising and singing. All his corporeal faculties are denied their natural requirements, being devoted entirely to religious service, as if there were in him no animal element at all.[163]

It is generally said that Halevi is philosophical in his poetry even as he is poetic in his philosophy. This is so, in certain measure, because some of his central concepts appear in both the *Kuzari* and his poetry. This is especially evident in his poems on God, the Sabbath, the centrality of the Land of Israel, and the suffering of his people.[164]

What follows are several illustrations of Helevi's ideas appearing in both his poetry and in the *Kuzari*:

Underlying Halevi's explanation of divine attributes is the belief that the knowledge of God's essence or His nature is beyond human capacity. In the conclusion of Book V, he states explicitly, "We therefore dwell on His works, but refrain from describing His nature."[165] The very same thought appears in one of his liturgical poems, recited by the Sephardim on Rosh Hashanah, *Yah Shimkha Aromimkha* (O Lord I Will Extol Thy Name). The last line of this *pizmon* reads,

Search His works, only upon Himself
Stretch not your hand By delving into the beginning and the end,
the wondrous and the deeply hidden.[166]

One of the contrasts drawn by Halevi between the God of the philosophers and the God of Abraham is that the latter serves God and perceives Him out of his deepest yearning; his greatest joy is to be near Him." In the poem "Lord, Where Shall I Find Thee?" Halevi says,

Lord, I have sought Thy nearness;
With all my heart have I called Thee.[167]

One of the central concerns of Halevi is to prove the superiority of Judaism ("the despised faith") to the more powerful faiths of Christianity and Islam. In Book III, # 8–9, he declares that Judaism is the absolute religion, as opposed to which Christianity and Islam can only claim devitalized imitations. Thus, the king of the Khazars comments that other people attempt to imitate the Jewish practice of circumcision, but they only had the pain without the joy experienced by the Jews. Halevi, agreeing with the king, responds, "Just so it is with other imitations; no people succeeded in equaling us. Look at those who appoint a day of rest in the place of the Sabbath. Could they reach a higher plane of resemblance than that which exists between statues and living human bodies?" The very same thought is expressed even more forcefully in one of Halevi's poems for the Sabbath, quoted by Heinemann (at the end of his abridged version of the *Kuzari*):

Thou hast bestowed great splendor on the Sabbath
Through the bond of peace and life.
And Thou hast sanctified it, that it may distinguish
Between Israel and the other nations.

Who utter mere empty words
When they would compare their days with my holy day—
Edom later on the first day—and Arabia earlier on the sixth—
Can the deceit of Ishmael and Edom mislead the men of truth?
They compare dross with jewels,
The dead with the living.[168]

Halevi says that philosophy does not bring man closer to God, nor does it entail a way of life designed to bring him near God.[169] In one of his famous poems, *Devarekha be-mor* . . . (Thy words are compounded of sweet-smelling myrrh), one of the lines reads:

> And let not the wisdom of the Greeks beguile thee,
> Which hath no fruit, but only flowers.[170]

Finally, Halevi's poetry is famous for his love of God, the people of Israel, and above all, for his Zionist poems which are intensely and passionately nationalistic. The same intense nationalism is woven throughout the *Kuzari* in such doctrines as "Israel is the pick of mankind," prophecy is the unique heritage of Israel, and the Land of Israel is "the land of prophecy" chosen by God for His chosen people. The *Kuzari* ends with Halevi's call for the return of the Jewish people to the Land of Israel as a precondition for Israel's redemption. His last discourse with the king of the Khazars concludes with the following: "If we provoke and instill love of this sacred place among men, we may be sure of obtaining reward and hastening the [Messianic] aim; for it is written: 'Thou shalt arise and have mercy upon Zion; for it is time to favor her, the moment is come. For thy servants love her stones and pity her dust' (Ps. 102:14, 15). This means: Jerusalem can only be rebuilt when Israel yearns for it to such an extent that we sympathize even with its stones and its dust."[171]

CONCLUSION

Speaking of the influence of the *Kuzari* on subsequent generations, Eliezer Schweid writes that it is "a popular work which exercised great influence on Judaism throughout history." He adds, "It was particularly influential in kabbalistic circles in the thirteenth century, and among the anti-Aristotelians in the 14th and 15th centuries. In more recent times, it had a marked influence on Hassidism." As for its influence on modern Jewish thought, Schweid notes that "some philosophers of the 19th and 20th centuries, such as Samuel David Luzzatto, Franz Rosenzweig, and Abraham Isaac Kook saw in the *Kuzari* the most faithful description of the particular qualities of the Jewish religion."[172]

8.

THE THREE-FOLD ZIONIST LEGACY
OF RABBI YEHUDAH HALEVI

Rabbi Yehudah Halevi[1] is most representative of the Jewish Golden Age in Spain and its glorious legacy. He was a rabbi, a theologian, a successful physician, and an enormously popular secular and religious poet. As stated above, his verse represents the zenith of Hebrew poetry in Spain, and he is generally considered the greatest of all post-biblical Hebrew poets, truly *ne'im zemirot yisrael*—"the sweet singer of Israel."

In Chapter Five, which deals with medieval Hebrew poetry in Spain, we have seen some of the unique features of Halevi's poetry as well as some of the literary techniques he used, quoting samples exemplifying these features and techniques. We have likewise seen that what makes his poetry unique and famous is, above all, his intense nationalism which is evident in both his poetry and in his philosophical work, the *Kuzari*.[2]

This chapter will focus on Halevi's Zionist legacy. I submit that Halevi's passionate love for the Land of Israel manifested itself in three ways: poetically, ideologically, and pragmatically. First, this chapter will outline briefly each of these aspects of his legacy, and then it will show how they continued to be part of the Sephardic tradition, culminating in massive immigration of Sephardim to Eretz Israel, both leading up to and following the establishment of the State of Israel in 1948.[3]

THE POETIC ASPECT OF HALEVI'S ZIONISM

In his poetry, Halevi sings of his great love for God, the Torah and its commandments, the people of Israel, and the Land of Israel. It is no wonder that his religious poetry became an integral part of the liturgy of both Ashkenazim and Sephardim for all sorts of occasions, and most espe-cially, for the Sephardic liturgy for the High Holidays.[4]

Perhaps it is worth recapitulating several illustrations of what may be termed the great loves of Yehudah Halevi. First and foremost was his great love for the God of Israel; it could be said of him that he was God-intoxicated. He sought and felt the nearness and intimacy of God as few other Jews in history (with the exception of the prophets) ever did. Thus, in his liturgical poem for the Day of Atonement, "Before Thee, O Lord is my Whole Desire" (*Hashem Negdekha Kol Ta'avati*), he proclaims,

> Lord, all my longing is before You,
> And though it does not pass my lips.
> Grant me Your favor for even a moment, and I will die.
> If only You would grant my wish.

In the same *bakkashah* (supplication), he continues:

> When I am far from You my life is death;
> But if I cling to You my death is life.

> * * * * *

> Does time hold anything for me beyond Your favor?
> And if You are not my lot, what other lot do I have?[5]

Love of God is a motif that runs throughout his religious poetry. Thus, in the poem "Lord, Where Shall I Find You?" (*Yah Ana Emtza'akha*), he states,

> I have sought to come near You, I have
> Called to You with all my heart;
> And when I went out towards You,
> I found You coming towards me.[6]

Similarly, the last line of the poem "The Servant of God" (*Mi Yiteneni Eved Elo'ah 'Oseni*) reads,

> If only I could be the servant of God who made me.
> My friends could all desert me, if He would but befriend me.[7]

Halevi's love for the Torah and its commandments was as consuming a passion. Perhaps no other poem exemplifies this love for both as does his delightful poem for the Sabbath, "To Love of Thee I Drink my Cup . . ." ('*Al Ahavatekh Eshteh Gevi'i, Shalom lakh Shalom Yom Ha-Shevi'i*), which is very popular among most Sephardim. Here are several stanzas from it:

> To love of thee I drink my cup:
> Peace to thee, peace, O Seventh Day!
>
> Six days of work are like thy slaves.
> While toiling through them, full of restlessness,
> All of them seem to me but a few days,
> For the love I have of thee, O day of my delight!
>
> I go forth on the first day to do my work,
> To set in order the next Sabbath day's array;
> For God hath placed the blessing there:
> Thou alone art my portion for all my toil.

* * * * *

> How sweet to me the time between the lights
> To see the face of the Sabbath with mien renewed!
> O, come with apples, bring ye many raisin cakes—
> This is the Day of my rest, this my love, my friend.
>
> I will sing to thee, O Sabbath, songs of love:
> So it befitteth thee, for thou art a day of enjoyments,
> A day of pleasure, yea, of banquets three,
> Pleasure at my table, pleasure of my couch.
>
> Thou hast bestowed great splendor on the Sabbath
> Through the bond of peace and life.
> And Thou hast sanctified it, that it may distinguish
> Between Israel and other nations.
>
> Who utter mere empty words
> When they would compare their days with my holy day—

Edom later on the first day—and Arabia earlier on the sixth—
Can the deceit of Ishmael and Edom mislead the men of truth?
They compare dross with jewels,
The dead with the living.[8]

Halevi also had a boundless love for his people, the people of Israel. His concern for their suffering is the dominant theme of many of his poems. Indeed, the very titles of some poems such as "Zion Complains to God" (*Yedidi ha-Shakhahta*), and "Save My People" (*Ya'avor 'Alay Retzonekha*) are indicative of this concern. In these and similar poems, Halevi not only aches for the suffering of his people, but also pleads with God for their redemption. Indeed, at times he not only pleads, but demands of God an end to their sufferings. The poem "Zion Complains to God" concludes with one of his most moving lines: "There is no savior but You; no prisoner of hope but I."[9] The poem "Save My People" concludes,

You who dwells on cherubs' wings, outstretched above the ark,
Arise, look down from Your dwelling.
Save my people, my Redeemer.

Similarly, the poem, "The Servant of God" (quoted above) concludes with the bold demand:

Do not delay Your healing power in the days of my sickness.
Answer, my God. Do not chastise. Do not withhold reply.
Employ me again as Your servant. Say: Here am I.

And while the overall tone of this poem is personal, it seems that in the last two lines, Halevi is speaking on behalf of his people.[10]

These lines show Halevi's boundless love for God, for the Torah and its Commandments, and for the People of Israel. But he is most famous for his Zionistic poems in which he expresses his love for Eretz Israel—the land of his dreams. His many beautiful and moving poems on Zion, Jerusalem, and the Temple include these: "My Heart is in The East" (*Libbi ba-Mizrah*); "Jerusalem" (*Yefeh Nof Mesos Tevel* . . . —Beautiful Heights, Joy of the World, City of a Great King); "Mount Avarim" (*Shalom Lekha Har Ha-Avarim*); and of course his immortal "Ode to Zion" (*Zion ha-lo Tish'ali*). These and other similar poems are permeated with a passionate love for Eretz Israel and a consuming yearning for the restoration and re-demption of the Jewish People.[11]

THE IDEOLOGICAL ASPECT OF HALEVI'S ZIONISM

Halevi's intense nationalism (or Zionism), however, was not lim-ited to his poetic outpourings, and it was not merely romantic sentimental-ism. Rather, it had philosophical and pragmatic dimensions as well. At the end of his philosophical work, the *Kuzari*, his love for Zion is given a philo-sophical formulation. Simply stated, his position was that the Jews can-not—must not—sit idly by in exile while waiting for the Messiah. The Messiah will come, he maintained, only when the Jews take the first steps in his direction. If the Messiah did not come to the Jews, then let the Jews go to the Messiah. Interestingly, he found support for this revolutionary idea in these biblical verses:

Thou surely will arise and take pity on Zion,
For it is time to be gracious to her; the appointed time has come.
For Thy servants love her stones and pity her dust (Ps. 102:14–15).

This means, he maintained, that "Jerusalem can only be rebuilt when Israel yearns for it to such an extent that we sympathize even with its stones and dust."[12]

Halevi's nationalistic ideology was no doubt influenced if not de-termined by contemporary circumstances. He was born and grew up in the difficult times toward the end of the Golden Age and the beginning of the Christian Reconquista of Spain from the Arabs. These were times of intense conflict between Muslims and Christians both in Spain and in the Holy Land, with the Jews feeling somehow trapped in the middle. As certain cities (Toledo, Cordova) changed hands, the Jews, and Halevi among them, felt like a pawn in this game. Indeed, Halevi himself commutes, as it were, between Muslim and Christian Spain. Thus, he complains often in his po-etry of being caught between "Edom and Arab" or "Edom and Ishma'el," which is to say, Eretz Israel under Crusader rule (even as northern Spain was under Christian rule) and Andalusia under Muslim rule.[13]

This situation often left Spanish Jewry in a very precarious posi-tion. It is against this historical background that Halevi's intense national-ism must be understood.[14] He became ever more convinced that Jews faced imminent disaster and that they had to do something to avoid it. He believed that their redemption would be accomplished only by their return to the Land of Israel. He was thus the first "active Zionist" anticipating Theodor Herzl by almost eight centuries.[15] It is truly amazing how contemporary all this sounds. Indeed, his position is the linchpin of modern Zionist ideology as reformulated by Rabbis Yehudah Alkalai of Sarajevo, and Zvi Hirsch Kalisher of Prussia, both considered precursors of Herzl.[16]

THE PRAGMATIC ASPECT OF HALEVI'S ZIONISM

As stated above, Halevi's nationalism was not only poetic or even philosophical, but pragmatic as well. In addition to being a poet, a theologian, and a physician, he was also a man of action—that is, one who lived by his own convictions. So, acting on his nationalistic feelings, and no doubt wishing to set an example for his contemporaries, he decided to leave Spain for the Holy Land. As was expected, his contemporaries were stunned by his decision; they pleaded with him not to take his Zionist ideology that seriously, but to no avail. In 1140, to the dismay of his family and friends, he left Spain, abandoning his family, his lucrative medical practice, and many friends and admirers as he set out for the Land of Israel—the land of his dreams.

After a stormy journey which he describes in a series of stirring sea poems, his ship arrived at Alexandria.[17] Everywhere he went in Egypt, he was received with great honors—his good name having preceded him. Egyptian communal and rabbinic leaders pleaded with him to stay and become their spiritual leader, claiming that Egypt was as important as Eretz Israel as the first prophecy as well as great miracles had taken place there.[18] Friends tried to dissuade him from proceeding with the trip, pointing out the danger and grave risks it entailed. Halevi's answer was: "How can Egypt hold me when all my thoughts and desires are woven around Mount Zion?"

Finally, he boarded a ship in Alexandria bound for the Holy Land, but its departure was delayed by inclement weather. What ultimately happened to him is unknown. Some believe that he died in Egypt and was buried there.[19] Israel Zinberg conjectures on the basis of statements made by Halevi's pupil, the scholar Solomon Farhoun, that Halevi returned to Spain where he died shortly thereafter.[20] However, the end of his journey is still shrouded in a beautiful legend befitting his poetic genius and his consuming love for Eretz Israel. It holds that Halevi managed to reach Jerusalem, but as he knelt down kissing its stones, a passing Arab horseman trampled him just as he was reciting his "Ode to Zion" (*Zion ha-lo Tish'ali*), and he fell dead on the spot with his "Ode" on his lips.[21]

This in brief is the three-fold legacy of Halevi's nationalism or Zionism, the poetic, the ideological or philosophical, and the pragmatic. It is my contention that the Sephardim were inspired by all three aspects of this legacy, which continues to be a very important component of Sephardic culture and tradition.

THE IDEOLOGICAL LEGACY OF HALEVI'S ZIONISM AMONG SEPHARDIM

Related to the ideological aspect of Halevi's Zionism is the halakhic attitude of Sephardim toward residence in the Land of Israel during the time of exile. One of the central questions discussed in Jewish law with regard to this issue is whether or not residence in Eretz Israel is a continuous obligation (*mitzvah*) incumbent on the individual Jew for all generations. A secondary question is, assuming that it is a continuous obligation, can it be overridden by the fear of danger involved in travel (*sakkanat derakhim*)—whatever the nature of the danger. In order to follow the sometimes entangled arguments and discussions, it is useful to review briefly the halakhic background of this question.

The Mishnah in *Ketubboth* states, "All may be compelled to go up to the Land of Israel but none may be compelled to leave it." A *baraita* cited in the same Talmudic passage spells out this rule in more detail: "If [the husband] desires to go up [to the Land of Israel] and his wife refuses to go up, she is to be compelled to go up; and if she still does not consent, she may be divorced without payment of the *ketubbah* (the marriage contract). Conversely, if she [the wife] desires to go up to the Land of Israel and the husband refuses to go up, he may be compelled to go up, and if he does not consent, he is forced to divorce and pay *ketubbah*"(Ket. 110b).

So far, the Talmudic rule is clear and succinct. The matter is complicated, however, by the Tosafot, who state that this rule was not in force in their day for two reasons: the danger of travel and the opinion of Rabbi Haim ben Hananel ha-Cohen (one of the Tosafists—Franco-German scholars of the eleventh and twelfth centuries) who maintained that residence in Eretz Israel was not obligatory in his day. His reason is that residence in Eretz Israel entails the obligation to fulfill numerous commandments which depend on the land (*mitzvoth ha-teluyot ba-'aretz*), which, during the many centuries have fallen into disuse, a fact which renders the commandments' careful observance very unlikely.

The statement of the Tosafot is somewhat problematic, capable of two interpretations, and too complex to be dealt with here. The point to be emphasized, however, is that subsequent Sephardic tradition ignored the opinion of the Tosafot and continued to maintain that residence in Eretz Israel is a continuous obligation for all generations.

For example, Nachmanides (1195–1270) maintains that the obligation to settle in Eretz Israel is a positive biblical commandment, and therefore constitutes a continuing obligation for all generations. Thus, in his commentary on the verse, "You shall inherit the land and you shall dwell therein (Num. 33:52)," he writes, "In my opinion, this is a positive commandment. [God] commands them to dwell in the land and to inherit it for He has given it to them and [commanded them] not to disdain the inheritance of God. And should it occur to them to go and conquer the land of Shin'ar or the land of Assyria or any other [land] and settle therein, they would [thereby] transgress the commandment of God. . . . This verse constitutes a positive commandment and [God] reiterates it in many places."

In his commentary on Maimonides' *Sefer ha-Mitzvot* (The Book of the Commandments), Nachmanides adds, "This is a positive commandment incumbent upon each of us even during the period of exile." It is worth noting that, like Yehudah Halevi, Nachmanides acted on his convictions and left Spain for Eretz Israel where he spent the rest of his life, dying there in 1270.

Similarly, Rabbi Joseph Caro, the author of the *Shulhan Arukh* also ignores the opinion of the Tosafot and rules that residence in the Land of Israel is a continuous obligation. Thus, in his code (*Even ha'Ezer*, 75:4), he essentially repeats the Talmudic rule that either spouse may compel the other to go up to Eretz Israel, and that if the husband refuses to go up, he is forced to divorce and pay the *ketubbah*, and should the wife refuse to go up, she forfeits her right to the *ketubbah*. Likewise, in *Yoreh De'ah* (267:82), Rabbi Caro rules, "If a resident of the Land of Israel sells his slave to someone residing in the Diaspora, the slave is to be freed by the new master who loses his money." According to this ruling, one may not force even a slave to leave Eretz Israel for the Diaspora. As is well known, Rabbi Joseph Caro, was another Spanish Jew who had left Spain with his family in 1492, and who, after his family's wandering through several way stations—Constantinople, Salonika, and Egypt—settled in Safed where he ultimately headed the *bet din* there. (See chap. 6, n. 56)

Finally, in my research on Moroccan Jewry's relations with Eretz Israel, I examined a number of responsa and several entries in commentaries on the *Shulhan Arukh*. These texts emanate from different periods and different cities in Morocco and were authored by eminent jurist-decisors (*poskim*), all recognized as undisputed legal authorities of their times. These texts deal with various issues revolving around emigration to Eretz Israel. Here are some examples:

- Can a man compel his wife against her will to accompany him to Eretz Israel?

- In the event that she refuses to join her husband and he divorces her, must he pay the *ketubbah*, or does she forfeit her right to it?

- When, following a divorce, the mother retains custody of minor children, can a father intending to make aliyah take the children with him?

- When a man makes a vow to go up to Eretz Israel and is then unable to do so, may his vow be annulled retroactively as is the case with ordinary vows?

These texts and the rabbinic decisions they portray are most revealing. They show, for example, that emigration to Eretz Israel was continuous; it really never stopped. People made aliyah at all periods (from the end of the sixteenth century through the twentieth century), and they took it very seriously to the point of selling their homes and liquidating their businesses in preparation for aliyah.

In general, the tenor of most of these rabbis' decisions is that residence in Eretz Israel (even in their time) is a great mitzvah, and an important obligation. Some of the decisors do not refer to "the danger of travel"; others bring up the argument of *sakkanat derakhim* only to dismiss it on the ground that the performance of the mitzvah of aliyah will provide protection against any chance of danger. This is based on the Talmudic principles: "No harm befalls those engaged in the fulfillment of a mitzvah" (*shomer mitzvah lo yeda' davar ra'*), and "He who is involved in the observance of a mitzvah will know no evil" (*Sheluhe mitzvah einan nizokin*).

The bias of these decisors and commentators in favor of Eretz Israel is evident not only from their decisions, but also from the very language and the choice of biblical and rabbinic expressions and statements in which they couch their legal decisions. These expressions and formulations reveal a strong attachment to Eretz Israel transcending the legal parameters of the particular issues discussed. While it is impractical to quote all or most of these texts, the following three brief examples will serve as good illustrations.[22]

One of the great Moroccan rabbinic authorities, Rabbi Raphael Berdugo of Meknes (1742–1829), discusses aliyah in connection with the laws governing the sale of a Torah scroll (*Sefer Torah*). Commenting on Caro's rule that one may not sell a Torah scroll except in order to fulfill the commandment of studying Torah (*Talmud Torah*), Rabbi Berdugo reports that people have been permitting the sale of a Torah scroll in order to go to Eretz Israel (that is, to defray the cost of the journey), "for aliyah is the equivalent of the study of Torah," he explains.[23]

Another Moroccan rabbi who treats the issue of emigration to the Land of Israel is Rabbi Joseph Toledano (d. 1788), a rabbinic scholar of Meknes. He discusses residence in Eretz Israel in connection with Rabbi Caro's rule that "if a person makes a vow to go up to Eretz Israel (and is then unable to go), the vow may be annulled retroactively, just as in the case of ordinary vows" (*Yoreh De'ah*, 228:36). Rabbi Toledano's discussion of Caro's rule is rather complicated, and too lengthy to quote here. However, he concludes his discussion of the issue with a very passionate personal prayer, which reveals his attitude toward residence in the Land of Israel. It reads, "And God (only) knows that were it possible for me to go, even alone, I would travel day and night with neither rest nor repose until I reach the land of tranquility and inheritance. Grant my wish, O, God (while I am) in this world, for the sake of Thy great and Holy Name. Amen."[24]

The final example is a responsum by another Moroccan decisor from Meknes, Rabbi Ya'akov ben Yekutiel Berdugo (1783–1843). In a case of a divorced couple where the wife has custody of their two three-year-old daughters, and the father wants to take them with him to Eretz Israel, Rabbi Berdugo rules for the husband for a number of considerations. This is a very lengthy responsum, and Rabbi Berdugo offers many halakhic arguments in support of his ruling. But his most decisive argument, and the one he presents most forcefully, is that a mother's right to custody of minor children was bestowed on her by our sages for the benefit of the children on the assumption that they will be happier in their mother's company (*de-betzavta de-imam niha leho*). But Rabbi Berdugo argues that the merit (*zekhut*) and privilege of residing in the Land of Israel serves the children's welfare far better than staying with their mother. He states, "For it is a great merit for them (*zekhut gedolah*) to go to the Holy Land and strike roots (literally, pitch a tent, build a home) in a secure place and in the company of their father who will bring them up, educate them, and eventually find them a spouse, 'like an eagle who rouses his nestlings, gliding down to protect his young,' and he will have a compassion for them 'as a father has compassion for his children.'"[25]

But beyond the Sephardic halakhic attitude toward residence in Eretz Israel, Halevi's "active Zionism"—that is, the notion that the Jews cannot wait passively for the miraculous coming of the Messiah (articulated in his *Kuzari*)—was picked up later by numerous Sephardic activists, most notably by Don Yosef Nasi who attempted to renew the Jewish settlement in Tiberias during the latter half of the sixteenth century, and Rabbi Hayim Abulafia who actually succeeded in renewing the Jewish settlement there in 1740, ushering in a worldwide wave of immigration to Tiberias. Finally, "active Zionism" was given its fullest expression by Rabbi Yehudah Alkalai of Sarajevo, who is rightly regarded as the precursor of Theodore Herzl. As early as 1834, Rabbi Alkalai published a Hebrew booklet, *Shema Israel*, in which he advocated the creation of Jewish colonies in the Land of Israel as a precondition to redemption. This became a dominant theme throughout his writings, especially after the "blood libel" of Damascus in 1840.

In his first book *Darkhei No'am* (Pleasant Ways), a Ladino-Hebrew textbook published in 1839, he gave the concept of *teshuvah* (according to the Talmud, a precondition for redemption) a Zionistic twist, distinguishing between *teshuvah peratit* (personal return) which means repentance in the traditional sense, and *teshuvah kelalit* (general return) which he interpreted to mean a return of all Israel to the Land of Israel. This approach is the foundation of his preaching for a return to Zion within the traditional religious framework. Actually, as a young man, Rabbi Alkalai was introduced to the concept of Jewish nationalism by the rabbi of Corfu, Rabbi Yehudah Bibas, one of the originators of *Hibbat Zion* and settlement in the Land of Israel. Rabbi Alkalai was to develop this idea further in his writings.[26]

Rabbi Alkalai, like Halevi before him, became more and more convinced that Jews must do something about their own precarious situation by returning to the Land of Israel, rather than waiting passively for the coming of the Messiah. Throughout his writings in both Hebrew and Ladino, Rabbi Alkalai continued to maintain that redemption is primarily in the hands of man himself, that is, the people of Israel. Miraculous redemption, he believed, can only come at a later stage.[27]

Actually, his position is a modern reformulation of that of Halevi seven centuries earlier. But Alkalai went much further. His writings provide specific and pragmatic suggestions. He actually formulated a full program of action including the establishment of agricultural colonies and an industrial infrastructure, a mode of self-rule, a world Jewish assembly (anticipating Herzl's Zionist Congress), methods of raising funds from Jews of the Diaspora, the securing of international political support, and the revitalization of the Hebrew language. In short, Rabbi Alkalai worked out a real "blueprint" for political Zionism as it was later outlined by Herzl in his book, *The Jewish State*. Indeed, one must agree with Rabbi Marc Angel's assessment that Rabbi Alkalai's advocacy of active Jewish participation in their own redemption in their own land was "a historic innovation of the first magnitude."[28]

And while we cannot establish any direct link between the ideas of Alkalai and those of Herzl, it is not altogether improbable that Herzl might have been directly or indirectly influenced by the Zionist thought of Rabbi Alkalai. The parallels and similarities between Herzl's program and Alkalai's are too numerous to be accidental or coincidental. Interestingly, Herzl's grandfather, Simon Loeb Herzl was a disciple and a great admirer of Rabbi Alkalai. As if to return the favor, one of Rabbi Alkalai's granddaughters was among the delegates to the First Zionist Congress. In a memoir that appeared in 1922 (in honor of the twenty-fifth anniversary of the Congress) she wrote, "I thought about my grandfather, Rabbi Yehudah Hai Alkalai, who spent his life preaching the return to the Land of Israel. And I remembered my grandmother, his wife, who, in joyous dedication, had sold her jewels to enable my grandfather to publish his books in which he broadcast his idea of the return to the Land of Israel."[29]

To conclude this section, it is worth noting that the late Israeli Hebrew novelist and short-story writer, Yehudah Burla, himself a Sephardi from Izmir, Turkey, toward the end of his life wrote three historical novels revolving around Rabbi Yehudah Halevi and Rabbi Yehudah Alkalai, as if to underscore the connection between the two precursors of modern Zionism. The novel about Halevi, *Ellei Mas'ei Yehudah Halevi* (These Are the

Travels of Yehudah Halevi)—published in Tel Aviv, 1959—describes Halevi's journey to Eretz Israel. The other two novels, *Ma'avak* (Struggle, two volumes; Tel Aviv, 1946) and *Kissufim* (Yearnings; Tel Aviv, 1955) deal with Rabbi Alkalai's dedicated preaching for the redemption and return to Eretz Israel.[30]

POETIC LEGACY OF HALEVI'S ZIONISM AMONG THE SEPHARDIM

As stated in chapter one, following their expulsion from Spain, the Spanish exiles cherished the rich and diversified legacy of the Golden Age in Spain and carried it wherever they went. They preserved it, amplified it, and continued to create in its spirit. The poetic legacy of Andalusian Jewry was preserved and enriched by many Sephardim. Thus, for example, Syrian and Moroccan *paytanim* or scholar-poets composed *piyyutim* and *pizmonim* for all occasions in both Hebrew and Arabic.

While the general content of these poems is religious, within the religious framework, their dominant themes are the love of Eretz Israel, the yearning for the coming of the Messiah, and the ingathering of exiles on the one hand, and lamentations (*kinot*) for the destruction of the Temple and the Jewish suffering in exile on the other. In fact, these themes constitute a major section of every collection or anthology of Sephardic *piyyutim*.

One of the most illustrious and popular poets of Moroccan Jewry is Rabbi David ben Hassin of Meknes (1727–92). His *piyyutim* are highly representative of the poetic creativity of Moroccan Jewry of which he is unquestionably the most outstanding *paytan*. His *piyyutim* were first published in Amsterdam in 1807 in a collection entitled *Tehilah Le-David* (Praise of David), which was republished in Casablanca in 1930, and again in Israel in 1973.[31] One section of *Tehilah Le-David* (in the original arrangement of the 1807, 1930, and 1973 editions) is called *Zimrat ha-Aretz* (Songs of the Land of Israel) comprised of poems in praise of the Land of Israel. Another section is called *Ahavat David* (Love of David); it includes poems about the Messiah, Elijah the Prophet, and redemption. A third section contains *kinot* in which the poet laments the destruction of the Temple and the ensuing exile, and prays for the ultimate end of exile and its unbearable suffering. It is worth noting that the *piyyutim* of Rabbi Ben Hassin gained widespread acceptance and popularity even during his lifetime throughout Morocco and North Africa. There was no festive event or celebration, whether religious, social, or familial, that was not crowned by the singing of his *piyyutim*.

Another illustrious Moroccan *paytan* is Rabbi Jacob Aben-Tzur (1673–1753) of Fez, one of the most celebrated halakhic authorities of his time, known popularly by his acronym, Ya'betz. His *piyyutim* were published in Alexandria, Egypt in 1893 in a collection entitled *'Et le-Khol Hefetz* (Poems for All Occasions). It includes four hundred of his *piyyutim*, *kinot*, and *bakkashot*. His poetry reveals the extent to which he ached for the suffering of the Jewish people in exile as well as his yearning for their redemption. In many of his poems, he laments the destruction of the Temple as well. All his *piyyutim* express his fervent hope and prayer for the return of the Jewish people to Zion and the redemption of Eretz Israel. Indeed, according to Binyamin Bar Tikvah, an authority on Rabbi Aben-Tzur's poetry, a distinct characteristic of his poems is that every one of them concludes with a prayer for redemption.[32]

Likewise, a Syrian rabbi and mystic, Rabbi Israel ben Moses Najara (1555–c.1625) wrote numerous poems full of yearnings for redemption and love of Eretz Israel. He was born in Damascus and died in Gaza. In 1587, he published his books *Zemirot Israel* and *Mesaheket Ba-Tevel* in Safed. The enlarged edition of *Zemirot Israel* (Venice, 1599–1600) includes 346 poems. His other works include *Pizmonim* (1558) containing 129 poems, and *She'erit Israel*, a large collection of poems.

In his youth, he wrote secular love poems (as did all the Hebrew poets in Spain), but his chief compositions are sacred. They are distinguished by their deep religiosity, by their references to Jewish sufferings, and by his yearning for redemption. His *piyyutim* achieved wide circulation among North African and Near Eastern Sephardim, and are sung in their synagogues. Well known is his *Ketubbah le-Hag ha-Shavu'ot* (Marriage Contract for Shavuot). It is a beautiful and charming poem written in the style and with all the details of a real marriage contract, describing the symbolic marriage between God and the people of Israel. It is read in many Sephardic communities on Shavuot before the Torah is taken from the ark.[33] His popular Sabbath song, *Yah Ribon 'Alam ve-'Almaya* (God of the World, Eternity's Sole Lord), was adopted by Ashkenazic communities as well.

Rabbi Najara's poetry was influenced by the Hebrew poetry of the Golden Age in both content and form. Some of the common themes in his poetry are exile, hatred of the oppressors, and yearning for redemption. According to Aaron Mirsky, the poetry of Najara and that of Yehudah Halevi have in common their preoccupation with matters relating to the people of Israel.[34] Najara, however, also employed original forms. He was the innovator of a new genre of *piyyutim* designed to be sung to Spanish, Andalusian, and Arabic music. In composing such *piyyutim*, the poet selects a melody (*lahan*) of a well-known song, and uses its style and structure as a model for his Hebrew poem.[35]

Finally, Rabbi Shalem ben Yoseph al-Shabazi, the greatest of Yemenite poets (born in 1635, he died near the end of the seventeenth century) wrote a voluminous amount of poetry. About half the poems in the Yemenite *diwan* (collection of poems, published in many editions) are his. Living in a period of persecutions of Yemenite Jewry, Shabazi gave faithful expression to the sufferings and messianic yearning of his generation. His poetry treats primarily the religious themes of exile and redemption, the Jewish people and God, wisdom and ethics, Torah and the life to come. Many of his poems deal with the glorious past of the Jews in their own land, from which the poet draws faith and hope for renewed greatness in the future. His style is simple, making his poetry readily accessible to the masses. Not surprisingly, his poems are accorded a place of honor in Yemenite synagogues in the liturgy of the holy days and family celebrations.[36]

Some of these *piyyutim* gained widespread acceptance in most of the Sephardic world, east and west. Thus, poems of Rabbi Israel Najara were chanted in Morocco and elsewhere, and Moroccan *piyyutim* were published in Amsterdam and Alexandria. For example, the poems of Najara were very popular among Moroccan Jews. Moroccan *paytanim* were greatly influenced by their mystical and nationalistic content as well as by their poetic style.[37] One of his most popular poems, *Yadekha Tanheni . . .* (Let Your Hand Direct me, O Lord My Maker), was sung by Moroccan Jews almost on all occasions, but especially on the last day of Passover and on Shavu'ot, both in the synagogues and in their homes. Its dominant theme is the yearning for the coming of the Messiah, and each of its six stanzas concludes with the word *ben Yishay* (the son of Jesse—referring of course to the Messiah, a descendant of David). Both its lyrics and the various tunes to which it was sung evoke deep nationalistic feelings.

Similarly, two popular Zionist poems of Rabbi David ben Hassin, *Ohil Yom Yom Eshta'eh*, glorifying the newly rebuilt Tiberias,[38] and *E'erokh Mahalal Nivi*, a poem dedicated to the Prophet Elijah which was sung usually during the *havdalah* ceremony and during the circumcision ceremony, were both spread throughout the Sephardic world by itinerant rabbis and emissaries from Eretz Israel who visited Morocco fairly regularly.[39] These and other Syrian and Moroccan *piyyutim* appear in a considerable number of anthologies of the poetry and rituals of most Sephardic communities.

One of the most significant aspects of this poetry is its popular and folkish nature. Sephardi rabbis and laymen alike composed *piyyutim* for every occasion in a very lucid and simple Hebrew, and often in the local Arabic dialects as well. Moreover, these *piyyutim* were chanted both in the synagogue and in the homes on holy days and at family celebrations to classical and contemporary Andalusian, Spanish, and Arabic music, a fact which made them and their melodies very popular. Some of the techniques used by the *paytanim* were ingenious. For example, a poet writing Hebrew lyrics for a popular Arabic or Andalusian melody would select his Hebrew words so cleverly as to have them sound exactly like the original Arabic lyrics. This usually enhances and even insures the widespread popularity of the Hebrew poem. All this means that these *piyyutim* were not intended exclusively for the intellectual and scholarly elite. Rather, they were written to be sung and enjoyed by everyone and on all possible occasions. Why is this important? It's important because it is this popular aspect of the *piyyutim* which led to the pragmatic aspect of Sephardic Zionism. This brings us to the pragmatic legacy of Halevi's Zionism.

THE PRAGMATIC LEGACY OF HALEVI'S ZIONISM AMONG SEPHARDIM

The *piyyutim* served to spread and intensify the Zionist feelings among the Sephardim. Because of their popular character, they reached scholars and laymen alike. In a sense, these Zionist *piyyutim* served the same purpose and achieved the same results as the Zionist press and leaflets did in the West. That is, they kept the attachment to Eretz Israel and the messianic yearnings at the forefront of the Sephardic religious consciousness. As a result, when the shofar of modern Zionism was heard in Islamic lands, the Sephardim were ready and eager to respond en masse. And while the mass immigration of these Sephardim to Israel after 1948 may have been partly motivated by other factors (such as the insecurity they must have felt in Arab lands in the wake of Israel's victory in the war of independence or fear of a possible change in their legal and economic status that might follow the gaining of independence by some Arab states), there is no doubt that the chief catalyst which sped their emigration was their religious nationalism, always at a high pitch as a result of the *piyyutim* and other religious literature.

I still remember the joyous mood that gripped the Jews in the *mellahs* (Jewish quarters) throughout Morocco the Saturday Israel was declared a state in May 1948. Fortunately for the Jews then, the French were still in Morocco, and the *mellahs* were well protected, so that the Jews had no reason to fear an adverse Arab reaction. A kind of a messianic fervor seized everyone. There were celebrations everywhere. In the synagogues, a festive atmosphere filled the air. There was singing and there was dancing with the Torah as on *Simhat Torah*. In the homes, the mood was Purimlike: eating, drinking, embracing each other and singing. In the streets, the youth of new Zionist movements, Bnei Akiva, Habonim, and others, danced the hora. Most of the songs sung in the synagogues, in the homes, and in the streets were *piyyutim* of Rabbi Ben Hassin and Rabbi Najara, among others, about the Messiah, redemption, and Eretz Israel. In short, the mood was electrifying. Immigration to Israel—aliyah—was on everyone's mind. The awaited moment had come.

But Sephardic immigration to Israel did not begin with the establishment of the state of Israel, for it pre-dated it. Indeed, it was the Spanish exiles who, in the fifteenth and sixteenth centuries, reestablished a significant presence in Eretz Israel by settling in Safed and its surrounding villages. Similarly, according to Rabbi Jacob Moshe Toledano, a group of mystics (*mekubbalim*) from southern Morocco immigrated to Safed in 1577, joining other Moroccan rabbis who were studying Qabbalah under the famous mystic master Rabbi Isaac Luria—known popularly as the Ari. In the middle of the sixteenth century, Dona Gracia Mendes and her nephew, Don Yosef Nasi, the statesman and leader, attempted to rebuild Tiberias and renew its Jewish settlement. Their attempt met with initial success. The rebuilt city began attracting Jewish settlers from Safed and from the Diaspora. However, their success was short-lived, and by the time of Don Yosef's death, Tiberias was again in decline.

Its Jewish settlement was once again renewed in 1740, however, by Rabbi Hayim Abulafia. The Turkish governor of the region at the time, Zahir al-Omar, who had extended his rule over the Galilee, invited Jews of Turkey and especially Rabbi Abulafia to come and settle in Tiberias. Rabbi Abulafia accepted this invitation and arrived in the city in 1740. Seizing this historic opportunity, he immediately and energetically set about renewing the city's Jewish settlement. In a relatively short time, he managed to build houses, a synagogue, and even a bathhouse. He apparently saw in this the beginning of the "ingathering of exiles" (*kibbutz galuyot*) and the resettlement of the Land of Israel as a whole. Rabbi Abulafia's efforts had impressed many Jews in the Diaspora who saw in his initiative "the beginning of redemption" (*athalta de-ge'ullah*).

At about the same time, Rabbi Hayim ben Attar, a Moroccan scholar and mystic, known especially among the Hasidim as the *Or ha-Hayim ha-Kadosh* (the Saintly Or ha-Hayim), impressed by Rabbi Abulafia's success, arrived in Israel with a group of his Moroccan students and established a yeshivah, *Kenesset Israel*, in Jerusalem in 1742.

Meanwhile, Tiberias continued to attract Jews from all over the Diaspora. In particular, it attracted Jews from Morocco for whom the city had a special appeal because of its sanctity and because of the tombs of Rabbi Me'ir Ba'al Ha-Nes and other saintly rabbis buried in and around the city. Many Moroccan rabbis flocked to Tiberias to study Torah in its yeshivot, and the renowned Moroccan *paytan*, R. David ben Hassin expressed Moroccan Jews' affection for Tiberias in his popular *piyyut*, *Ohil Yom Yom Eshta'eh*, glorifying the newly rebuilt Tiberias.[40]

These immigrants were generally pious rabbis and laymen who were motivated by the same religious and nationalistic feelings that had compelled Rabbi Yehudah Halevi to set out on his journey. Moreover, the aliyah of Sephardim continued without interruption up to the establishment of the state of Israel in 1948. Thus, in the nineteenth century, Moroccan Jews immigrated to Tiberias and Jerusalem by the hundreds, so much so that by the end of the nineteenth century, Tiberias was nicknamed "the Little Meknes" (*Meknes ha-ketanah*) because many Jews from Meknes, hundreds of them, settled there. Likewise, it was members of the *maghrebi community* (*ha-'Edah ha-Ma'aravit*) in Jerusalem—Moroccan Jews under the able and inspiring leadership of Rabbi David ben Shim'on, known popularly as *Tzuf devash* (literally, drink of honey, *devash* being an acronym of his Hebrew name)—who were the first to buy land and build homes outside the walls of the Old City.[41]

Commenting on the immigration of Sephardim to Israel before the establishment of the state, Daniel Elazar writes, "Waves of immigrants from the Sephardic communities paralleled every one of the *aliyot* from Eastern Europe. Sephardim from Greece, Yemenites, Bokharans, and Moroccans came in the 1870s and 1880s at the time of the first aliyah. Syrian Jews made up the bulk of the Sephardic migration during the second aliyah. The third aliyah, after World War I, brought a large mixture from every part of the Sephardic Diaspora while the aliyot of the 1930s brought the fruit of modern Zionist education work, particularly from the Balkans and North Africa."[42]

Moreover, Hayim Cohen has shown that between 1919 and 1948, the scale of immigration was especially large from Yemen, Kurdistan, Syria, and Turkey. Thus, approximately one-third of Yemenite and Syrian Jews and one-sixth of Kurdistani and Turkish Jews immigrated to Israel between 1919 and 1948. As Cohen points out, as far as is known, there was no other Jewish community from which such a high percentage emigrated during this same period.[43]

Finally, in addition to reestablishing and maintaining Jewish presence in Eretz Israel, a fact which in a great measure made the realization of the modern Zionist enterprise feasible, the early Sephardic *olim* made another significant contribution, namely, urban pioneering in the Land. As mentioned above, the urban pioneering tradition was begun by the settling of Safed in the fifteenth and sixteenth centuries and the founding of modern Tiberias in the eighteenth century. This tradition was continued by the settlements outside the Old City of Jerusalem by Moroccans and Bokharan Jews in the nineteenth century. According to Elazar, "This Sephardic urban pioneering enterprise was again manifested by the Jews of Salonika who built the port of Haifa in the 1930s."[44] Following the establishment of the state of Israel, this tradition was maintained by the Sephardic majorities in the development towns, where they became the pioneers of the Israeli urban frontier.

CONCLUSION

The above survey shows how, following their expulsion from Spain, the Sephardim have preserved and acted on the Zionistic legacy of Yehudah Halevi in all its ideological, poetic, and pragmatic aspects. This is a telling example of how the Sephardic legacy of the Golden Age in Spain continued to inspire and inform Sephardic culture and tradition after 1492 throughout the Sephardic Diaspora.

9.

THE SPANISH LEGACY AMONG MOROCCAN JEWS

The settlement of Jews in Morocco dates back to Greco-Roman and even Phoenician times. The Jewish presence during the Greco-Roman period (beginning in 150 BCE) is historically attested to by archaeological remains, Jewish tombstones with both Hebrew and Latin inscriptions, and slabs from ancient synagogues. There are various interesting theories as to the origins of this community, some of a purely legendary nature, others more historical.[1]

It is with the beginning of the Islamic period, however, that Moroccan Jewry achieves cultural prominence. Soon after the establishment of Fez in the ninth century, that city became a great center of Jewish learning, attracting to its yeshivot students from Qayrawan, Baghdad, Andalusia, and other parts of the Jewish world. But Fez was not the only center of Jewish life and learning; there were others equally as important: Dar'a, Sijilmasa, and Marrakesh in the south, and later on, Sale, Sefrou, Meknes, and Tetouan in central and northern Morocco. Great yeshivot and centers of kabbalah were to flourish in all these cities.

Beginning with the middle of the twelfth century, however, a curtain of darkness, as it were, descended on all the Jews of North Africa, especially on those of Morocco. The Almohad persecutions that lasted from 1148 to 1276 decimated most Jewish communities in North Africa. These persecutions swept like wildfire across Andalusia and all of North Africa, and left the Moroccan Jewish community spiritually and numerically exhausted.[2] Following the expulsion of the Jews from Spain in 1492, the community in Morocco was infused with new blood, but Moroccan Jewry's contact with Spanish Jewry antedates the arrival of Spanish exiles in Morocco after 1492.

EARLY CONTACTS BETWEEN MOROCCAN AND SPANISH JEWS

During the first two centuries of Islamic rule in Spain, Spanish Jewry continued to depend for its spiritual guidance on the Babylonian yeshivot in Baghdad. It was not until the days of Hasday Ibn Shaprut (915–75) that it began to develop its own culture.[3] In this process, Moroccan Jewry served as a cultural bridge between the great Babylonian centers of Jewish learning and the newly emerging Jewish community in Spain. They were in a very good position to do so. Not only were their rabbis scholars in their own right, but they were also in constant contact with both communities and commanded the respect of both. Indeed, responsa from the Babylonian yeshivot to the Jewish communities of Fez and Sijilmasa address them with the utmost reverence. According to Simha Assaf, no other Jewish community maintained such continuous contact with the Babylonian academies throughout the Geonic period as did those of North Africa who received thousands of responsa from the Babylonian academies for nearly three hundred years. Furthermore, According to Assaf, responsa addressed to Fez and Qayrawan dealt not only with halakhic issues, but with historical, theological, and philosophical matters as well.[4]

Moreover, Morocco even provided the young Jewish community in Spain with its first teachers in Hebrew poetry, philology, and rabbinic learning. From Morocco in the tenth century came the first Hebrew grammarians, linguists, and poets (Rabbi Yehuda Ibn Hayyuj and Dunash Ibn Labrat among others), and the great Talmudist and halakhist, Rabbi Isaac Al-Fasi, known also as the Rab Alfes or the Rif. Ibn Hayyuj's philological discoveries revolutionized the scientific study of Hebrew grammar and lexicography; Ibn Labrat was the first to adapt features and conventions of Arabic prosody to Hebrew, thereby providing future Hebrew poets in Spain with an important tool and models for their poetry; Rabbi Al-Fasi headed the great yeshivah in Lucena. These three individuals may be rightly regarded as the founders of the Spanish school of Jewish learning and science which was to culminate in the Golden Age of Jewish culture and creativity in Spain.[5] Throughout the Golden Age in Spain, Moroccan Jews continued to maintain close cultural and intellectual ties with Spanish Jewry.

MAIMONIDES AND MOROCCAN JEWRY

Maimonides' most important contact with Moroccan Jews was from c.1159 to 1165 when he and his family lived among them. The circumstances of Moroccan Jewry at the time led Maimonides to compose one of his most important epistles, The Epistle on Martyrdom (*Iggeret ha-Shemad*).

In 1148, Cordova fell under the rule of the Almohads who had adopted a policy of forced conversion to Islam. Non-Muslims in Spain, as in Northwest Africa, were given only three choices: conversion to Islam, emigration, or death. Apparently, Maimonides' family chose emigration. From 1148 to 1159 they wandered from place to place in Spain, and in 1159, emigrated to settle in Fez where they stayed until 1165.[6]

At this junction, many Moroccan Jews had chosen exile, while others found refuge in outlying areas among friendly Berber tribes. Many, however, were forced to live a double life as crypto-Jews (*anusim*)—professing Islam in public while adhering to Jewish practices in private. But this double life proved to be too dangerous and too troubling to the conscience. They were experiencing something of a religious crisis. Their predicament prompted Rabbi Maimon (Maimonides' father) to write his *Iggeret ha-Nehamah* (Letter of Consolation) assuring them that he who says his prayers even in their shortest form and who does good works remains a Jew. In conclusion, he urged them "to cling to our holy teachings as steadfastly as a drowning person clings to a lifeline that is thrown out to save him."[7]

Meanwhile, one of the forced converts in Fez inquired from a foreign rabbi whether he could gain merit by observing secretly as many commandments of Judaism as he could. The rabbi responded with a halakhic ruling that any Jew who had made a profession of Islam could no longer be regarded as a Jew, but only as an idol-worshiper and a renegade, and that he would be committing an additional sin with each commandment of Judaism that he performed. The only course of action he recommended was to accept martyrdom, for a Jew must hold religion more precious than life.

The impact of this response on the community of Fez was disastrous. Many felt that they were "damned if they did and damned if they didn't" and even considered giving up Judaism altogether, while loyal Jews were overwhelmed by feelings of guilt and dismay. Horrified by the ruling, Maimonides composed The Epistle on Martyrdom to refute the rabbi's ruling and to offer the forced converts some sounder advice.[8]

The Epistle is full of love and compassion for the Jews of Fez; his heart aches for the suffering of his people. Maimonides' tone is angry. He is furious at the rabbi whom he attacks personally, which is rather unusual for him. The Epistle is divided into four chapters; it is well structured, and his attack on the rabbi is well orchestrated.[9] First he attacks his credibility and competence: the rabbi gives opinions on matters in which he has no competence; he tries to do good and ends up causing endless harm; he talks too much—too much babble; it is easy for him to give his harsh advice as he himself did not experience what the Jews of Fez were experiencing; and finally, with biting sarcasm, Maimonides shows that all the proofs cited by the rabbi in support of his ruling are irrelevant.

Next, Maimonides summons his vast knowledge of the Bible, the Mishnah and the Talmud, and all relevant sources to prove that (a) it is not a sin to disguise oneself in order to avoid death (citing specific instances when great sages did the same in order to save their lives); (b) God reprimands Moses, Elijah, and Isaiah for briefly criticizing Israel (How dare the rabbi then "let his tongue loose against Jewish communities of sages and their disciples, priests, and Levites . . . [calling them] sinners, evildoers, gentiles, disqualified to testify, heretics who deny the Lord God Of Israel?"); and (c) God does not deny reward for a good deed (*mitzvah*) even to the most wicked persons such as King Ahab, and Eglon King of Mo'ab, among others (Why would He not reward the Jews who keep the commandments in private?).

Next, Maimonides goes on to analyze objectively the whole issue of apostasy (*shemad*) and the concept of "desecration of God's name" (*hillul ha-Shem*). It is one of the finest dissertations on the subject. He argues that while it is true that he who does not prefer martyrdom and chooses to confess (Islamic faith—*Shahadah*) has profaned God's name under compulsion, not a single instance is to be found in the Torah in which an individual is punished for profaning God's name under coercion. True, he concedes, it is incumbent on one to surrender to death in sanctification of God's name (*Kiddush ha-Shem*), but if he does not, he is not guilty. How can anyone believe that the law is the same with regard to a person who acted under duress and one who acted voluntarily? This distinction is so clear, he adds, it requires no proof or argument.

Finally, Maimonides draws a clear distinction between the situation of the Jews of Fez and other historical cases of apostasy. This compulsion of the Almohads is different, he asserts, as "it imposes no action [on the part of the convert] only speech.[10] They know very well that we do not mean what we say, and that what we say is only to escape the ruler's punishment and to satisfy him with this simple confession." Maimonides adds that God holds great reward in store for "anyone who suffered martyrdom in order not to acknowledge the apostleship of 'that man' [Muhammad] . . . for he has given his life for the sanctity of God. . . . But if anyone comes to ask me whether to surrender his life or acknowledge, I tell him to confess and not choose death." He then advises people to leave Morocco as soon as it becomes possible to do so; it is foolish, he adds, to wait for the coming of the Messiah to save the situation.[11]

Maimonides concludes his epistle on a hopeful note and a prayer. Noting that we frequently find in the Talmud that persecution is likely to pass, he prays: "May God put an end to this one, and may the prediction be realized. *In those days and in that time—declares the Lord—the iniquity of Israel shall be sought, and there shall be none; the sins of Judah, and none shall be found; for I will pardon those I allow to survive* (Jer. 50:20). May it be His will. Amen."

The reassurance provided by The Epistle on Martyrdom undoubtedly kept many of the Moroccan forced converts from forsaking Judaism altogether. In recent years, Rabbi Haim Soloveitchik criticized Maimonides' position rather harshly as being in outright violation of halakhah. But Rabbi David Hartman defended Maimonides, forcefully adducing many arguments in his defense. One of the compelling arguments offered by Rabbi Hartman is that the epistle was not meant to be a responsum or a halakhic treatise. Rather, Maimonides' overriding concern was to save an entire Jewish community and give them hope to continue to cling to Judaism. Maimonides was convinced that the rule of the Almohads was temporary, and history proved him right. The rule of the Almohads did not last forever. By 1212, their empire was breaking at the seams, breaking into what corresponds to today's Morocco, Tunisia, and Algeria. And by the end of the thirteenth century, it had disintegrated completely.[12] As expected, the fall of the Almohads meant a new lease on life for North African Jews— and Moroccan Jews in particular. Those who had converted under duress returned to Judaism openly, while those who had found refuge among Berber tribes returned to the cities.

Another interesting example of Maimonides' connection with Moroccan Jewry is his acquaintance and close relationship with his illustrious disciple, Joseph ben Yehudah Ibn Shim'on the Maghrebi (*ha-ma'arabi*) to whom Maimonides dedicated his philosophical magnum opus, *The Guide of the Perplexed*. Ibn Shim'on is especially known for the Dedicatory Epistle attached to the *Guide*, which Maimonides addresses to him. Ibn Shim'on was born in Ceuta in northern Morocco where he received his extensive education in both Jewish and secular subjects. His relationship with Maimonides began when both men were in Morocco, Ibn Shim'on in Ceuta and Maimonides in Fez. After leaving Morocco, Maimonides continued to correspond with Ibn Shim'on, who eventually followed him to Cairo where he studied under him.

At some point, Ibn Shim'on left Cairo for Aleppo, and Maimonides continued to instruct him in philosophical matters, sending him one chapter of the *Guide* after another, as soon as he finished composing them. In a sense, *The Guide of the Perplexed* was the result of this "correspondence course" between Maimonides and his Moroccan disciple.[13] Incidentally, from Maimonides' Dedicatory Epistle we learn of his close relation with Ibn Shim'on, the esteem and respect in which he held him, the scope of Ibn Shim'on's education, as well as Maimonides' theory of education, progressing from such sciences as mathematics, astronomy, and logic to the study of metaphysics (speculative divine matters or philosophy).

Morocco is connected with the fortunes of another Joseph ben Yehudah, better known by his surname Ibn Aknin, a colleague of Maimonides.[14] We know almost none of the particulars of his life. He left Spain probably for the same reason Maimonides did, stayed for some time in Ceuta, and then proceeded to Fez where he became a close colleague of Maimonides. In his writings, he mentions Maimonides repeatedly with great respect and deference, but feels free to disagree with him when he finds Maimonides' views unacceptable. Like most Jewish scholars of his days, he probably was a physician by profession. He witnessed the mental distress and social degradation of the forced converts to Islam and described their insecure position during the later stage of the Almohad persecutions. On this basis, Abraham Halkin decides that Ibn Aknin himself was forced to embrace Islam, although it is clear that he and other forced converts continued to study Torah even under these harsh circumstances.

Ibn Aknin was a greater writer and scholar than Ibn Shim'on. He wrote numerous books on various subjects (mostly in Arabic and only some in Hebrew).[15] These works are a testament to the fact that even in the darkest hours for Moroccan Jewry, the study of Torah did not cease among the forced converts.

Thus, a rabbi like Ibn Aknin, forced to pose as a Muslim, continued to study and disseminate Torah even after Maimonides' departure from Morocco. He stayed in Fez after 1165 and even composed a couplet expressing his extreme sadness and loneliness in the wake of Maimonides' departure from Fez, concluding, "My soul left me with his departure."[16]

SPANISH EXILES IN MOROCCO

As stated above, the Almohad persecutions left the Moroccan Jewish community spiritually and numerically exhausted, but following the expulsion of the Jews from Spain and Portugal in 1492 and 1497, it was infused with new blood. Beginning with the summer of 1492, refugees from Spain began to stream to Morocco. Most of them settled in Fez because of its political and commercial importance at the time, as well as the friendly and warm welcome extended to them by Moulay Muhammad al-Shaykh (1472–1505), the first king of Fez of the Wattas dynasty. This favorable attitude toward the Spanish exiles on the part of this king is attested to in a number of Jewish sources and confirmed by an account of a non-Jewish writer, Leon Africanus.[17] As to the number of Spanish exiles who settled in Fez, approximate figures suggested by different sources vary from 10,000 to 20,000.[18]

At any rate, notwithstanding the friendly and kind attitude of the king of Fez, the lot of the Spanish exiles in Fez during the first years (until 1498) was not a happy one. Suffering from a number of calamities— famine, disease, harsh weather conditions such as floods—many of them left Fez, some going to Middle Eastern countries, while others were even compelled to return to Christian Spain. Beginning with 1498, however, their situation began improving markedly both economically and culturally. Thus, the illustrious Rabbi Haim Ganin, native of Fez who had spent some time studying in Spain but returned with the exiles after 1492, writes, "From 1498 onwards, God, may His name be blessed, bestowed on us many blessings so that we were able to build spacious homes full of elaborate decorations; God blessed us also with yeshivot and students [of Torah] , and beautiful synagogues of solid and elegant construction, and Torah scrolls dressed in embroidered silk mantles and crowned with silver Torah finials, so much so that nowadays the fame of the *mellah* has spread throughout all Arab lands [literally, in all the domain of Ishma'el]."[19]

Subsequently, the exiles, known as the *megorashim*, succeeded in consolidating their position and adapting to their new life in Morocco. They established themselves in the major cities of the interior—Fez, Meknes, and Sefrou—as well as in some cities along the seaports. They benefited

Moroccan Jewry both materially and spiritually. They brought with them much commercial and diplomatic talent and expertise, which were mobilized in the service of succeeding rulers of Morocco. But the more important legacy of the *megorashim* was the rich cultural and spiritual heritage they brought with them from Spain, thereby quickening and reinvigorating Moroccan Jewish life and culture.

Immediately after their arrival, these exiles began enacting ordinances, known as *Tekkanot Hakhme Castilya*, to ensure that their communal and religious life in Morocco would continue to be conducted as it had been in Spain. One example of the early *takkanot* is the one requiring a husband to include in the marriage contract (*ketubbah*) a clause barring him from marrying a second wife without the explicit and voluntary permission of the first wife. This ordinance virtually eliminated the practice of bigamy. It achieved for the Sephardim essentially the same result as Rabbenu Gershom's *herem* (ban) on bigamy (which is not binding on Sephardim) had for the Ashkenazim. Moroccan rabbis continued to enact *takkanot* as needed through the centuries, down to the 1950s. These ordinances helped to protect the rights of women and children and promote the stability of the Jewish family—and respond to contemporary economic and social needs.[20]

Initially, the *megorashim* met with some resistance on the part of the indigenous community, known as the *toshabim*, especially in matters of rituals and some religious practices, but eventually, the *megorashim* and their customs and practices (*minhagim*) prevailed throughout Morocco.[21] Until the massive immigration of Moroccan Jews to Israel of the 1960s and 1970s, however, the *toshabim* maintained their own synagogue, known as the Ibn Danan synagogue, and their own prayer book, *Ahavat ha-Kadmonim* (published by Rabbi Raphael ben Shim'on in Jerusalem in 1898). But, as Rabbi Moshe Amar correctly points out, that is not indicative of the existence of a separately organized community of *toshabim*. In fact, the differences in ritual reflected in *Ahavat ha-Kadmonim* relate only to *pizmonim* and *bakkashot* (that is, supplementary liturgical poems), but the core prayers are identical to those of the *megorashim*.[22]

THE SEPHARDIC LEGACY

When the Spanish exiles arrived in Morocco in 1492, they found themselves among people whose culture they considered to be inferior to the one they had left in Spain, for Arab culture in Morocco, as elsewhere in the Arab world, was on the decline at the time. Finding no new or fresh intellectual challenges, the exiles bent their intellectual energies and talents to conserving and preserving the cultural legacy they had brought with them from Spain. They not only preserved and cultivated this heritage zealously, but also did their utmost to amplify it. They continued to develop their own Jewish culture very much in the spirit and within the literary framework and context of the Sephardic tradition.

The attachment of Moroccan Jews to the Sephardic legacy found expression in many ways and on many levels. These included the liberal sprinkling of Spanish words and phrases in their Judeo-Arabic dialect, personal and family names, liturgy for the High Holidays and other special religious occasions, love of Andalusian music, and many customs, rituals, and religious practices. Above all, this legacy manifested itself in Moroccan scholarship and creativity in the fields of halakhic literature, religious poetry in Hebrew and Arabic, critical biblical exegesis, kabbalah, philology, and even historiography.

SPECIFIC EXAMPLES

LANGUAGE

There are a considerable number of Spanish words in Moroccan Judeo-Arabic dialect, some of which are shared by non-Jewish Arabic dialects while others are peculiar to the Judeo-Arabic dialect. Here are some typical examples:

ARABIC DIALECT	SPANISH ORIGIN	ENGLISH
abrigeu	*abrigo*	overcoat
banco	*balcon*	upper apartment; balcony or terrace
bizita	*visita*	visit
blusa	*blusa*	blouse
camiza	*camisa*	shirt
cuchara	*cuchara*	spoon
famelia	*familia*	family
forma	*forma*	form
fruta	*fruta*	fruit
pallebe (or *pallibi*)	*pan leve*	large cookie

sala	*sala*	living room
sobri	*sobre*	envelop
swirti	*suerte*	luck
sotano	*sotano*	basement
tasa	*taza*	cup

NAMES

Jewish names in Morocco—family names and, to a lesser extent, first names—betray definite Spanish origin. They include a considerable number of family names such as Abensur (or Aben-Tzur), Aboab, Albo, Arama, Azulay, Benattar, Benezra, Bengwalid (or Ben-Walid), Benaim, Betito, Berdugo, Bibas, Caro, Corcos, Dabela (or De-Abila), Danon, Deloya, Elmaleh, Elmoznino, Enkawa (or Ankawa), Haliwa (or Halewa), Hatchwell, Laredo, Maimran (or Maymeran), Malka, Marciano (or Murciano), Messas, Monsonego, Moreno, Mrejen (or Moregon), Nahamias, Nahon, Nahor, Pariente, Petito, Pinto, Portal, Sasportas, Sarfati, Serrero, Tapiero, Toledano, and Zamiro. Less common are Spanish first names. They include Leon, Vidal, Victor, Clara, Donna, Gotha, Gracia, Ledicia (or Leticia), Luna, Reina, Revida (or Rubida), Rosa, and Sol. It is to be noted that Spanish first names are more common among Moroccan Jewish women than among men. Perhaps that is because, with few exceptions, parents prefer giving their sons Hebrew names, and occasionally Arabic names such as Makhlouf, Mas'od, Maymon, Sa'adiah, and Yahya. Worth noting also is the fact that some Hebrew names such as Abner, Nissim, and Rahamim, seem to be peculiar to Moroccan Jews, and perhaps to some other Sephardim as well.[23]

LITURGY

The religious poetry of the Golden Age of Spanish Jewry was incorporated in the liturgy of Moroccan Jews for all occasions. Thus, for example, the special liturgical poems (called *pizmonim, piyyutim, bakkashot,* or *selihot*) sung by Moroccan Jews as well as other Sephardim on the High Holidays and in the *selihot* service during the month of *Elul* are all gems of medieval Hebrew poetry composed by Solomon Ibn Gabirol, Yehudah Halevi, Moses and Abraham Ibn Ezra, and others.[24] In addition, on *Shabbat Zakhor*, the Sabbath before Purim, Moroccan Jews, like all Sephardim, sing Halevi's long historical poem, *Mi Kamokha*, which is essentially a masterful poetic rendition of the story of Purim. Likewise, on the seventh day of Passover, they sing Halevi's poem of redemption, *Yom Le-Yabbashah* . . .

Shirah Hadashah Shibbehu Ge'ulim (The Day the Depths Were Turned into Dry Land, a New Song Sang the Redeemed), celebrating the miraculous crossing of the Red Sea by the Israelites.

On Shavu'ot, Moroccan Jews recite the *Azharot* (poetic enumeration of the commandments) of Solomon Ibn Gabirol at the conclusion of the morning service, a practice common to all Sephardim, although some Sephardim recite them before the afternoon service. Following the afternoon service, Moroccans also recite the *Azharot* of Rabbi Isaac ben Reuben al-Bargeloni. On *Tish'ah be-Av* (the ninth of *Av*), they recite many *kinot* composed by Yehudah Halevi and Moses Ibn Ezra, including Halevi's immortal Ode to Zion, *Tzion Halo Tish'ali*, as well as several special *kinot* lamenting the expulsions from Spain and Portugal.[25]

Moroccan songs for the Sabbath table (*zemirot*) include *Deror Yikra le-Ben 'Im Bat* (He Will Proclaim Freedom to All His Children) by Dunash Ibn Labrat; *'Al Ahavatekh Eshteh Gevi'I, Shalom Lakh Shalom Yom ha-Shevi'I* (To Love of Thee I Drink My Cup; Peace to Thee, Peace O Seventh Day) by Yehudah Halevi; and *Ki Eshmerah Shabbat El Yishmereni* (As I Observe the Sabbath, So Will God Guard Me) and *Tzame'ah Nafshi Lelohim le-El Hai* (My Soul Thirsts for the Living God) by Abraham Ibn Ezra.

Finally, besides the liturgy for the High Holidays, the Sabbath, and other special occasions, some medieval religious poems have become part of the popular repertoire of *piyyutim* sung by Moroccan Jews at all types of social gatherings. These *piyyutim* include *Yedidi Ha-Shakhahta?* (Israel complains) by Yehudah Halevi; *Shehi la-El Yehidah ha-Hakhamah* (Bow Down Before God, My Precious Thinking Soul), *Shefal Ru'ah Shefal Berekh ve-Komah* (Humble of Spirit, Lowly in Knee and Stature), *Shahar Avakeshkha Tzuri u-Misgabi* (At Dawn I Come to You, My Rock, My Strength) by Solomon Ibn Gabirol; and *Agadelkha Elohei Kol Neshamah* (I Glorify You, Lord of All Souls) by Abraham Ibn Ezra. All these are popular *piyyutim* that appear in numerous Moroccan anthologies of *piyyutim* and *bakkashot*. To quote Andre Chouraqui, the hymns and poems of Ibn Gabirol "that had become part of the liturgy were known by heart, like the Psalms and many parts of the Bible, among all who attended the synagogue."[26] The same is true of certain poems of Halevi and Abraham Ibn Ezra. It is important to note that these poems were not recited as poetry, but sung to popular Andalusian and contemporary Arabic music.

It should be pointed out also that on festive occasions (other than the High Holidays), services in Moroccan synagogues were characterized by improvisation in both content and music. The central liturgy was often supplemented by poetic compositions of Moroccan *paytanim* (scholar-poets), and regular prayers and supplementary *piyyutim* were chanted to Andalusian or even contemporary Arabic music.[27]

CUSTOMS, RITUALS, AND RELIGIOUS PRACTICES

Essentially, the *minhagim* (customs and practices) of Moroccan Jews are similar to those of all Sephardim, for all Sephardim cherish and take pride in a common cultural and religious heritage that goes back to the Golden Age in Spain. This is certainly true in matters of halakhah and liturgy. For example, all Sephardim regard Rabbi Joseph Caro's *Shulhan Arukh* as the supreme halakhic authority whose rulings are binding on all of them. Nonetheless, Sephardim from various parts of the world differ from each other in the precise manner in which they express and practice this tradition. This is especially true with respect to food, music, and folklore, which inevitably reflect local influence. Colorful local customs lend to the celebrations of certain holidays and festive occasions an element of charm and local fragrance that give them their unique character. Such are, for example, the Moroccan celebrations of the *Mimuna* on the last night of Passover, and the *Hillula* on *Lag ba-Omer*, as well as the institution of *bakkashot*, all of which are quintessentially Moroccan.[28]

But even in matters of halakhah, Moroccans depart from Caro's rulings in favor of Castilian practices. Such are, for examples, the practices included in Rabbi Raphael Berdugo's *Kitzur ha-Takkanot*, and *Kitzur ha-Minhagim*, summaries of ordinances or enactments of the Castilian rabbis, and the Castilian judicial practices with regard to the laws of ritual slaughtering (*shehitah*) and the examination of the lungs (*bedikat ha-re'ah*), both of which had acquired the force of binding authority in Morocco.[29]

RABBINIC CREATIVITY

The output of Moroccan rabbis in halakhic literature, religious poetry, biblical exegesis, philology, and even historiography are most impressive. Every city and every period produced its rabbis, poets, and Jewish scholars of great renown. These rabbis and poets wrote a voluminous quantity of works in all branches of Jewish and rabbinic literature. Because of the high scholarly quality of these works and the general Jewish interest of their contents, these works were to gain widespread acceptance throughout the Jewish world. Such were, for example, the biblical commentary of Rabbi Hayim ben Attar, known especially among the Hasidim as the saintly *Or ha-Hayim* or *Or ha Hayim ha-Kadosh*, (Leghorn, Italy, 1739);[30] the responsa of Rabbi Ya'akov Aben-Tzur (Alexandria, Egypt, 1894), Rabbi Repha'el Berdugo (Krakow, Poland, 1891), Rabbi Itzhak Bengwalid (Leghorn, Italy, 1855), and Rabbi Repha'el ben Shim'on (Alexandria, Egypt, 1912); the *piyyutim* of Rabbi David ben Hassin (Amsterdam, 1807; Casablanca, Morocco, 1931; Israel, 1973, 1999), Rabbi Ya'akov Aben-Tzur (Alexandria, Egypt, 1898), Rabbi Repha'el Moshe Elbaz (Jerusalem, 1935), and Rabbi Ya'akov Berdugo (London, 1855); the numerous historical works on Moroccan Jewry by Rabbi Abner Tzarfati (Jerusalem, 1979), Rabbi Ya'akov Moshe Toledano (Jerusalem, 1911, 1975), Rabbi Yoseph ben Naim (Jerusalem, 1930), and Rabbi Yoseph Messas (Jerusalem, 1969–75); and finally the philosophical and theological works of Rabbi Yehuda ben Nissim Ibn Malka (Paris, 1954), Rabbi Repha'el Berdugo (Jerusalem, 1905; Djerba, 1940) and Rabbi A. Eliyahu Benamozeg (Jerusalem, 1967). These are only some of the better known ones; there are many more.[31]

It should be emphasized in this connection that Moroccan rabbinic creativity was unique and came closest to the ideal established by the Spanish masters of the Golden Age in that it was multidimensional. Moroccan rabbis wrote works on biblical and Talmudic exegesis, halakhah, poetry, history, and theology. The following profiles of several Moroccan rabbis from different cities and different periods provide an exemplary illustration of the multidimensional aspect of rabbinic creativity in Morocco.

Rabbi Repha'el Moshe Elbaz (1823–1898) of Sefrou is one.[32] Known as *al-ribbi al-kbir* (the great teacher), he was the *Dayyan* of his generation—as well as a great Talmudic scholar, halakhist, poet, and mathematician. His many works include *Halakhah le-Moshe*, a collection of responsa (Jerusalem, 1901); *Shir Hadash*, a collection of poems (Jerusalem, 1935); *Ko'ah Ma'asav*, a special work on the Jewish calendar; *Kise ha-Melakhim*, a history of ancient kings and the Jewish community of Sefrou; *Zivhei Tzedek*, a commentary on the laws of ritual slaughter; as well as numerous commentaries on the Bible and the Talmud under various titles.

Rabbi Joseph ben Naim of Fez (1882–1961) provides another example.[33] He was a lifelong bibliophile who collected the largest library of books and manuscripts in Morocco. After his death, his heirs sold it to the Jewish Theological Seminary in New York (where part of it was damaged by an unfortunate accidental fire). A prolific author, he wrote some seventy works on a variety of subjects. Following is a sampling of his works: *Malkhei Rabanan* and *Kevod Melakhim* (Jerusalem, 1931), a bio-bibliographical dictionary of Moroccan rabbis and their works, a most indispensable primary source for any and all research on Moroccan Jewry; *Nifle'otekh Asiha* (Fez, n.d.), a collection of *piyyutim*; *Tson Yosef* (Israel, n.d.), a collection of responsa; *Kol Hadash* (Israel, n.d.), a collection of responsa dealing with all halakhic problems raised by new technology such as electricity, the telephone, various means of transportation, and so on; *Noheg be-Hokhmah* (Israel, 1987), an anthology of customs and religious practices in Morocco, with their origins and rationales, another indispensable primary source for the study of Moroccan Judaism; *Derakhav le-Moshe*, a biography of Maimonides; *Teranen Leshoni*, a work in praise of the revival of the Hebrew language; *Olam ha-Teva'*, a treatise on the world of nature and modern discoveries drawing on Jewish sources as well as contemporary journals; *Hayot Ketanot 'Im Gedolot*, a work on zoology; and numerous commentaries on the Bible and the Talmud under various titles, one of which is an extensive commentary on Abraham Ibn Ezra's popular commentary on the Torah. This sampling shows Rabbi ben Naim's voracious intellectual appetite and the encyclopedic scope of his erudition.

The last and most compelling example is provided by Rabbi Repha'el Berdugo (1747–1821), son of Rabbi Mordekhai, a noted *Dayyan* in Meknes.[34] He was a scion of a family of Spanish exiles, a family of distinguished scholars, rabbis, and communal leaders. Rabbi Repha'el is recognized as one of the most original rabbinic minds produced by Moroccan Jewry in the last four hundred years. His prolific works cover every genre of rabbinic literature, including responsa, novellae on Caro's *Shulhan Arukh*, *takkanot* (judicial reforms or enactments), biblical and Talmudic commentaries, and even a translation of the Bible into the Moroccan dialect of Arabic. He was respected and venerated by all his contemporaries as "The Teacher" par excellence of their generation, usually referring to him simply as *ha-Rav*—the master, *rav* being also the acronym of Repha'el Berdugo. His extraordinary industriousness in the study of Torah and his extreme piety also earned him the title *ha-mal'akh Repha'el*—the Angel Rephael, by which he is generally known in Moroccan rabbinic literature.

His halakhic works include *Mishpatim Yesharim* (Right Rules), a collection of responsa in two volumes (Krakow, Poland, 1891); and *Torot Emet* (True Teachings), a commentary on Caro's *Shulhan Arukh* (Meknes,

1939), in which were published also his *Kitzur ha-Takkanot* and *Kitzur ha-Minhagim*, summaries of the judicial ordinances or enactments of the Castilian rabbis and the Castilian judicial practices with regard to the laws of ritual slaughtering (both of which had acquired halakhic authority), as well as Berdugo's own *takkanot*. His works on the Talmud include *Sharbit ha-Zahav* (The Golden Scepter), a two-volume commentary on the Talmud (Israel, 1975–78); and *Rokah Merkahat* (A Mix of Spices), novellae on the *aggadot* in the Talmud (still in manuscript in my private collection).

His commentaries on the Bible include *Me Menuhot* (Green Pastures), a two-volume work comprising homilies (*derashot*) on the weekly readings of the Torah (*parashiyot*—Jerusalem1905; Djerba, 1940); *Rav Peninim* (Jewels Abundant), a series of homilies for special occasions covering the life cycle and the year cycle (Casablanca, 1969); and *Mesamehe Lev* (Rejoicing the Hearts), a commentary on most of the Bible according to the plain meaning of the text (*peshat*—Jerusalem, 1990). Also, *Me Menuhot* includes a full commentary on the tractate *Avot* woven into the homilies of the Sabbaths between Passover and Shavu'ot, and a commentary on the *Amidah* prayer woven into the homily of *parashat va-ethanan*, apropos of Moses' prayer. Likewise, Berdugo's third homily for *Shabbat ha-Gadol* in *Rav Peninim* constitutes a verse-by-verse commentary on the Passover *Haggadah*. *Rav Peninim* includes also a commentary on Maimonides' Thirteen Principles of the Jewish Faith.

Another work deserving mention is his *Kaf ha-Zahav* (The Golden Spoon), a didactic poem constituting his ethical will as well as his ideal curriculum for rabbinic education.[35] It was published together with the second volume of his *Me Menuhot* (Djerba, 1940). On a more popular level, Rabbi Berdugo wrote *Leshon Limmudim* (Skilled Tongue), a translation of most of the Bible into spoken Moroccan Arabic (*sharh*), published recently in a scholarly annotated edition by Professor Moshe Bar Asher (3 vols: Israel, 2001).

All of Berdugo's works are characterized by brevity, clarity, and originality of approach. His legal decisions are innovative even as his theological views are bold and daring. In his commentaries on the Talmud, he continues the tradition of the early Sephardic masters Alfasi, Rabbenu Nissim, and other North African commentators. He emphasizes straightforward understanding and clear, sharp reasoning (*yosher ha-Havanah ve-harifut*). He dislikes and harshly criticizes the dialectical hair-splitting methods (*pilpulim*) cultivated mostly in Eastern European yeshivot. With regard to his biblical commentaries, Berdugo leaves no doubt as to the source of his inspiration and who his "model commentators" were. Among them, he lists as his first preference those he designates as belonging to the "first group" (*kat alef*), namely, Maimonides in his *Guide*, Abraham Ibn Ezra, Kimhi (Radak), Gersonides (Ralbag), Nachmanides (Ramban), and their like, whom he describes as "the great giants who, in their pursuit of the *peshat*, dare disagree with our sages in their interpretation of biblical narratives— i.e., nonlegal material." He also approves of the method followed by Isaac Arama (*ba'al ha-'akedah*) and Abrabanel, who combine rabbinic dicta with philosophy, quoting frequently the works of important non-Jewish philosophers. It is to be noted that all the above commentators belong to the Spanish school of biblical exegesis, although in his *Kaf ha-Zahav*, Berdugo also lists Rashi among those he recommends as the best. Moreover, throughout his homiletic work, *Me Menuhot*, as well as in his *Mesamehe Lev*, he quotes most frequently these and other Sephardic masters.

A measure of Berdugo's stature and originality is to be found in the sort of issues he grapples with throughout his works. They reveal a remarkable degree of originality and sophistication truly atypical of most premodern commentators. Thus, in his commentary on the Talmud, *Sharbit ha-Zahav*, he is not content merely to explain difficult Talmudic passages or decide the meaning of a controversial text—although he does that, too, in his inimitable way, which is lucid, straightforward, and succinct—but more importantly, he goes beyond that. Anticipating the school of *Wissenschaft des Judentums* of the nineteenth century, Berdugo deals with fundamental issues and concepts relating, for example, to the meaning and contents of the "Oral Torah" (*torah she-be-al-peh*), the composition and structure of the Mishnah, and the ways of the aggadah and how it should be understood.

Likewise, while his *Me Menuhot* was meant as a series of homiletic discourses (*derashot*) arranged according to the weekly readings of the Torah, Berdugo exploits every opportunity presented by the biblical text, or the midrashim based on such a text, to discuss questions of faith, theology, and philosophy—such as the purpose of the commandments (and whether each commandment has an innate value), the purpose of sacrifices, the nature of the knowledge acquired by Adam after eating from the tree of knowledge and the prior state of his knowledge, as well as Maimonides' explanation of it (with which he disagrees), the nature of Divine Providence and its scope, and the all-important theological problem that exercised the minds of most medieval Jewish philosophers, namely, the seeming irreconcilable contradiction between the doctrines of God's foreknowledge and that of man's free will.

In short, although Berdugo produced no work on philosophy as such, nor did he deal with issues of purely philosophical nature, within the framework of his weekly homilies, he addressed all sorts of questions that engaged the interest of medieval Jewish philosophers, most especially Maimonides in his *Guide*. Indeed, in most of these instances, his frame of reference and point of departure seem always to be Maimonides' *Guide*, which he quotes frequently, although he quotes other Sephardic philosophers such as Bahya Ibn Paquda's *Hovat ha-Levavot* and Y. Halevi's *Kuzari* as well. For example, in his first two homilies for *parashat Bereshit* alone (vol. I, pp.1–10a), he quotes Maimonides' *Guide* (three times), Ibn Gabirol's *Keter Malkhut*, what he calls *hakhme ha-tikhonim* (by which he no doubt means astronomers), Isaac Arama, the *Zohar*, and even the Lurianic doctrine of *tzimtzum* (contraction of the Godhead). He seems to have been also greatly impressed by Gersonides, whom he calls, in one connection, the "genuine [or pure] philosopher" (*ha-pilosoph ha-'amitti*).

Even in his *Mesamehe Lev*, which consists of plain explanations of words or phrases in the Bible, Berdugo deals with weighty issues relating to the authorship or the composition of the Torah. Also, he frequently quotes a midrashic interpretation of a given biblical text and proceeds to show how absurd or far-fetched some interpretations are when taken literally. He often suggests a rational figurative interpretation of the midrash in question.[36]

Finally, even the most cursory examination of some of his homilies of the various *parashiyot*, or his *peshat* explanations of the text impresses one with the vast and phenomenal erudition of the man, as well as his intimate familiarity with and mastery of all Geonic and Sephardic works of philosophy and exegesis, in addition to all Talmudic and halakhic sources. The influence of the Sephardic tradition and his bias in its favor are unmistakable.

MOROCCAN *PIYYUTIM*

Moroccan *piyyutim* provide yet another excellent example of the multidimensional aspect of rabbinic creativity in Morocco. Of all the manifestations of the Sephardic legacy noted above, it was in poetry that the two functions of preservation and creative amplification are most apparent. Of all the major literary genres, none was more jealously preserved and zealously cultivated than was poetry. Moroccan poets preserved and enriched the poetic legacy of Andalusian Jewry. They faithfully guarded both the form and the substance of the *piyyut* in terms of the traditional themes and the techniques of composition.

Most Moroccan rabbis considered the composition of *piyyutim* and *melitzah* (rhymed prose) to be a desirable achievement of a *talmid hakham* (rabbinic scholar). Thus, almost all great (and not so great) rabbis in Morocco composed *piyyutim* for various occasions, some more than others, but all did. It is no accident that all the great religious poets in Morocco, in most cases, were also the pillars of rabbinic scholarship and the halakhic authorities of their time. For example, Rabbi Ya'akov Aben-Tzur (1673–1753), one of the greatest halakhic authorities of his time, was equally famous for his *Mishpat u-Tzedakah be-Ya'akov*, a two-volume collection of responsa and *takkanot* and his *'Et le-Khol Hefetz* (Poems for All Occasions), a collection of his *piyyutim* and *kinot* (lamentations). The same was true of all Moroccan religious poets; they were all renowned rabbinic scholars.

By far the most illustrious of Moroccan poets was Rabbi David ben Hassin who died in Meknes in 1792. His collection of *piyyutim* and *kinot*, entitled *Tehilah le-David* (Praise of David) was first published in Amsterdam in 1807 shortly after his death; it was republished in Casablanca, Morocco in 1931, and again in Israel in 1973. Most recently, Professors Ephrayim Hazan and Andre Elbaz published a scholarly and annotated edition of this work (Lod, Israel, 1999).[37]

The Moroccan *piyyut* was strongly religious; it was inspired by ardent faith, permeated with devotion, and distinguished by a deep attachment to the values of Judaism and a great love for Eretz Israel. Noteworthy also is its popular character. Moroccan rabbis and laymen composed *piyyutim* for every occasion in a very lucid and simple Hebrew and in the local Arabic dialect. Moreover, these *piyyutim* were sung both in the synagogue and in the homes on holidays and at family celebrations to classical and contemporary Andalusian and Arabic music, a fact that made them and their melodies very popular. All this means that these *piyyutim* were not intended exclusively for the intellectual and scholarly elite; they were sung and enjoyed by everyone on all possible occasions. It is this popular aspect more than the literary one that accounts for their centrality in Moroccan

Jewish life. There was no festive occasion, whether in the synagogue or in the home, which was not marked by the singing of appropriate *piyyutim*.

BAKKASHOT

Connected with the centrality of *piyyutim* in Moroccan Jewish life is the institution of *bakkashot*, one of the most popular Moroccan cultural institutions. It may be described in popular terms as a concert or a "sing-in" that took place around 3:00 a.m. every Friday night between *Sukkot* and *Pessah*, a season of long winter nights. This service was held by a number of *hevrot* or groups bearing the names of one of the biblical prophets, such as *hevrat Yehizkel Ha-Navi*, or *hevrat Eliyahu ha-Navi*. The *bakkashot* gatherings provided lovers of music and *piyyutim* an opportunity to get together and entertain themselves by singing *piyyutim*. This is reminiscent of the poetic tradition in medieval Spain, when Arab and Hebrew poets would entertain themselves by reciting and discussing poetry at nocturnal wine parties, testing each other's poetic mettle.

Other members of the community, including rabbis and *Dayyanim*, attended these gatherings as well and enjoyed the experience as much. The *bakkashot* service would begin with the singing of *Shir ha-Shirim* followed by *Tikkun Hatzot* (special midnight liturgy that included the chanting of many psalms, especially Psalm 51, the Psalm of Repentance). Following these preliminaries, the *Paytan*—and every such group had its own *paytan*—introduced the musical theme of the night. He led the participants in singing the appropriate *piyyutim*, selected for their thematic connection to the weekly portion of the Torah and for their melodic adaptability to the particular mode of Andalusian music chosen for the night. All participants, especially those with pleasant voices and a rudimentary knowledge of *piyyutim*, took turns, each singing a stanza. Toward morning, young boys joined in the singing of popular *piyyutim* and even modern Israeli songs. Throughout the service, participants were served refreshments. In short, this was a very festive religio-social gathering enjoyed by all, and reflecting Moroccan Jews' love for Andalusian music and *piyyutim*. Religiously speaking, it was perhaps inspired by the words of the Psalmist: "I arise at midnight to praise You for Your just rules" (Ps. 119:62).

The institution of *bakkashot* encouraged the composition of *piyyutim*, the training of *paytanim*, and the publication of anthologies of *piyyutim*. While every city had its *hevrot* of *bakkashot*, the city of Mogador was particularly renowned for its many expert *paytanim*, and for its own anthology of *piyyutim* entitled *Shir Yedidot*. Towering head and shoulders over all Moroccan *paytanim* was Rabbi David Bouzaglo of Casablanca, a rabbinic scholar, a superb Hebraist and grammarian, a prolific poet, and above all *ne'im zemirot yisra'el*, "the sweet singer of Moroccan Jewry," whose many disciples are still active as *hazanim* and *paytanim* in Israel, France, Canada, and other diasporic Moroccan Jewish communities.

CONCLUSION

Moroccan Jewry's involvement with Sephardic culture spans a millennium or more, contributing significantly to its development during its formative period, and to its preservation after 1492. During the first two centuries of Islamic rule in Spain, it served as a cultural bridge between the great Babylonian centers of Jewish learning and the newly emerging Jewish community in Spain. Later, in the tenth century, it provided the young Jewish community in Spain with its first teachers in Hebrew poetry (Dunash Ibn Labrat), and Hebrew philology (Judah Ibn Hayyuj), as well as its first major codifier of Jewish law (Rabbi Isaac Alfasi). In addition, two of Maimonides' major works were the direct result of his connection with the Jews of Morocco when he lived among them from 1159 to 1165, during the Almohad persecutions. The circumstances of Moroccan Jewry at the time led him to compose one of his most important epistles, The Epistle on Martyrdom (*Iggeret ha-Sgemad*). During those same years, Maimonides developed a close relationship with his illustrious Moroccan disciple from Ceuta, Joseph ben Yehudah Ibn Shim'on, for whose continued instruction in philosophy he composed his magnum opus, *The Guide of the Perplexed*, and to whom he dedicated it in his Dedicatory Epistle, addressed to that beloved student.

Finally, after 1492, the Spanish exiles, the *megorashim*, brought with them their rich cultural and spiritual heritage, thereby reviving and reinvigorating the Jewish community in Morocco which had been sapped of its strength in the wake of the Almohad persecutions and other intermittent outbursts against the Jews of Fez in the course of the fifteenth century.[38] Once they established themselves in Morocco, the Spanish exiles devoted their intellectual energies and talents to conserving and preserving this cultural legacy. They not only preserved and cultivated it zealously, but also did their utmost to amplify it by continuing to develop their own Jewish culture very much in the spirit and within the literary framework and context of the Sephardic tradition. As a result, the Sephardic legacy among Moroccan Jews after 1492 was manifested in many ways and on every level, especially in liturgy, customs and religious practices, love of Andalusian music, and above all in Moroccan scholarship and rabbinic creativity. This creativity was unique and came closest to the ideal established by the Sephardic masters of the Golden Age in Spain in that it was multidimensional. As we have seen, Moroccan rabbis wrote halakhah, responsa, religious poetry in both Hebrew and Arabic, as well as important works on biblical and Talmudic exegesis, philology, theology, and even historiography.

APPENDIX

THE *"HEITER NEFIHAH"* CONTROVERSY
BETWEEN THE
MEGORASHIM AND THE *TOSHAVIM*

Initially, there was some dissent and friction between the *megorashim* and the *toshabim*, known respectively as *kehal Kadosh megorashim* and *kehal Kadosh toshabim*. First, there was a problem of communication between the two groups: the *toshabim* spoke only Arabic and the *megorashim* spoke only Judeo-Spanish. Thus, for example, the first ordinances—*takkanot* enacted by the rabbinic leaders of the *megorashim*—were written in Judeo-Spanish.

More important was the appreciable gap in the level of education and culture between them. The *megorashim*'s pride in their superior culture and their alleged nobility aroused the envy and even resentment of the *toshabim*. But from the responsa and *takkanot* literature as well as other sources we know that, notwithstanding striking differences in communal organization and the way of life between the two groups, we do not find among them divisions into congregations according to cities of origin, as we find in the Muslim East and Palestine. But there were exceptions.

One of the most contentious controversies between the two groups centered on the issue of *heiter nefihah*, that is, the examination of the lung of a properly slaughtered animal by inflating it while immersing it in tepid water to determine whether or not the lung had been punctured before *shehitah*. If the water bubbles, this is an indication of a puncture in the lung, and the animal is *terefah*—otherwise it is kosher. This is known as *heiter nefihah*. The halakhic background of this controversy is as follows. Halakhically, to slaughter and eat a live animal or bird, suffering from a wound or illness that will cause it to die within twelve months, is forbidden (*terefah*). The rabbis describe in great detail the possible illnesses or defects

227

that would render the animal *terefah*. For example, if one of the eleven vital organs of the animal has been punctured before *shehitah*, the animal is *terefah*. In most cases, however, the rabbis do not require that the organs of a properly slaughtered animal be checked for these defects, on the assumption that most live animals are healthy, unless they had been ill before *shehitah*. A notable exemption is the lungs. Because lesions or adhesions (*sirkhah*, pl. *sirkhot*) are common in the lungs, they must be checked, since adhesions could be indicative of a puncture in the lung (although it is also possible that they may not be).

The adhesions discussed in halakhic literature are of several types: some connect the lungs to the chest or the ribs, some connect one lobe of one lung to another, and some connect the lung to other organs found in the chest cavity. Halakhic authorities differ in each instance. Some, like the *Tosafot*, are most stringent; others, like *Rabbenu Tam*, are most lenient. Without going into the complex details entailed in the differing opinions, it is important to point out that if the adhesion connects one lobe of the lung to another (not to the adjacent lobe, but to the one beyond it as from the first lobe on the right lung to the third one), most authorities agree that the animal is *terefah*, and so did the *megorashim*. On the other hand, if the ribs or the chest of the animal to which the lung is connected by the *sirkhah* is injured in some way (such as a fractured rib or similar injuries—*makkah ba-dofen*), most authorities agree that the animal is kosher and requires no special examination of the lung because it is assumed that the wound in the chest (not a puncture in the lung) is the cause of the adhesion; in such a case, even the *Tosafot* and the *toshabim* agree that if it can be determined by means of an examination of the lung (*bedikat ha-re'ah*) that it is not punctured, it is kosher.

The controversy between the two groups centers only on cases in which the adhesion connects the lung to the ribs (or to other organs in the chest cavity), and when there is no injury on the side or the ribs of the animal. The *megorashim* allowed *heiter nefihah* in such cases and the *toshabim* did not. The rabbis in Spain had allowed such leniency in the practice of examining the lungs ever since the Church had prohibited Christians from buying *terefah* animals from Jewish butchers, a prohibition which meant that a *terefah* animal resulted in total economic loss (*hefsed merubbeh*). The *megorashim* in Fez continued to adhere to this practice (*minhag*), while the *toshabim* continued their age-old practice of disallowing *nefihah* examination of the lungs in such cases.

Because the lenient practice of the *megorashim* resulted in less *terefot*, and consequently less economic loss, some of the *toshabim* eventually adopted the *minhag* of the *megorashim* (until 1500). In 1500, a Tunisian rabbi, Rabbi Shalom Masnot, on a business visit to Fez, told the *toshabim* that their original *minhag* was the correct one and advised them to revert to it. Rabbi Moshe Haliwa, a leader of the *megorashim*, responded by issuing a responsum asserting that *heiter nefihah* was permissible even for the *toshabim*. However, once the Tunisian rabbi left Fez, the controversy subsided and things went back to normal until 1526. In 1526, an incident involving a ritual slaughterer (*shohet*) from among the *toshabim* resulted in a serious mishap (*takalah*), causing the controversy between the two groups to flare up again with ever increasing fierceness on both sides.

The *toshabim* accused the *megorashim* of eating *terefot*, thereby defaming the memory of Rabbi Haliwa (who had died in the intervening years), and the *megorashim* responded by excommunicating those who defamed their rabbi as well as anyone asserting that the examination of the lung through *nefihah* is forbidden. As a result of the continuing controversy, the *toshabim* set up their own separate butcher shops. The conflict got fiercer and uglier to the point that both groups sought the intervention of the government on their behalf. The controversy continued with nasty twists and turns until 1535, after which the tempers of both groups seemed to calm down.

Ultimately, the *minhag* of the *megorashim* of allowing *heiter nefihah* prevailed and eventually spread to other Moroccan cities. The triumph of the *megorashim* was due, no doubt, to their superior numbers, economic considerations, and the fact that it became realistically impractical for the Jewish community of Fez to sustain two separate types of *shehitah*, one for the *megorashim* and another one for the *toshabim*.

For a good summary of the controversy and its halakhic implications, see the introduction of Rabbi Moshe Amar to his edition of Rabbi Hayim Ganin's *Etz Hayim*, pp.16–22. Rabbi Ganin was a leader of the *toshabim*, and his work is a detailed presentation of the controversy from their point of view.

NOTES

1. SEPHARDIC CULTURE—DEFINITIONS

1. Although Saadiah Gaon was born (and, we presume, educated) in Egypt, he was such a towering rabbinic scholar that he went on to become the Gaon of Sura, one of the two prestigious rabbinic academies in Baghdad, and an important leader of Babylonian Jewry. For an overview of Saadiah's rabbinic career, his conflict with Aaron ben Meir, the head of the Jerusalem academy in the matter of the Jewish calendar, his writings against heretics (such as Hiwi ha-Balkhi) and the Karaites, his considerable contributions to rabbinic Judaism, as well as a brief description of his many pioneering works in Jewish law, philosophy, liturgy and poetry, biblical studies, and Hebrew philology, see "Saadiah Gaon" in *Encyclopedia Judaica*, XIV, cols. 543–45.

2. For details on Hasdai Ibn Shaprut and his patronage of Jewish culture in Spain, see chap. 4, pp. 44, n. 12 below.

3. According to Simha Assaf, no other Jewish community maintained such continuous contact with the Babylonian academies throughout the Geonic period as did the Jewish communities of North Africa who received thousands of responsa from the Babylonian academies for nearly three hundred years. Moreover, according to Assaf, Geonic responsa addressed to Fez and Qayrawan dealt not only with halakhic issues, but with historical, theological, and philosophical matters as well (the Epistle of Sherira Gaon to Rabbi Nissim of Qayrawan is but one such example). See Assaf, *Tekufat Ha-Geonim*, p. 212.

4. For details on Ibn Labrat and Ibn Hayyuj, see chap. 4, pp. 44–47, n. 21 below.

5. For Alfasi, see chap. 6 below.

6. See Freehof, *The Responsa Literature*, p. 80.

7. In the case of Ethiopia, the Islamic influence was due to the presence of a substantial number of Muslims there at various periods. In the case of Italy, it was due to the occupation of Sicily and other parts of Italy by the Arabs through the

end of the ninth century. For a detailed discussion of this occupation and the influence of Arab civilization on Italy in matters of "gracious living," see Watt, *The Influence of Islam on Medieval Europe*, pp. 4–5, 14, 28–29. (Also note that many of the Spanish exiles following the persecutions in Aragon in 1391 went to Leghorn, Italy.)

2. DISTINGUISHING FEATURES OF SEPHARDIC CULTURE

1. For the terms of Muhammad's agreement with the Jews of Khaybar and other Jewish and Christian communities, see Baron, *A Social and Religious History of the Jews*, III, pp. 79–80, 86.

2. Typical examples are provided by the careers of Joseph ben Phineas and Aaron ben Amram as bankers to the Abbasid Caliph Al-Muqtadir (c.911–24) in Baghdad; Hasdai Ibn Shaprut (915–75) as court physician and advisor to the Umayyad Caliph 'Abd Al-Rahman III in Cordova, Spain; and Samuel Ibn Nagrela (Hanagid) (993–c.1054) as diplomat, statesman, general commanding Muslim armies, and prime minister (vizier) to Habbus, King of Granada. See Baron, *History of the Jews*, III, pp. 155–57; Fischel, *The Jews in the Economic and Political Life of Medieval Islam*, pp. 6–32. For a fuller discussion of the careers of these individuals, see chap. 3, n. 27; chap. 4, n. 12; chap. 5, n. 15 below.

3. For the role played by the translation of the Bible into Arabic in the development of Hebrew philology, see Goitein, *Jews and Arabs*, pp. 131–40.

4. See introduction to Altmann, tr., *Saadya Gaon*, p. 20.

5. See preface to Twersky, *A Maimonides Reader*, p. xvi.

6. This popular hymn summarizes Maimonides' "Thirteen Principles" and was most likely composed by Rabbi Jehudah Dayan (c.1300). See Shapiro, *The Limits of Orthodox Theology*, pp. 17–18; see also Messas, *Mayim Hayim*, p. 50a, # 102.

7. For an overview of Maimonides' life, his wanderings, a brief description of his many works, and his lasting legacy, see "Maimonides, Moses," in *Encyclopedia Judaica*, XI, cols. 754–81.

8. See Shapiro, *The Limits of Orthodox Theology*, pp. 107–9.

9. For Abraham Ibn Ezra as a poet and for samples of his poetry, see chap. 5, n. 64 below.

10. For a detailed discussion of Abraham Ibn Ezra's biblical commentaries and his works on astrology, as well as an evaluation of A. Ibn Ezra as an intellectual, see Carmilly-Weinberger, "Two Biblical Scholars in Transylvania-Banat."

11. In his introduction to *Sefer ha-Rikmah* of Jonah Ibn Janah, Ibn Tibbon writes, "The Jews of the Diaspora, from France to the land of *Edom* [Christendom], did not know the Arabic language [thus they could not take advantage of the books that the Spanish scholars wrote in Arabic] until the scholar Ibn Ezra came to their countries and helped them in this with short works [summaries] containing pleasant and precious teachings." See *Encyclopedia Judaica*, VIII, col. 1165.

12. See Goitein, *Mediterranean Society Volume II: The Community*, p. 242.

13. See Goitein, *Jews and Arabs*, p. 70.

14. See Baron, *History of the Jews* III, p. 147.

15. See Altmann, tr., *Saadya Gaon*, pp. 36–39.

16. See Jacobs, *Jewish Biblical Exegesis*, p. 13.

17. See Maimonides, *The Guide of the Perplexed*, Part III, pp. 502–613; see also Isaac Husik's discussion of Maimonides' treatment of the reason and purpose of the commandments in Husik, *A History of Medieval Jewish Philosophy*, pp. 294–97.

18. See Heinemann, *Ta'ame ha-Mitzvot be-Sifrut Yisrael*, I, pp. 46–128. Heinemann discusses various rationales for the commandments offered by medieval Sephardi philosophers and biblical commentators from Saadiah, Maimonides, and Gersonides to Abraham Ibn Ezra, Nachmanides (Ramban), and Abrabanel. See also a thorough discussion of the medieval classification of the commandments into rational laws (*mitzvoth sikhiliyot*) and traditional laws (*mitzvoth shim'iyot*), and Maimonides' opposition to such a classification in Faur Halevi, *Studies in the Mishneh Torah Book of Knowledge* (Hebrew), pp. 160–76.

19. See Schirmann, *Ha-Shirah ha-Ivrit*, I, pp. 524–25, 521–22, 466–67; for the English translation, see Carmi, *Book of Hebrew Verse*, p. 338.

20. Scheindlin, *Wine, Women, and Death* discusses this question in great detail and offers several arguments to prove that these poems on wine, women, and love did reflect the experience of the poets. See his introductions to the sections "Wine" and "Women" (pp. 19–33; 77–89). Toward the end of his introduction to the section

234 / THE SEPHARDIC LEGACY

"Women," he writes, "And yet the same reasoning that led us to affirm the partic-ipation of Jews in wine parties would lead us to affirm cautiously their participation in the kind of love life fashionable in their milieu." He then adds, " Even if the Hebrew poetry could be proved a mere aping of literary conventions, we should still be left to account for the poets devoting so much intellectual energy and cre-ative power to these particular conventions, so removed from those of traditional Judaism. The intellectual problem does not disappear even if we assume that the poets were merely fantasizing; for the fact remains that in the minds of the religious and intellectual leadership of Andalusian Jewry, two different ideals coexisted. That is exactly what makes them so interesting" (pp. 86–87). See also Chapter 3, n. 14 below.

21. See Pool, *Prayers for the Day of Atonement*, p. 161.

22. See Y. Halevi, *Kuzari: The Book of Proof and Argument*, II, p. 77.

23. For a detailed discussion of this poem, see Scheindlin, *Wine, Women, and Death*, pp. 46–49. It is worth noting that the notion of giving God half of one's time and taking the other half for oneself is not entirely new. Rabbi Joshua, one of the Talmudic sages, makes the same recommendation with regard to the celebration of holidays. He says, "Divide it [the holiday], half for God and half of it for your-self (*halekehu hetzio la-Shem ve-hetzio la-khem*)," that is, devote half of the holi-day to God's service, praying and studying, and spend the other half celebrating, eating, drinking, and so on (TB Pesahim 68b; Betzah 15b).

24. For these and other synagogues showing Arab architecture and decorative influences, see Folberg, *And I Shall Dwell among Them: Historic Synagogues of the World*.

25. For a detailed discussion of the celebration of *Sukkot* and *Simhat Torah* in Morocco, as well as the Moroccan institution of *piyyutim* and *bakkashot*, see my article, Henry Toledano, "The Practice of Judaism in Morocco," in *The Encyclo-pedia of Judaism*. For a detailed discussion of Hebrew poetry in medieval Spain and representative excerpts of this poetry, see chap. 5 below; see also Zafrani, *Etudes et Recherches*.

3. HISTORICAL AND CULTURAL ROOTS OF SEPHARDIC JUDAISM

1. In his Epistle to Yemen, Maimonides refers to Muhammad no fewer than five times as *meshuga'* and only once as Muhammad. Abraham Halkin and others offer several explanations as to why Maimonides chose to refer to the founder of Islam as a madman. In my opinion, Maimonides calls him madman simply out of

contempt for his daring to call himself a prophet, let alone the acme and "seal" of prophecy and prophetic ministry. Indeed, Maimonides refers also to the Yemeni "false messiah" as *meshuga'* for the same reason. For, as Maimonides explains, by claiming to be the Messiah, "he is indeed arrogating to himself the role of prophet." This is so, Maimonides continues, "because the Messiah is more illustrious than all the prophets except Moses." See A. Halkin's translation of this Epistle in Halkin, tr., *Crisis and Leadership*, pp. 100, 107–10, 121–23, 126, ns. 48, 227.

2. It is no wonder that this medieval period seems to have had a special appeal for the leaders of the *haskalah* (Jewish Enlightenment) in Europe. Thus, Moses Mendelssohn (1729–1786), the philosopher of the movement, studied Maimonides' *The Guide of the Perplexed* in his youth under the guidance of his tutor, Rabbi David Fraenkel, a fact that no doubt predisposed him to rationalism and philosophy. Later, he wrote *Milot ha-Higayon*, explaining in Hebrew Maimonides' book on logic, and he translated Judah Halevi's immortal "Ode to Zion" (*Tzion Halo Tish'ali)* into German as part of his efforts to publicize Judaism's literary and spiritual treasures. Also, both his German translation of the Pentateuch and its accompanying Hebrew commentary (*Be'ur*) were conceived in the spirit of rationalism and followed the simple or literal exegetical approach of Abraham Ibn Ezra, David Kimhi, and Nachmanides, among others. Likewise, Nachman Krochmal (Ranak; 1785–1840), philosopher, historian, and one of the founders of "the science of Judaism" (Wissenschaft des Judentums), was inspired in his Jewish thinking by Maimonides and A. Ibn Ezra. Maimonides was truly his model. He wanted to do for his generation what Maimonides did for his. Thus, ten years before his death, he wrote to S. D. Luzzatto that he was about to write "a major work in the study of religion, which would include a number of chapters on the most fundamental aspects of our pure faith (*emunah tzerufah*) . . . and following the model of Maimonides in his *Guide*, as required by the perplexities of our time." This work turned out to be his *Moreh Nebukhei ha-Zeman* (Guide to the Perplexed of the Time), which was edited by L. Zunz and published posthumously in 1859. Incidentally, the last and longest chapter of this work deals with the works of Abraham Ibn Ezra and is entitled *Hokhmat ha-Misken* (A Poor Man's Wisdom). (Ibn Ezra was indeed very poor.)This work analyzes his philosophy and includes extensive quotations from his biblical commentaries. (See chap. 17, pp. 284–394 in S. Rawidowicz's edition, 1961.) See also Arthur Hyman's concluding comments on the influence of Maimonides' *Guide* on the development of modern Jewish philosophy (see chap. 7, n. 93 below). Similarly, Solomon Judah Leib Rapoport (Shir; 1790–1867), rabbi, scholar, and a pioneer of *haskalah* and *Wissenschaft des Judentums*, devoted his scholarly research to the Geonic period, writing a series of biographical studies of the Geonic leaders Saadiah, Hai, Hanan'el ben Hushi'el, Nissim ben Jacob, Hefez ben Yazli'ah, Elazar ha-Kalir, and Nathan ben Yehi'el of Rome (au-

thor of the *Arukh*). Finally, Samuel David Luzzatto (Shadal; 1806–65), a great He-braist, biblical commentator, philosopher, and expert on medieval Hebrew poetry, contributed greatly to the revival of medieval Hebrew poetry with his pioneering works in the field, including his edition of Halevi's Hebrew poetry (*Betulat Bat Yehudah*, 1840), as well as his anthology of medieval Hebrew poetry (*Tal Orot*, 1881). One gets the impression that the thinkers and writers of the *haskalah* were particularly attracted to medieval Sephardic culture in an attempt to justify their own embracing of rationalism and secular learning. Indeed, Isaac Barzilay, in dis-cussing the reasons why Rapoport chose to devote his research to the Geonic pe-riod, quotes him as having written in 1829, "Few times can compare with the time from the *Geonim* to Rabbi Nathan in terms of the serious approach to the pursuit of both Talmudic and secular studies, and in terms of the diffusion of such studies from land to land and from country to country." Barzilay then comments, "It is obvious that the cultural dynamism of the period which witnessed the decline of the old centers and the rise of new ones . . . constituted a subject of great attraction to the dynamic and vigorous Shir. He found an additional attraction in the strong secular tendencies of that period, which, in his view, deserved emphasis in order to strengthen the theoretical basis justifying the haskalah of his own day." See Klausner, *Kitzur ha-Historiah*, I, pp. 20–40; Urinovsky, *Toledot ha-Sifrut*, pp. 31–38, 88–116; Krochmal, *Kitvei Ribbi Nachman Krochmal*, pp. 284–394; Barzilay, *Shlomo Yehudah Rapoport*, pp. 51–52.

3. See Baron, *History of the Jews*, III, pp. 66–72; Katsh, *Judaism in Islam*.

4. But the early chapters of the Koran (the Meccan Surahs) show that, at that time, Muhammad knew the Jewish Scriptures only from hearsay and through the mirror of their current homiletic interpretations. See Baron, *History of the Jews*, III, p. 81.

5. See M. Pearlman's prolegomenon to Geiger, *Judaism and Islam*, p. xvii.

6. After a mock trial, all males were condemned to death unless they converted to Islam. Baron notes, "Remarkably, only three or four week-kneed men chose apostasy, while all remaining Jews, estimated at between 600 and 750, after a night spent in study, suffered martyrdom." Baron notes sadly, "They died unsung by their fellow Jews," and only in modern times did their tragic fate become the sub-ject of a great poem, "The Last Sons of Qurayza" (*Ha-Aharon livnei Qorayta*) by Saul Tchernichovsky, written in 1896. See Baron, *History of the Jews*, III, p. 79. For a detailed account of Muhammad's treatment of these tribes, see Stillman, *The Jews of Arab Lands*, pp. 129–44; see also Lewis, *The Jews of Islam*, p. 10. In a different context, Lewis observes that the martyrdom of Banu Qurayza "is a part of the semi-sacred biography of the Prophet, and is treated with respect, at times bordering on admiration" (Ibid. p. 83).

7. See Baron, *History of the Jews*, III, pp. 86, 172.

8. See n. 11 below.

9. See Goitein, *Jews and Arabs*, pp. 9–61. Goitein attributes these and other resemblances between the two traditions to several factors: (a) Judaism was a fully developed system at the time of the Arab conquest, (b) Muslim religious law developed mainly in Iraq, the chief center of Jewish studies at the time, (c) Islam by its very nature was prone to learn from other religions, and (d) Muhammad's uncompromising monotheism must have impelled at least some of his believers to seek instruction from equally strict monotheists.

10. See Schacht, *An Introduction to Islamic Law*, p. 21. Schacht notes also that "the influence of Jewish law [on Islamic law] is particularly noticeable in the field of religious worship" (Ibid.).

11. Lewis, "The Pro-Islamic Jews" discusses an interesting phenomenon, the dominant role played by Jews in the field of Islamic scholarship. Lewis observes that Jews—in particular, orthodox Jews—"played a disproportionate role" in the development of Islamic studies in European and later in American universities. Thus, he asserts, the first grammars, dictionaries, and critical histories of Arabic, Persian, and Turkish were all pioneered by Jews. Lewis gives an impressive list of these scholars and their pioneering works. Of all the Jewish scholars on Islam discussed by Lewis, perhaps the most outstanding one is Ignaz Goldzhier, an orthodox Hungarian rabbi, who wrote a most significant series of studies on Muslim theology, law, and culture. He is ranked by most scholars in the field as one of the more important founders and masters of modern Islamic studies. Some of his writings, according to Lewis, "had been translated into Arabic and are used for teaching Muslim Students their own heritage." It should be pointed out that Lewis himself is an illustrious example of this very phenomenon. He is an eminent Turkologist, Arabist, Islamicist, and Hebraist, whose many works in all these fields are must reading for any serious study of Islamic civilization. Finally, Lewis asks the obvious question, "Why did the Jews, European Jews in particular, rally to the cause of Islam?" He suggests a number of answers and concludes with the passage quoted here. See *Judaism* (Fall 1968), pp. 391–404. For a detailed discussion of these and other affinities between Judaism and Islam, as well as various theories as to Muhammad's source(s) of inspiration, see the chapter, "Judaeo-Islamic Tradition" in Lewis, *The Jews of Islam*, pp. 67–106. Lewis points out that while it is often difficult to determine, with regard to any idea or religious practice, which tradition inspired or influenced the other, "in some matters, the simple facts of chronology indicate beyond a reasonable doubt which is the source, which is the recipient of influence." He then proceeds to discuss specific examples of both Ju-

daic influence on Islam and Islamic influence on Judaism. For general works on the Judaic elements in Islam, see Geiger, *Judaism and Islam*; Katsch, *Judaism in Islam*; Rosenthal, *Judaism and Islam*.

12. See Goitein, *Jews and Arabs*, p. 141.

13. See Lewis, *The Jews of Islam*, p. 80.

14. In discussing the apparent dichotomy, in medieval Hebrew and Arabic poetry of wine and women, between the religious piety of the poets on the one hand, and their commitment to temporal things such as political power, material success, and simple physical pleasures as sources of meaning, beauty, and joy, Raymond P. Scheindlin writes, "More important for Jewish culture than any specific cultural institution acquired from the Arabs—language, philosophy, social habits, and communal organization—was the centuries-old habit of living in allegiance to two opposing principles, one of which finds its natural expression in poetry and the other in scripture. In the process of acculturation to Hispano-Arabic society, the Jewish aristocracy adapted to Judaism the double life lived by sophisticated Muslims, with its contradictions, ambivalences, and occasional pangs of conscience." Scheindlin later adds, "For the most part, these tensions between the demands of religion and the attraction of the larger society were simply overlooked in the poetry, and poets kept their religion and their social life carefully separated in their work." Scheindlin, *Wine, Women, and Death*, pp. 30, 33.

15. See Goitein, *Studies in Islamic History and Institutions*, pp. 3–53.

16. See Stillman, *The Jews of Arab Lands*, p. 156.

17. Ibid., pp. 154–55; see also Baron, *History of the Jews*, III, pp. 88–89.

18. For the "Pact of Omar," see Stillman, *The Jews of Arab Lands*, pp. 157–58; for an evaluation of the Pact, its historical evolution, and the particulars of its terms, see Baron, *History of the Jews*, III, pp. 120–72; Lewis, *The Jews of Islam*, pp. 24–33.

19. See n. 17 above.

20. See Baron, *History of the Jews*, III, p. 104; Al-Baladhuri, *Kitab Futuh al-Buldan*, p. 127—in Hitti's English translation, pp. 194–95.

21. See Baron, *History of the Jews*, III, p. 100, n. 37.

22. Ibid., p. 107.

23. See Stillman, *The Jews of Arab Lands*, p. 45.

24. See chap. 4 below.

25. See Goitein, *Jews and Arabs*, p. 7.

26. Ibid.

27. See Fischel, *The Jews*, pp. 6–32. Fischel also surveys in detail the career of Ya'aqub Ibn Killis, the powerful vizier under the Fatimids in Egypt, as well as that of other Jewish viziers and courtiers in the employ of other Muslim dynasties, especially in the East.

28. See chap. 4, n. 12; chap. 5, n. 15 below.

29. Maimonides states, "Anyone who makes up his mind to study Torah and not work but live on charity profanes the name of God, and brings the Torah into contempt . . . and deprives himself of the world to come, for it is forbidden to benefit from Torah study in this world" (*Mishneh Torah: Hilkhot Talmud Torah*, 3:10).

30. See Goitein, *Jews and Arabs*, p. 121.

31. See Lewis, *The Arabs in History*, p. 55.

32. The other factors were the military and financial exhaustion of the Byzantine and Persian Empires who had just emerged from two long wars; the presence of military geniuses and able caliphs; the lack of appreciation of the danger from Bedouins; the military strategy and effective use of desert power; native Aramean and Arab populations sympathetic to the Arab conquerors—they were next of kin; and finally, the religious persecutions endured by Jews and certain Christian sects under the Byzantines, which caused these oppressed minorities to welcome the Arab invaders as liberators. For a general discussion of the Arab conquest, see Lewis, *The Arabs in History*, pp. 49–56.

33. See Goitein, *Jews and Arabs*, pp. 131–32.

34. See ; Elon, *Jewish Law*, III, pp. 1159–61; Assaf, *Tekufat Ha-Geonim*, pp. 188–202.

35. See Goitein, *Jews and Arabs*, p. 132. Goitein notes that the deviations

from the ancient models of Arabic style found in Judeo-Arabic literature used by medieval writers only reflect "the stage of development reached by Arabic in the Middle Ages," and because the Jewish writers used Hebrew characters, they "felt themselves less bound by the classical models than the Muslims."

36. See Lewis, *The Arabs in History*, pp. 131–32. Lewis notes further that although "this civilization is usually known as Arabic, it was not brought ready-made from the desert, but was created after the conquest by the collaboration of many peoples, Arabs, Persians, Egyptians and others." Nor, adds Lewis, was it even purely Muslim, "for many Christians, Jews and Zoroastrians were among its creators. But its chief medium of expression was Arabic, and it was dominated by Islam and its outlook on life. It was these two things, their language and their faith, which were the great contributions of the Arab invaders to the new and original civilization which developed under their aegis."

37. See chaps. 4 and 5 below.

38. See n. 33 above.

39. See Lewis, *The Jews of Islam*, p. 78.

40. See n. 20 above.

41. See Baron, *History of the Jews*, III, p. 99. To be sure, many Jews also converted to Islam mostly for convenience, that is, in order to attain high government positions or to advance economically or socially in Muslim society. The number of Jewish converts to Islam, however, was minimal compared to that of Zoroastrian or Christian converts. Thus, Bernard Lewis, after stating that "large numbers of Christians, Jews, and Zoroastrians adopted the Muslim religion and became part of Islamic society," goes on to point out that "there are significant differences in the fates of the three religions under the Muslim conquest." He explains these differences thus: "Zoroastrians fared worst. The pre-Islamic Persian state, unlike the Christian state, was completely overcome and destroyed, and its territories and peoples were brought within the embrace of the Islamic caliphate. . . . Possessing neither the stimulation of powerful friends abroad enjoyed by the Christians nor the bitter skill in survival possessed by the Jews, the Zoroastrians fell into discouragement and decline. Their numbers dwindled rapidly." Lewis continues, "[Christianity] was defeated, not destroyed by the rise of Islam and the establishment of the Islamic state. But the processes of Arab settlement, of conversions to Islam and assimilation to the dominant culture, gradually reduced the Christians from a majority . . . to a minority of the population. In some places, notably in Central Asia, southern Arabia, and North Africa, where Christianity before the advent of

Islam occupied a significant or even, in the last-named, a dominant position, it died out completely. For many Christians, the transition from a dominant to a subject status with all the disadvantages involved, was too much to endure, and large numbers of them sought refuge from subjection by adopting Islam and joining the dominant faith and community. Judaism in contrast survived. Jews were more accustomed to adversity. For them, the Islamic conquest merely meant a change of masters, in most places indeed for the better, and they had already learned to adapt and endure under conditions of political, social, and economic disability." See Lewis, *The Jews of Islam*, pp. 17–18.

42. See Lewis, *The Arabs in History*, p. 56.

43. See ns. 8–10 above.

44. See n. 41 above.

4. BIBLICAL EXEGESIS AND HEBREW PHILOLOGY IN MEDIEVAL SPAIN

1. See Sarna, "Hebrew and Bible Studies in Medieval Spain," in Barnett, ed., *The Sephardi Heritage*, p. 332.

2. Ibid.

3. Ibid., p. 323.

4. Ibid.

5. For a sampling and discussion of the works of these commentators and their respective exegetical approach, see Jacobs, *Jewish Biblical Exegesis*, pp. 8–21, 37–45, 46–60, 76–88, 108–19, 120–33.

6. Ibn Al-Rawandi harshly criticized the notion of prophecy in general and that of Muhammad in particular. He maintained further that religious dogmas are unacceptable to reason and must, therefore, be rejected. Likewise, he regarded the miracles attributed to the prophets, whom he compared to sorcerers and magicians, as pure invention. Finally, he ridiculed the notion, held by orthodox Muslims, that the Koran was the greatest miracle of all, declaring it to be neither a revealed book nor even an inimitable literary masterpiece. For a fuller discussion of Ibn Al-Rawandi and his heretic views, see "Ibn Al-Rawandi or Al-Rewendi Abu'l Husayn Ahmad ben Yahya. ben Ishak," *The Encyclopedia of Islam*, III, pp. 905–6. On the notion of "I'jaz al-Kor'an" in Islam, see Ignaz Goldzhier's essay on "Imitation of the Koran," in Goldzhier, *Muslim Studies*, II, pp. 363–65.

7. For a detailed discussion of ha-Balkhi's criticism of the Bible and Saadiah's replies, see Baron, *History of the Jews*, VI, pp. 299–306.

8. Baron sums up these internal and external factors best. He writes, "Jewry of the Great Caliphate, however, was spared this lapse into one-sided talmudism by the new intellectual ferment which seized the intelligentsia of all faiths; by the example of endless debates among the Muslim themselves about text and interpretation of the Qur'an; and by the need of defending the Jewish tradition against the onslaught of powerful enemies. Above all, the internal sectarian controversies enforced constant appeals to the text and meaning of Scripture" (Ibid., p. 236).

9. See Goitein, *Jews and Arabs*, p. 132.

10. See Lewis, *The Jews of Islam*, p. 81.

11. See Goitein, *Jews and Arabs*, p. 136.

12. See Sarna, "Hebrew and Bible Studies," p. 327.

13. See Goitein, *Jews and Arabs*, p. 135.

14. See "Saadiah Gaon" in *Encyclopedia Judaica*, XIV, cols. 543–45.

15. The origin of this practice goes back to the Talmud, which states, "Rav Huna says in the name Ribbi Ammi: A man should always complete the *parashah* with the congregation [reading each verse] twice in Hebrew and once in the Aramaic *targum*" (TB Ber. 8a).

16. For a description of the Epistle and its contents, as well as a full bibliography on the subject, see Becker, *The Risala of Judah Ben Quraysh*; see also *Encyclopedia Judaica*, VIII, cols. 1192–93.

17. For example, the letter *shin* in Hebrew corresponds to *t* in Aramaic and *th* in Arabic. Thus, the word *snow* is *sheleg* in Hebrew, *talga* in Aramaic, and *thalj* in Arabic; the word *three* is *sahalosh* in Hebrew, *telat* in Aramaic, and *thalath* in Arabic. Similarly, the Hebrew letter *zain* becomes *d* in Aramaic and *dh* in Arabic. Thus the word *gold* is *zahab* in Hebrew, *dehaba* in Aramaic, and *dhahab* in Arabic.

18. Linguists of later generations, Menahen Ibn Seruq and Dunash Ibn Labrat, were still grappling with the structure of the Hebrew language.

19. On the importance of the Epistle of Ibn Quraysh to the science of comparative semitic linguistics, Sarna writes, "It was left to another North African,

Judah Ibn Quraish (born c.900) to put the study of comparative Semitic linguistics on a methodical, organized basis. He may be regarded as the real founder of the science and he went so far as to utilize Berber dialects and even Greek and Latin to elucidate otherwise intractable biblical words." See Sarna, "Hebrew and Biblical Studies," p. 343.

20. It is not known whether Ibn Quraysh wrote his *Risalah* in Tahert and sent it to the community of Fez, or wrote it after he (ultimately) moved to Fez.

21. See Sarna, "Hebrew and Biblical Studies," pp. 337–38.

22. Ibid., p. 339. For Hanagid's poetry, see chap. 5, n. 15 below.

23. Sarna, "Hebrew and Biblical Studies," p. 339. According to Abraham Halkin, Ibn Chiquitilla "seems to have written commentaries on the bulk of the Bible." Nevertheless, most of his works perished; we know of them only from relatively few remnants culled from citations by others. Yet, from these citations it is obvious that he was a rational, original, and innovative thinker. Thus, for example, he attempted to apply all prophetic predictions to the immediate time of the Prophet rather than to a distant Messianic future. Likewise, he believed that chapters 40 on of Isaiah form a separate section. Halkin observes that "while it may not be warranted to credit him with the recognition of a 'Second Isaiah,' he sensed the difference between the two portions of the book." Ibn Chiquitilla also recognized that a number of psalms were of exilic date. In short, concludes Halkin, "it may be stated that Ibn Chiquitilla is a clear example of the rational, enlightened spirit of the Jewish Arabic age as it manifested itself in exegesis." See Halkin, "Judeo-Arabic Literature," in Finkelstein, ed., *The Jews*, II, p. 1127.

24. Sarna, "Hebrew and Biblical Studies," pp. 341–42; see also *Encyclopedia Judaica*, VIII, cols. 1163–70.

25. See Goitein, *Jews and Arabs*, p. 138.

5. HEBREW POETRY IN MEDIEVAL SPAIN

1. See Lewis, *The Arabs in History*, p. 135.

2. See Lewis, *The Jews of Islam*, p. 81.

3. See Goitein, *Jews and Arabs*, pp. 155–56.

4. See chap. 4 above.

5. Maimonides, *Responsa*, # 14. For a detailed discussion of Saadiah Gaon's rich legacy and its significance, see chap. 2 above; see also "Saadiah Gaon" in *Encyclopedia Judaica*, XIV, cols. 543–55.

6. Dunash Ibn Labrat (c.910–c.990) was born in Fez, Morocco in the first half of the tenth century. He studied under the great rabbinic scholar, Hebrew grammarian, and philosopher, Saadiah Gaon in Baghdad, and returned to Fez after Saadiah's death in 942. As noted above, Dunash Ibn Labrat was also one of the first two linguistic scholars who flourished in Spain under the patronage of Hasdai Ibn Shaprut.

7. See Ibn Daud, *The Book of Tradition*, p. 102; Hebrew text, p. 73.

8. See Goitein, *Jews and Arabs*, pp. 155–56.

9. Schirmann, *Ha-Shirah ha-Ivrit*, I, pp. 525, 521–22; translation, Carmi, *Book of Hebrew Verse*, pp. 336, 338. For all the poems quoted in this chapter, I used several sources as follows: For the Hebrew source I used either the poetic collections of the individual poets (where possible), or in most other cases, I used Schirmann, *Ha-Shirah ha-Ivrit*; for the English translation I used my discretion in choosing between Carmi's translations in *The Penguin Book of Hebrew Verse*, Goldstein, *Hebrew Poems from Spain*, or Zinberg, *A History of Jewish Literature Vol. I: The Arabic-Spanish Period*. Whenever possible, I tended to use Carmi's translations. On occasion, I also used the Jewish Publication Society's Halevi, *Selected Poems of Jehudah Halevi*, and Ibn Gabirol, *Selected Poems of Solomon Ibn Gabirol*. However, for S. Hanagid's wine poem, "Reward" (*'Alekhem le-Fo'alkhem*), and Abraham Ibn Ezra's penitential poem (*Agadelkha Elohei Kol Neshamah*), I provided my own translations.

10. See Abraham Ibn Ezra's harsh criticism of Hakalir's *piyyutim* in his (Ibn Ezra's) commentary to Ecclesiastes (5:1). For a detailed discussion of this criticism, see my section on Moses Ibn Ezra in this chapter.

11. See n. 8 above.

12. See Zinberg, *A History of Jewish Literature*, I, p. 163; see also "Maqama" in *Encyclopedia Judaica*, XI, cols. 937–38.

13. See, Schirmann, *Ha-Shirah ha-Ivrit*, I, p. 365.

14. Ibid.; translation, Halevi, *Selected Poems*, p. 88.

15. Samuel Hanagid (993–1055 or 1054) was one of the most versatile medieval personalities. He was a rabbi, statesman, diplomat, and general, as well as a patron of Jewish learning and culture. He was a prime minister (vizier) of the Caliphs of Granada, Habus and his son Badis, and even led the Caliph's armies in battle. Born in Cordova, he received an excellent Jewish and general education, including training in Arabic and the Koran. He studied Talmud and halakhah in one of the academies established by Hasdai Ibn Shaprut under Rabbi Hanokh ben Moses of Cordova. Hanagid was also interested in Hebrew language and grammar and wrote numerous philological treatises. He was the first Hebrew poet in Spain who, utilizing meter and rhyme modeled on Arabic poetry, composed poems covering all subjects and poetic themes popular in Arabic poetry such as love, wine, nature, and friendship. Hanagid's poetry and erudition were praised by Muslims and Jews alike. Rabbi Solomon Ibn Gabirol, the famous Spanish Hebrew poet and philosopher was one of his protégés. In 1027, the Jews of Spain conferred upon him the title of *Nagid* (Prince) of Spanish Jewry.

16. See Zinberg, *A History of Jewish Literature*, I, p. 27.

17. See Scheindlin, *Wine, Women, and Death*, p. 26.

18. This is one of a number of short poems called *Tefilot* (prayers) having for a common theme strong nationalistic feelings. Source, Hanagid, *Divan Samuel Hanagid*, p. 318; translation, Goldstein, *Hebrew Poems from Spain*, p. 58.

19. Source, Schirmann, *Ha-Shirah ha-Ivrit*, I. p. 141; translation, Goldstein, *Hebrew Poems from Spain*, p. 35. This short poem from *Ben Mishlei* (The Son of Proverbs), no doubt, reflects Hanagid's own experience; he rose from obscurity, as a shopkeeper in Malaga, to become prime minister (vizier) to the ruler of Granada, due to the power of his pen. According to A. Ibn Daud, Samuel was among those forced to flee Cordova in 1013 in the wake of the Berber conquest of the city. Samuel opened a spice shop in Malaga, and soon afterward he was asked by an Arab maidservant to write for her a letter to her master, Ibn Al-'Arif, the vizier of King Habus of Granada. The vizier was so impressed by Samuel's Arabic style and calligraphy that he advised King Habus to appoint him to his staff. Hanagid advanced from one high position to another until he became the vizier to the king in 1020. See Ibn Daud, *The Book of Tradition*, pp. 72–73; Hebrew text, pp. 55–56.

20. Source, Hanagid, *Divan Samuel Hanagid*; translation, Carmi, *Book of Hebrew Verse*, p. 297. See also his delightful wine poem, "Reward" (*'Alekhem le-Fo'alkhem*) in chap. 2, n. 23 above.

21. Source, Schirmann, *Ha-Shirah ha-Ivrit*, I, p. 142; translation, Carmi, *Book of Hebrew Verse*, p. 291. This is another short poem from *Ben Mishle*, also reflecting Hanagid's personal experience on the battlefield.

22. The first and second Temples in Jerusalem were both destroyed on the ninth of Av.

23. Source, Hanagid, *Divan Samuel Hanagid*, pp. 4–14, especially the verses 45–55, 59–61, 65–72, pp. 7–9; translation, Carmi, *Book of Hebrew Verse*, pp. 286–88.

24. In his childhood, Samuel had a vision, in which the archangels Michael and Gabriel brought him God's promise of protection. Hanagid took this vision very seriously, referring to it often in his poetry (almost as if quoting from Scripture). This vision is the subject of one of Hanagid's early poems, *Hazon Nevu'i* (Prophetic Vision). In this vision, the angel Michael assures him, "On the day that you cross waters of sorrow, I am with you . . . the rivers will not drown you," and the angel Gabriel promises "When you walk into the fire, it shall not burn you." Clearly Hanagid was invoking these promises in this "Short Prayer." See Schirmann, *Ha-Shirah ha-Ivrit*, I, pp. 78–79, and Goldstein translation titled, "God's Assurance," in Goldstein, *Hebrew Poems from Spain*, p. 45.

25. Source, Schirmann, *Ha-Shirah ha-Ivrit*, I, p. 93; translation, Carmi, *Book of Hebrew Verse*, p. 283.

26. Source, Hanagid, *Divan Samuel Hanagid*, pp. 16–26, especially the verses 5–9, 10–11, 16–17, 21–22, 29–30, 52–54, 58–60, 84–85, 137–40, 145–49; translation, Goldstein, *Hebrew Poems*, pp. 46–47, 49, 51, 54. It is to be noted that the number of verses in this poem (149) corresponds to that of psalms in the Book of Psalms, not counting psalm 150, Halleluyah. Hanagid always attributed his battlefield victories to God's providence, and he considered them not only his personal victories, but victories of his people as well. Interestingly, at the end of the poem *Shirah* celebrating his victory over Ben Abbas, he compares his poem to the Book of Esther, celebrating the victory of Esther and Mordecai over Haman, and like Mordecai, one of his biblical heroes, he recommends that his poem be written by all Jews so that this victory is remembered forever.

27. Solomon Ibn Gabirol was born in Malaga in 1021 or 1022, and lived the greater part of his life in Saragosa. He was orphaned at an early age. Crippled from his childhood with disease, he spent most of his life bedridden. His illness and suffering are constant themes in his poetry. In one of his poems, *"Nihar be-kor'i geroni"* (My Throat is Parched with Crying), he complains, "I am full of pain, I

am motherless and fatherless, young and lonely and oppressed—I am alone, I have no brother, and I have no friend except my thoughts" (Schirmann, *Ha-Shirah ha-Ivrit*, I, p. 208). His physical suffering, however, seems not to have hindered his consuming passion for wisdom, in which he found his only solace. His literary legacy includes works in biblical exegesis, Hebrew grammar, philosophy and ethics, and, above all, poetry. Abraham Ibn Ezra speaks of Ibn Gabirol's commentary on the Torah, the Book of Isaiah, and the Book of Psalms. At the age of seventeen, he composed a 400-verse poem on Hebrew grammar, of which A. Ibn Ezra speaks in the highest terms of praise. Of his many works on philosophy and ethics, three survived (all in Arabic). They are *Kitab Ihsan al-'Akhlaq* (Book on improvement of moral qualities—Hebrew, *Tikkun Middot ha-Nefesh*); *Mukhtar al-Jawahir* (An anthology of ethical maxims—Hebrew, *Mivhar Peninim*); and his major philosophical work, *The Fountain of Life* (Hebrew, *Mekor Hayim*—the Arabic original was lost, and the work was preserved only in a Latin version, *Fons Vitae*, authored by Avicebron). Because the last work deals with universal philosophical issues with no particular reference to traditional Jewish sources, it was thought to be the work of a Christian monk, Avicebron, and as such, it had great influence in medieval Christian circles. It was not until the middle of the nineteenth century, when Solomon Munk discovered its Hebrew version, that its true author, Ibn Gabirol, became known. See "Gabirol Solomon ben Judah, Ibn" in *Encyclopedia Judaica*, VII, cols. 235–46.

28. Source, Schirmann, *Ha-Shirah ha-Ivrit*, I, p. 194; translation, Goldstein, *Hebrew Poems*, p. 67. This is a typical example of Ibn Gabirol's complaints about his illness and his suffering. Similar reference to his suffering appears in his *Keter Malkhut* (The Kingly Crown). In stanza 38, he writes, "And when Thou dost put my sins into one of the scales, put my affliction in the other. And when Thou rememberest my wickedness and rebellion, Remember my misery and my misfortunes." (See quotation of full passage from this stanza below.)

29. Source, Schirmann, *Ha-Shirah ha-Ivrit*, I, p. 203; translation, Goldstein, *Hebrew Poems*, p. 66. Ibn Gabirol refers to Rab Hai as the "ark buried in Babylon." The "ark of the law" (*aron ha-Torah*) seems to be a common metaphor for rabbinic scholars. Thus, in Morocco, for example, the epitaph "*po nignaz aron ha-Torah*" (Here lies buried the ark of the law) is a typical inscription on the tombstones of great rabbinic scholars.

30. SourceSchirmann, *Ha-Shirah ha-Ivrit*, I, p. 192; translation, Zinberg, *A History of Jewish Literature*, p. 36. This short poem is typical of the egocentricity and arrogance found in Ibn Gabirol's secular poetry. And while boasting is generally in line with one of the common themes of Arabic poetry, it also reflects Ibn Gabirol's own character. At the tender age of sixteen, he considered himself superior to his contemporaries.

31. Source, Schirmann, *Ha-Shirah ha-Ivrit*, I, p. 235; translation, Ibn Gabirol, *Selected Poems*, p. 17. In sharp contrast to the arrogance and overconfidence expressed in the poem, "I am the Master" (see n. 30 above) and in similar poems, this short poem expresses Ibn Gabirol's extreme humility and the outpouring of his soul evident in all his religious poetry.

32. Source, Schirmann, *Ha-Shirah ha-Ivrit*, I, p. 237; translation, Carmi, *Book of Hebrew Verse*, p. 315. This short poem is an illustration of the poem addressed to one's soul introduced by Ibn Gabirol into Hebrew poetry.

33. Source, Schirmann, *Ha-Shirah ha-Ivrit*, I, p. 238; translation, see Raymond P. Scheindlin, *The Gazelle*, p. 170. This and the preceding two poems, "*Shefal Ru'ah*" and "*Shehi la-El*" are examples of a new genre of Hebrew poems innovated by Ibn Gabirol. It is called *reshut* (pl. *reshuyot*) prefacing each of the three prayers, *Nishmat Kol Hai, Kadish,* and *Barekhu* in the morning service of the Sabbath and festivals. The *reshut* usually has the acrostic of the poet's first name at the beginning of the lines. Also, the last line of the *reshut* alludes to one of the above-mentioned three prayers. In the case of the three *reshuyot* quoted here, the last line of each of them alludes to the prayer *Nishmat kol hai*, the basic theme of which is the spontaneous praise of God by all his creation. According to Schirmann, because the *reshuyot* consist of no more than four or five lines, they require of the poet concentration of thought, as well as concision and delicacy of expression that only a great poet like Ibn Gabirol, a master of condensation, could achieve. For a discussion of *reshuyot* and their poetic significance, see Schirmann, *Ha-Shirah ha-Ivrit*, I, pp. 181–82; for an extensive discussion of the *reshuyot* as a new genre, the poetic techniques involved in their composition, their place in the context of liturgical history, and their significance as an Andalusian contribution to Hebrew poetry, see Scheindlin, *The Gazelle*, pp. 144–48.

34. See Ibn Gabirol, *The Kingly Crown*, pp. 8–9.

35. Ibid., stanza 1, p. 42.

36. Ibid., stanza 15, p. 64.

37. Ibid., pp. 40–42, 92–94, 96, 102, 112–14, 116–18.

38. Moses Ibn Ezra (1055–1135) was an important official in the kingdom of Granada until it fell to the Berbers in 1090. At some point before that, he went to Lucena to study under Rabbi Isaac Ibn Ghiyath. Back in Granada, he gathered around him a circle of scholars and poets, both Jewish and non-Jewish, among whom was the young Yehudah Halevi. His early poetic achievements in Granada

met with great acclaim. However, sometime after Granada fell to the Berbers in 1090, his family became scattered. Moses seems to have remained in Granada for a time, impoverished and destitute. Because of a quarrel with the family (details of which are not clear), Moses left Granada for good and spent the last years of his life wandering in Christian Spain, away from his family and friends, longing for the physical and intellectual environment of his birthplace. His suffering and alienation find echo in many of his secular poems.

39. See n. 10 above.

40. See Pool, *Prayers for the Day of Atonement*, pp. 294–95.

41. Source, Schirmann, *Ha-Shirah ha-Ivrit*, I, p. 371; translation, Carmi, *Book of Hebrew Verse*, p. 323.

42. Source, Schirmann, *Ha-Shirah ha-Ivrit*, I, p. 372; translation, Carmi, *Book of Hebrew Verse*, p. 323. Like the other major Spanish poets, Moses Ibn Ezra wrote poems of nature, friendship, wine, women, and love. This and the preceding poem are typical examples of his wine and nature poems.

43. SourceSchirmann, *Ha-Shirah ha-Ivrit*, I, p. 401; translation, Goldstein, *Hebrew Poems*, p. 85.

44. Source, Schirmann, *Ha-Shirah ha-Ivrit*, I, p. 403; translation, Goldstein, *Hebrew Poems*, p. 87. This and the preceding poem, "Let Man Remember," are examples of the poet's reflections on the brevity of life and the inevitability of death. Like the other great Jewish poets of the age, Moses Ibn Ezra wrote many poems on death. For this particular genre, he seems to have followed, in particular, the example of Samuel Hanagid, who devoted one of his three poetic collections, *Ben Kohelet* (The Son of Ecclesiastes) to meditations on life, old age, death, cemeteries, and those buried in them. For comparative purposes, the following are several of Hanagid's poems on death:

Man Runs towards the Grave
(*Merutzat Ish el Kubbah*)

> Man runs to the grave,
> And rivers hasten to the great deep.
> The end of all living is their death,
> And the palace in time becomes a heap.
> Nothing is further than the day gone by,
> And nothing nearer than the day to come.

And both are far, far away,
From the man hidden in the heart of the tomb.
(Schirmann, *Ha-Shirah ha-Ivrit*, I, p. 135;
Goldstein, *Hebrew Poems*, p. 39)

The Old Man's Warning
(*Tesahek bi be-Yaldutekha*)

You laugh at me, now that you are young,
Because you see me old, and grey-haired.
I am an old man, but I have seen workmen
Make a coffin and a bier for a young lad.
(Schirmann, *Ha-Shirah ha-Ivrit*, I, p. 135;
Goldstein, *Hebrew Poems*, p. 40)

The Root
(*Ohavei Yamim*)

Oh, you merry-makers on earth's back,
do you know that your life is nothing?
You grow from the root of death—
and every branch to its own root returns!
(Schirmann, *Ha-Shirah ha-Ivrit*, I, p. 133;
Carmi, *Book of Hebrew Verse*, p. 292)

The Two Cries
(*Shit Libbekha*)

Reflect, and you will realize how shameful is your heart's delight, which
Comes between two cries; you cry when you come into the world.
And others cry when you leave it.
(Schirmann, *Ha-Shirah ha-Ivrit*, I, p. 133;
Carmi, *Book of Hebrew Verse*, 292)

According to Scheindlin, this poetic genre, in which the thoughts of death play a great part, was also inherited by the Jewish poets from the Arabs. For a detailed discussion of this poetic genre, the Arab influence, and the liturgical precedent of *Tokhehot*, see his introduction to the section on death in Scheindlin, *Wine, Women, and Death*, pp. 135–41.

45. That is, God, the all-encompassing Soul.

46. The motif of shamefulness and contrition for the sins of his youth expressed in this and the following poem ("*Be-Levav Mar*") recurs in many of his *selihot* and other religious hymns. Thus, for example, in the prayer "*Zeman Havli*," he writes, "In grievous sin did my youthful years pass; I have misspent my years, my life!" See M. Ibn Ezra, *Liturgical Poems*, p. 48.

47. Ibid., p. 68; translation, Carmi, *Book of Hebrew Verse*, pp. 331–32.

48. M. Ibn Ezra, *Liturgical Poems*, p. 43; translation, Zinberg, *A History of Jewish Literature*, pp. 76–77.

49. The following two *selihot* are chanted by all Sephardim as part of the *selihot* service during the month of *Elul* and the days between Rosh Hashanah and Yom Kippur. M. Ibn Ezra, *Liturgical Poems*, pp. 18, 81; for the English translation, see Pool, *Prayers for the New Year*, pp. 40–42.

50. Yehudah Halevi was born in Toledo, Spain no later than 1075. He was educated in Muslim Spain, first in Granada where he befriended Moses Ibn Ezra, and then in Lucena where he studied under Rabbi Isaac Alfasi. From Lucena he returned to Toledo. Following the persecution of Jews in Castile in 1109, he returned to Muslim Spain, this time to Cordova. Halevi is most representative of the spirit of the Golden Age period and its glorious legacy. In addition to his Jewish learning, he was also steeped in the contemporary culture of both Christian and Muslim Spain. He was a rabbi, a theologian, a successful physician, and an enormously popular secular and liturgical poet. He was born and grew up in difficult times, toward the end of the Golden Age, at the beginning of the Christian Reconquista of Spain from the Arabs. Those were times of intense conflict between Muslims and Christians, both in Spain and in the Holy Land, with the Jews feeling somewhat trapped in the middle. As certain Spanish cities changed hands, the Jews, Halevi among them, felt like a football in this game. Thus Halevi complains often in his poetry of being caught between "Edom and Arab," or "Edom and Ishma'el," that is Israel and Jerusalem being under the Crusaders (even as northern Spain was under Christian rule), while Andalusia was under the Muslims. This same concern seems to be behind the writing of his major philosophical work, *The Kuzari* (see n. 52 below). In 1140, to the dismay of his family and friends, he left Spain, abandoning his family, his lucrative medical practice, and his many friends and admirers, and set out for the land of Israel, the land of his dreams.

51. Thus, Heinrich Brody, who translated many of Halevi's poems into English for the J.P.S. publication, writes in his introduction, "The gift of song, cherished and tended as it was by the Spanish Jews of the Middle Ages, reached its highest development in the poems of Yehudah Halevi" (Halevi, *Selected Poems*, p. xiii).

Likewise, Hayim Schirmann, the dean of scholars on medieval Hebrew poetry, writes, "The cultural development in Andalusia reached its zenith in the times of Yehudah Halevi. He integrated in his poetry all the features and conventions characteristic of the Spanish school." (My translation—see Schirmann, *Ha-Shirah ha-Ivrit*, I, p. 425.) Finally, Abraham Halkin, another authority on Judeo-Arabic literature, calls Halevi "the most beloved medieval Jewish poet" (see chap. 7, n. 98 below). Needless to say, this also happens to be my personal opinion.

52. See Halevi, *Selected Poems*, pp. 99–100. Halevi's complaint echoes that of the psalmist in Psalm 44. Following a litany of complaints that God has abandoned Israel to its enemies, the psalm concludes: "It is for your sake that we are slain all day long, that we are regarded as sheep to be slaughtered. Rouse Yourself, why do You sleep O Lord? Awaken, do not reject us forever! Why do You hide Your face, ignoring our affliction and distress?" (Psalm 44:23–25). Even a stronger complaint along these lines is expressed in the Book of Lamentations (3:42–44). See also n. 59 below.

53. Halevi, *Selected Poems*, pp. 87–89.

54. Interestingly, Halevi applies the same poetic device of wordplay in the full Arabic title of his philosophical work, *The Kuzari*. The Arabic title is *Kitab al-hujja **wa-dalil** -fi nasri al-din **al-dhalil*** (The Book of Argument and Proof in Defense of the Despised /Scorned Religion). The words proof (***dalil***) and despised (***dhalil***) rhyme and alliterate; thus one word refers to the other; the proof is the answer to the scorn and the spiritual oppression it produces.

55. Heine's poem is quoted by Zinberg, *A History of Jewish Literature*, p. 84.

56. This refers to the wandering of the Israelites in the desert after the exodus from Egypt.

57. *Seir* refers to the Christian nations while *Kedar* refers to the Muslim nations. In other poems, he uses the terms *Edom* and *Arab* (as in the poem "My Heart is in the East . . ." below), or *Edom* and *Ishma'el*, to refer to the Christian and Muslim nations.

58. Source, Schirmann, *Ha-Shirah ha-Ivrit*, I, pp. 466–67; translation, Carmi, *Book of Hebrew Verse*, p. 334. This poem had become very popular among Moroccan Jews in the last half century; it was sung to a very lively and popular tune in both the synagogue and the homes on every festive occasion. Following the mass emigration of Moroccan Jews from Morocco in the 1950s and 1960s, it continued to be as popular in their diaspora. Indeed, in Israel, it acquired in recent years the status of a quasi national hymn.

59. Source, Schirmann, *Ha-Shirah ha-Ivrit*, I, p. 159; translation, Goldstein, *Hebrew Poems*, p. 96. This poem and others like it show to what extent Halevi was God-intoxicated, so to speak. Yet, in the last two lines, he not only pleads with God, he demands, "Answer. . . . Do not chastise. Do not withhold reply." And while the overall tone of the poem is personal, it seems that in the last two lines, Halevi is speaking on behalf of his people.

60. Source, Schirmann, *Ha-Shirah ha-Ivrit*, I, p. 489; translation, Carmi, *Book of Hebrew Verse*, p. 347. This poem belongs to a series of poems, including the three poems quoted below, that express Halevi's intense nationalism. In some poetic anthologies, they are appropriately grouped under the rubric, *Shirei Tzion* (Songs of Zion). Halevi plays on the words *yekal be-'enay* (lit. it would be light/easy in my eyes) and *yekar be-'enay* (lit. it would be dear/precious in my eyes) to underscore how all the goods of Spain are meaningless to him compared to the glorious experience of beholding even just the ruins and dust of the Temple in Jerusalem. On the use of *Edom* and *Arab* to refer to Christians and Muslims, see n. 57 above.

61. Source, Schirmann, *Ha-Shirah ha-Ivrit*, I, p. 489; translation, Goldstein, *Hebrew Poems*, p. 102.

62. *Source, Schirmann, Ha-Shirah ha-Ivrit*, I, p. 490; translation, *Goldstein, Hebrew Poems*, p. 101. *The first line of this poem in Hebrew reads, "Shalom lekha har ha-'avarim—Shalom lekha mi-kol avarim."* Halevi brings greetings to Mount Avarim from all sides (*avarim*); his clever play on the name *Mount Avarim* is all too obvious.

63. Source, Schirmann, *Ha-Shirah ha-Ivrit*, I, pp. 485–89; translation, Carmi, *Book of Hebrew Verse*, pp. 347–49. The poems "Ode to Zion" and "My Heart is in the East" are perhaps Halevi's most celebrated nationalistic poems. It is not surprising that Moses Mendelssohn (1729–86) translated Halevi's "Ode to Zion" into German, as part of his effort to publicize the literary and spiritual treasures of Judaism. According to Joseph Klausner in his *Abridged History of Modern Hebrew Literature* (vol. I, p. 23), when Goethe read this poem in Mendelssohn's German translation, he commented, "This lamentation expresses such warm and heart-felt yearnings as few other poems do." Appropriately, Sephardim chant this lamentation (*kinah*) on *Tish'ah be-Av* (the Ninth of Av, commemorating the destruction of both the first and second Temples in Jerusalem). A recent practice of some Ashkenazim (especially, Hasidim) to sing this *kinah* (often to band music, no less) at happy occasions such as weddings and the like, seems to be not only incongruous, but outright inappropriate.

64. Like Yehudah Halevi before him, Abraham Ibn Ezra was born in Toledo around 1092. Also, like Halevi, Ibn Ezra left Spain in 1140. But unlike Halevi, he did not set out for Palestine. Instead, he journeyed to various places in Italy, France, and England—where he probably died in 1161. Abraham Ibn Ezra suffered from abject poverty throughout his life, but took his misfortune with equanimity and good humor. His poverty and bad luck are often the subject of his humor and satire. For a fuller discussion of A. Ibn Ezra's literary and scientific legacy, as well as a description of his commentary on the Pentateuch, see chap. 2, ns. 8–11 above.

65. Source, Schirmann, *Ha-Shirah ha-Ivrit*, I, p. 578; translation, Zinberg, *A History of Jewish Literature*, p. 162. His characterization of peoples according to the songs they sing is clever and witty. It also reflects his familiarity with their respective cultures. It is worth noting that although he assigns the composition of riddles and fables to the Indians, he himself indulged in composing many clever and witty riddles. See Kahana's chapter, "Riddles," in A. Ibn Ezra, *Rabbi Abraham Ibn Ezra*, I, pp. 87–108.

66. SourceSchirmann, *Ha-Shirah ha-Ivrit*, I, pp. 575–76; translation, Carmi, *Book of Hebrew Verse*, pp. 353–54. In the above three poems, Abraham Ibn Ezra laments his poverty and misfortune with humor and sarcasm, but it could be assumed that behind the laughter there must have lurked tears.

67. This poem is a *reshut* (an introductory short poem) prefacing the *Kadish* prayer. In Morocco, however, it became a very popular *piyyut* sung on all occasions to lively and popular melodies. Source, A. Ibn Ezra, *The Religious Poems*, pp. 43–44; translation, my own.

68. See Schirmann, *Ha-Shirah ha-Ivrit*, I, pp. 605–6; translation, Carmi, *Book of Hebrew Verse*, pp. 354–55. In most Sephardic communities, the *selihot* service during the month of *Elul* begins with Yehudah Halevi's penitential poem, *Yashen al Teradam* (O Sleeper, Sleep No More). In my native city of Meknes, Morocco, however, we began the service with Abraham Ibn Ezra's *selihah*, "*Eshtahaveh Appayim Artzah*," which was chanted with great fervor and to a very stirring and plaintive melody.

69. Most Ashkenazim sing this poem during the circumcision (*brit*) ceremony because of a reference made in one of the verses to circumcision as a sign of the covenant between God and Israel:

They that have come to Thee—Under Thy seal to be
They from birth are Thine—Bound by a holy sign.

However, some Ashkenazim sing this poem also on the seventh day of Passover. See *The Traditional Prayer Book for Sabbath and Festivals*, pp. 501–2.

70. See for example, Attiya, *Shirei Dodim ha-Shalem*, pp. 260, 331, 355.

6. SEPHARDIC CODIFICATION OF JEWISH LAW

1. See Elon, *Jewish Law*, p. 1148. It must be pointed out at the outset that most of the information in this chapter is drawn from Elon's work quoted above (chap. 3, n. 34). Elon is the preeminent historian of Jewish law, and the highest authority on various developments in Jewish jurisprudence, including, of course, that of codificatory literature, the focus of this chapter. Other sources consulted are Assaf, *Tekufat Ha-Geonim*; and Twersky, *Introduction to the Code of Maimonides* (*Mishneh Torah*).

2. See Elon, *Jewish Law*, pp. 1139–40.

3. Ibid. The outstanding examples of this third type are, of course, the complementary works of Rabbi Joseph Caro, the *Bet Yosef* and the *Shulhan Arukh*. (See a fuller discussion of Caro's works below.)

4. Elon, *Jewish Law*, pp. 1184–85; ns. 7–9.

5. Ibid., pp. 1156–57; n. 28.

6. Ibid., p. 1150.

7. Ibid., pp. 1150–55. Elon notes that perhaps due to the completely negative attitude toward codification expressed by Paltoy Gaon (Gaon of Pumbedita, 842–57), during the entire Geonic era, hardly any additional works in the style of *Halakhot Pesukot* and *Halakhot Gedolot* were composed. Elon adds that for about a century, until Saadiah Gaon, no codificatory work was written, and that halakhic creativity during this period took the form of responsa which were becoming numerous. Ibid., p. 1158.

8. The Muslims developed an entire legal system, which absorbed and digested many foreign elements, Jewish, Roman, and Persian, as well as local customs, and molded them into a legal system uniquely and particularly Islamic in character, comparable only to halakhah in Judaism, in the sense that it covered all aspects of life—civil, criminal, commercial, family, and ritual. This system branched off into four official schools of Islamic law, each with its "authoritative handbooks" or codes reflecting the differing doctrines of the school as well as local

customary practice. All of the handbooks were systematically and logically structured in their literary form and content. While elements of Jewish law influenced Islamic law during its formative period, it is very probable that the codification of Jewish law during the late Geonic period by Saadiah and those who followed his model was influenced by the systematic organization and logical and topical structure of the handbooks of Islamic law. This is especially so in the case of Saadiah whose works in numerous fields reflect a definite Islamic and Arabic influence. For the Jewish influence on Islamic law, see Schacht, *An Introduction to Islamic Law*, p. 21; see also chap. 3, ns. 9, 11 above. For the influence of Islamic Law on the halakhic works of such *Geonim* as Saadiah, Rab Hai, and especially Rabbi Samuel ben Hofni, see B. Cohen, "The Classification of the Law in the *Mishneh Torah*," pp. 525–26. Cohen points out, for example, that twenty of the titles of the 27 sub-divisions in Hofni's *Sefer ha - Mitzvot* "are manifestly borrowed from the standard works of Fikh and Hadit." He also notes, "Nine of these titles are found as divisions in Maimonides' Code." For the Islamic influence on the halakhic works of the *Geonim* in general, see also Leibson, "Jewish Muslim Comparative Law." See also ns. 11, 28, 35 below.

9. See Assaf, *Tekufat Ha-Geonim*, p. 189; Elon, *Jewish Law*, pp. 1159–61. Of all the halakhic monographs of Saadiah, only one, *Sefer Ha-Yerushot* (Book of Inheritance), survived intact; the others are known only from Genizah fragments or quotations in the works of subsequent authors.

10. See Elon, *Jewish Law*, pp. 1159–61, n. 10. Samuel ben Hofni was Gaon in Sura in the years 977–1013. Like Saadiah, he too wrote works not only on Jewish law but in many other fields as well—including biblical exegesis, philosophy, and philology. He too wrote numerous monographs summarizing various topics of the law: Book of the Laws of Acquisition, Book of Gifts, Book of Contracts, Book of Pledges, Book of Purchase and Sale, Book of Partnership, Book of the Laws of Robbery, Book on the Law of Neighbors, Book of Ordinary and Special Contractual Suretyship, Book of Oaths, Book of Minority and Adulthood, Book of Family Law, and what Elon describes as a "long list of other monographs treating all the areas of civil law, evidence and procedure, as well as some of the criminal law." According to Elon, Samuel ben Hofni's monographs "set a record of halakhic literature for quantity," and were "remarkably systematic, organized topically according to consistent classification, and written in an easy straightforward style." Unfortunately, they suffered the same fate as the works of Saadiah; not one of the dozens of his works has been printed in its entirety, and all that survived of most of them is their name.

Hai Gaon (939–1038) was the last, and one of the greatest and most famous of the *Geonim*. With his death in 1038 (at the ripe age of 99), the Geonic period came to its end. He was the son of the equally famous Sherira, Gaon of Pumbedita, and was himself appointed Gaon of Pumbedita while his father was still alive. Like Saadiah and Samuel ben Hofni, Hai Gaon also was highly productive in various fields including biblical exegesis, philology, and philosophy. However, his preeminence was primarily in halakhah; his responsa, for example, constitutes more than a third of all extant responsa of the *Geonim*, issued over a period of approximately four hundred years. Hai Gaon continued the pattern of composing halakhic monographs on particular subjects: Book of Judges, Book of Oaths, Book of Purchase and Sale, Book of the Laws of Contracts, Book of Laws of Loans, Book of the Laws of Adjoining Property Owners (*matzranut*), and others. Like Saadiah and Samuel ben Hofni, he wrote these monographs in Arabic, but two of them survived (Elon suggests) as a result of having been translated into Hebrew at an early period. Thus, his *Sefer Shevu'ot* (Book of Oaths), and *Sefer HaMikah ve-Ha-Mimkar* (Book of Purchase and Sale), which, according to Elon, is Hai's "greatest work, and one of the classics of codificatory literature," survived intact. The first was translated by an unknown translator, and entitled *Mishpetei Shevu'ot* (Laws of Oaths), and the latter was translated by Rabbi Isaac ben Reuben al-Bargeloni in 1078, barely forty years after Hai's death. (Ibid., pp. 1161–66.) Elon points out that the monographs of these three *Geonim* dealt in most part with subjects within the purview of *Mishpat ivri*—that is, civil, criminal, and public law—and responded to the needs of the Jewish communities and their courts, which adjudicated according to Jewish law. (Ibid., p. 1158.)

11. Ibid., p. 1214. See also B. Cohen, "The Classification of the Law," pp. 525–36. In his meticulous and detailed analysis of the classification of the law in the *Mishneh Torah*, Cohen discusses the possibility of Islamic influence on Maimonides' Code (see n. 28 below). He also notes that the halakhic works of Saadiah, Hai, and Rabbi Samuel ben Hofni influenced Maimonides in regard to the arrangement and classification of the law. He points out, for example, that "Saadia, by force of his originality and independence of treatment of the halakhah was undoubtedly a great stimulus to Maimonides," that Hai "wrote some books on law in Arabic which Maimonides undoubtedly studied," and that nine of the titles of the subdivisions in Hofni's *Sefer ha-Mitzvot* are found as divisions in Maimonides' Code. See n. 8 above.

12. Elon notes, however, that "with all the assistance that Maimonides could derive from works of his predecessors, he was, as a practical matter, compelled to plow deeply through all the available halakhic material, break it down into individual rules, and insert each rule in its proper place under the appropriate general heading." While this is true, it does not change or negate Elon's preceding statement that "the concentration of material on a particular subject in each of the monographs greatly assisted Maimonides in his efforts to classify the law and organize it topically." Ibid., pp. 1196–97; see also Assaf, *Tekufat Ha-Geonim*, pp. 188–89.

Likewise, Twersky notes, "The Gaonic literary achievement provided a partial precedent in the sense that there were individual halakhic monographs in existence from which Maimonides benefited, but there was no synoptic presentation of all the material." Elsewhere, in further discussion of this literature's influence on Maimonides' topical classification of the law, he writes, "While aligning himself with this monographic approach and extolling it as the most effective and appropriate, Maimonides was fully aware that not a single predecessor produced a total regrouping of halakhah." Twersky adds, "This salient fact of total regrouping provides the correct perspective for assessing the many specific influences of the Gaonic literature on Maimonides; *they should not, per se, be dismissed or downgraded* [emphasis is mine], but the radical difference between the Gaonic works and the *Mishneh Torah* in scope and structure should be sharply perceived." See Twersky, *Introduction to the Code*, pp. 256, 274.

13. See Elon, *Jewish Law*, pp. 1196–97.

14. Ibid., p. 1161, n. 39; Abramson, *"Ha-Genizah she-ba-Genizah."*

15. See Elon, *Jewish Law*, pp. 1167–68.

16. Rabbi Isaac Alfasi was born in 1013 in the town of Qal'at Hamad in North Africa, and studied in the yeshivot of Qayrawan and in those of Rabbi Nissim ben Jacob (Nissim Gaon) and Rabbenu Hananel ben Hushiel. Eventually, he settled in Fez where he taught Torah to many students. At the age of seventy-five, forced to flee Fez, he moved to Spain and settled in Lucena, which was then the spiritual center of Spanish Jewry. (Dr. Gershon Cohen, the late Chancellor of the Jewish Theological Seminary, once described Lucena as the "Harvard of medieval Spain; anyone who was anybody sent his son to study in Lucena.") Upon the death of Rabbi Isaac ben Judah Ibn Ghiyath, he was succeeded as the head of the yeshiva in Lucena by Alfasi, who attracted many distinguished students, including Rabbi Joseph Ibn Migash (Ri Migash) and Yehudah Halevi. Alfasi died in 1103, having designated Ri Migash to succeed him. Ibid., p. 1168.

17. Ibid., p. 1171, n. 77. Elon points out that in one of his responsa, Maimonides writes that his rulings in the *Mishneh Torah* differ from those of Alfasi in about thirty places. At any rate, it is clear then that with the exception of ten or at most thirty instances, Maimonides' rulings follow those of Alfasi. The Rashba also states in one of his responsa, that "Alfasi and Maimonides agree all the time except in a few places" (*Teshuvot ha-Rashba*, I, # 253). See also ns. 63, 69 below.

18. Elon, *Jewish Law*, p. 1172.

19. Ibid., pp. 1168–69; see also n. 69 for more examples.

20. Ibid., p. 1170.

21. Ibid., p. 1171.

22. Interestingly, despite Maimonides' high opinion of Alfasi's *Sefer ha-Halakhot*, cited above, he did not follow Alfasi's arrangement of the laws, preferring instead that of Saadiah's monographs, as he pointed out in his letter to Rabbi Phinehas ben Meshullam of Alexandria. (See full quotation in discussion of Maimonides below.)

23. See Elon, *Jewish Law*, p. 1181.

24. Ibid., pp. 1181–84. Maimonides wrote of Ri Migash, "That man's grasp of the Talmud amazes everyone who studies his writings and perceives the depth of his analysis, so that I may say of him, 'His methodology surpasses that of his predecessors.'" Ibid., n. 6.

25. Ibid., p. 1184.

26. Ibid., pp. 1214–15. According to D. Z. Baneth, the recipient of this letter was not Ibn Aknin but Joseph ben Yehudah Ibn Shim'on to whom Maimonides dedicates the *Moreh Nebukhim*. Indeed, Baneth's opinion is that Ibn Aknin (or Ibn Aqnin) was not a student of Maimonides, but his colleague. See Baneth, ed., *Iggerot ha-Rambam*, pp. 31–2; Hirschberg, *Toledot ha-Yehudim*, I, pp. 267–70, n. 89. See also chap. 9, ns. 13, 14 below.

27. Twersky's suggestion finds possible support in the very words of Maimonides: "I am zealous for the Lord, God of Israel, when I see before me a nation that does not have a comprehensive book [of laws]... (Twersky's translation of this statement differs slightly from Elon's). One can almost hear the mental and spiritual agony felt by Maimonides when comparing his nation's lack of a code with the fact that such codes were common in contemporary Islam. Moreover, in discussing the possible influence of Maimonides' cultural milieu on his systematization of the law, Twersky writes, "To be sure, there was a sharp contrast between the diffuse and associative Talmud and systematic works of other kinds, and the cultural milieu could sharpen one's awareness of this. In this sense, academic taste of Hellenistic stimulation, the saturation of Jewish thought in Spain and Africa with Islamic methods and models, themselves an embodiment of the Greek spirit which places a premium on systematization, may certainly have played a role." Similarly, Twersky lists the "possible external influences and stimuli emanating

from the *fiqh* literature and the classification of Islamic law," among the various factors that could have influenced Maimonides' classification of the law. See Twersky, *Introduction to the Code*, pp. 358–59. See also B. Cohen, "The Classification of the Law," pp. 528–29. After discussing the pros and cons of possible Islamic influence on Maimonides' Code, Cohen concludes, that "the direct influence of Muslim law upon Maimonides is *quantite negligeable*. . . . In another and more important sense, however, Maimonides was even more deeply indebted to Islam for his unsurpassed systematization of Jewish Law. . . . In short, he learned from the Muslims what we, today, term the scientific method." See also Kramer, "The Influence of Islamic Law on Maimonides." Kramer shows that Maimonides was familiar with the five religious qualifications recognized by Islamic Law: (1) obligatory (*wajib, fard*), (2) recommended (*sunna, mandub*), (3) indifferent (*mubah*), to be distinguished from allowed, unobjectionable (*ja'iz*), (4) reprehensible, disapproved (*makruh*), and (5) forbidden (*haram*) as opposed to *halal* (everything not forbidden). Kramer shows that Maimonides, in *Mishnah Avot* and in his *Mishneh Torah*, uses the very same qualifications: obligatory (*hobah*), recommended (*mumlatz, meshubbah*), indifferent, permitted (*muttar*), disapproved, reprehensible (*meguneh*), and forbidden *(assur)*. Kramer points out that Maimonides uses two of the qualifications *meshubbah* and *meguneh* more often than the other three. Kramer indicates that some scholars point out the Jewish origin of these two qualifications. At any rate, he concludes, it is clear that Maimonides was aware of the five Islamic qualifications and was influenced by them. And if we accept the opinion of the Jewish origin of the two qualifications, then we have here a case of mutual borrowing or interplay between two legal systems.

28. See Twersky, *Introduction to the Code*, pp. 74–75.

29. See Elon, *Jewish Law*, p. 1186.

30. Twersky, *Introduction to the Code*, p. 20.

31. For a full description of these sources, see Twersky, *Introduction to the Code*, pp. 24–48 where Maimonides' statements are quoted *in extenso*. The following samples, however, are quoted from Elon's work (used throughout this chapter).

32. See Elon, *Jewish Law*, p. 1191. Commenting on this aspect of the *Mishneh Torah*, Twersky discusses at some length the views of a number of scholars such as Abraham Ibn Ezra and Bahya Ibn Pakuda, who disapproved of the study of laws that were no longer relevant for one reason or another. He then points out that although Maimonides was influenced by these scholars, shared some of their concerns regarding excessive emphasis on Talmudic studies, and agreed with them

that "Talmudic studies not related to or rooted in philosophic knowledge was in-adequate," when it came to the issue of which laws are relevant and which ones are not, he parted ways with them. Thus, at one point, in his *Commentary on the Mishnah*, he states, "It is, therefore, proper for man to preoccupy himself with the subject of sacrifices and to delve into them. He should not say, 'After all, these are matters for which there is no use in the present,' as most people do in fact say." Twersky adds that the *Mishneh Torah* presents itself as a major intellectual break-through, insisting that the present time, when part of the law is in abeyance, should be viewed as a historical anomaly and should not arbitrarily determine the scope of the study. The real historical dimensions were to be those in which the Torah and its precepts would be fully realized (as they were in the past), that is, in the time after the restoration of the Davidic dynasty, when "all the ancient laws will be reinstated...." For Twersky's full discussion of this aspect of Maimonides' *Mishneh Torah*, see Twersky, *Introduction to the Code*, pp. 195–220.

33. See Elon, *Jewish Law*, p. 1191.

34. See Twersky, *Introduction to the Code*, pp. 259–61. Some believe that Maimonides' idea of an all-inclusive legal work that also includes nonlegal aspects may have been influenced by al-Ghazali's monumental work, *Ihya 'Ulum al-Din* (Revival of the Religious Sciences), which is divided into forty books, the first of which, interestingly enough, is entitled "Book of Knowledge." Thus, Lawrence Berman, in his entry on al-Ghazali in the *Encyclopedia Judaica* ("Ghazali, Abu Hamid"), writes, "The parallel between al-Ghazali, who attempted to reconcile Islam with Sufism in his *Revival*, and Maimonides, who attempted to reconcile the law of Judaism with philosophy in his *Guide* is instructive, and Maimonides' idea of an all-inclusive legal work including non-legal aspects may have been in-fluenced by al-Ghazali's *Revival* as well." Similarly, according to Franz Rosenthal, in his *Knowledge Triumphant*, quoted by Steven Harvey (see below), "Without a work like al-Ghazali's *Revival of the Religious Sciences*, and without the 'cultural tradition out of which it grew,' all these subjects [of Maimonides' "Book of Knowledge"] could hardly have been united by a Jewish scholar under the title 'Book of Knowledge.'" In concluding his discussion of the impact of al-Ghazali's "Book of Knowledge" on Maimonides, he writes: "It is obvious that this 'Book of Knowledge,' occurring as it does at the beginning of the legal code, owes its title, its being, and its place to the attitude of Muslim civilization toward 'knowledge' and the trends and developments described in this chapter" (pp. 95–96). Finally, in a seminal article, "Alghazi and Maimonides and Their Books of Knowledge," Steven Harvey reviews the opinions of several scholars who consider al-Ghazal's possible influence on Maimonides' *Guide*, including the views of L. Berman and F. Rosenthal quoted above, and then focuses on the more striking similarities between al-Ghazali's and Maimonides' "Books of Knowledge." More specifically, Harvey

discusses in detail al-Ghazali's opinions regarding the duties of students and teachers to each other outlined in the fifth section of his "Book of Knowledge," entitled "On the Rules of Conduct for the Student and the Teacher" (*Adab al-muta'allim wal-mu'allim*) and their parallels in the sections on "Laws of the Study of Torah" and "Laws of Basic Fundamentals" in Maimonides' *Sefer ha-madda'*. Examples of the similarities include their opinions regarding the duties of the teacher "to have compassion for his students and treat them as his own children," that he not seek a fee for his teaching, that he not allow the student to study the "hidden sciences" before the completion of the "clear ones," and that he act in accordance with his knowledge, that he practice what he preaches, so that his act not give the lie to his word. Harvey also points to "significant differences" between the two "Books of Knowledge," such as the lack of a decisive linguistic similarity, the fact that Maimonides supports his views with quotations from the Bible and the Talmud, as well as the fact that Maimonides' treatment of the mutual duties of students and teachers are not numbered in a systematic list as they are in al-Ghazali's work. Incidentally, Harvey observes that Joseph ben Judah Ibn 'Aqnin (or Ibn 'Aknin)—Maimonides' close colleague—in chapter twenty-seven of his major work *Tibb al-nufus al-salimah* (The Hygiene of Healthy Souls) entitled *Adab al-mu'allim wal-muta'allim* (Rules of Conduct for the Teacher and the Student), enumerates and discusses the various obligations of the teacher and the student and provides a list of those duties, which is very similar to that of al-Ghazali. Harvey observes further that "scholars suggested the influence of Alghazali on this text, and it is, in fact, certain that Ibn 'Aqnin had Alghazali's account of the duties of the teacher and the student in front of him when he wrote this chapter."

Another striking similarity between al-Ghazali's and Maimonides' views, also noted briefly by Harvey, is their criticism of legal scholars who devote themselves to mastering the intricate details of legal argumentation and neglect or are ignorant of the knowledge of theology and philosophy. Thus, according to W. Montgomery Watt in his *Muslim Intellectual* (pp. 111–13), al-Ghazali "devoted most of the preface of *The Revival of the Religious Sciences* to commenting on the shortcomings of contemporary 'scientists,' that is, the scholar-jurists." Essentially, according to Watt, al-Ghazali blames those scholar-jurists who claim to be religious scholars for over-exercising themselves "in academic trifles [by which he means judicial and legal argumentation] while neglecting the real business of religion, the preparation of man for the life of the world to come," that is, via the study of correct religious and theological opinions. Similarly, at the beginning of his *Ma'amar tehiyyat ha-metim* (The Essay on Resurrection), explaining the reason that led him to include philosophical-theological sections in his legal writing, Maimonides writes,

> When I applied myself to this task [writing a legal compilation],
> I realized that it was not correct to strive to explain the ramifi-

cations of the religious law, and to leave its roots neglected, un-explained, and its essentials undiscussed, providing no guidance. This is especially urgent since I have met some who think they are among the sages of Israel . . . but they are not certain if God is corporeal. . . . When I learned of these exceedingly deficient folk and their doubts, who, although they consider themselves sages in Israel, are in fact the most ignorant, and more seriously astray than beasts, their minds filled with the senseless prattle of old women and noxious fantasies . . . I concluded that it was necessary that I clearly elucidate religious fundamentals in my work on law.

Commenting on this passage in "The Essay of Resurrection," Twersky notes that Maimonides "emphasizes the inclusion of theological-philosophical principles in all his works. . . . He had never dealt with any aspect of Judaism without paying attention to philosophical issues and implications. . . . It was particularly impossible for him to compose a comprehensive work on the details of practical precepts while ignoring the fundamentals of essential beliefs." He refers here to those command-ments which, according to Maimonides, "are the 'root' (*ikkar*) of Mosaic religion, and which should be known before anything else." Twersky adds that Maimonides' "pejorative characterization of those people who think that they are scholars but who are actually engaged in trivial scholastic endeavors, also reflects his concep-tion of proper Talmudism and his repeated criticism of scholarly stereotypes." After an evaluative discussion of the similarities and differences between the two "Books of Knowledge," Harvey concludes,

Yet, if it is known that Maimonides lived amidst a people whose great legal works were often preceded by initial discussions of "Knowledge" and even chapters and books on knowledge with the title *Book of Knowledge*, and it is known that among the most famous, if not the most famous, of these books of knowledge was one that contained a section on duties of the student and the teacher, then we must begin to consider influence. The similar-ities uncovered in our comparison of the two sections on these duties make the case for influence even more compelling. Here, the influence is not so striking as that upon Ibn 'Aqnin, but is rather the influence of one great mind upon another, one of sug-gestion, stimulation, example, and reinforcement.

Harvey adds, "The question of the overall influence of the *Revival* on the *Mishneh Torah*, in general, and on the *Book of Knowledge*, in particular, should be seen in this perspective." See Harvey, " Alghazali and Maimonides and Their Books of

Knowledge"; "The Essay on Resurrection," in Maimonides, *Crisis and Leadership*, pp. 212–13, 246–52; Twersky, *Introduction to the Code*, pp. 201–2, 260, 503; for al-Ghazali's influence on Jewish philosophy, see "Ghazali, Abu Hamid Muhammad Ibn Muhammad Al" in *Encyclopedia Judaica*, VII, cols. 538–40.

35. Elon, *Jewish Law* cites illuminative examples from the *Mishneh Torah* for all these features. See pp. 1187–95. For a thorough discussion of Maimonides' statements and the significance of his objectives, as well as illustrative examples of how Maimonides implemented these objectives, see pp. 1185–1214.

36. Maimonides anticipated criticism from "envious evildoers," ignoramuses and simpletons, "starry-eyed and confused neophytes," and "pious thick-headed and dyed-in-the-wool conservatives," and their like who would not appreciate his work or would not understand it. See text of passage from Maimonides' letter to his disciple, quoted in Elon, *Jewish Law*, p. 1222.

37. Ibid., pp. 1216–17. After quoting this explanation of Maimonides in full, Elon comments, "In principle, Maimonides was certainly correct. Rabbi Judah Ha-Nasi also omitted the names of some of the transmitters of the tradition, stated the law as he thought correct without mentioning the particular Sages who held that view, and used other similar methods." But, Elon continues, "This parallel does not solve the problem entirely. The Mishnah of Rabbi Judah Ha-Nasi, despite its manner of transmitting and declaring the law, is replete with the names of *tana'im* and records differences of opinion as to the law. The body of *Mishneh Torah* [not the introduction], however, does not mention even one name of a transmitter of the law, and the entire book states the law monolithically and without attribution of source" (Ibid., p. 1219).

38. Ibid., pp. 1219–20; n. 113.

39. For the full text of Maimonides' letter to Phinehas ben Meshullam and Elon's detailed discussion of its main points, see ibid., pp. 1216–21.

40. Abraham ben David (Rabad) of Posquiere was known as one of the great halakhic authorities, and was the head of a yeshiva in Posquiere.

41. See Elon, *Jewish Law*, pp. 1224–25.

42. Asheri (Asher ben Yehiel, also known as the Rosh) was the outstanding disciple of Meir of Rothenberg (Maharam). Following the death of his teacher, Asheri became the leader of Ashkenazi Jewry, and later settled in Spain, where he became one of the foremost halakhic authorities and leaders in Spain as well. Ibid., p. 1226.

43. Ibid., p. 1227.

44. According to Elon, Asheri's criticism of Maimonides was triggered, so to speak, by a case referred to him for review after it had been decided by another judge named Mazliah on the basis of the *Mishneh Torah*. After examining the underlying Talmudic sources of Maimonides' ruling, Asheri concluded that Mazliah misunderstood Maimonides' meaning. This led him to conclude that relying solely on such a book for determining the law and in rendering judgment is likely to lead to misunderstanding of what has been written in categorical and monolithic form— hence, his criticism of the *Mishneh Torah*. Ibid., p. 1226.

45. Rabbi Solomon ben Abraham ben Aderet, known as the Rashba, was an outstanding halakhic authority and the recognized leader of Spanish Jewry in the second half of the thirteenth century and the beginning of the fourteenth. Ibid., p. 1273.

46. Ibid., p. 1275.

47. Ibid., p. 1273; n. 156.

48. Ibid., pp. 1277–78.

49. Jacob ben Asher was born in Germany c.1270 and, together with his father, fled from there to Spain in 1303. He was the third son of Asheri, who was sharply opposed to the methodology of the *Mishneh Torah*, and had composed his own book of *halakhot*, *Piskei Ha-Rosh*. Jacob served as a judge in the rabbinical court of Toledo, and died in 1343. Ibid., pp. 1278–79.

50. Ibid., p. 1285.

51. Elon adds that "the adoption of the principle of *hilkheta ke-vatra'ei* with regard to Asheri was particularly appropriate in that he, as the leader of Ashkenazic Jewry and, later, one of the leading authorities in Spain, had considered a substantial portion of the opinions of the halakhic authorities in both centers and, in the event of conflict, had decided between them." In a sense, continues Elon, "acceptance of Asheri's rulings resolved conflicts between the halakhic authorities of these great Jewish centers" (Ibid., pp. 1284–85; n. 186).

52. As we have seen, Maimonides' response to the criticism of the *Mishneh Torah* by Phinehas ben Meshullam contended that the *Mishneh Torah* had in fact followed the method of Rabbi Judah Ha-Nasi in that the Mishnah had also not given the chain of tradition of every law. But Elon points out that this comparison is flawed. See n. 37 above, which explains Elon's reason for his reservation.

53. See Elon, *Jewish Law*, pp. 1287–92.

54. Elon explains that Maimonides' order was influenced by the order of the tractates of the Talmud, in which the Order of *Nezikin* begins with *Baba Kamma*, dealing with the laws of damages, robbery, theft, and assault and battery, and ends with Tractates *Sanhedrin, Shevu'ot*, and *Makkot*, which deal with the composition of the courts and the laws of evidence. Elon suggests that the *Tur Hoshen Mishpat* departed from the conventional organization of halakhic codes and followed the inner logic of the subject matter in accordance with the author's aim "so that every point may be easily found." Ibid., pp. 1292–93.

55. Ibid., pp. 1301–2.

56. Joseph Caro was born in Spain in 1488, and at the tender age of four went into exile with his parents in 1492. His family wandered through several way sta- tions—Constantinople, Nikopol in northern Bulgaria, Salonika, and Egypt, and fi- nally settled in Safed, in the Land of Israel. In Safed, Caro was appointed to the *bet din* presided by Jacob Berab, who reintroduced the ancient practice of rabbini- cal ordination. Joseph Caro was one of the first rabbis ordained by Berab. When Berab died, Caro, together with Moses ben Joseph Trani (Mabit), headed the *bet din* of Safed. Ibid., p. 1310; n. 2.

57. Elon observes that this approach to codification was not entirely new. A similar approach was suggested by Maimonides himself in his letter to Phinehas ben Meshullam of Alexandria (discussed above). It will be recalled that Mai- monides stated that he intended to write a separate work, a companion to the *Mish- neh Torah*, which would cite the sources of his rulings. However, Elon points out, Maimonides' plan was meant to include in such work only the sources of the opin- ions he adopted in the *Mishneh Torah* (not all opinions), and only for the laws for which the source was not readily available in the Talmud (such as the laws of the Sabbath that are not found in Tractates *Shabbat* and *Eruvin*, but are scattered throughout other tractates). But Maimonides never carried out even this limited project, and in this respect, Elon adds, Rashba's two-part work, the Long *Torat ha-Bayit* and the Short *Torat ha-Bayit* was a much larger step in the direction of Caro's approach. As pointed out above, however, Rashba's work, though original and innovative, was limited in scope, covering only what Elon calls "religious laws" (*issur va-heter*), and "did not in its time noticeably influence the methodol- ogy of codificatory literature." Ibid., p. 1313.

58. Ibid.

59. Ibid., p. 1314.

60. Ibid., p. 1315.

61. Ibid., pp. 1317–18.

62. Ibid., pp. 1318–19. The practical implication of this methodology of Caro, however, is that when Maimonides and Alfasi agree with each other and disagree with Asheri, Caro rules most often in accordance with the view of Maimonides and Alfasi—against Asheri. Since, according to Maimonides' own statements, his rulings in the *Mishneh Torah* differ from those of Alfasi only in ten or thirty places at most (see n. 17 above), Caro ends up ruling in accordance with their view against that of Asheri most of the time. There are, however, a few instances in which Caro rules against both Maimonides and Alfasi in favor of Aheri's opinion. Rabbi Shlomo Toledano discusses these instances in detail and tries to explain why Caro rules as he does in these exceptions. See his *Divrei Shalom ve-Emet*, I, pp. 242–54, 263–64.

63. Elon, *Jewish Law*, pp. 1319–20.

64. Ibid., n. 30.

65. Ibid., pp. 1323–25.

66. For the full text of Elon's comparative discussion of these examples, see ibid., pp. 1327–40.

67. It might be well to remember in this connection also the contributions of Geonic codification, especially that of Yehudai Gaon and Saadiah Gaon. Yehudai Gaon's *Halakhot Pesukot* was the first attempt at codification of halakhah, and, in the words of Elon, "opened an era in codificatory literature," and "substantively facilitated subsequent halakhic research." As for Saadiah Gaon, his innovative scientific and systematic classification and topical organization of the law in halakhic monographs on particular topics was followed by two illustrious *Geonim*, Samuel ben Hofni and Hai, and together their works no doubt provided a model for Maimonides' goal of topical organization of Jewish law, and even facilitated his task in implementing that goal.

68. Since Maimonides follows Alfasi's rulings in most cases, given Caro's methodology for determining the law, he ends up ruling like both of them against Asheri in all but a few cases. We have then, a direct line leading from Alfasi's rulings through Maimonides to Caro. Or, to put it differently, Alfasi's rulings constitute the underpinnings of Sephardic halakhah, which regards Caro as its supreme halakhic authority. See ns. 17 and 62 above.

7. MEDIEVAL JEWISH PHILOSOPHY

1. See Goitein, *Jews and Arabs*, p. 141

2. See Altmann, "Judaism and World Philosophy," p. 964.

3. See Halkin, "Judeo-Arabic Literature," p. 1136.

4. See Lewis, *The Jews of Islam*, p. 80.

5. The Arab conquest resulted in an influx of Greek thought which profoundly influenced Islamic thought. Essentially, most of the Greek learning came to Islam from the translation of Greek texts into Arabic. First, under the Abbasid Caliph Ma'mun (813–33), a school of translators was established in Baghdad. Then, in the tenth century, when Arabs were no longer proficient in Greek, translations into Arabic were based on Christian Syriac intermediate renderings. As a result, a very considerable part of the scientific and philosophical literature of classical and Hellenistic Greek thought was made accessible to the Islamic world. See Altmann, "Judaism and World Philosophy," p. 966.

6. Ibid.

7. See Patai, *The Jewish Mind*, p. 126.

8. Maimonides, *Guide*, II, chap. 16, pp. 293–94. For Maimonides' justification of his choice, see his position on creation discussed in the sub-section, "Classification of the Commandments," later in this chapter (pp. nnn–nn); see also ibid., II, chap. 25, pp. 328–29.

9. Actually, Isaac Israeli of Qayrawan was interested in science before Saadiah. As a physician he was probably more at home in purely physical sciences than Saadiah. But according to Husik, "There is no evidence that he had the larger interest of the Gaon of Sura, namely, to construct a system of Judaism upon the basis of scientific doctrine." See Husik, *Medieval Jewish Philosophy*, p. 24.

10. For a full discussion of his halakhic monographs and their contribution to the ultimate topical codification of Jewish law, see chap. 6, ns. 9–13.

11. See Husik, *Medieval Jewish Philosophy*, p. 24.

12. See Altmann, *Saadya Gaon*, introduction, p. 17.

13. Ibid.

14. They were opposed by the Ash'ariyya who insisted on a literal interpretation of the Koran. Ibid., p. 12; see also Watt, *Islamic Philosophy*, pp. 85–86; Wensinck, *The Muslim Creed*, pp. 88–90.

15. See Watt, *Islamic Philosophy*, p. 66; Wensinck, *The Muslim Creed*, p. 60.

16. Maimonides, who was a strong opponent of the Mutakallimun, gives a detailed outline of their fundamental principles and their arguments for the existence, unity, and incorporeality of God as well as a sarcastic criticism of their "atomic theory" (see below). See Maimonides, *Guide*, I, chaps. 71–76, pp. 175–231. Watt and Wensinck offer a more detailed discussion of their views as well as the historical and intellectual context or backdrop of their views. See Watt, *Islamic Philosophy*, pp. 58–71; Wensinck, *The Muslim Creed*, chaps. 4 and 5, pp. 58–101.

17. See Halkin, "Judeo-Arabic Literature," p. 1137; Husik, *Medieval Jewish Philosophy*, introduction, p. xxii, p. 25. An example of Maimonides' sarcastic criticism of the atomic theory follows: "When the pen is put into motion, God creates four accidents, no one of which is the cause of the other. . . . The first accident is my will to put the pen into motion; the second accident, my power to put the pen into motion; the third accident, human motion itself—I mean the motion of the hand; the fourth accident, the motion of the pen." For they think, Maimonides continues, "that when a man wills a thing, and, as he thinks, does it, will is created for him, his power to do that which he wills is created for him, and his act is created for him." Ridiculing this theory further, Maimonides observes that, according to the Mutakallimun, life and death are also accidents created and recreated by God continually since accidents last only an atomic unit of time. He creates a unit of death following upon the disappearance of the accidents of life. Since we find molars of dead individuals that are thousands of years old, it follows that according to them, God would be creating in these remains the accident of death all through these thousands of years creating one unit of death as soon as another unit disappears, since no unit of life or death lasts more than one atom of time. See Maimonides, *Guide*, I, chap. 73, pp. 194–214, especially, pp. 202–4. For a detailed discussion of the historical development of the theory, who were its supporters and its opponents, as well as a very positive evaluation of Maimonides' ironic critique of it, see Fakhry, *Islamic Occasionalism*, pp. 22–43, 83–92.

18. In fact, according to Alexander Altmann, all of Saadiah's works were devoted to the same end. Altmann adds that "there is a singular purpose and design running through all the extensive writing which he did, and which incidentally, made him the pioneer of the 'scientific' learning of the Middle Ages." Thus his

Arabic translation of the Bible (*Tafsir*) "was destined to save the Jewries of the Arabic-speaking world from falling into spiritual decay." Indeed, the *Tafsir* has remained the standard Arabic Bible for all Arabic-speaking Jews down to the present. For the more learned readers, he composed also an extensive commentary (*sharh*) on the Bible. According to Altmann, the same educational purpose was behind the composition of his *Siddur*, the first Jewish Prayer Book of which we know. Saadiah "recognized the need for supplying the communities with a textbook of prayers instead of the mere halakhic rules for prayers, with which his predecessors in the field of liturgy, Rabbi Natronai and Rabbi Amram Gaon were chiefly concerned. But Altmann adds, for those of his people who had lost their way, or were "lacking in faith," or tormented by "doubts," to them he had to offer religious guidance in the language of philosophy. So, in 933, he produced his magnum opus, "The Book of Doctrines and Beliefs" (in Arabic, *Kitab al-Amanat wa'l-I'tikadat*; known, in Yehudah Ibn Tibbon's Hebrew translation, as *Sefer ha-Emunot ve-ha-De'ot*). See Altmann, *Saadya Gaon*, introduction, pp. 15–16.

19. See Altmann, *Saadya Gaon*, prolegomena, p. 29. This statement is followed by a most humble declaration about "the shortcoming of [his] knowledge, which is far from being perfect, and the deficiency of [his] understanding, which is far from being complete." This sense of extreme humility on the part of Saadiah contrasts markedly with Maimonides' self-confidence and even arrogance evident in numerous statements throughout his *Guide*.

20. Altmann, *Saadya Gaon*, prolegomena, p. 26. Note the contrast between this inclusive approach and Maimonides' elitism expressed in his dedicatory introduction to his student, Joseph ben Yehudah Ibn Shim'on: "Your absence drove me to compose this Treatise, which I composed for you and for those like you, however few they are" (*Guide*, p. 4); or when he writes, "It is not the purpose of this treatise to make its totality understandable to the vulgar or to beginners in speculation" (ibid., I, p. 5). At the very beginning of the *Guide*, he says that, in teaching the truth, he prefers to please "a single virtuous [that is, intelligent] man while displeasing ten thousands ignoramuses—I am he who prefers to address that single man by himself and I do not heed the blame of those many creatures" (ibid., p. 16).

21. Altmann, *Saadya Gaon*, prolegomena, p. 30.

22. Ibid., pp. 36–43. The third source of knowledge, "logical inference," is crucial for Saadiah who relies on it to prove such central Judaic concepts as the existence of God, creation in time, and the justice of God.

23. Ibid., pp. 43–47; see also Husik, *Medieval Jewish Philosophy*, p. 28.

24. Husik, *Medieval Jewish Philosophy*, p. 31; see also Altmann, *Saadya Gaon*, pp. 40–68.

25. Altmann, *Saadya Gaon*, pp. 69–80.

26. Ibid., pp. 80–84. According to Husik, Saadiah, his contemporary and associate David ben Merwan al-Mukammas, and later Jewish philosophers "owed their interest in the problem of attributes to Muslim schools in which we know it played an important role." But from the discussion of the problem by Saadiah and al-Mukammas, it is clear that "the problem originated in the Christian schools in the Orient, who made use of it to rationalize the dogma of the Trinity." Husik notes further that monotheism is a fundamental dogma in both Judaism and Islam. Hence their rationalizing theologians felt it necessary "to meet the Trinitarians [Christian theologians] with their own weapons and show that the multiplicity of divine attributes which they could not deny, . . . does in no way affect God's unity." See Husik, *Medieval Jewish Philosophy*, pp. 17–19, 33–35.

27. See Altmann, *Saadya Gaon*, pp. 84–92; see also Husik, *Medieval Jewish Philosophy*, p. 36. This is in agreement with Maimonides who devotes the greater part of Part I of his *Guide* to the allegorical interpretation of such biblical passages. See the sub-section, "Allegorical Interpretation," later in this chapter (pp. 143–45, ns. 49–55).

28. See Altmann, *Saadya Gaon*, p. 66, n. 1; p. 93, n. 4; see also Husik, *Medieval Jewish Philosophy*, p. 32.

29. Essentially, Saadiah echoes the rabbinic dictum in Mishnah *Avot* that "The Holy One, blessed be He, was pleased to make Israel worthy [of rewards], therefore he gave them a copious Torah and many commandments" (*Avot*, I, 18).

30. See Altmann, *Saadya Gaon*, pp. 94–105. For Maimonides' classification of the commandments, which differs markedly from that of Saadiah, see the sub-section, "Explanation of the Commandments," later in this chapter (pp. 156–57, ns. 86–91).

31. See Altmann, *Saadya Gaon*, pp. 105–14. Husik notes that Saadiah's emphasis on tradition, apart from its intrinsic importance for Judaism, has its additional motive in rejecting Karaism. Husik notes further that Saadiah's argument (at the end of the chapter on commandments) against the possibility of the Law being abrogated is directed no doubt against the two sister religions, Christianity and Islam. See Husik, *Medieval Jewish Philosophy*, p. 40.

32. See Altmann, *Saadya Gaon*, pp. 118–21.

33. Ibid., pp. 121–25. Maimonides' solution to this problem seems to be more realistic. He maintains that God's knowledge is so different from our knowledge that we have no way of knowing how He knows, just as we are unable to know His essence, for His essence and His knowledge are one. See Maimonides, *Guide*, III, chap. 21, pp. 480–85. See also my discussion, "God's Omniscience and Its Limits," in connection with Maimonides' interpretation of the biblical instances of *nissayon* (trial) which seem to imply that God is testing individuals or nations in order to find out that which he did not know before (ibid., III, chap. 24). However, Gersonides and the Moroccan sage Rabbi Raphael Berdugo disagree with Maimonides' interpretation, and maintain that God's foreknowledge does not embrace the contingent acts of man—that is, actions which result from man's exercise of his free choice. See Henry Toledano, "The Centrality of Reason," pp. 171–205, especially, pp. 181–82, ns. 41–47.

34. Here again, Maimonides' explanation seems more satisfactory. According to him, God did indeed cause Pharaoh to refuse to let the children of Israel go, but this was part of his punishment for drowning all Jewish male children in the river. God forced him to refuse to let Israel go in order to visit on him the full measure of the punishment— the ten plagues. See Maimonides, *Mishneh Torah, Hilkhot Teshuvah*, 6:3.

35. See Altmann, *Saadya Gaon*, pp. 137–39.

36. Ibid., pp. 141–48.

37. Ibid., pp. 181–91; see also Husik, *Medieval Jewish Philosophy*, pp. 43–44.

38. For a detailed discussion of this work and its significance in the codification literature, see the section, "The *Mishneh Torah* of Maimonides" in chap. 6 above (pp. 93–105, 23–35).

39. See the section on philosophy in "Maimonides, Moses" in *Encyclopedia Judaica*, XI, col. 768.

40. See Halkin, "Judeo-Arabic Literature," p. 1143.

41. Ibid.

42. See "Maimonides, Moses" in *Encyclopedia Judaica*, XI, col. 769.

43. See Husik, *Medieval Jewish Philosophy*, p. 239; see also Strauss' introductory essay to Maimonides, *Guide*, p. xiv.

44. See "Maimonides, Moses" in *Encyclopedia Judaica*, XI, col. 769. The introduction to Mishnah *Avot*, known as the *Shemonah Perakim* (Eight Chapters) is a philosophical and ethical treatise in which Maimonides harmonizes Aristotle's ethics with rabbinic teachings on the subject. In his introduction to the eleventh chapter of Mishnah *Sanhedrin* (*Perek Helek*), he dealt at length with the fundamental doctrines of Judaism, which he formulated as the "Thirteen Articles of Faith." The first book of *Mishneh Torah*, *Sefer ha-Madda'*, is devoted to a discussion of God and His attributes, angelic beings, the structure of the universe (consistent with contemporary astronomical views), prophecy, ethics, repentance, free will and providence, and the afterlife. The last section of *Mishneh Torah*, *Hilkhot Melakhim*, includes a discussion of the Messiah and the messianic age.

45. See Husik, *Medieval Jewish Philosophy*, p. 239.

46. Maimonides, *Guide*, p. 4.

47. Ibid. In describing Ibn Shim'on's adequate preparation and capacity for the study of philosophy, Maimonides incidentally outlines his theory of education, progressing from such secular sciences as mathematics, astronomy, and logic to the study of metaphysics (speculative divine matters or philosophy).

48. Ibid.

49. Maimonides, *Guide*, I, chap. 1.

50. See Maimonides, *Guide* (Strauss), p. xiv.

51. See Husik, *Medieval Jewish Philosophy*, p. 244.

52. See introductions to Parts I and III of Maimonides, *Guide*. This principle is based on the inverse reading of the biblical verse: "It is time to do for the Lord, for they have infringed Thy Law (*heferu toratekha*)" (Ps. 119:126); that is to say, they infringed Thy Law in order to do for the Lord (T. B. Berakhot, 63a). See also other Talmudic applications of this principle cited in Elon, *Ha-Mishpat Ha-Ivri*, II, p. 412.

53. Thus, in the introduction to Part I, Maimonides describes seven types of contradictions which appear in literary works, and states explicitly that he will make use of two of them. Maimonides, *Guide*, pp. 17–20.

54. See Maimonides, *Guide* (Strauss), pp. xiv–xv.

55. See "Maimonides, Moses" in *Encyclopedia Judaica*, XI, col. 770.

56. Ibid., col. 771.

57. See Husik, *Medieval Jewish Philosophy*, p. 241.

58. Maimonides, *Guide*, I, chap. 71, p. 179. He no doubt had Saadiah, among others, in mind.

59. Ibid., p. 180.

60. Commenting on Maimonides' discussion of *kalam*, Husik writes, "Maimonides' exposition and criticism of the principles of the Mutakallimun is of special interest, too, because up to recent times his sketch of the tenets of this school was the only extensive account known; and it has not lost its value even yet." More important, referring to Maimonides' argument against proving the existence of God from creation, Husik states, "This is a new contribution of Maimonides. All Jewish writers before Halevi followed in the proofs of the existence of God the method designated by Maimonides as that of the *kalam*. . . . Maimonides is the first who takes deliberate account of the Mutakallimun, gives an adequate outline of the essentials of their teachings, and administers a crushing blow to their principles as well as their method" (pp. 246–48). For a brief discussion of *kalam*'s "atomic theory" and Maimonides' biting criticism of it, see the discussion of *kalam* in the sub-section, "Source of Saadiah's Inspiration and Model" above (pp. 128–30, ns. 14–17). For an evaluation of Maimonides' criticism of the atomic theory by Majid Fakhry, see n. 17 above.

61. Maimonides, *Guide*, II, chaps. 1, 25, pp. 252–53, 328–29; see also a fuller discussion of his view on creation in the sub-section "Creation Ex Nihilo" in this chapter (pp. 148–49, ns. 65–66).

62. Maimonides' cosmogony follows closely that of Aristotle, according to which the universe is constituted of ten concentric spheres, each of which is endowed with a soul and moved by an intelligence. Parting with Aristotle, who held that the spheres coexisted with the Prime Mover—as well as with the Neoplatonists who maintained that the spheres emanated from God (theory of emanation)—Maimonides says that the spheres were created by God and are identical with the angels of the Jewish tradition. Maimonides maintains that the tenth sphere, which is the "Active Intellect" is the sphere under whose influence stands the sublunar world, and through which knowledge is bestowed on the human mind. See Patai, *The Jewish Mind*, p. 130, n. 62.

63. Maimonides, *Guide*, II, chap. 1, p. 243; see also Hyman's succinct summary of this argument in "Maimonides, Moses" in *Encyclopedia Judaica*, XI.

64. Maimonides, *Guide*, II, chap. 1, pp. 243–44; Husik, *Medieval Jewish Philosophy*, pp. 257–68.

65. According to Hyman, Maimonides even attempted to show from an analysis of Aristotle's texts that "Aristotle himself did not consider his arguments as conclusive demonstrations but only as showing that eternity is more plausible than creation." Therefore Maimonides says that a conclusive demonstration of the creation or the eternity of the world is beyond the capacity of human reason. See "Maimonides, Moses" in *Encyclopedia Judaica*, XI, col. 772. For a more detailed analysis of Maimonides' argument(s) for creation ex nihilo, see the extensive and informative exploration of the subject in Gluck, "Maimonides' Arguments for Creation Ex Nihilo in the Guide of the Perplexed." In this groundbreaking study of the subject, Gluck reexamines meticulously Maimonides' arguments and provides a brief and schematic synopsis of all the twelve chapters in the *Guide* devoted to the argument for creation (II, chaps. 13–24). He also reviews the diverse scholarly opinions regarding the nature of Maimonides' argument. Gluck notes, for example, that some scholars interpret Maimonides' argument for creation to be based on revelation while others maintain that it is based on reason. (He quotes A. H. Wolfson, who thought that Maimonides' argument for creation was not demonstrative nor based on revelation, but on some other kind of reasoning.) Gluck wonders how there can be confusion on such a fundamental distinction. He suggests, by way of an explanation, that the reason for the confusion seems to be that "at times Maimonides stresses one [view] and at times the other." According to Gluck, Maimonides creates the confusion "by saying that in the absence of demonstrative proof one ought to follow prophecy and that it will also be possible to employ rational argument for creation." Following an intricate and detailed exploration of what such rational argument may be, Gluck concludes that "Maimonides argues for creation *ex-nihilo* on the basis of the fact of revelation and not on any particular authoritative traditional opinion. Revelation is assumed and from that assumption everything else follows." Fleshed out, this argument runs as follows:

> If revelation is a fact, God did something quite novel in the world; this is consistent with creation but inconsistent with an eternal universe where nothing essentially novel occurs.

> Aside from creation and eternity, there are no tenable explanations for the existence of the universe.

> We, heretofore, have believed in revelation as a fact as well as its teaching regarding creation.

The eternity of the universe has not been logically proved nor has creation been disproved.

Therefore, we have no reason to revise our belief in revelation and creation and the Aristotelian theory of the eternity of the universe is rejected.

Gluck notes, however, that while this argument is logically valid, it can be attacked in terms of its premises. As he puts it, "It proceeds from belief to belief, not from facts to belief." For "if revelation was a generally agreed upon belief (as in the Middle Ages) and no alternatives to creation and eternity were plausible, then his argument would indeed come close to being demonstrative. Revelation, however, is no longer conventional wisdom but the object of specific religious faith and his argument may not mean much to those who do not already believe in it." Gluck adds, however, that Maimonides' argument, "can be shared by a number of religious communities and Maimonides acknowledged that belief in creation was shared by Judaism, Christianity, and Islam despite their differences on many other issues."

66. Maimonides, *Guide*, II, chap. 25, pp. 328–29. Patai, *The Jewish Mind* observes, "No better example could be found to illustrate the point that despite their adoption of the Arabic literary and poetic forms, Greco-Arab science and philosophy, and many other aspects of Arab culture, when it came to fundamentals, the Jews in the Muslim world remained impenetrably Jewish" (pp. 128–29).

67. Maimonides, *Guide*, II, chap, 32, pp. 360–63. Maimonides' attitude toward the first two theories is that while the prophet is necessarily a philosopher, he is superior to the latter in that he succeeds in acquiring that knowledge of God that comes only through illumination from God via the Active Intellect. As for the possibility of God choosing an ignorant person as a prophet, Maimonides states categorically that God is likely to turn an ignorant person into a prophet no more than He is likely to turn an ass or a frog into one. Ibid., p. 362.

68. Ibid., chaps. 36, 41, pp. 370, 385. For a definition of the Active Intellect and its function in imparting knowledge (including prophecy) to humans, see n. 62 above.

69. Ibid., chaps. 38, 39, pp. 377–81; see also "Maimonides, Moses" in *Encyclopedia Judaica*, XI, col. 773. Hyman adds, "In line with the view of the Islamic Aristotelians, particularly al-Farabi, Maimonides conceived of the prophet as a statesman who brings the law to his people and admonishes them to observe it." This conception of the prophet-statesman, Hyman continues, is based on Plato's

notion, found in the *Republic*, of the philosopher-king who establishes and administers the state" (ibid.).

70. Maimonides, *Guide*, II, chaps. 35, 39, pp. 367–69, 378–81.

71. See his *Hilkhot Yesode ha-Torah*, 7:6. Interestingly, Rabbi Habib Toledano (c.1800–70), the author of *Terumat ha-Kodesh* and *Peh Yesharim*, composed a *piyyut* in honor of Moses entitled "Ben Amram" modeled after the *piyyut*, "Bar Yohay," popular among the Sephardim. Just as "Bar Yohay" glorifies the legendary and mystical qualities of Rabbi Shim'on Bar Yohay, Toledano's poem glorifies the unique qualities of Moses, incorporating the distinguishing features of his prophetic experience enumerated in the *Mishneh Torah*. See Habib Toledano, *Peh Yesharim*, p. 9–10.

72. Maimonides, *Guide*, I, chap. 71, p. 178.

73. Ibid., II, chap. 25, pp. 328–29. See also the sub-section "Creation Ex Nihilo" (pp. 148–49, ns. 65–66) in this chapter.

74. See Patai's comment in n. 66 above.

75. Maimonides, *Guide*, II, chap. 29, especially pp. 345–48.

76. Ibid.

77. Ibid., ns. 60, 61.

78. Ibid., III, chaps. 10, 11, pp. 438–41.

79. Ibid., chap. 12, pp. 441–48. Maimonides discusses his theory on the purpose of creation ibid. chap. 13, pp. 448–56. He rejects as wrong the notion that the world was created for the sake of man. Everything was created for its own sake, he asserts, and everything was created as a result of God's volition—His free will.

80. Ibid., chap. 12, pp. 441–42.

81. Ibid., pp. 442–48.

82. Saadiah suggests also several possible reasons why the wicked prosper. See a fuller discussion of his solution to the problem in the sub-section "God's Justice and Man's Free Will" (pp. 137–38, ns. 32–35) in this chapter.

83. Maimonides discusses four views of divine providence which he rejects. His position is that there is individual providence (in addition to general providence), and it is determined by the degree of development of the individual's intellect. The more developed a man's intellect is, the more subject he is to divine providence. Maimonides, *Guide*, III, chaps. 22–24, pp. 486–502.

84. Ibid., chap. 21, pp. 480–85; see also n. 33 above.

85. See Maimonides, *Mishneh Torah, Hilkhot Teshuvah*, 6:3; see also Saadiah's explanation of the same passage in the sub-section, "God's Justice and Man's Free Will," (pp. 137–38, ns. 32–35) in this chapter.

86. Maimonides, *Guide*, III, chap. 26, pp. 506–10.

87. Ibid.

88. Ibid., chap. 27, pp. 510–12.

89. Ibid., chap. 31, pp. 523–24.

90. According to Maimonides, "The knowledge of those opinions and practices [of the pagans] is a very important chapter in the exposition of the reasons for the commandments." His own familiarity with those beliefs and practices is based on his study of the books of the Sabians (his name for the pagans at the time of the Patriarch Abraham), notably *The Nabatean Agriculture*, which were in his possession in Arabic translation. After describing some of their basic beliefs and some of the stories they told regarding Abraham and Adam, Maimonides adds, "I shall now return to my purpose and say that the meaning of many of the laws became clear to me and their causes known to me through my study of the doctrines, practices, and cult of the Sabians, as you will hear when I explain the reasons for the *commandments* that are considered to be without a cause. I shall mention to you the books from which all that I know about the doctrines and opinions of the Sabians will become clear to you so that you will know for certain that what I say about the reasons for these laws is correct." Later in the chapter (III, chap 29, p. 521), Maimonides provides a long list of those books of the Sabians including what he calls "the big book by the same author [Ishaq al-Sabi] concerning the laws of the Sabians, the details of their religion, their festivals, their sacrifices, their prayers, and other matters belonging to their religion." Ibid., chaps. 29–30, pp. 514–23, especially pp. 514, 518, 521. It seems that in view of the above, Maimonides could be regarded as having pioneered the "comparative religion" approach to the study of religion.

91. Ibid., chaps. 32, 46; pp. 525–31, 581–92.

92. The Arabic original *Dalalat al-Ha'irin* was composed around 1200, and shortly thereafter was translated twice in Hebrew as *Moreh Nebukhim*, first by Samuel Ibn Tibbon (completed in 1204), and shortly later by the Hebrew poet Judah al-Harizi. See "Maimonides, Moses" in *Encyclopedia Judaica*, XI, col. 769.

93. Ibid. See also my detailed discussion of the influence of the Jewish works of the Golden Age in Spain on the thinkers of the *haskalah* movement, chap. 3, n. 2 above.

94. See Zinberg, *A History of Jewish Literature*, p. 119.

95. See Husik, *Medieval Jewish Philosophy*, p. 153.

96. See Baneth, "Judah Halevi and Al-Ghazali," p. 183. For further details on Halevi's life, education, and a sampling of his poetry, see chap. 5, n. 50 above; see also Husik, *Medieval Jewish Philosophy*, pp. 151–52.

97. The book was translated into Hebrew in the middle of the twelfth century by Judah Ibn Tibbon under the title "*Sefer ha-Hokhahah ve-ha-Re'ayah le-Hagganat ha-Dat ha-Bezuyah*," but was more commonly known as *Sefer ha-Kuzari* (The Book of the Kuzari). Halevi worked on the *Kuzari* for twenty years and completed it shortly before his departure for Eretz Israel. It was translated into English by Hartwig Hirschfeld (1905), and was reprinted with an introduction by Henry Slonimsky. An abridged version with an introduction by Isaac Heinemann appeared in 1947. Heinemann also attached four of Halevi's poems to his abridged version. Passages quoted in this essay are from Heinemann's abridged edition. Slonimski's edition is used for passages not included in Heinemann's edition. See "Judah Halevi" in *Encyclopedia Judaica*, X, cols. 355–66.

98. See Halkin, "Judeo-Arabic Literature," p. 1140.

99. See "Judah Halevi" in *Encyclopedia Judaica*, X, col. 363.

100. See Baron, *History of the Jews*, VIII, pp. 62, 126.

101. For the text of the correspondence and biographical details of Ibn Shaprut, see Leviant, *Masterpieces of Hebrew Literature*, pp. 158–69.

102. See Husik, *Medieval Jewish Philosophy*, p. 153.

103. Halevi, *Kuzari* (Heinemann's commentary on book I), p. 51.

104. See ibid., p. 59. Referring to the participation of the philosopher in the discussion along with representatives of the three religions, Baron writes, "In so far as they belonged to the group calling itself 'philosophers,' many such persons could almost be classified as members of another faith. . . . That is why in his famous dialogue, Halevi could present a 'philosopher' as the spokesman of an independent outlook on life, even as a 'belief' at variance with the three faiths." See Baron, *History of the Jews*, VIII, p. 67, n. 21.

105. Halevi, *Kuzari* (Heinemann's commentary on book I), p. 51.

106. Halevi, *Kuzari* (Heinemann), I, # 8–9, pp. 32–33.

107. See "Judah Halevi" in *Encyclopedia Judaica*, X, cols. 364–65.

108. Halevi, *Kuzari* (Heinemann), I, # 10, p. 33.

109. Ibid., # 11, p. 33.

110. Ibid., # 25, p. 35.

111. Ibid., # 26–27, p. 35.

112. Ibid., # 95, pp. 45–47.

113. Baron, *History of the Jews*, VIII, p. 125.

114. Halevi, *Kuzari* (Heinemann), I, # 97, pp. 47–49.

115. See Halevi, *Kuzari* (Heinemann's commentary on book I), pp. 57–58.

116. See Baneth, "Judah Halevi and Al-Ghazali," p. 192.

117. See Guttmann, *Ha-Pilosophia shel ha-Yahadut*, p. 120.

118. See Heinemann, *Ta'ame ha-Mitzvot*, p. 24.

119. It is true that Halevi's view that a proselyte cannot attain the gift of prophecy runs counter to the Talmudic assertion that the prophet Obadiah was a proselyte (*Sanhedrin* 39b), but perhaps Obadiah's case was an unusual exception because of his great merit of having saved 100 prophets from the murderous Jezebel by hiding them in caves.

120. Halevi, *Kuzari* (Heinemann), II, # 36–44. At the end of # 44, Halevi concludes, "Now we are oppressed whilst the whole world enjoys rest and prosperity. But the trials which meet us serve to purify our piety, to cleanse us, and to remove all taint from us." See also Husik, *Medieval Jewish Philosophy*, p. 164.

121. See n. 96 above.

122. Halevi, *Kuzari* (Heinemann), I, # 25, p. 35.

123. See Halevi, *The Kuzari* (Slonimsky), V, # 14, pp. 268–69.

124. See Baneth, "Judah Halevi and Al-Ghazali," pp. 184–85; Halevi, *Kuzari* (Heinemann), IV, # 16–17, pp. 118–19.

125. Halevi, *Kuzari* (Heinemann), I, # 2, p. 29.

126. Halevi, *The Kuzari* (Slonimsky), V, # 14, pp. 268–74; see also Husik, *Medieval Jewish Philosophy*, pp. 176–79; Baneth, "Judah Halevi and Al-Ghazali," p. 184.

127. See Husik, *Medieval Jewish Philosophy*, p. 150.

128. Halevi, *The Kuzari* (Slonimsky), IV, # 19, pp. 224–25.

129. Ibid., V, # 14, pp. 272–74.

130. See Baron, *History of the Jews*, VIII, pp. 84–85, n. 42.

131. See Halkin, "Judeo-Arabic Literature," pp. 1140–41.

132. Abu Hamid al-Ghazali began his career as a philosopher and jurist. Then, after a crisis of conscience, he lost interest in the logical method of proof, pointed to the contradictions of the philosophers, to their disagreement among themselves, and opted for the way of the Sufis, the pietists of Islam. See Husik, *Medieval Jewish Philosophy*, p. 153. For a summary of al-Ghazali's criticism of philosophy and a synopsis of *The Inconsistency of the Philosophers* (al-Ghazal's major work on the subject), see Watt, *Muslim Intellectual*, pp. 57–71; see also Watt, *The Faith and Practice of Al-Ghazali*, pp. 26–43.

133. Husik, Guttman, and Baneth all credit David Kaufmann for having been the first to trace Halevi's relationship to al-Ghazali in detail, but Baneth and Guttmann point out also the many differences between the two thinkers. See Husik,

Medieval Jewish Philosophy, pp. 152–53; Guttman, *Ha-Pilosophia*, p. 116, n. 320; Baneth, "Judah Halevi and Al-Ghazali," p. 182. See also Kaufmann, "Rabbi Yehudah Halevi."

134. For Halevi's and al-Ghazali's views on prophecy, see the sub-section on prophecy (pp. 177, ns. 147–49) in this chapter.

135. See n. 96 above.

136. Baneth, "Judah Halevi and Al-Ghazali," p. 83.

137. Ibid., pp. 184–85.

138. Ibid., p. 186.

139. Halevi, *Kuzari* (Heinemann), I, # 67, p. 38. Halevi's stand on creation in time is somewhat similar to the one adopted by Maimonides. See the sub-section, "Creation Ex Nihilo," (pp. 148–49, ns. 65–66) earlier in this chapter.

140. Baneth, "Judah Halevi and Al-Ghazali," p. 187.

141. Ibid., p. 190.

142. Ibid., pp. 191–92.

143. Ibid., p. 195.

144. Halevi, *Kuzari* (Heinemann), II, # 50, p. 77.

145. See Halkin, "Judeo-Arabic Literature," pp. 1140–41.

146. Halevi, *Kuzari* (Heinemann), I, # 25, p. 35.

147. Al-Ghazali makes almost the same distinction between the prophet and the philosopher. After discussing the various stages of man's knowledge, he adds,

> Beyond intellect there is yet another stage. In this, another eye is opened, by which he [the prophet] beholds the unseen, what is to be in the future, and other things which are beyond the ken of intellect. . . . Just as intellect is one of the stages of human development in which there is an "eye" which sees the various types of intelligible objects, which are beyond the ken of the

senses, so prophecy also is the description of a stage in which there is an eye endowed with light such that in that light the unseen and other supra-intellectual objects become visible.

Speaking of the superiority of the prophetic illumination, al-Ghazali states, "Behind the light of prophetic revelation there is no other light on the face of the earth from which illumination may be received." See Watt, *The Faith and Practice of Al-Ghazali*, pp. 60, 64–65.

148. Salo Baron observes that Halevi's doctrine that prophecy is the exclusive heritage of Israel, is in line with other Jewish thinkers who sought to establish in various ways the exclusivity, or at least the unique character of Old Testament prophecy. He cites the examples of Abraham Ibn Ezra and Maimonides among others: Ibn Ezra, Baron explains, "felt prompted to interpret away the biblical statements concerning the prophecies of Balaam, and declared him to be a simple magician inspired by God solely for the glorification of Israel," while Maimonides, in his attempt to undermine Muhammad's claim to prophecy, refers to him often as the "madman." Baron notes, however, that Abraham Bar Hiyya and Halevi went further. "They pushed the doctrine of the chosen people to the extreme of postulating that Israel stands above the nations as men above the animals." Finally, Baron adds, "In fact, this idea of selection permeates all medieval Jewish philosophy, whether it be amply discussed, as in Halevi, or merely referred to or implied, as in most of the other writers." See Baron, *History of the Jews*, VIII, pp. 133–34.

149. See "Judah Halevi" in *Encyclopedia Judaica*, X, col. 364.

150. Halevi, *Kuzari* (Heinemann), II, # 9–14, pp. 64–65.

151. Ibid., # 14–end, p. 67.

152. Ibid., # 24, pp. 69–70.

153. Halevi, *The Kuzari* (Slonimsky), IV, # 23, pp. 226–28. After quoting this passage from *The Kuzari*, Baron observes, "This was a realistic appraisal of the position of Jewish converts to Islam. By merely verbal adherence to the new faith, any Jew could get rid of his disabilities and even join the highest ranks of Muslim society" (Baron, *History of the Jews*, VIII, p. 127, n. 91).

154. At the end of book II, # 44, Halevi tells the king, "Now we are oppressed, while the whole world enjoys rest and prosperity. But the trials which meet us serve to purify our piety, cleanse us and remove all taint from us."

155. In describing the typical pious Jew, Halevi states, "The pious man is deeply convinced of the justice of God's judgment. . . . He enjoys looking forward to reward and retribution which await him" (Halevi, *Kuzari* (Heinemann), III, # 11, pp. 94–95).

156. Speaking of the pious Jew who recites his prayers in certain order and enjoys doing so, Halevi states, "Whoever pronounces all this context with pure intention, is a true Israelite, and may hope to obtain that contact with the Divine power which is exclusively connected with the Israelite among all nations; he is worthy to stay before the Shekhinah and to receive an answer as often as he asks." Ibid., III, # 17, pp. 96–98. See also ibid., I, # 95, pp. 43–47.

157. For their respective classification and explanation of the commandments, see the sub-sections, "Classification of the Commandments" (pp. 136–37, ns. 29–31) and "Explanation of the Commandments" (pp. 156–57, ns. 86–91), in this chapter.

158. Halevi, *Kuzari* (Heinemann), II, # 48–50, pp. 76–79.

159. Ibid.

160. Ibid., # 26, pp. 70–72.

161. Ibid., II, # 2, pp. 61–63. Compare Saadiah's and Maimonides' treatment of divine attributes. See sub-sections, "Nature of God" (pp. 134–35, ns. 25–26) and "Divine Attributes" (pp. 145–46, ns. 56–57) in this chapter.

162. Ibid., # 7, p. 64.

163. Ibid., III, # 3–5, pp. 86–89.

164. After discussing some of the central themes of the *Kuzari* in his introduction, Heinemann adds, "This line of thought in the *Kuzari* finds its complement in his poems, of which we give a few examples. If the *Kuzari* may be said to show the poet as a thinker, the reverse holds true of the poems. Just as reading in the former we realize that Halevi does not disdain to clothe his intuitive feelings in the garment of thought, so in the latter he builds up on the foundation of clear thinking a genuine religious life, comprising the apprehension of God, of the Sabbath, and Zion" (Halevi, *Kuzari* (Heinemann), p. 15).

165. Halevi, *The Kuzari* (Slonimsky), V, # 21, p. 291.

166. See Halevi, *Kol Shirei Yehudah Halevi*, p. 305.

167. Halevi, *Kuzari* (Heinemann), IV, # 13–14, pp. 116–19; see also Baneth's discussion of Halevi's sharp distinction between rationalistic and theistic concepts of God in Baneth, "Judah Halevi and Al-Ghazali," pp. 184–85. For Halevi's poem, see the translation in Halevi, *Kuzari* (Heinemann), Song III, p. 132.

168. See Halevi, *Kuzari* (Heinemann), Song III, p. 134. The preceding quote, which ended by comparing statues to human bodies, is from Halevi, *Kuzari* (Heinemann), pp. 90–91.

169. Ibid., I, # 2, p. 29.

170. See Schirmann, *Ha-Shirah ha-Ivrit*, I, p. 493; see also Baron, *History of the Jews*, VIII, p. 85, n. 42.

171. Halevi, *Kuzari* (Heinemann), V, # 27, pp. 128–29. For a sampling of Halevi's Zionist poems, see chap. 5, ns. 60–63 above.

172. See "Judah Halevi" in *Encyclopedia Judaica*, X, col.365.

8. THE THREE-FOLD ZIONIST LEGACY OF RABBI YEHUDAH HALEVI

1. For a fuller biography of Halevi, see chap. 5, n. 50.

2. Ibid., ns. 50–63.

3. The term *Zionism* is used here in its broader traditional sense rather than in the narrow sense of Herzlian political Zionism. Defined in broad religious nationalistic terms, Zionism is the attachment to Eretz Israel, the messianic yearning for the redemption of the Jewish people, the prayer and hope for the restoration of the national homeland and the ingathering of exiles. Such Zionism is as old as exile itself and has been widespread among all Jews at all times. It antedates the political Zionism of Herzl as well as the cultural Zionism of Ahad Ha-'am. It may be called "pre-Herzlian Zionism." The Midrash states that the Messiah was born on the very same day the Temple in Jerusalem was destroyed (Num. *Rabbah*, 7). Clearly, the general idea conveyed by this Midrash seems to be that the messianic yearning for redemption set in as soon as the Jews found themselves in exile outside their homeland, with the Temple, the symbol of their national existence, in ruins. Naturally, the intensity of these nationalistic feelings varied from time to time depending on the actual condition of the Jews in a given period and in a given country. The manifestation of these feelings also varied from time to time and place to place de-

pending on the political and social milieu and the intellectual mode of thinking of the Jews at a given period. The same nationalistic feelings that produced messianic pretenders, when Jewish thought was highly mystical and religious, produced political Zionism at times when the general milieu of the Jews was marked by a drive for individual liberty, national freedom, and economic and social justice. But essentially, these nationalistic feelings themselves were shared and cherished by all Jews at all times. See Henry Toledano, "Zionism in Moroccan Judaism,"; "Poetic and Pragmatic Aspects of Sephardic Zionism."

4. See "Concluding Comments" in chap. 5, ns. 69 and 70.

5. See chap. 5, n. 9.

6. Ibid.

7. See chap. 5, ns. 58 and 59.

8. Source, Halevi, *Kol Shirei Ribbi Yehudah Halevi*, pp. 246–47; translation, Halevi, *Kuzari* (Heinemann), Songs II and III, pp. 133–35.

9. See chap. 5, n. 58.

10. See n. 7 above.

11. For the full text and discussion of these Zionist poems (including several passages from the long "Ode to Zion"), see chap. 5, ns. 60–63. See also n. 21 below.

12. See Halevi, *Kuzari* (Heinemann), Book V, # 22–28, pp. 126–29.

13. This same concern seems to have been behind the writing of his major philosophical work, *The Kuzari*. See chap. 5, ns. 50 and 54 above.

14. Theodor Herzl's Zionism was also influenced by the "Alfred Dreyfus Affair" and the anti-semitism that swept all of Europe in its wake. See Hertzberg, *The Zionist Idea*, pp. 201–6.

15. See n. 3 above.

16. Merely fifty years before Herzl, these two rabbis began preaching for and advocating the return of the Jews to Eretz Israel and the rebuilding and recultivating of the land as a prerequisite for the coming of the Messiah. Actually, both

rabbis were basically reformulating the "active Zionism" of Yehudah Halevi, articulated first in his *Kuzari* seven centuries earlier. (See a fuller discussion of Alkalai's Zionist ideas below). See Hertzberg, *The Zionist Idea*, pp. 103–14.

17. According to both Hayim Schirmann and Israel Zinberg, Halevi's sea poems are unique in the entire corpus of medieval Hebrew poetry. Describing these poems as well as Halevi's mood during this stormy journey, Zinberg writes,

> Now the poet is already far from home. He sees around himself "only water, heaven, and the ship." The sea is angry, but Halevi's soul is filled with quiet joy; the ship is "bringing him closer to the sanctuary of the almighty God." Halevi, however, is not only a pious pilgrim going up to God's holy city; he is also a great poet. He stands on the ship enthralled by the sea with its splendor and powerful beauty. His soul leaps up with joy, and he composes on the ship a series of marvelous sea poems that have no peer in all of medieval literature.

Zinberg then quotes several of these sea poems:

> I cry to God with a melting heart and knees that smite together,
> While anguish is in all loins,
> On a day when the oarsmen are astounded at the deep,
> When even the pilots find not their hands.
> How shall I be otherwise, since I, on a ship's deck,
> Suspended between waters and Heavens,
> Am dancing and tossed about?—But this is but a light thing,
> If I may but hold the festal dance in the midst of thee, O Jerusalem!
>
> I say in the heart of the seas to the quaking heart,
> Fearing exceedingly because they lift up their waves:
> If thou believest in God who made
> The sea, and whose Name doth stand unto all eternity,
> The sea shall not affright thee when the waves thereof arise,
> For with thee is One who hath set a bound to the sea.

After quoting the above poems, Zinberg adds, "These verses are fragments of the great symphony in which Jehudah Halevi portrays with tremendous poetic power the storm wind on the sea, the fierce roar of the waves that boil and seethe, the demonic laughter of the bottom of the sea that has sundered the chain of the abysses." See Schirmann, *Ha-Shirah ha-Ivrit*, I, pp. 430–31; Zinberg, *A History of Jewish Literature*, pp. 97–98, ns. 25–27.

18. One of the arguments of Halevi in his *Kuzari* was that prophecy was possible only in the Land of Israel. See Halevi, *Kuzari* (Heinemann) Book II, # 9–24, pp. 64–69.

19. From the elegies written in Egypt and from the *Genizah* letters which mention his death, it could be concluded that he died about six months after reaching Egypt, and that he was buried there. See "Judah Halevi" in *Encyclopedia Judaica*, X, cols. 355–58; see also S. D. Goitein, "The Biography of Rabbi Judah ha-Levi."

20. See Zinberg, *A History of Jewish Literature*, p. 102, n. 31.

21. For details of his journey as well as the legend regarding his death, see Schirmann, *Ha-Shirah ha-Ivrit*, I, pp. 430–32; see also ns. 19–20, just above. See also a recent important study of Halevi's poetry by Raymond Scheindlin. It focuses on Halevi's poetry, especially as it relates to his pilgrimage to the Land of Israel. Parts I and III of the work are devoted to a discussion of Halevi's pilgrimage poems and other poems having a bearing on the subject, while Part II focuses on a detailed narrative of the pilgrimage and its unique character. Scheindlin notes, for example, that Halevi's pilgrimage was unique in that, unlike typical pilgrims who travel to a shrine, pray there, and return home "feeling uplifted through their encounter with the sacred," Halevi "did not go to Palestine in order to visit Jerusalem and other holy sites and return, but rather to die there and mingle his body with the stones and soil of the Land of Israel." According to Scheindlin, the unique nature of Halevi's pilgrimage "cries out for an explanation." In a sense, the discussion of Halevi's poems and the pilgrimage narrative are Scheindlin's attempt to provide such an explanation. In telling the story of Halevi's pilgrimage (in Part II), he draws mostly on letters and epistles from the *geniza*, and in attempting to understand the religious impulse behind it, he draws mostly on Halevi's poems (in Parts I and III). See Scheindlin, *The Song of the Distant Dove: Judah Halevi's Pilgrimage*, pp. 3–8.

22. For a summary and a full discussion of these responsa, see Henry Toledano, "The Attachment of Moroccan Jewry to the Land of Israel."

23. See Berdugo, *Torot Emet, Eben ha'Ezer*, sec. 1, p. 38a.

24. His discussion is published in a work of Novella on the *Shulhan Arukh* by Rabbi Moshe ben Daniel Toledano, *Ha-Shamayim Ha-Hadashim*, pp. 30b–31b.

25. See Berdugo, *Shufreh De-Ya'akov*, secs. 61–62, pp. 51b–52b.

26. Rabbi Yehudah Bibas (1780–1852) is a scion of a Spanish family of rabbis and physicians who settled in Morocco after 1492, where its members became

leaders of the Castilian community in Fez. Subsequently, members of the family settled in various cities including Safed, Jerusalem, Cairo, Leghorn, Amsterdam, and Gibraltar. Yehudah was born in Gibraltar and studied there and in Italy—where he pursued secular studies, earning a doctoral degree from an Italian university. A prominent rabbi and precursor of modern Zionism, Bibas conceived the idea of the return to Zion in active contemporary terms on a religious basis, and is considered the originator of *Hibbat Zion*. In 1852, after a stay in London and another ten-year period in the rabbinical post in Corfu, he went to Eretz Israel and settled in Hebron. See "Bibas" in *Encyclopedia Judaica*, IV, col. 813.

27. These include a series of books and pamphlets first in Ladino and then in Hebrew: *Darkhei No'am*, *Shema' Israel*, *Minhat Yehudah*, *Shalom Yerushalayim*, and *Mevasser Tov*, among others.

28. See Angel, *Voices in Exile*, pp. 138–44.

29. See Hertzberg, *The Zionist Idea*, pp. 103–7; see also "Alkalai, Judah ben Solomon Hai" in *Encyclopedia Judaica*, II, cols. 638–40.

30. Incidentally, Burla was criticized in Israeli literary circles for having written his novel on Halevi in rhymed prose (maqama-style), but the criticism missed Burla's intent, which was to recreate in the novel the poetic literary environment of Halevi's times.

31. In 1999, Ephrayim Hazan and Andre Elbaz published the first scholarly edition of this work. It includes several analytical essays by Hazan as well as a French translation by Elbaz of Ben Hassin's widely known *piyyutim*. (The arrangement of the *piyyutim* differs from the original.)

32. See Binyamin Bar-Tikvah, *Piyyutei R. Ya'akov Aben-Tzur*, pp. 30–31.

33. In Morocco, for example, it was read responsively by the Hazan and the congregation in the traditional melody in which an actual *ketubbah* was read at weddings.

34. See Mirsky, *Shirim Hadashim mi-She'erit Yisrael le-Ribbi Yisrael Najara*, pp. 169–89.

35. For a biography of Rabbi Israel Najara, see "Najara, Israel ben Moses" in *Encyclopedia Judaica*, XII, cols. 798–99.

36. For a biography of Rabbi Shabazi as well as a full bibliography on his poetry, see "Shabazi, Shalem" in *Encyclopedia Judaica*, XIV, col. 1215.

37. The influence of Najara's poetry in terms of both content and form is most evident in the poetry of Rabbi Jacob Aben-Tzur and Rabbi David ben Hassin. Because their poems, as well as those of other Moroccan poets, were meant to be sung, the term *paytan* which originally meant a poet-scholar who composed the *piyyutim*, came to mean the singer who sang them, and who usually was very familiar with the full range of Andalusian and Arabic melodies to which they were to be sung. For the decisive influence of Najara's poetry on that of North African poets in general and Aben-Tzur and Ben Hassin in particular, see Fenton, "Les bakkashot D'Orient et D'Occident"; Hassin, *Sefer Tehilah Le-David*, pp. 18, 20, 59, 79, 121, 141 in the Hebrew section, and pp. 105–6 in the French section; see also n. 31 above.

38. This is one of Ben Hassin's most popular poems which was sung by everyone throughout the Moroccan Jewish communities. Its first stanza reads,

> *Ohil yom yom eshta'eh*
> *'eni tamid tzofiyah*
> *E'berah na ve-'er'eh*
> *admat kodesh Tebaryah*

> I wait daily and wonder
> my eyes searching yonder
> Let me, pray, go and see
> the holy city of Tiberias.

In this poem, the poet immortalizes the glories of the newly rebuilt city of Tiberias and expresses the special affection Moroccan Jews felt for it. In the last stanza, he praises the role played by Rabbi Hayim Abulafia in the rebuilding of the city. (On this role of Abulafia, see below). This *piyyut* was sung by all to various melodies, and was popular not only in Morocco but in many other Sephardi communities as well.

39. For the significance of these emissaries' activities in Morocco and the generous assistance extended to them by the Moroccan communities, see the section, "Financial Assistance to the Old *Yishuv*," in Henry Toledano, "Zionism in Moroccan Judaism," pp. 2294–96.

40. For an extensive discussion and a full documentation of Moroccan Jewish immigration to the Land of Israel from the sixteenth century onward, see Henry Toledano, "*Yahadut Maroko ve-Yishuv Eretz Israel*"; "Zionism in Moroccan Judaism"; and *The Attachment of Moroccan Jewry to the Land of Israel*.

41. For a detailed account of Rabbi ben Shim'on's immigration to Israel in 1854, and his inspiring leadership of the *maghrebi* community in Jerusalem, see the section, "Moroccan Jews in Jerusalem," in Henry Toledano, "Zionism in Moroccan Judaism."

42. See Elazar, "Israel's Sephardim: The Myth of the 'Two Cultures.'"

43. See H. Cohen, *The Jews of the Middle East: 1860–1972*, pp. 177–78.

44. See n. 42 above.

9. THE SPANISH LEGACY AMONG MOROCCAN JEWS

1. For the early history of the Jews of Morocco and the various theories as to their origin, see Chouraqui, *Between East and West*, pp. 3–21; Hirschberg, *Toledot ha-Yehudim*, I, pp. 3–17, 59–67; II, pp. 35–36; Zafrani, *Mille Ans*, pp. 11–13. For the founding of Fez by Moulay Idriss II at the beginning of the ninth century, see Hirschberg, *Toledot ha-Yehudim*, I, pp. 69–70.

2. On the Almohad persecutions, see Chouraqui, *Between East and West*, pp. 50–55; Hirschberg, *Toledot ha-Yehudim*, I, pp. 84–86.

3. For the role of Ibn Shaprut in the development of Jewish culture in Spain, see chap. 4, n. 12.

4. See Assaf, *Tekufat Ha-Geonim*, p. 212.

5. For the significance of Ibn Labrat's and Ibn Hayyuj's pioneering works in Hebrew philology, see chap. 4, n. 21; for a detailed account of Rabbi Alfasi's contribution to rabbinic scholarship as well as an evaluation of his Major code of Jewish law, *Sefer ha-Halakhot*, see chap. 6, pp. 90–93,ns. 16–20.

6. Many scholars wonder what made Rabbi Maimon seek refuge for his family in Fez, Morocco's capital, the very place of origin of the Almohads. Was that not like jumping from the frying pan into the fire? A number of explanations have been suggested. According to Muslim authorities, the Maimon family became formally (outwardly) converted to Islam somewhere between 1150 and 1160. But Ibn Danan, *Hemdah Genuzah*, p. 16a, asserts that Muslims maintain the same thing about many Jewish scholars. Ibn Danan states further that in his old age, 'Abd al-Mu'min, the Almohad ruler, somewhat changed his attitude toward the Jews, becoming more moderate toward those who lived in the central, Moroccan part of his realm. Ibn Danan reports also that at the time, there lived in Fez Rabbi Judah

ha-Cohen Ibn Susan, whose fame for learning and piety had spread to Spain, and that his presence in Fez was another reason why Rabbi Maimon deemed it worthwhile to emigrate to Morocco and settle in Fez where his son Moses could study under Rabbi ha-Cohen Ibn Susan. Some believe that because of Maimonides' wide learning in philosophy, he befriended many Muslim scholars who provided him with protection. For these and other explanations, see Maimonides, *Iggerot HaRambam* (Rabinowitz), pp. 22–23; see also "Maimonides, Moses" in *Encyclopedia Judaica*, XI, cols. 754–55.

7. See Maimonides, *Iggerot HaRambam* (Rabinowitz), pp. 24–25.

8. According to Rabinowitz, the epistle was written in 1162–63 when Maimonides was twenty-seven years old, while David Hartman believes that it was written in 1165, shortly before Maimonides and his family left Fez. Ibid., pp. 25–26; see also the introduction to The Epistle on Martyrdom, in Halkin and Hartman, *Crisis and Leadership*, p. 13.

9. But before attacking the rabbi's ruling, Maimonides quotes extensively from it, in order to repudiate it more forcefully.

10. Maimonides believed that the declaration that Muhammad was a prophet of God does not alter the monotheistic nature of Islam.

11. Maimonides acted on his own advice, and in 1165, he and his family left Morocco for the Holy Land, eventually settling in Egypt. Many Moroccan scholars followed his example and left Morocco. Al-Harizi (c.1165–?) reports having encountered some who emigrated to Syria, Palestine, Egypt, and southern Italy.

12. For a fine translation of The Epistle on Martyrdom, see Halkin and Hartman, *Crisis and Leadership*, pp. 13–45; for the Soloveitchik-Hartman controversy, see Rabbi Hartman's discussion, pp. 46–83.

13. In Aleppo, Ibn Shim'on became friendly with the Muslim historian, Ibn Qifti (who, like Ibn Shim'on, was a physician). This was fortunate because Ibn Qifti included the biography of Ibn Shim'on in his *Lives of Scholars*, which together with Maimonides' dedicatory epistle and al-Harizi's *Tahkemoni* afford us all we know about Ibn Shim'on. See Baneth, *Iggerot ha-Rambam*, pp. 1–2; see also Hirschberg, *Toledot ha-Yehudim*, I, pp. 267–70, n. 89.

14. His full name is Yosef ben Yehudah ben Yosef ben Ya'akob ha-Sepharadi (or ha-Dayyan hal-Bargeloni). Because of the same name and father's name as well as the fact that both he and Ibn Shim'on lived in Ceuta when Maimonides

was in Fez, he is sometime confused with Ibn Shim'on. For example, another important letter of Maomonides to his pupil, Joseph ben Yehudah, was a response to the latter's outrage at the criticism and anti-Maimonides polemics generated at the Yeshiva of Baghdad under the *Gaon* Samuel ben Eli, and his pupil's eagerness to retaliate in kind. Maimonides counseled his pupil to ignore critics and concentrate on his studies instead. Among other matters, Maimonides explains to him the purpose of his writing the *Mishneh Torah*. David Z. Baneth also believes that this letter was addressed to Ibn Shim'on. Twersky, likewise, identifies the recipient of this letter as Ibn Shim'on who "was the immediate cause of the composition of the *Moreh*." Elon, however, mistakenly identifies the recipient of this letter as Ibn Aknin. See Baneth, *Iggerot ha-Rambam*, pp. 31-2.; Twersky, *Introduction to the Code*, pp. 41–43; Elon, *Jewish Law*, p. 1184; see also n. 13 above.

15. His books include (a) *Sefer ha-Musar* (*Book of Ethics*), a commentary on Mishnah *Avot*; (b) *Introduction to the Talmud* (published by Graetz); (c) a treatise on weights and measures mentioned in the Bible and the Talmud; (d) an allegorical commentary on the Songs of Songs ; (e) *Tibb al-nufus al-salimah* (*The Hygiene of Healthy Souls*), a philosophical treatise on ethics; and (f) two other works, lost and known to us only by reference to them—"The Book of Laws and Judgments," on precepts applicable after the destruction of the Temple, and an Epistle on the rationale for the commandments and principles of faith. From chapter 27 of his *The Hygiene of Healthy Souls* (called in Arabic *Adab al-mu'allim wal-muta'allim*— Rules of Conduct for the Teacher and the Student), it appears that his theory of education corresponds to the rules of the study of the law set out by Maimonides in the section, "Laws of the Study of Torah," in his *Mishneh Torah*. It is safe to assume that this method and sequence of subjects was followed in the education of outstanding individuals. This is quite evident from Maimonides' dedicatory epistle to Ibn Shim'on outlining more or less the same sequence. For details of Ibn Aknin's program of Jewish education outlined in this work, see Hirschberg, *Toledot ha-Yehudim*, I, p. 269. For the possible influence of Al-Ghazali's "Book of Knowledge"—the first book of his monumental *The Revival of the Religious Sciences*—on Maimonides' "Laws of the Study of Torah" and Ibn Aknin's "Rules of Conduct for the Teacher and the Student," see chap. 6, n. 35.

16. Hirschberg, *Toledot ha-Yehudim*, I, pp. 267–68.

17. The Jewish sources include *Sefer ha-Kabbalah* of Abraham ben Solomon Torrutiel who continued the work of Abraham Ibn Daud, *Shevet Yehudah*, by Solomon Ibn Vargas, and *Sefer Yohasin ha-Shalem* by Abraham Zacuto. See Hirschberg, *Toledot ha-Yehudim*, I, pp. 298–99.

18. Abraham Torrutiel asserts that 20,000 Jews came to Fez after 1492, and

an undetermined number died there or left during the first winter, while Hirschberg finds the number of 10,000 suggested by Marmol to be exaggerated. Leon Africanus, on the other hand, does not suggest a specific number but states, "In fez itself, which became a commercial metropolis, a center of international trade, the number of Jews increased enormously, especially after the expulsion from Spain." Ibid., p. 299; see also Gerber, *Jewish Society in Fez*, p. 47.

19. See Ganin, *Etz Haim*, p. 15.

20. Commenting on the development of rabbinic jurisprudence in Morocco during the past 450 years, Menahem Elon says, "Moroccan decisors (*poskim*) show great sensitivity to changing circumstances and the exigencies of modern times. They show a readiness to deal with the issues head on; and when the situation demands bold initiatives, they do not hesitate to resort to enacting *takkanot*." He adds that "the Israeli chief rabbinate is timid by comparison," and suggests that the chief rabbis of Israel and elsewhere can use Moroccan rabbis as a model of openness and innovation. See Elon, "*Yihudah shel Halakhah*."

21. For a detailed discussion of the relations between the two groups, see the Appendix on *Hetter Nephihah* below.

22. See Amar, *Ha-Mishpat ha-Ivri*, p. 10, n. 3.

23. For these and other typical Moroccan family names including those of Arabic or Berber origin, see Laredo, *Les Noms Des Juifs Du Maroc*.

24. Incidentally, the melodies for the liturgy of the High Holidays are almost uniform among many Sephardim. Thus, for example, with very few nuanced exceptions, Moroccan melodies for most of the *pizmonim* and *selihot* are not that different from those of the Spanish and Portuguese synagogues in New York and Amsterdam. The same is true of the melodies used for the cantillation of the Torah and *haftarah*.

25. See, for example, the *kinot*, "*Halanofelim Tekumah*," "*Eikhah Tzon ha-Haregah*," and "*Tzion Halo Tish'ali*," by Yehudah Halevi, and "*Nir'eh le-Helil'al Shibrenu*" by Moses Ibn Ezra, as well as "*Golat Sefarad be-Khol Levavkhem*" and "*Yom Me'ori Hashakh be-Gerush Castilia*"—all in *Kol Tehinah he-Hadash*, pp. 16–19, 20–21, 157–59, 212–13, 216–17, 219.

26. See Chouraqui, *Between East and West*, pp. 102–3.

27. For a full discussion of Hebrew poetry in Spain as well as representative

samples of it, see chap. 5 above. For Moroccan's love of *piyyutim* and Andalusian music, see a fuller discussion in connection with the Moroccan *piyyut* and the institution of *bakkashot* below.

28. For a full description of these celebrations as well as other Moroccan customs and practices, see Henry Toledano, "The Practice of Judaism in Morocco," especially pp. 1853–63. For the institution of *bakkashot*, see a full discussion below.

29. These works are in Berdugo, *Torot Emet*, pp. 80a–84b, 139b–144a. On the binding authority of Caro's rulings on Moroccan Jews and the Sephardim in general, see a recent essay by Rabbi Shalom Messas, the late Chief Sephardic Rabbi of Jerusalem (formerly, the Chief Rabbi of Morocco), and an important contemporary decisor. In this essay, Rabbi Messas outlines the desirable features of a model responsum (*pesak halakhah*) in terms of both content and form. Among these features, he emphasizes "adherence to the rules of Sephardic jurisprudence which regard Joseph Caro as the supreme halakhic authority." Rabbi Messas declares further that "when Caro's ruling with regard to any particular issue is clear and unambiguous (and when it has not been superseded by a local or regional judicial practice—*minhag* or *takkanah*), it must prevail, regardless of who and how many halakhic authorities differ with it." See Messas, *Shemesh u-Magen*, II, # 54, pp. 91–93.

30. The place names and dates of publication given next to the following works indicate that Moroccan Jewry was in no way isolated from other centers of Jewish life. Moroccan rabbis traveled to, published their works, and at times served as spiritual leaders in Amsterdam, Leghorn, London, Egypt, and most of all Eretz Israel.

31. Besides rabbis, poets, and scholars, Moroccan Jews also produced statesmen, diplomats, bankers, and courtiers, whose diplomatic skills and commercial abilities were mobilized in the service of the various dynasties that ruled over Morocco. These Jewish merchants and statesmen were trusted by their respective kings to negotiate for them commercial agreements, diplomatic treaties, and military alliances with such contemporary European powers as Holland, England, and Italy. The family names of Corcos, Levi-Yuly (or Yulee), Maymeran, and Toledano, among others, figure prominently in these diplomatic and commercial activities. For example, Samuel Ibn Sunbal was vizier of the Sultan Moulay Muhammad (1757–1790). Joseph Maimeran (d. 1721) and his son Abraham (d. 1723) served as financial advisers to the Sultan Moulay Isma'il (1672–1721), at the same time that Rabbi Daniel Toledano (d. c.1680) and his son Joseph (d. c.1700) served as counselors to the same monarch. In addition, Joseph Toledano was commissioned

by the king to the Netherlands to conduct negotiations that led to a peace treaty and a commercial agreement between the two countries; in 1688, he presented his credentials as Moroccan ambassador to the States General. Likewise, in 1772, Jaime (Haim) Toledano asked to present his credentials to the British Secretary of State as the emissary from Morocco. Another favorite of Moulay Isma'il was Rabbi Samuel Levy Aben-Yuly, a scholar and statesman who also served as a counselor to the sultan, and later served as adviser to Moulay Abd Allah (1729–1752), the all-powerful secretary of Mouilay Isma'il, who appointed him *nagid* (prince or leader) of Moroccan Jewry. His son Judah Aben-Yuly, one of the founders of the Jewish community of Mogador, was appointed "merchant of the Sultan" around 1767, and his son Elijah Levy Yuly was also appointed "merchant of the Sultan" and became vizier at the end of the reign of Moulay Abd Allah in 1757. His son Moses Levy Yuly (d. c.1782), who was educated in England, left England for St. Thomas in the Caribbean in 1800 and settled in Florida in 1819. His son David Yulee was the first U.S. Senator from Florida, and the first U.S. Senator of Jewish origin. The Corcos family produced its share of merchants and statesmen. Maimon ben Isaac Corcos (d.1799), another one of the founders of the Jewish community of Mogador, was an influential merchant and one of the pillars of British politics in Morocco. Solomon ben Abraham Corcos (d. 1854) was a banker and adviser to the sultan and was accredited as consular agent of Great Britain from 1822. His sons Jacob (d. 1878) and Abraham (d. 1883) were entrusted with important missions by three successive sultans. In 1862, Abraham was appointed U.S. Consul in Mogador. Clearly these Moroccan merchants and statesmen were continuing the tradition of such predecessors as Joseph ben Phinehas and Aaron ben Amram of Baghdad and Hasdai Ibn Shaprut and Samuel Hanagid of Spain, among others. See Bentov, *"Li-Demuto shel ha-Sar Shemuel Ibn Sunbal"*; Stillman, *The Jews of Arab Lands*, p. 307; "Corcos" in *Encyclopedia Judaica*, V, cols. 960–61; "Maymeran" in *Encyclopedia Judaica*, XI, cols. 1148–49; "Toledano" in *Encyclopedia Judaica*, XV, cols. 1193–97; "Yuly (Aben-Yuly, Yulee, Levy-Yuly)" in *Encyclopedia Judaica*, XVI, cols. 895–96; "Yuly, David Levy" in *Encyclopedia Judaica*, XVI, cols. 894–95. (No year of birth is provided by the sources for any of these individuals.)

32. See Ben Naim, *Malkhe Rabbanan*, pp. 107a–b; see also *Encyclopedia Judaica*, VI, col. 572.

33. See the introduction to Amar, ed., *Tzon Yosef*, which provides a comprehensive list of Rabbi Ben Naim's works; the biography of Rabbi Ben Naim in Zafrani, *Pedagogie Juive en Terre D'Islam*, pp. 113–17; and *Encyclopedia Judaica*, IV, col. 459.

34. For Rabbi Berdugo's approach to biblical and Talmudic exegesis as well

as some of his daring theological views, see Henry Toledano, "The Centrality of Reason," pp. 171–205.

35. For the Hebrew text and an English translation of his poem, see ibid., pp. 190–94.

36. For a sampling of Berdugo's exegesis, see the section "Samples of Berdugo's Exegesis," ibid., pp. 180–90.

37. For a fuller discussion of the poetry of Rabbi Aben-Tzur and Rabbi Ben Hassin, see chap. 8, ns. 31, 32.

38. See Hirschberg, *Toledot ha-Yehudim*, I, pp. 288–96.

BIBLIOGRAPHY

Abramson, S. "*Ha-Genizah she-ba-Genizah*" (The Genizah within the Genizah), *Proceedings of the Rabbinical Assembly of America* 15 (1951): pp. 227–28.

Al-Baladhuri. *Kitab Futuh al-Buldan*. Cairo, 1959. (See Hitti, Philip K. *The Origins of the Islamic State*.)

Altmann, Alexander. "Judaism in World Philosophy." In Finkelstein, ed., *The Jews*, II, pp. 954–1009.

———, tr. *Saadya Gaon: Book of Doctrines and Beliefs* (abridged). In *Three Jewish Philosophers*, edited by Hans Lewy et al., pp. 9–190. New York, 1945.

Amar, Moshe. *Ha-Mishpat ha-Ivri bi-kehilat Maroco: Sefer ha-Takkanot . . . Mo'etzat ha-Rabbanim be-Maroco* [in Hebrew]. Jerusalem, n.d.

———. *Tzon Yosef*. Lod, n.d.

Angel, Marc D. *Voices in Exile: A Study in Sephardic Intellectual History*. New York, 1991.

Arberry, A. J. *Revelation and Reason in Islam*. London, 1957.

Assaf, Simha. *Tekufat Ha-Geonim Ve-Siufrutah* (The Geonic Period and Its Literature) [in Hebrew]. Jerusalem, 1968.

Attiya, Meir Elazar. *Shirei Dodim ha-Shalem: Piyyutim mi-Masoret Yehudei Maroko* (Complete Anthology of Songs from the Tradition of Moroccan Jewry) [in Hebrew]. Israel, n.d.

Baneth, David Zvi. "Judah Halevi and Al-Ghazali." In *Studies in Jewish Thought: An Anthology of German Jewish Scholars*, edited by Alfred Jospe, pp. 181–99. Detroit, 1981.

————, ed. *Iggerot ha-Rambam* (The Epistles of Maimonides) [in Hebrew]. Jerusalem, 1946.

Barnett, R. D., ed. *The Sephardi Heritage: Essays on the History and Cultural Contributions of the Jews of Spain and Portugal*, Vol. I. New York, 1971.

Baron, Salo Wittmayer. *A Social and Religious History of the Jews*. 2nd ed. rev., 18 vols. New York and Philadelphia, 1952–83.

Bar-Tikvah, Binyamin. *Piyyutei R. Ya'akov Aben-Tzur* (The Poems of Rabbi Jacob Aben-Tzur) [in Hebrew]. Jerusalem, 1988.

Bar Yuda, M., ed. *Halakhah u-Ftihut: Hakhme Maroco ke-Poskim Le-Dorenu*. Israel, 1985.

Barzilay, Isaac. *Shlomo Yehudah Rapoport (Shir), 1790–1867, and His Contemporaries: Some Aspects of Jewish Scholarship of the Nineteenth Century*. Ramat Gan, 1969.

Becker, Dan. *The Risala of Judah Ben Quraysh: A Critical Edition* [in Hebrew]. Tel Aviv, 1984.

Ben Naim, Joseph, *Malkhei Rabanan* [in Hebrew]. Jerusalem, 1931.

Bentov, Haim. "*Li-Demuto shel ha-Sar Shemuel Ibn Sunbal*" (Profile of the Vizier Samuel Ibn Sunbal). In *Zakhor Le-Abraham: Melanges Abraham Elmaleh*, edited by H. Z. Hirschberg, pp. 47–68. Jerusalem, 1972.

Berdugo, Raphael. *Torot Emet* (True Teachings – commentary on Caro's *Shulhan Arukh*). Meknes, Morocco, 1939.

Berdugo, Jacob ben Yekuti'el. *Shufreh de-Ya'akob* (Jacob's Splendor; Responsa). Jerusalem, 1910.

Burla, Yehudah. *Elleh Mas'ei Yehudah Halevi* (The Travels of Yehudah Halevi) [in Hebrew]. Tel Aviv, 1959.

————. *Ma'avak* (Struggle) [in Hebrew], 2 vols. Tel Aviv, 1946.

————. *Kissufim* (Yearnings) [in Hebrew]. Tel Aviv, 1953.

Carmi, T., ed. *The Penguin Book of Hebrew Verse*. Philadelphia, 1981.

Carmilly-Weinberger, Moshe. "Two Biblical Scholars in Transylvania-Banat: Professor Leopold Fleischer and Dr. Lipot Keeskemet," *Studia Judaica* (2004): pp. 13–27.

Chouraqui, Andre. *Between East and West: A History of the Jews of North Africa*. Philadelphia, 1968.

Cohen, Boaz. "The Classification of the Law in the *Mishneh Torah*," *Jewish Quarterly Review* 25 (1934–35): pp. 519–40.

Cohen, Hayim. *The Jews of the Middle East: 1860–1972*. Jerusalem, 1973.

Elazar, Daniel. "Israel's Sephardim: The Myth of the 'Two Cultures,'" *The American Sephardi* (June 1967): pp. 34–38.

Elon, Menahem. *Jewish Law: History, Sources, Principles—Ha-Mishpat Ha-Ivri*, Vol. III. Translated by Bernard Auerbach and Melvin J. Sykes. Philadelphia, 1990.

————. *"Yihudah shel Halakhah ve-Hevrah be-Yahdut Tzefon Africa mi-le-ahar Gerush Sepharad ve-' 'ad Yamenu."* In Bar Yuda, *Halakhah u-Ftihut: Hakhme Maroco ke-Poskim Le-Dorenu*, pp. 15–38.

Encyclopedia Judaica, new English edition, 16 vols. Jerusalem, 1972.

The Encyclopedia of Islam: New Edition. Edited by B. Lewis et al. Leiden, 1971.

The Encyclopedia of Judaism. Edited by Jacob Neusner et al. Leiden: Brill,

Volume IV, Supplement One, 2003. pp. 1847–63; Volume V, Supplement Two, 2004. pp. 2293–2307.

Fakhry, Majid. *Islamic Occasionalism and Its Critique by Averroes and Aquinas*. London, 1955.

Faur Halevi, Jose. *Studies in the Mishneh Torah Book of Knowledge* [in Hebrew]. Jerusalem, 1978.

Fenton, Paul. *"Les Bakkashot D'Orient et D'Occident," Revue Des Etudes Juives* (REJ) 134 (1975): pp. 101–21.

Finkelstein, Louis, ed. *The Jews: Their History, Culture, and Religion*, 2 vols., 3rd ed. Philadelphia, 1960.

Fischel, Walter. *The Jews in the Economic and Political Life of Medieval Islam*. New York, 1969.

Folberg, Neil. *And I Shall Dwell among Them: Historic Synagogues of the World*. New York, 2001.

Freehof, B. Solomon. *The Responsa Literature*. Philadelphia, 1955.

Ganin, Hayim. *Etz Hayim* (The Tree of Life) [in Hebrew]. Edited by Moshe Amar. Jerusalem, 1987.

Geiger, Abraham. *Judaism and Islam* (The original title was *Was hat Mohammed dem Judenthume aufgenommen?*—What did Muhammad Accept/Borrow from Judaism?). Translated by F. M. Young, with a prolegomenon by Moshe Pearlman. Reprint. New York, 1970.

Gerber, Jane. *Jewish Society in Fez*. Leiden, 1980.

Gibb, H. A. R., and J. H. Kramers, eds. *Shorter Encyclopedia of Islam*. Ithaca, NY, 1953.

Gluck, Andrew L. "Maimonides' Argument for Creation Ex Nihilo in *The Guide of the Perplexed*," *Medieval Jewish Philosophy and Theology* 7 (1998): pp. 221–54.

Goitein, S. D. *Jews and Arabs: Their Contacts through the Ages*, 3d ed., rev. New York, 1974.

————. *Mediterranean Society, Volume II: The Community*. Berkeley, CA, 1971.

————. *Studies in Islamic History and Institutions*. Leiden, 1966.

————. "The Biography of Rabbi Judah ha-Levi in the Light of the Cairo Geniza Documents," *Proceedings of the American Academy for Jewish Research* (PAAJR) 28 (1959): pp. 41–56.

Goldstein, David. *Hebrew Poems from Spain*. New York, 1966.

Goldzhier, Ignaz. *Muslim Studies (Muhammedanische Studien)*, 2 vols. Edited by S. M. Stern; translated by C. R. Barber and S. M. Stern. London, 1967–71.

Guttman, I. Julius. *Ha-Pilosophia shel ha-Yahadut* (The Philosophy of Judaism) [in Hebrew]. Jerusalem, 1961.

Halevi, Yehuda. *Kol Shirei Yehudah Halevi* (All of Yehudah Halevi's Poems) [in Hebrew]. Edited by Israel Zamora. Tel Aviv, 1955.

————. *The Kuzari: An Argument for the Faith of Israel*. Reprint of H. Hirschfeld's English translation; introduction by Henry Slonimsky. New York, 1964.

————. *Kuzari: The Book of Proof and Argument*. Edited by Isaac Heinemann et al.; abridged East and West Library Edition. Oxford, n.d.

————. *Selected Poems of Jehudah Halevi*. Edited and translated by Henrich Brody. Philadelphia, 1974.

Halkin, Abraham. "Judeo-Arabic Literature." In Finkelstein, ed., *The Jews*, II, pp. 1116–48.

————, and David Hartman, tr. *Crisis and Leadership: Epistles of Maimonides*. Philadelphia, 1985.

Hanagid, Samuel. *Divan Samuel Hanagid: Ben Tehilim* (The Collected Poems of Samuel the Prince, 993–1056: The Son of Psalms) [in Hebrew]. Edited by Dov Jarden. Jerusalem, 1966.

Harvey, Steven. "Alghazali and Maimonides and Their Books of Knowledge." In *Be'erot Yitzhaq: Studies in Memory of Isadore Twersky*. Edited by Jay M. Harris, pp. 99–117. Cambridge, MA, 2005.

Hassin, David ben. *Sefer Tehilah le-David: Kobetz Shirato shel Ribbi David Ben Hassin Z. Tz. L—Paytanah shel Yahadut Maroko—Mahdora Mada'it* (Praise of David: Collection of the Poems of Rabbi David ben Hassin, the poet of Moroccan Jewry—a critical edition) [in Hebrew]. Edited by Ephrayim Hazan and Andre Elbaz. Lod, 1999.

Heinemann, Isaac. *Ta'ame ha-Mitzvot be-Sifrut Yisrael* (The Rationales for the Commandments in Jewish Literature) [in Hebrew], 2 vols. Jerusalem, 1954.

Hertzberg, Arthur. *The Zionist Idea*. Philadelphia, 1960.

Hirschberg, H. Z. *Toledot ha-Yehudim be-Africa ha-Tzefonit* (History of the Jews in North Africa) [in Hebrew], 2 vols. Jerusalem, 1965.

Hitti, Philip K. *The Origins of the Islamic State*: *Being a Translation of* Kitab Futuh al-Buldan. New York, 1916.

Husik, Isaac. *A History of Medieval Jewish Philosophy*. Philadelphia, 1958.

Ibn Danan, Saadiah. *Hemdah Genuzah* (A Hidden Treasure) [in Hebrew]. Edited by Zvi Hirsch Edelman. Konigsberg, 1856.

Ibn Daud, Abraham. *Sefer ha-Kabbalah: The Book of Tradition*. Edited and translated by G. D. Cohen. Philadelphia, 1967.

Ibn Ezra, Abraham. *The Religious Poems of Abraham Ibn Ezra* [in Hebrew]. Edited by Israel Levin. Jerusalem, vol. 1, 1975.

———. *Rabbi Abraham Ibn Ezra: Kobetz Hokhmat Haraba'* (Rabbi Abraham Ibn Ezra: A Collection of Ibn Ezra's Wisdom) [in Hebrew], 2 vols. Edited by David Kahana. Warsaw, 1894.

Ibn Ezra, Moses. *The Collected Liturgical Poems of Moses Ibn Ezra* [in Hebrew]. Edited by Shimeon Bernstein. Tel Aviv, 1957.

Ibn Gabirol, Solomon. *Selected Poems of Solomon Ibn Gabirol*. Edited and translated by Israel Davidson. Philadelphia, 1974.

———. *The Kingly Crown: Keter Malkhut*. Translation, introduction, and notes by Bernard Lewis; additional introduction and commentary by Andrew L. Gluck. Notre Dame, IN, 2003.

Jacobs, Louis. *Jewish Biblical Exegesis*. New York, 1973.

Katsh, Abraham I. *Judaism in Islam: Biblical and Talmudic Background of the Koran and Its Commentaries*. New York, 1954.

Kaufmann, David. "Rabbi Yehudah Halevi" [in Hebrew]. In *Studies in Hebrew Literature of the Middle Ages*, pp. 166–211. Jerusalem, 1965.

Klausner, Joseph. *Kitzur ha-Historiah shel ha-Sifrut ha-Ivrit ha-Hadashah* (An Abridged History of Modern Hebrew Literatrure) [in Hebrew], 2 vols. Edited by B. Netanyahu. Jerusalem, 1954.

Kol Tehinah he-Hadash (Moroccan Prayer Book for *Tish'ah be-Av*). Edited by Jacob Levi. Jerusalem, 1988.

Kramer, Joel. "The Influence of Islamic Law on Maimonides: The Case of the Five Qualifications" [in Hebrew], *Te'udah* 10 (1996): pp. 225–44.

Krochmal, Nachman. *Kitvei Ribbi Nachman Krochmal* (The writings of Rabbi Nachman Krochmal) [in Hebrew]. Edited by S. Rawidowicz. London, 1961.

Laredo, Abraham I. *Les Noms Des Juifs Du Maroc: Essai D'Onomastique Judeo-Marocaine*. Madrid, 1978.

Leibson, Gideon. "Jewish Muslim Comparative Law: A History of Its Study and Problematics" [in Hebrew], *Pe'amim* 62 (1995): pp. 42–81.

Leviant, Curt, ed. *Masterpieces of Hebrew Literature: A Treasury of 2000 Years of Jewish Creativity*. New York, 1969.

Lewis, Bernard. *The Arabs in History*. London, 1950.

————. *The Jews of Islam*. Princeton, NJ, 1984.

————. "The Pro-Islamic Jews," *Judaism* (Fall 1968): pp. 391–404.

Maimonides, Moses. *Crisis and Leadership: Epistles of Maimonides*. Translated by Abraham Halkin. Introduction and discussion by David Hartman. Philadelphia, 1985.

————. *The Guide of the Perplexed*. Translated by Shlomo Pines. Introductory essay by Leo Strauss. Chicago, 1963.

————. *Iggerot Ha-Rambam* (Epistles of Maimonides) [inHebrew]. Edited by D. Z. Baneth. Jerusalem, 1946.

————. *Iggerot Ha-Rambam* (Epistles of Maimonides) [in Hebrew]. Edited by M. D. Rabinowitz. Jerusalem, 1960.

————. *Mishneh Torah: Hilkhot Talmud Torah*. Rambam edition; New York, 1957.

————. *Responsa* [in Hebrew]. Edited by Joshua Blau. Jerusalem, 1960.

Messas, Joseph. *Mayim Hayim* (Responsa). Fez, 1913.

Messas, Shalom. *Shemesh u-Magen* (Collection of Responsa), 3 vols. Jerusalem 1986–2000.

Mirsky, Aaron. *Shirim Hadashim mi-She'erit Israel le-Ribbi Yisrael Najara* (New Poems from the She'erit Israel Collection by Rabbi Israel Najara). In Nash, ed., *Between History and Literature*, (Hebrew section), pp. 169–89.

Nash, Stanley, ed. *Between History and Literature: Studies in Honor of Isaac Barzilay.* Israel, 1991.

Patai, Raphael. *The Jewish Mind.* Detroit, 1996.

Pool, David De Sola, ed. and trans. *Prayers for the Day of Atonement According to the Customs of the Spanish and Portuguese Jews,* 3rd ed. New York, 1949.

————. *Prayers for the New Year According to the Customs of the Spanish and Portuguese Jews.* New York, 1987.

————. *The Traditional Prayer Book for Sabbath and Festivals.* New York, 1960.

Rosenthal, Franz. *Knowledge Triumphant.* Leiden, 1970.

Rosenthal, Irwin I. J. *Judaism and Islam.* London, 1961.

Sarna, Nahum. "Hebrew and Bible Studies in Medieval Spain." In *The Sephardi Heritage: Essays on the History and Cultural Contributions of the Jews of Spain and Portugal,* edited by R. D. Barnett, pp. 323–66. New York, 1971.

Schacht, Joseph. *An Introduction to Islamic Law.* Oxford, 1964.

Scheindlin, Raymond P. *The Gazelle: Medieval Hebrew Poems on God, Israel, and Soul.* Philadelphia, 1991.

————. *The Song of the Distant Dove: Judah Halevi's Pilgrimage,* Oxford, 2006.
————. *Wine, Women, and Death: Medieval Hebrew Poems on the Good Life.* Philadelphia, 1986.

Schirmann, Hayim. *Ha-Shirah ha-Ivrit bi-Sefarad uve-Provence* (Hebrew Poetry in Spain and Provence) [in Hebrew], 2 vols. Israel, 1959.

Shapiro, Marc. *The Limits of Orthodox Theology: Maimonides' Thirteen Principles Reappraised.* Oxford, 2004.

Stillman, Norman A. *The Jews of Arab Lands: A History and Source Book.* Philadelphia, 1976.

Toledano, Habib. *Peh Yesharim*, a commentary on the Passover Haggadah. Leghorn, Italy, 1838.

Toledano, Henry. "The Attachment of Moroccan Jewry to the Land of Israel According to Rabbinic Literature." In *Haham Gaon Memorial Volume*, edited by Marc D. Angel, pp. 197–221. New York, 1997.

———. "The Centrality of Reason and Common Sense in the Biblical and Talmudic Exegesis of Rabbi Rephael Berdugo (1747–1821)." In Nash, ed., *Between History and Literature*, (English section), pp. 171–205.

———. "Poetic and Pragmatic Aspects of Sephardic Zionism," *Focus. Zionist Council of Arts and Sciences* (Fall 1975): pp. 1–5.

———. "The Practice of Judaism in Morocco." In *The Encyclopedia of Judaism*, Volume IV, Supplement One, pp. 1847–63.

———. "Zionism in Moroccan Judaism." In *The Encyclopedia of Judaism*, Volume V, Supplement Two, pp. 2293–2307.

———. "*Yahadut Maroko ve-Yishuv Eretz Yisrael: Toledot ha-'Aliyyot ha-Shonot shel Yehudei Maroko meha-me'ah ha-Shesh 'esreh ve-'ad Reshit ha-me'ah ha-'Esrim.*" In *Hagut Ivrit be-Artzot ha-Islam* [in Hebrew]. Edited by Menahem Zohari et al, pp. 229–52. Jerusalem, 1981.

Toledano, Moshe ben Daniel. *Ha-Shamayim ha-Hadashim* (The New Heavens – Novellae on Caro's *Shulhan Arukh*). Casablanca, 1937.

Toledano, Shlomo. *Divrei Shalom ve-Emet* (Words of Peace and Truth) [in Hebrew], 3rd ed., 2 vols. Jerusalem, 2003.

Twersky, Isadore. *Introduction to the Code of Maimonides* (Mishneh Torah), *Yale Judaica Series*, vol. xxii. New Haven, CT, 1980.

———. *A Maimonides Reader.* New York, 1972.

Urinovsky, Aaron. *Toledot ha-Sifrut ha-Ivrit ha-Hadashah Kerach I, Tekufat Ha-Haskalah be-Yisrael* (A History of Modern Hebrew Literature: Vol. I: The Haskalah Period) [in Hebrew], 3 vols. Tel Aviv, 1963.

Watt, W. Montgomery. *The Faith and Practice of Al-Ghazali*. London, 1953.

————. *The Influence of Islam on Medieval Europe*. Edinburgh, 1972.

————. *Islamic Philosophy and Theology*. Islamic Survey I. Edinburgh, 1962.

————. *Muslim Intellectual: A Study of Al-Ghazali*. Edinburgh, 1963.

Wensinck, A. J. *The Muslim Creed*. London, 1965.

Zafrani, Haim. *Etudes et Recherches sur la Vie Intellectuelle Juive au Maroc: Deuxieme Partie, Poesie Juive en Occident Musulman*. Paris, 1977.

————. *Mille Ans de Vie Juivce au Maroc: Histoire et Culture, Religion et Magie*. Paris, 1983.

————. *Pedagogie Juive en Terre D'Islam*. Paris, 1969.

Zinberg, Israel. *A History of Jewish Literature: Vol. I, The Arabic-Spanish Period*. Philadelphia, 1972.

INDEX